THE SECRET VOYAGE OF
SIR FRANCIS DRAKE

THE SECRET VOYAGE OF

Sir Francis Drake

᛭1577–1580᛭

SAMUEL BAWLF

DOUGLAS & McINTYRE
Vancouver / Toronto

Douglas & McIntyre
2323 Quebec Street, Suite 201
Vancouver, British Columbia
Canada V5T 4S7
www.douglas-mcintyre.com

National Library of Canada Cataloguing in Publication Data
Bawlf, R. Samuel
The secret voyage of Sir Francis Drake, 1577–1580 / Samuel Bawlf.—
Canadian ed.
Includes bibliographical references and index.

ISBN 1-55054-977-4 (bound) ISBN 1-55365-041-7 (pbk)

1. Drake, Francis, Sir, 1540?–1596—Journeys. 2. Drake, Francis, Sir,
1540?–1596—Journeys—Northwest Coast of North America.
3. Northwest Coast of North America—Discovery and exploration—British.
4. Voyages around the world. I. Title.

F851.5.B38 2003   910'.92   C2003-910539-3

Cover design by Jessica Sullivan
Cover image from Mary Evans Picture Library
Printed and bound in Canada by Friesens
Printed on acid-free paper

The publisher gratefully acknowledges the financial support of the
Canada Council for the Arts, the British Columbia Arts Council,
and the Government of Canada through the Book Publishing Industry
Development Program (BPIDP) for its publishing activities.

For my dear Chauney, Natasha, and
Marni; my brother, Nicholas; and Pamela, Allan, and Kathy.

He was more skilfull in all poyntes of Navigation than any that ever was before his time, in his time, or since his death. He was also of a perfect memory, great Observation, Eloquent by Nature, Skilfull in Artillery, expert and apt to let blood and give Physicke unto his people according to the Climats. He was Low of stature, of strong limbs, broade Breasted, round headed, brown hayre, full Bearded, his eyes round, Large and cleare, well favoured, fayre, and of a cheerefull countenance.

His name was a terrour to the French, Spaniard, Portugal, and Indians. Many Princes of Italy, Germany and others, as well enemies as friends in his lifetime desired his Picture. He was the second that ever went through the straights of Magellan, and the first that ever went round about the world. He was married unto two wives, both young, yet he himselfe and ten of his brethren dyed without Issue. He made his youngest brother Thomas his heir who was with him in most and chiefest of his Imployments. In briefe, he was as famous in Europe and America as Tamberlaine in Asia and Africa.

In his imperfections hee was   Ambitious for Honour
                                          Unconstant in amity
                                          Greatly affected to Popularity.

—JOHN STOW, *THE LIFE AND DEATH OF SIR FRANCIS DRAKE* (1615)

CONTENTS

ঌ PART ONE ৼ

The Quest for Riches

ঌ PART TWO ৼ

Round About the Whole Globe of the Earth

◊ PART THREE ◊

Celebrity amid Secrecy

◊ PART FOUR ◊

The Northern Voyage, April to September 1579

ACKNOWLEDGMENTS

This book is the product of a research project that I could not have undertaken and completed without the support, advice, and encouragement of many people. I sincerely thank Bob Ward for supplying me in the first instance with copies of some of the scholarly literature, including his own publications on the subject, and for sharing with me his discovery of the altered latitude in the "Anonymous Narrative"; Dr. Tim Ball for tutoring me in the climate of the Little Ice Age, and for his many other efforts; Grant Keddie of the Royal British Columbia Museum for sharing his deep knowledge of the archaeological record of the coast; the staff of the British Columbia Archives for their assistance; Francis Herbert of the Royal Geographical Society for his advice, and for translating the text of the Hondius Broadside; Dr. Michelle Brown and Dr. Justin Clegg of the British Library for assisting my investigation of the altered numerals in the "Anonymous Narrative," and Anthony Payne of Bernard Quaritch, Ltd. for examining the manuscript with me; Peter Barber and Geoff Armitage of the British Library map room and Dr. Alan Jutsi of the Huntington Library for facilitating my examination of the cartographic record; Wayne Jensen of the Tillamook County Museum for the details of the archaic survey at Nehalem; Niki Ingram of the National Trust for access to the Molyneux globe at Petworth House; the Library of the Middle Temple for permission to photograph their Molyneux globe; Professor Richard Ruggles for his wonderful insights into the mapping of discovery and the secrecy aspect; Sir Ian Gourlay and Professor Thomas Symons for linking me to their Frobisher archival research group; Robert Baldwin for his examination of the Grenville manuscripts, and for other valuable insights; Dr. Marcel van den Broecke for reviewing my Ortelius findings; Professor Robin Winks for his unstinting support; Jim Thomson of the U.S. National Park Service for his many kind endeavors; Mark McCallum, Jane Smith, and the U.S. Forest Service for facilitating my Alaska investigations, and Dr. Frank Norris, Doug Scott, and Melissa Scott for joining us in that voyage; Doug Scott again for digging into the records at the Smithsonian; Lieutenant Commander Michael Brooks for his work on the navigation; and Dr. Andrew Cook for his advice and numerous kindnesses.

Sincere thanks to Dianne Fidler for the countless hours she spent transcribing the many drafts of my handwritten manuscript; to Jan Whitford, Bruce Westwood, and Jackie Kaiser for their determined support; and especially to Scott McIntyre and George Gibson for wanting me to tell this story, and for their infinite patience.

NOTE TO THE READER

ost of the quotes in this book have been taken from the compendia of documents assembled by Martin A. S. Hume, Zelia Nuttall, N. M. Penzer, E. G. R. Taylor, W. S. W. Vaux, Henry R. Wagner, and Irene A. Wright; or from other contemporary works reprinted through the auspices of the Hakluyt Society. For ease of reading, the spelling and punctuation have been modernized. The forms of personal names adopted are those most commonly used by English scholars. Where an English version of a place-name existed, it is used; otherwise the foreign or modern place-name is given. Aside from quotes, footnotes are provided only where an important interpretation by another author is adopted, or where the information is not represented in previous works about Drake. No attempt has been made to provide detailed references for the general course of events widely covered in other works. Unless otherwise noted, all dates cited are according to the old-style Julian calendar. To adjust a date to the modern calendar, ten days must be added.

THE SECRET VOYAGE OF
SIR FRANCIS DRAKE

PROLOGUE

And the 26 of Sept . . . we safely with joyfull minds and thankful hearts to God, arrived at Plymouth, the place of our first setting forth, after we had spent 2 years 10 months and some few odd days beside, in seeing the wonders of the Lord in the deep, in discovering so many admirable things, in going through with so many strange adventures, and overcoming so many difficulties in this our encompassing of this nether globe, and passing round about the world.

—THE WORLD ENCOMPASSED BY
SIR FRANCIS DRAKE, 1628

It was *nightfall on September 26, 1580, when the weatherworn bark came to* anchor in the outer harbor of Plymouth. The next day trumpeter John Brewer was dispatched to London to inform Sir Christopher Hatton, captain of Queen Elizabeth's bodyguard, of their return. Brewer reached London on September 29, and within hours the news created great excitement in the city. Francis Drake was back at last, his bark *Golden Hinde* laden with a huge haul of treasure. This time he had plundered Spanish shipping on the far side of America and then become the first captain to sail completely around the world.

Nearly three years had passed since Drake set sail from Plymouth, on December 13, 1577, with a company of 164 men and boys in five small ships. When they departed, only a handful among them knew their true destination. By order of Queen Elizabeth, the expedition had been cloaked in secrecy from the outset. To conceal its purpose from King Philip II of

Spain, the story had been given out that Drake was bound for Alexandria on a trading voyage. Instead he had taken his squadron southward across the equator, farther than any English ship had gone before, and farther still, to the dreaded Strait of Magellan at the southern extremity of America.

The plan of the voyage had been several years in the making. In 1570 Drake had commenced a private war of retribution against King Philip for losses suffered two years earlier in a treacherous Spanish attack on an English trading fleet in the harbor of San Juan de Ulúa, Mexico. Operating from hideouts along the Caribbean coast of Central America, Drake had plundered dozens of Spanish vessels and eluded all attempts to capture him. His crowning achievement had come when he formed an alliance with a band of runaway Negro slaves and seized 100,000 pesos of gold from a Spanish mule train carrying bullion across the Isthmus of Panama from the Pacific coast.

In the course of these exploits Drake had trekked across the isthmus to within sight of the South Sea,* and there conceived the idea of sailing through the strait discovered half a century before by Ferdinand Magellan to raid the coasts of Chile and Peru, where the Spanish ships carried rich cargoes of treasure. No such expedition could depart England without the Queen's consent, however, and her senior minister, Lord Burghley, was unalterably opposed to any such venture on the grounds that it would inflame already tense relations between England and Spain.

Drake persisted and found support from a more aggressive faction within Elizabeth's Privy Council. Led by her favorite, Robert Dudley, the Earl of Leicester, and Secretary of State Francis Walsingham, its members aimed to disrupt the flow of New World treasure with which King Philip was financing his increasingly menacing campaign against Protestant religious reform in Europe, and to share in Drake's plunder.

At the same time, others were reviving a long-standing English interest in discovery of a sea passage around the northern extremity of America to access the storied riches of Cathay and the Oriental Indies. Among the advocates of a search for a northern passage was Dr. John Dee, England's foremost cosmographer, and personal astrologer to the Queen. In 1575 a license to explore for the supposed northwest passage was granted to shipmaster Martin Frobisher, and the following year he sailed westward below

---

*Also referred to by this time as the Pacific Ocean.

Greenland into a broad opening between two headlands and returned to report that he had found its eastern entrance.

The pivotal question for Dee then came to the fore: Was America a separate continent from Asia, or were they joined north of the Pacific Ocean, as many geographers believed? If the latter, there would be no possibility of entering that ocean via a northern passage.

Dee was acquainted with the respected Flemish geographer Abraham Ortelius, who theorized that America and Asia were separated by a Strait of Anian that ran northward from the Pacific to a junction with the supposed passage from the Atlantic Ocean. However, Ortelius also projected that North America was comparable in breadth to Asia, leavng only a narrow strait between them. Therefore, if an expedition were to sail from Frobisher's entrance all the way across the top of this great expanse and fail to locate this Strait of Anian, its members would likely perish in the icy grip of the arctic winter before they could get back to the Atlantic.

The only other means of confirming the existence of the strait was to send an expedition southward, all the way around South America, or Africa and Asia, and onward into the North Pacific to look for its outlet, and this became the key that unlocked Drake's project. In consideration for being permitted to pass through Magellan's Strait to raid Spanish shipping, Drake undertook to continue northward and search for the Strait of Anian. If successful, he would attempt to return to England through the northwest passage, completing a circumnavigation of America.

Thus, Drake had embarked in great secrecy upon both the most daring naval expedition and the most ambitious voyage of exploration ever conceived.

The first word of Drake's progress had come when his principal consort, the Queen's bark Elizabeth, returned to England in June of 1579, and the news was not good. Drake's squadron, by then reduced to three ships, had passed through the Strait of Magellan, but emerging into the Pacific in September 1578, had been struck by violent storms and driven far to the south, toward the unknown region of the Antarctic. The bark Marigold had disappeared, and the Elizabeth had turned back for England, leaving Drake and the crew of the Golden Hinde to continue the voyage on their own.

In August 1579, however, word of Drake's spectacularly successful raid had reached Seville, where English merchants, nervous that his actions might provoke a war, chartered a ship to carry the news to England. According to the dispatches from Mexico, the last the Spaniards had seen of Drake had been at the little Pacific port of Guatulco in April 1579, after which he had vanished. From London, Spanish ambassador Bernardino de Mendoza reported that officials at Plymouth had been instructed to assist Drake in landing and guarding his treasure as soon as he arrived. But several more months passed without further word of him, and in February 1580 Mendoza reported that Drake's backers had begun to despair.

After many more months, however, Drake was finally back, and once again the veil of official secrecy descended. On October 16 Mendoza wrote an urgent dispatch to King Philip relating what his informants at Elizabeth's court had learned about Drake's first meeting with her. They had met for six hours, and Drake had presented her with a large chart and a journal of everything that had happened on the voyage. Her councillors were "very particular not to divulge the route by which Drake returned," and his men had been warned not to disclose anything or they would suffer "pain of death." Moreover, Drake was proposing to return to the Pacific and was saying that he would be able to make the round-trip in a year, "as he has found a very short way."[1]

Soon afterward Walsingham drafted a proposal for a new enterprise. In consideration for his "late notable discovery," Drake was to serve as lifetime governor of the venture and receive 10 percent of the profits, while the Queen's share would be 20 percent.[2] In January 1581 Mendoza reported that Drake was to take ten ships out to the Pacific and rendezvous with the Earl of Leicester's brother-in-law, who would bring six more. In April, Elizabeth led a procession past throngs of Londoners to the deck of the *Golden Hinde* and knighted Drake. Two days later Mendoza reported that she had decided Drake would not go back to the Pacific after all; someone else would take his place.

The follow-up expedition was organized under the command of Edward Fenton and finally set sail on May 1, 1582. Fenton's secret instructions called for "the better discovery of the Northwest Passage," and he was authorized to leave behind at an undisclosed place, "to inhabit and dwell therein," as many of his company as he thought advisable.[3] In the meantime, however, King Philip had sent a fleet with 3,500 men to fortify Magellan's Strait against further intrusions into his dominions. When Fenton reached South America and learned that the Spanish fleet lay ahead, he turned back.

Immediately upon Drake's return in 1580, Queen Elizabeth had ordered a ban on publication of any details of his voyage. In time, Drake began giving hand-drawn maps depicting his route around the world to important friends. In an early rendition, drawn with pen and ink on the world map of Abraham Ortelius, his route extended northward along the coast of North America to latitude 57 degrees—the latitude of southern Alaska—before returning south and homeward via the East Indies. Then, with the help of a young Flemish artist named Jodocus Hondius, Drake produced several more maps. On these maps his track northward terminated at a lower latitude, where an inscription read "turned back on account of the ice," and then returned southward to a place called Nova Albion* before heading across the Pacific. On some of the maps Nova Albion was at the head of an inlet in the coast, but on another it was an island: one of a chain of islands stretching some 500 miles along the Pacific coast of North America.

In 1584, with England and Spain on the brink of war, Drake resurrected his proposal for a great Pacific enterprise, and Elizabeth gave her consent. This time he planned to take fifteen ships and 1,600 men. Yet as he was preparing his fleet, she changed his mission to the sacking of King Philip's Caribbean possessions. Drake set sail for the Caribbean in September 1585 and returned triumphant in July 1586, whereupon he discovered that a new expedition had been dispatched to the Pacific during his absence.

Shortly thereafter Drake's mapmaker Hondius began revising Abraham Ortelius's atlas maps of northwest America and sending them to Ortelius for publication on the Continent. On the maps, Ortelius's imaginary coastline remained unchanged, but arrayed along it were many descriptive place-names—capes, bays, and rivers—reaching up the coast to his Strait of Anian.

The conflict with Spain entered a new phase in 1587 with Drake's brilliant raid on Cadiz. Then in 1588 his career reached its zenith with his role

---

*Albion was an ancient name for England.

in the defeat of the great Spanish Armada sent to invade England and depose Elizabeth. With each triumph books, pictures, and ballads were published in Drake's praise. Across Europe friend and foe alike regarded him as the finest seaman and naval commander of the age. Nevertheless, in England the official ban on publication of anything about his great voyage continued.

Finally, in 1589 Richard Hakluyt, England's leading propagandist for overseas colonization, announced on the title page to his forthcoming book of English voyages that it would include an account of a voyage to Chile, Peru, and "*Nova Albion* upon the backside of *Canada*, further than any Christian hitherto hath pierced."[4] But when Hakluyt's book was printed, the account was not included.

Hakluyt's account, which was withheld by official order, had been adapted from a longer narrative Drake had loaned to him. Drake subsequently revised this narrative, and on New Year's Day 1593 he presented the manuscript to Elizabeth, requesting her permission to publish it, "that Posterity be not deprived" of such knowledge as had been gained from his efforts.[5] The manuscript was suppressed, however, and a carefully edited rendition of Hakluyt's shorter account was published instead.

In 1595 Drake sailed with another expedition for the Caribbean, where he died at sea the following January. Thirty-two years later, with England and Spain again at war, his narrative finally appeared in print, "offered now at last to public view, both for the honour of the actor, but especially for the stirring up of heroic spirits to benefit their Country, and eternize their names by like noble attempts."[6]

Together with other contemporary sources, including a wealth of Spanish documents, Drake's narrative enables a vivid account of events up to the point where he departed Guatulco, Mexico, on April 16, 1579. Like the official account published by Richard Hakluyt so many years before, however, it concealed the true extent of his northern explorations, and unfortunately, the original charts and journals of his voyage subsequently disappeared. But the cartographic information that he gave out privately to his friends, Ortelius, and others, much of it enciphered to comply with certain rules of secrecy, was designed to preserve knowledge of his discoveries, and has recently been deciphered to reveal the true extent of his voyage.[7]

The name Sir Francis Drake is emblazoned in history as one of England's greatest heroes. His innovative and often brilliant exploits in the New World and in defense of his homeland mark the beginning of England's rise as a great sea power. Among his many adventures, his voyage around the world has long been celebrated as one of the most remarkable of the age. Yet because his discoveries on the northwest coast of America were tightly wrapped in official secrecy and then lost to memory, the voyage is remembered as a consummate display of his genius and audacity as a gold-seeking privateer. Rarely is he thought of as an explorer. However, his maps reveal that Drake performed an astonishing feat of exploration, and enable the full story of his voyage to be told at last.

PART ONE

The Quest for Riches

San Juan de Ulúa

*I*n the second week of August, 1568, a fleet of eight seaworn ships sailed through the Yucatán Channel, bound for the Straits of Florida and thence home to England. Aboard his flagship, the *Jesus of Lubeck*, their captain-general, John Hawkins, was satisfied with the results of their voyage. As in his previous expeditions, he had had to contend with King Philip's injunction against his Spanish colonies trading with foreigners. However, Hawkins had assembled a sufficiently imposing force to overcome the reluctance of Philip's officials at several ports, and he had managed to sell most of his goods.[1]

The principal ships in Hawkins's fleet were the two old men-of-war that Queen Elizabeth had loaned to the venture in consideration for her share of the profits. At 700 tons—the vessel's "burden," or carrying capacity—the *Jesus* was one of England's largest ships, but she was nearly thirty years old and had been condemned by the Queen's navy as too costly to maintain; and the *Minion*, 350 tons, was in hardly better condition. Nevertheless, they provided the heavy armament that Hawkins needed to back up his demands. With four smaller ships as escorts, and a company of 408 men and boys, he had sailed from Plymouth in October 1567. On the coast of Africa he had added a French privateer and a captured Portuguese caravel to his fleet before setting sail across the Atlantic.

After stopping at the islands of Dominica and Margarita, they had followed the coast of South America westward into the Caribbean. At most of their ports of call virtually the same scene had played out: Indeed it had become a practiced charade on both sides. Upon arriving, Hawkins re-

quested permission to trade with the colonists, but the local Spanish governor replied that no one could do so without a license for the purpose, duly
issued from Seville. Hawkins then landed a party of armed men and threatened the town, and after secret negotiations to fix his share of the proceeds,
the governor capitulated and the trading began.

The goods Hawkins sold included English cloth and manufactures, but
principally were Negro slaves. The Spanish colonies were clamoring for
slave labor, and Hawkins was determined to seize the opportunity for profit
regardless of the commodity. On this voyage he had brought 450 men,
women, and children from the coast of West Africa. Most had survived the
eight-week crossing, and he had obtained good prices for them. With
29,743 gold pesos plus quantities of silver and pearls in hand, he was anxious to sail clear of the Caribbean before the season of great storms set in.

Serving as a captain under Hawkins was Francis Drake. In his
midtwenties, Drake had already spent half his life in the seagoing profession. When he reached the age of twelve or thirteen his father had arranged
for him to apprentice under the old captain of a small bark* plying the
coastal trade between England, France, and the Low Countries, or
Netherlands, and Drake had learned to read current, wind, and tide, and to
handle a ship in all weather on those treacherous coasts. Then at age twenty
he had gone into the service of his wealthy ship-owning kin, the Hawkins
brothers of Plymouth, and this was his third voyage to the Caribbean in
their employ.[2] His skill in directing men, and the alacrity with which he performed his duties, had marked him for advancement, and on the present
voyage John Hawkins had given him command of the fifty-ton bark *Judith*
when they departed Africa.

On August 12 Hawkins's fleet rounded the western cape of Cuba into the Strait of Florida.
At eight o'clock in the morning, as they did every day, the crew of each ship
assembled around their mainmast for the daily religious service. Removing
their caps and kneeling on the deck, they recited the Psalms, the Lord's Prayer,
and the new Creed in English, and then one of the ship's officers delivered the
sermon. On the *Judith* it probably was Drake himself who did so, for like his

---

* A bark was a three-masted vessel that was square-rigged on her fore and main masts and had a tri-
angular, or lateen, sail rigged fore and aft from her mizzen mast.

father he had become a fervent preacher of the Protestant faith. After the service the men began to reduce sail, as the wind had stiffened noticeably. Normally, they would have gathered again for the evening service, but as the day wore on the velocity of the wind grew steadily, and by late afternoon they were engulfed in a violent storm.

As the tempest grew in intensity, Hawkins signaled his ships to turn and run before the wind. Soon afterward the bark *William and John* disappeared from sight. Through the night and the next day Hawkins and his crew were driven northward until they found themselves off the west coast of Florida. In the pounding seas the *Jesus's* seams began to open up, so much so that when men were sent below to plug the leaks they found fish swimming in her ballast. Hawkins searched in vain for a sheltered anchorage. After four days the wind subsided, but the calm lasted for only a day: No sooner had Hawkins begun to assess the damage to his ships than another powerful storm struck, this time from the northeast. Over the next four days they were driven continually to the southwest, and when this storm finally abated they were far into the Gulf of Mexico, where no English ship had been before.

Sighting the southern coast of the gulf, they followed it westward, but again there was no sheltered anchorage. Then they intercepted a Spanish vessel whose captain informed Hawkins that the only refuge on the entire coast was the harbor of San Juan de Ulúa. Located 15 miles from Vera Cruz and 200 miles from Mexico City, San Juan de Ulúa was no less than the principal port of Mexico.

For a year prior to Hawkins's departure from England, the Spanish ambassador had demanded assurances from Queen Elizabeth that Hawkins would not be permitted to return to the Caribbean. As if to enforce this, when Hawkins was fitting out the expedition at Plymouth, seven Spanish warships had sailed boldly into the harbor and had only turned away when he loosed his cannons on them.[3] England and Spain were not at war, but there was considerable tension over Hawkins's efforts to break King Philip's trade embargo, and he fully understood the danger of taking his battered ships into San Juan de Ulúa.

However great the risk, Hawkins resolved that there was no alternative. His ships were in need of repair, the *Jesus* urgently so, and there was no possibility of his getting his company and profits home unless they replenished their water and provisions. On September 16, more than a month after their ordeal began, they entered the harbor of San Juan de Ulúa. As soon as they had anchored, Hawkins landed a party of men to commandeer the cannons guarding the entrance to the harbor. Then he dispatched a letter to the governor of Vera Cruz, assuring him that he had come in peace, would pay the current price for water, provisions, and the materials needed for repairs to his ships, and that as soon as these repairs were completed he would be gone.

The next morning, however, thirteen Spanish ships appeared on the horizon. A merchant fleet from Seville escorted by two warships, it was carrying the newly appointed Viceroy of New Spain, Don Martin Enriquez. Hawkins was faced with a terrible dilemma. His cannons and those on the quay were sufficient to deny the Spaniards access to their own harbor, but doing so would surely have been an act of war. However, if he let them in and they then resorted to treachery, he risked his men being overwhelmed at close quarters.

After three days of negotiations, Enriquez agreed to allow Hawkins to make his repairs and depart without harm, and Hawkins allowed the Spanish fleet into the already crowded harbor. The English ships were lined up side by side from one end of the quay and the Spaniards from the other, with little space remaining between the two fleets, and for the next three days they exchanged courtesies. However, Enriquez had secretly ordered soldiers brought down from Vera Cruz and preparations made for an assault on the English.

On the morning of September 23, Hawkins saw that the Spaniards had placed a big merchantman in the gap between the fleets, adjacent to the *Minion*. They had cut new gunports in her side, and large numbers of men from the other Spanish ships were massing aboard her. Alarmed, Hawkins sent the master of the *Jesus*, Robert Barrett, to complain to Enriquez aboard the Spanish flagship. Barrett returned with the Viceroy's assurances that he would protect the Englishmen; but the offending activities continued, so Hawkins sent him back to Enriquez with a stronger protest. Realizing that the element of surprise was rapidly disappearing, Enriquez had Barrett placed in irons and gave the order for the attack to begin.

Suddenly, a trumpet sounded, and the Spaniards poured over the side of the merchantman onto the *Minion*. Hawkins's men rushed to repulse them, but simultaneously hundreds of Spanish soldiers streamed onto the quay, slaughtering the English sailors there and turning its guns on

John Hawkins

Hawkins's ships. Hauling furiously on their stern moorings, his men pulled their ships away from the quay, and a fearful cannonade commenced at point-blank range.

The battle raged all afternoon. After six hours of fighting, the Spanish fleet lay heavily damaged, its two warships sunk. Hawkins's ships were in scarcely better condition: Four were hopelessly mangled, and the foremast of the *Jesus* had been carried away by chain shot while five shots had passed through her mainmast. Only the *Minion* and Francis Drake's *Judith* were sufficiently intact to be sailed. To have any hope of seeing England again, they had to escape before they suffered any more damage. With a Spanish fire ship drifting toward them, Hawkins and the crew of the *Jesus* hastily transferred to the *Minion* and then Drake led the way out of the harbor. Sometime in the night, however, the two ships became separated.[4]

The next morning Hawkins faced an appalling scene. Clinging to the *Minion* for survival with scarcely any provisions for the long trip home were 200 exhausted and in many cases wounded men. For two weeks they followed the coast, foraging as they might. Then 100 men volunteered to be put ashore so that the others would have a chance of reaching England.

Aiming to reach the French Huguenot colony in Florida, about thirty of those left behind banded together and set off on the 1,500-mile walk around the Gulf of Mexico. Five months later they reached Florida but were unable to find the French colonists because they had been massacred by the Spaniards three years earlier. The sailors turned north, following Indian trails from one tribal territory to another, invariably being greeted hospitably. As more of them elected to remain with their native hosts, the party steadily diminished. A year after the battle of San Juan de Ulúa, however, three of them, having trekked some 3,000 miles, were picked up by a French ship on the coast of present-day New Brunswick and eventually returned to England.[5]

However, most of the men who were left in Mexico were rounded up by the Spanish and suffered hideous cruelties at the hands of the Inquisition. Robert Barrett and three others were taken to Seville to be burned at the stake as heretics. Others were hanged or died of the tortures inflicted on them. Those who were not put to death either rotted in prison or were sentenced to spend the remainder of their lives working the oars of Spanish galleys. Only the boys were spared, being sent to monasteries.

Including the crew of the *William and John*, which had continued her voyage homeward after the storm, fewer than 100 of the men who had embarked on the expedition ever saw England again. Hawkins finally reached England four months after the battle. The voyage home was a horrendous ordeal. Reduced to eating boiled cowhides and vermin, the men on the *Minion* weakened and died by the dozen. Only fifteen survived the voyage. Francis Drake and what remained of the crew of the *Judith* had arrived at Plymouth just five days before. After listening to Drake's report, Hawkins's brother William had written to Secretary of State William Cecil and the Privy Council, informing them of the disaster, and dispatched Drake to London with the letters so that the council could hear a firsthand account of the affair.

Letters of Marque

or the young sea captain Francis Drake, the 200-mile horse ride from Plymouth to London with urgent letters for the Queen's ministers must have evoked memories of another hurried journey on the same road, probably on foot, when he was age six or seven.

The date of Drake's birth is uncertain, although sometime in 1542 or 1543 appears most likely. He was the eldest son of Edmund Drake, whose family had resided in the valley of the River Tavy, near Plymouth, for a century or more. They were of yeoman stock, tenant farmers of land originally leased from the Benedictine monks of Tavistock Abbey. After the dissolution of the Catholic monasteries by King Henry VIII, Lord John Russell had acquired title to the abbey lands and become the Drakes' landlord.[1]

Edmund married one of the Myllwaye family, whose first name is unknown, but who eventually bore him twelve sons. When their first was born, they christened him Francis after Lord Russell's son Francis, the future Earl of Bedford, who stood as his godfather. Only the names of four of Francis Drake's brothers are known: John, Joseph, Edward, and the youngest, Thomas. Some of the others probably died in infancy.

In Tavistock Edmund Drake found employment as a sheep shearer. As the Drakes were related to the noted Plymouth shipowner and privateer William Hawkins, father of William and John Hawkins, it is also possible that Edmund served as a sailor aboard one of the elder Hawkins's armed merchantmen during the war of 1543–45 with France. But then in 1548 or 1549 he took his young family and fled England's west country.

The cause of Edmund's sudden flight has never been fully explained.

Plymouth, England, ca. 1536

Francis Drake later said that his family was driven from Tavistock by religious strife, and this accords with the turbulent events of the time. Since early in the century there had been growing criticism throughout northern Europe of the Catholic Church and its clergy as being self-serving and corrupt, and of the doctrine and ritual of Catholicism itself. The most influential ideas were those of the adherents of Martin Luther, who rejected the Catholic concepts of penance and purgatory and the veneration of images and shrines, and sought to remove the priest as intermediary between God and man, arguing that salvation could be obtained only by direct faith in Christ.[2]

In England the first impetus for reform had come when Henry VIII, unable to sire a male heir by his first wife, Catherine of Aragon, sought an annulment of their marriage by the Pope so that he could take Anne Boleyn as his new bride. When the Pope declined to grant his request, Henry orchestrated a series of measures by Parliament severing the nation's religious governance from Rome and vesting the right to define religious doctrine in the English Crown. The property of the Church was confiscated, and the insular Church of England was created.

Upon Henry's death in 1547, the crown passed to his only son, Edward, a sickly ten-year-old, and his protectors pressed ahead with further reforms. These caused increasing unrest in the still predominantly Catholic nation. The majority wanted a Church free from foreign interference but preferred the old form of worship. In 1548 there were public disturbances over an edict requiring the removal of statues and images from all churches and chapels. The following year the imposition of a new Prayer Book and replacement of the Latin service by one in English sparked an uprising in Cornwall. As the rebels swept eastward into Devon, many Protestants abandoned their homes and took refuge in Plymouth Castle or on St. Nicholas Island in Plymouth Sound. The rebellion was put down later that year by forces under the command of Lord Russell.[3]

The Drake family disappeared from the records of Tavistock after 1549, and so it is quite possible that they did leave the valley as a consequence of the Catholic uprising. However, in 1548 Edmund Drake had been indicted in the county of Devon for stealing a horse, and on another occasion assaulting and robbing a man.[4] Some have therefore concluded that Edmund departed Tavistock as a fugitive of justice. Shortly afterward, however, he was granted a pardon for these incidents, and conceivably they were somehow linked to the religious unrest at the time.

Whichever the case, Francis Drake later recounted that his father took them across the south of England into Kent, where they found a home in the hull of an old ship lying in the River Medway, near the mouth of the Thames. The Medway was where the ships of the Royal Navy created by Henry VIII were laid up for repairs, and Edmund managed to eke out a living preaching the new faith to the seamen. So it was here that young Francis absorbed old sailors' tales and developed his fascination for the sea and ships. But soon unrest and insurrection invaded their lives again.

When Edward VI succumbed to illness in 1553, he was succeeded by Mary Tudor, daughter of Henry's first wife, Catherine of Aragon. Mary reinstated Catholicism and commenced persecuting adherents of the Protestant faith. Moreover, she accepted a proposal of marriage from Prince Philip, then heir to the throne of Spain. When word of the proposed union spread through the country, uprisings were plotted and a force raised in Kent by Sir Thomas Wyatt attempted to march on London, but they were defeated and brutally punished. Francis Drake, then eleven or twelve years of age, probably saw the remnants of their bodies displayed in Kent to discourage further uprisings.

Mary suspected that her half sister, Elizabeth, Henry's daughter by Anne Boleyn, had conspired with the rebels, and ordered her sent to the Tower of London, where she might not have survived but for her skillful appeals to the Privy Council. Fearful of the public reaction to their putting Henry's second daughter on trial for treason, Mary's councillors persuaded her to allow Elizabeth to retire to her estates.

Although Mary and Philip's marriage was consummated, it failed to produce an heir, and in August 1555 Philip departed England to take up his duties, at the behest of his father, as ruler of the Netherlands. The following year he became King of Spain, and thereafter he visited England only once, for three months in 1557.

Although Philip had attempted to moderate her policy, Mary continued dispensing savage punishments to persons accused of promoting a departure from Catholic doctrine. In all, some 300 Protestants were burned at the stake as heretics, and countless others were dispossessed, imprisoned, tortured, and mutilated for their beliefs.

The country was shocked by the magnitude of the tyranny, and in response to it Protestantism spread rapidly. By this time Drake was serving the apprenticeship his father had arranged with the old sea captain, and in his travels he would have gained his first sense of the widespread yearning for freedom from religious oppression, not only in England but in the Low Countries and France as well.

After a protracted illness, Queen Mary died on the morning of November 17, 1558, and with her death Philip ceased to be King of England. Around noon that same day Elizabeth, the last surviving offspring of Henry VIII, was proclaimed Queen of England at age twenty-five.

Elizabeth surprised everyone by the skill with which she gained her subjects' confidence and affection. Tactfully but firmly, she reestablished the Church of England as the foundation of English Protestant faith, while reassuring Catholics that their

Queen Elizabeth 1

private religious beliefs would be tolerated. She was quick-witted and possessed a powerful intellect nurtured by voracious reading. "There never was so wise woman born as Queen Elizabeth," wrote her chief minister, William Cecil, "for she spoke and understood all languages, and knew all estates and dispositions and princes, and particularly was so expert in the knowledge of her own realm as no councillor she had could tell her what she knew not before."[5]

Most especially, it was Elizabeth's vigor and personal magnetism that captured her subjects' hearts. Traveling regularly into the City and country to be seen and heard by the common people, she instilled in them a love of her majesty which transcended affairs of Church and State.

When Elizabeth ascended the throne, however, two decades of religious upheaval, war, and neglect had brought England near to ruin. Among the most serious problems, the steadily increasing flow of silver into Europe from Spain's colonies had debased England's economy. Prices had risen, and ordinary people were hard-pressed to survive. Landowners had raised rents and evicted tenants who could not pay; village commons, which provided part of the peasants' livelihood, had been enclosed; and plowland had been converted into pasture employing fewer hands.[6]

England's principal exports were wool and manufactured cloth, the latter traditionally providing work for a large part of the population, since spinning and weaving were peasant industries throughout the land. Due to the change in economic conditions, exports of these goods to continental Europe had declined. The cumulative effect of all this was impoverishment and vagrancy on an unprecedented scale. England had become a nation of unemployed "wandering idly up and down for lack of honest entertainment."[7]

To people of vision, the remedy for England's woes lay in finding new markets and developing new trade. Beginning in the reign of Edward, joint-stock ventures had been organized by the merchants of London to open up trade with Russia, the eastern Mediterranean, and Guinea, and had enjoyed some success. However, the enormous riches of the Orient and the New World held a greater allure, and the latter being nearer to hand, some of the most powerful men in England and the Queen herself had invested in the ventures organized by the Hawkins brothers with the aim of obtaining a share of Spain's lucrative colonial commerce. The battle of San Juan de Ulúa had brought their enterprise to an abrupt end, and when Francis Drake arrived in London bearing this news, there already were worrying signs that a deeper crisis was looming.

There is no surviving record of Drake's meeting with William Cecil and the Privy Council to give his eyewitness account of the treachery at San Juan de Ulúa. In the letters he delivered to them, William Hawkins urged that his captains be issued commissions of reprisal authorizing them to seize Spanish shipping in order to recover the losses suffered by his brother. The practice of issuing such commissions, or "letters of marque," giving legitimacy to what would otherwise be acts of piracy, had originated with the French and then been adopted by Henry VIII in his war against France as an inducement to private shipowners to augment the strength of his Royal Navy. The bearer of such a commission was known as a privateer, and the father of William and John Hawkins had been one of the most successful privateers in that war. However, Elizabeth decided on a different approach to the matter.

A rumor that John Hawkins's fleet had met with catastrophe had actually reached London from Spain in late November, two months before he returned, just as five Spanish ships carrying £85,000 to pay King Philip's army in the Netherlands were chased into Plymouth and Southampton by French privateers. Informed of the rumor concerning Hawkins, Elizabeth ordered the treasure seized and brought to the Tower of London. But this was as far as she was prepared to go toward an open confrontation with Philip.

In the eleventh year of her reign, Elizabeth had done much to stabilize England from within. The key to her and the nation's security, she well understood, was her ability to avoid a war with either of the principal Catholic powers, France and Spain. In its present circumstances England was ill equipped to fight either by itself. France and Spain were rivals, however, and Elizabeth could alter the balance of power between them by choosing to ally herself with one against the other. She had therefore made it the cornerstone of her foreign policy that if one threatened, she would promote improved relations with the other, holding out the prospect of an alliance as a deterrent to the aggressor. Of late, however, it had become increasingly difficult for her to apply this policy effectively.

Traditionally, France had been England's enemy and Spain its ally, and in the early days of Elizabeth's reign the threat from France had seemed greater than ever. Elizabeth's Catholic cousin Mary, Queen of Scotland and France, also had a legitimate claim to the crown of England, and together with her husband, King Francis II, had threatened to invade England and seize the throne. But Francis had died suddenly in 1560, and soon afterward France had become immersed in a series of insurrections by its Protestant Huguenot subjects. The first rebellion had ended with a compromise in 1563, but a second had broken out in 1567 and a third the following year. Thus torn by internal strife, France, for the moment at least, posed no threat to England. As France had weakened, though, England's relations with Spain had deteriorated.

When he succeeded to the throne of Spain in 1556, Philip II had become the most powerful monarch in Christendom. His inheritance included not only Spain, the West

Indies, New Spain, and most of South America but also most of Italy and all of the Low Countries. Philip's father, Charles V, Holy Roman Emperor, had spent his life building this empire, and his passing of the crown of Spain to Philip was the final step in a carefully laid plan of succession designed to prepare him for his duties and further secure his inheritance.[8]

Philip had begun to exercise power in 1543, at age sixteen, when his father appointed him regent of Spain. Next, in an effort to consolidate the two Iberian crowns, Charles had him marry Princess Maria of Portugal. Maria bore Philip a son but died shortly after giving birth, and their child, Carlos, subsequently proved to be mentally unstable. In 1554 Philip became king of Naples. Then Charles had directed Philip's attention to the security of the Netherlands.

Since they were the only practical place to base an army for the purpose, the Low Countries were the key to keeping Spain's great rival France in check. As well, the trading houses of Antwerp and the Dutch ports were a vital conduit for commerce with the German states. Nevertheless, support for Spanish rule in the Netherlands was being eroded by the spread of new ideas from Germany and England, and the English in particular posed a threat to the stability of the empire because they could disrupt the crucial sea route between the Netherlands and Spain.

Thus, when his cousin Mary Tudor sought his advice regarding marriage, Charles had wasted little time offering his son to be her husband. The restoration of England to Catholicism, he hoped, would strike a hard blow against the advance of heresy; the sea route through the English Channel to the Netherlands would be protected; and France would be further hemmed in. Moreover, if the marriage produced an heir, England would be joined to the Spanish empire.

After Philip dutifully wed Mary, Charles implemented the last step in his plan by abdicating the throne of Spain to him, and with it, responsibility for stemming the tide of Lutheranism. Backed by the Pope, the Holy Inquisition, and the Jesuits, Philip had assumed the mantle of leading protector of the Catholic faith.

The death of Mary Tudor and succession of Elizabeth to the throne of England had therefore presented serious concerns for Philip. Initially, he had attempted to resolve them by proposing marriage to Elizabeth provided that she would embrace Catholicism, but she had politely declined. Despite her heretical views, Philip had dissuaded the Pope from excommunicating Elizabeth because the alternative of replacing her with her cousin Mary carried with it the certain prospect of an Anglo-French alliance.

In 1564, however, believing that English traders were stirring up unrest in the Low Countries, Philip's officials closed first Antwerp and then all of the Dutch ports to them. Nevertheless, a major Protestant revolt soon erupted in several of the Dutch provinces, and in 1567 Philip sent an army under the command of the Duke of Alba to chastise the rebels and restore order.

The next year, while Francis Drake was adventuring in the Caribbean with John Hawkins, France's Huguenot leaders adopted the port of La Rochelle on the Biscay coast as their capital and sent out a swarm of privateers against all "papist" shipping, whether French, Spanish, or Portuguese. Lured by the prospect of sharing in the booty, English and Dutch captains flocked to La Rochelle to obtain Huguenot letters of marque, and Spain began to suffer losses to Englishmen engaged in what amounted to an international Protestant uprising.

Elizabeth denied any responsibility for the conflict, and indeed the rebellions in the Netherlands and France were not of her making. However, Philip knew well that she had tacitly supported them, and that senior officials of her navy as well as some of London's leading merchants had underwritten many of the privateers preying on Spanish shipping under Huguenot colors. Further complicating the situation, in May of 1568 Mary, Queen of Scots, had fled into England to escape an uprising by the Protestant lords of Scotland, and Elizabeth had ordered her placed under house arrest. Consequently, Philip's complaints to Elizabeth had grown progressively more strident, and she had begun to worry that matters had gone too far. At the time, the Duke of Alba was still engaged in his brutal purge of the Dutch rebellion, but Elizabeth had become increasingly concerned about Philip's plans for Alba's army once he had completed that mission.

England had fallen to invaders before, and the possibility of a Spanish assault on its sovereignty was deeply worrisome to Elizabeth and her council. The nation's chief defenses and fortresses were in a ruinous state after years of neglect, its arms and munitions were seriously depleted, and its navy was small and in poor repair. To restore them would require great sums, and Elizabeth's treasury was bare. Philip, on the other hand, could draw on the resources of his empire and the papacy to field an experienced,

King Philip II

professional army and superior naval forces. Moreover, there was the ever-present danger that dissidents within the country might organize an uprising of English Catholics to aid an invasion.

For all of these reasons, Elizabeth could ill afford to enter into open hostilities with Spain. It was abundantly clear that the Hawkinses' attempt to obtain a share of Spain's colonial wealth through trade had been dealt a terminal blow at San Juan de Ulúa. Philip was determined to stamp out these intrusions, so a new strategy was needed to bolster England's beleaguered economy. The formal commissions of reprisal that William Hawkins sought from Elizabeth therefore were not forthcoming. Yet there is every appearance that an understanding was reached by which Elizabeth looked the other way while the Hawkins' captains were unleashed in a new enterprise that was not in the nature of trade.

❧ 3. ❧

Drake's Private War

*O**n July 4, 1569, Francis Drake married a Plymouth girl, Mary Newman, at the* nearby church of St. Budeaux. Beyond the records of their marriage and her death fourteen years later, very little is known about Mary. Like many other wives in Plymouth, she would see her husband for only brief intervals between his long absences at sea, but they were able to spend a few months together after their wedding. Then, toward the end of the year, Drake set sail with two small barks, the *Dragon* and the *Swan*, bound for the Caribbean.

Little is known about Drake's 1569 voyage except that he later described it as a reconnaissance. However, his whereabouts may be at least partly surmised from subsequent events, for late in 1570 he set off again from Plymouth with the bark *Swan*, and this time he had a particular destination in mind.

The narrow Isthmus of Panama was a vital link in the route between Spain and its South American conquests. All of the treasure the Spaniards extracted from the former Inca empire in Ecuador, Peru, and Chile was carried by ship up the Pacific coast to the port of Panama, where it was transferred to mule trains for the journey across the isthmus to the Caribbean. From Panama the pack trains climbed for some fifteen miles to the outpost of Venta Cruces, at the head of navigation on the Chagres River. There some treasure was occasionally loaded onto small barks and shipped downriver to the Caribbean during the rainy season, from May until December, when the overland route was impassable. But most of the gold and silver was carried across the isthmus after the rains subsided, and from Venta Cruces the pack trains continued overland on a tortuous, forty-mile track through dense tropical rain forest to the shores of the Caribbean.

The terminus of both routes, where the treasure was stored pending shipment to Spain, was the town of Nombre de Dios, some 45 miles east of the mouth of the Chagres and 300 miles west of the principal port of the Spanish Main, Cartagena. Toward the end of each year, a fleet arrived from Spain carrying European merchandise and supplies for Philip's South American colonists, and the cargoes destined for the Pacific coast were off-loaded here for transport up the Chagres to Venta Cruces and thence Panama. Then the fleet continued on to Cartagena, where it remained into the New Year before returning to load the treasure stored at Nombre de Dios and carry it home to Spain. Thus Nombre de Dios and the overland and river routes connecting it to Panama regularly saw the richest traffic in the New World. It was here that Drake had decided to focus his efforts.[1]

By February 1571 Drake and about twenty men were employing a pinnace—an open boat with oars and sails—to intercept Spanish merchantmen coming and going around the mouth of the Chagres, taking from them merchandise, money, and other valuables. The annual fleet had arrived at Nombre de Dios, and three of the armed galleons were sent out but could not catch him. With his bark hidden, and operating in the light, shallow draft pinnace, Drake was able to run close inshore, in shoal waters where the Spaniards dared not risk their big ships pursuing him. Then he proceeded boldly up the river to Venta Cruces, where he seized a large quantity of goods off the wharf and disabled several barks. A second expedition was sent out to search for him, and then a third, but he always eluded them.

Drake had found a perfect hideaway in a small bay some ninety miles east of Nombre de Dios. Flanked by two pillars of rock, its entrance was barely 300 feet wide. Beyond lay a round bay half a mile in diameter and containing ten to twelve fathoms of water. Teeming with fish and its shores overhung by the forest, it was an ideal place to conceal his bark and Spanish prizes. Clearing an area for a camp, his men found that the forest was alive with fowl, so they named the bay Port Pheasant.

Although there is little information from the English side, it appears that Drake worked in concert with other Hawkins captains. In May he led

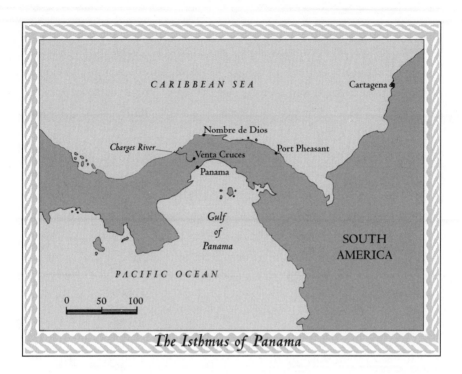

another raid up the Chagres, where they rounded up eighteen barks, transferred the most valuable cargoes to four, and made off with them. The
same month, frustrated colonial officials wrote to King Philip: "They are
so fully in control of the coast of Nombre de Dios, Cartagena, Tolu, Santa
Marta and Cabo de la Vela, that traffic dares not sail from Santo Domingo
thither, and trade and commerce are diminishing between the Windward
Islands and this Main."[2] However, Drake had all the plunder he could
manage, and after burying some provisions at Port Pheasant, he set sail for
England.

When he reached Plymouth, Drake anchored outside the harbor while
a messenger was sent to London. The situation called for caution. He had
acted without any written authority from the Crown, and if political tensions had escalated with Spain he knew the government could have charged
him with piracy to placate King Philip. Yet arrangements were soon made
for him to land his treasure, and no doubt a significant share was delivered
to London.

* * *

His efforts thus encouraged, Drake set about making preparations for another voyage, for which he had already formulated an ambitious scheme. Acquiring the seventy-ton bark *Pasco* from William Hawkins, he ordered three new pinnaces pre-fabricated and then stowed in pieces in her hold. While these were being constructed, Drake organized the provisions, arms, ammunition, and tools, and recruited the manpower he required.

Stories of Drake's exploits were becoming popular fare in Plymouth and the surrounding boroughs of Devon, and there were plenty of men eager to join him. He selected his company carefully, as he would need to depend on their courage and stamina at critical moments. Except for one man, all were in their twenties or younger. Drake was barely thirty himself. Among his recruits were two of his brothers, John serving as captain of the *Swan*, and Joseph as an ordinary seaman.

With a company of seventy-three men aboard the *Pasco* and the *Swan*, Drake set sail on May 24, 1572, arriving in the Caribbean thirty-seven days later and at Port Pheasant on July 12.[3] There he found a message left by a fellow captain warning that the Spaniards had discovered their camp and carried away the provisions he had buried. Undaunted, Drake had the pinnaces lifted out of the *Pasco* and brought ashore for assembly. The following day another Hawkins captain, James Raunse, arrived unexpectedly with two captured Spanish barks. After conferring, he agreed to support Drake's plan, and a few days later they moved to a new hideout, where Raunse remained to guard the ships while Drake and his men continued on in the pinnaces. Their objective was the treasure-house of Nombre de Dios, where all of the gold and gems were stored pending the arrival of the annual treasure fleet.

In his previous expeditions, Drake had formed a detailed picture of Nombre de Dios from the Spaniards he had detained and from their slaves. He knew the layout of the town and the location of the treasure-house, and that the town's defenses were weak and vulnerable to a well-organized assault. There were no walls or bastions, and a battery of six cannons was all that guarded the bay.

At an island thirty miles east of Nombre de Dios, Drake halted the pinnaces and distributed the arms he had selected for the raid: twenty-four harquebuses and calivers (match-fired muskets), sixteen bows, twelve pikes, six fire pikes, six spears, six shields, two trumpets, and two drums. His plan was to divide his force and enter the town from two sides, making as much noise as possible in the hope of frightening the inhabitants into withdrawing. After he drilled his men, they set off again and arrived outside the bay of Nombre de Dios late in the evening of July 28.

Drake had intended to rush the town at daybreak, but waiting out the long night made his men nervous, so when the moon appeared he launched the assault. Seeing them, a lone sentry ran to raise the alarm, and by the time they landed they could hear the commotion in the town. Leaving a dozen men to guard the pinnaces, Drake sent a party of eighteen around to the side of the town and then stormed up the main path with the remainder. When they reached the marketplace, they were confronted by a body of militia, who immediately fired a volley, and Drake's trumpeter pitched over dead. Drake's men fired their weapons, killing or wounding several Spaniards, and then charged. Moments later the second party of raiders arrived, and the defenders fled.

Proceeding first to the governor's house, they discovered in an adjoining shed a pile of silver bars seventy feet long, ten feet wide, and twelve feet high—far too much to carry away. Drake's priority was the more valuable gold and gems in the treasure-house. But as they prepared to smash the door to the strong-house, Drake suddenly fainted. Unnoticed by his men, he had been struck in the leg by a musketball during the exchange in the marketplace and had lost a considerable amount of blood. Fearing that they might lose the one man upon whom all their fortunes depended, they carried him down to the boats and departed.

Drake soon recovered from his wound, but the advantage of surprise was lost. There was no possibility of a second raid on the town. Fearing that they would be hunted down, Captain Raunse sailed away. By contrast, Drake's first concern was to bolster his company's morale. On the night of August 13, they stole into the harbor of Cartagena and snatched a ship from under the protection of the city's guns, and the next night they took two more, but there were no great prizes to be had there to make up for the lost opportunity of Nombre de Dios. Turning his mind again to the original object of the voyage, Drake decided on a new plan: to join forces with the *cimarrones* and intercept a mule train carrying gold across the isthmus from Panama.

The *cimarrones* were Negro slaves who had escaped from the Spaniards and banded together to live as outlaws. Intermarrying with the Indians, they knew the hinterland intimately and applied this knowledge with considerable success in attacks on their former masters. They would be invaluable allies for Drake's new project. Drake sent his brother John and a Negro named Diego, whom his men had liberated from Nombre de Dios, to make contact, and within a few days the *cimarrones* responded: They knew about his exploits along the coast and were prepared to assist him. However, it was mid-September, well into the rainy season, and five months before the mule trains resumed their journeys across the isthmus.

At a new hideout in the Gulf of San Blas, Drake put his men to work erecting a fort, and then, leaving a garrison under John's command, he set off eastward again with a raiding party in two of the pinnaces. For a fortnight contrary winds kept them in the outer harbor of Cartagena, and Drake took the opportunity to blockade the port and plunder several ships. Every effort by the Spaniards to dislodge him from the harbor's entrance proved futile. Then, seizing a bark loaded with victuals, Drake brought his men back to their haven in mid-November.

Upon their arrival, Drake received the tragic news that John had been killed attempting to board a Spanish ship armed only with a sword. Drake scarcely had time to grieve the loss of his brother, because an even worse catastrophe struck in early January. A terrible pestilence—possibly yellow fever—swept through the company, leaving nearly thirty men dead. Drake's younger brother Joseph died in his arms. Concerned to discover the cause, Drake resolved that one of their bodies should be cut open and examined. When his men recoiled at the suggestion, Drake ordered his surgeon to open up Joseph's body. Apart from a swollen liver, however, the crude autopsy revealed nothing useful, and a few days later the surgeon himself sickened and died. The company had been reduced to fewer than forty men. They named the place Slaughter Island.

In February 1573 word came from the cimarrones *that the mule trains were once again* moving across the isthmus. Drake set off with seventeen of his remaining men and thirty *cimarrones*, aiming to intercept the gold train where a raid would least be expected—on the road from the Pacific coast up to Venta

Cruces. Guiding them along hidden pathways, the *cimarrones* led the way through the dense jungle and across swift-flowing rivers.

On the seventh day of their march, they reached a ridge where the *cimarrones* had cut steps into the side of a tall tree, leading to a viewing platform at its top. Climbing the tree, Drake and his lieutenant, John Oxenham, were presented with a spectacular panorama: On one side, in the distance, lay the Caribbean, and on the other, nearer to hand, was the great Pacific Ocean. Drake later recounted that he "besought almighty God of his goodness to give him life and leave to sail once in an English ship in that sea."

Shortly afterward they reached the grassy pampas of the Pacific slope and descended to within a league of Panama, where they were able to count the ships that had come from Peru. One of the *cimarrones* slipped into the city and returned with news that the treasurer of Lima would be coming up the road that night with a pack train carrying a rich shipment of gold and gems. Backtracking toward Venta Cruces, they chose a place for an ambush and positioned themselves in the tall grass beside the road.

After a long wait the silence was broken by harness bells signaling the approach of the mule train. But then, from the direction of Venta Cruces came the sound of a solitary rider heading for Panama. Listening from his hiding place, Drake waited for the rider to pass. Suddenly the rider spurred his horse to a gallop; one of the sailors had leaped out of hiding prematurely and startled him. Another half hour passed and finally the mule train appeared, but it was only some slaves with the vanguard carrying supplies. Warned by the rider, the treasurer had turned back, sending them on as a decoy.

Again months of waiting and preparation had been wasted. When they were finally reunited with their shipmates after skirmishing with Spanish soldiers and briefly occupying Venta Cruces, Drake and his men were exhausted. In friendship, the *cimarrones* made them new shoes and vowed that they would continue to help him, so Drake resolved to try again when the furor died down. This time, he planned to intercept the gold train near the end of its journey, just before Nombre de Dios, when the escort would be tired and therefore less vigilant.

* * *

In March Drake was scouting the coast for more prizes when he encountered a French bark, a Huguenot privateer with a company of seventy men. Her captain, Guillaume Le Testu, was actually looking for Drake to join him in his next enterprise. Presenting Drake with a gilt scimitar that had belonged to Admiral Gaspard de Coligny, leader of the French Protestants, Le Testu told him about the horrible massacre of Huguenots in France on St. Bartholomew's Eve seven months before.

In 1570 French Catholics and Protestants had suspended hostilities, and to cement the peace a marriage was subsequently arranged between the young Huguenot prince Henry of Navarre and King Charles's sister, Marguerite de Valois. In July 1572 all of the leading Huguenots were in Paris for the wedding when, encouraged by Charles's scheming mother, Catherine de' Medici, supporters of the zealously Catholic Duke of Guise assassinated Admiral Coligny and then raged through Paris, dragging every Huguenot they could find into the streets and butchering them. The orgy of killing had then spread to the provinces and in four days had left 10,000 Protestants dead. After listening to Le Testu's account of the massacre, Drake agreed that he could join him in his next raid on the Spanish treasure train.

On March 31, 1573, Drake's pinnaces landed thirty-five English and French sailors at the mouth of the Río Francisco, a few miles east of Nombre de Dios, where they rendezvoused with the *cimarrones*. The pinnaces were to return for them three days hence. The *cimarrones* leading the way, they crept so close to Nombre de Dios that night that they could hear the Spaniards working aboard their ships in the bay. A few hours later they took up a position at the Campos River, two leagues from the town. Early the next morning the *cimarrone* scouts reported that the train was approaching. It comprised 190 mules tended by slaves and guarded by forty-five soldiers. This time everyone remained in hiding until Drake gave the command, and after a brief fight the soldiers abandoned the train and withdrew toward Nombre de Dios.

One of the *cimarrones* was killed, and Le Testu was wounded in the abdomen, but the treasure was theirs. In addition to quantities of gold and gems, there were some fifteen tons of silver, far more than they could carry away, so they hid as much of it as they could in the surrounding forest, hoisted the most valuable packs on their shoulders, and withdrew. Unable to keep pace, Le Testu insisted they carry on, and two French sailors volunteered to follow with him.

That night and the next day, the raiders staggered under their loads toward their rendezvous with the pinnaces. When they reached the mouth of the Río Francisco on the third day, however, the pinnaces were not there, and seven Spanish boats packed with soldiers were patrolling just offshore. They had captured one of the French sailors and forced him to reveal the rendezvous. However, they had already searched the estuary before Drake's arrival and concluded that he had escaped.

At midday the Spanish boats departed, and that evening Drake's pinnaces finally arrived. Fortunately, they had been delayed by contrary winds. After the raiders returned to their ships, Drake dispatched John Oxenham with the *cimarrones* to find Le Testu and his companions, but only one had escaped the Spaniards; Le Testu had been beheaded and the other sailor drawn and quartered.

The Spaniards had also found where most of the silver was hidden. Nevertheless, the mission had been a great success: In gold alone the raiders had seized some 100,000 pesos,* and including gems and what silver they managed to recover, the total value of the haul was likely well in excess of £40,000. It was a fabulous sum, equivalent to roughly one-fifth of Queen Elizabeth's annual revenues.[4] Le Testu's men were entitled to half, but Drake also had the spoils from the many ships he had plundered. The voyage was "made."

Invited by Drake to choose something as a keepsake, the *cimarrone* chieftain picked up the gilt scimitar that Drake had been given by Le Testu. Drake prized it as a memento of the gallant Huguenot captain, but nonetheless he surrendered it to him. It was a story Drake would be fond of retelling. In an account of these adventures written for him years later, Drake recalled the valiant service rendered by his Negro allies and credited them for the success of the expedition.

When Drake left the coast, King Philip's colonial officials were in a thorough state of alarm. The ease with which he had repeatedly struck and then vanished again both

*The peso was worth about eight shillings three pence of English money.

infuriated and frightened them. Especially troubling was his alliance with the dreaded *cimarrones*: If Drake armed the *cimarrones*, they warned, the shipments of treasure across the isthmus might be stopped altogether. The municipal council of Panama wrote to Philip:

> This realm is at the present moment so terrified, and the spirits of all so disturbed, that we know not in what words to emphasize to your Majesty the solicitude we make in this dispatch, for we certainly believe that if remedial action be delayed, disaster is imminent. . . .
>
> We hold it certain that the principal design of these English is to explore and study this land, and what strength there is in it, in order to come from England with more people to plunder and occupy . . .
>
> This league between the English and the negroes is very detrimental to this kingdom, because being so thoroughly acquainted with the region and so expert in the bush, the negroes will show them methods and means to accomplish any evil design they may wish to carry out and execute.[5]

At the same time, the colonials had begun to recognize that Drake was a remarkably gentle corsair in comparison to the French pirates, who were notorious for atrocities committed upon their prisoners. Although a number of people were killed offering armed resistance to his raids, Drake had gained a favorable reputation among the Spaniards for the civility and kindness he exhibited toward his captives. As Drake himself later summed up these exploits: There were in that region about 200 Spanish vessels,

> the most of which, during our abode in those parts, we took; and some of them, twice or thrice each: yet never burnt nor sunk any, unless they were made out Men-of-war against us, or laid as stales to trap us. And of all the men taken in these several vessels, we never offered any kind of violence to any, after they had come under our power; but either presently dismissed them in safety, or kept them with us some longer time, provided for their sustenance as for our ourselves and secured them from the rage of the Cimaroons.[6]

* * *

Francis Drake ca. 1575, by Isaac Oliver

On his homeward voyage Drake completed the passage from the Florida Strait to the Scilly Isles in just twenty-three days and reached Plymouth on the morning of August 9, 1573. It was a Sunday, and it was said that the townspeople rushed from church in midservice to see his ships.

However, Drake had returned at a most inconvenient time for the government. Faced with stronger resistance than he had anticipated in the Netherlands, and unable to reinforce his army via the English Channel due to the continual swarm of pirates, the Duke of Alba had made overtures for a peace accord with England, and Elizabeth had accepted.[7] As part of the bargain, she had agreed to discourage her seamen from further depredations on Spanish shipping. It was hardly an auspicious time, then, for Drake to arrive with a load of plunder from the Spanish Indies.

Indeed, Alba's initiative could not have come at a better time for Elizabeth, as he was genuinely interested in a peaceful resolution to the troubles, whereas King Philip was contemplating a more aggressive policy toward England. Early in 1574 Philip ordered Admiral Pedro Menéndez de Avilés to assemble a fleet capable of achieving supremacy in the English Channel. By summer Menéndez's armada had grown to 24 galleons, 12 barks, and 176 lesser vessels, and he was preparing to embark a force of 12,000 men. Alarmed by this ominous development, Elizabeth mobilized her navy—some 27 ships—and a large force of privateers to guard England's south coast.

Even after the terms of the new peace negotiated with Alba were signed, Menéndez's preparations continued. In September, however, a terrible epidemic broke out in the Spanish fleet, leaving hundreds, including Menéndez himself, dead. Scrambling to escape the sickness, the fleet scattered in disarray.[8] His project thus collapsed, Philip grudgingly accepted Alba's accord.

Nothing is known about Drake's whereabouts through this period. The only mention of his name is found in a heavily edited paper titled "For the Matter of Drake's Spoils"—evidently a draft of the government's reply to Spanish complaints about his activities. This paper contains a note stating that Drake "kept the seas till he had obtained his pardon."[9] It appears, then, that when he returned he was told to lay low for a while. Possibly, he was one of the privateers whom Elizabeth sent to guard the southern coast of Ireland against a Spanish attempt to land troops there. Regardless, there was no immediate prospect of his being permitted to return to the Caribbean. This mattered little to Drake, however, for he had been formulating a new plan since that day he climbed the tall tree on the isthmus and looked out upon the Pacific Ocean.

❧ 4. ❧

A Passage to Cathay

he aim to which Francis Drake aspired, of reaching the South Sea, was also an object of interest to a number of prominent men in England, for no English ship had ever done so. The quest for a passage through or around the New World had preoccupied cosmographers, mariners, and mapmakers ever since its vague outlines had been revealed by the first wave of European explorers eight decades earlier. But while others led the way, the English had made few efforts in exploration. Consequently, they had been mere onlookers as immense regions of the globe were discovered.

At the outset of the age of discovery, no one had dreamed of the existence of the American continent or the vast ocean lying beyond it. The great ambition was to find a sea route to the Oriental Indies and Cathay, where, so the memoirs of Marco Polo told, fabulous riches were to be had. For centuries the only routes by which the produce of those storied regions reached Europe had been via caravans across central Asia, or along the coasts of the Indian Ocean and thence through the Middle East. As the goods passed from trader to trader, and brigands and overlords along the way exacted their share, prices doubled and redoubled. They then passed through the empire of the Ottoman Turks, who imposed additional levies before they were loaded on ships and carried to Europe, principally via the wealthy and powerful city-state of Venice.

Besides gems, the most precious goods were the spices, essences, and drugs. By the time these reached their final market, the price was inflated by as much as fifty times their original cost. Some spices were literally worth their weight in gold. A sea route by which goods could be transported direct from the Far East would, it was projected, cut out all middlemen and generate enormous profits.

The Portuguese had been the first to recognize the opportunity and had spent half a century probing southward for the extremity of Africa. At last in 1487 Bartolomeu Dias rounded the Cape of Good Hope into the Indian Ocean. Five years later, however, Genoese navigator Christopher Columbus sailed westward across the Atlantic and returned to report his supposed discovery and claim, for Spain, of the easternmost islands of Asia.

The following year, amid mounting tension between Spain and Portugal over the right to discover and exploit the Indies, Pope Alexander VI stepped in to broker a resolution to the dispute. By the Treaty of Tordesillas, ratified in 1494, Spain and Portugal agreed to divide equally the right to occupy and trade in all non-Christian lands. From a north-south line, or meridian, plotted 1,300 miles west of the Azores, in the mid-Atlantic, Spain claimed the sole right to exploit all lands lying to the west, and Portugal all lands lying to the east until their empires met at a second line of demarcation 180 degrees around the globe.

Based on the treaty, Portugal eventually claimed Brazil, because it pro-truded eastward over the line of demarcation, as well as sub-Saharan Africa, India, the East Indies, and China. In 1497 Vasco da Gama reached the Malabar coast of India, and within three years Portuguese ships were re-turning annually with cargoes of precious goods from tropical Asia.

In the meantime Giovanni Caboto, a Venetian who had become known as John Cabot, had obtained a license from King Henry VII to discover a route to Cathay for England, and his report in 1497 of discovering land to the west had briefly raised the hope that he had reached the northeast coast of Asia. As more of its landmass was revealed by subsequent explorations, however, there had been a growing realization that Cabot's Newfound Land was part of a hitherto unknown continent standing in the way of Asia. While Columbus searched in vain for a passage westward from the Caribbean, Florentine navigator Amerigo Vespucci, for whom the new con-tinent would soon be named, followed its coast southward as far as the Río de la Plata* in 1501 with no better luck.

The English search for a passage around the Newfound Land had then

*The River Plate, whose vast estuary separates the modern countries of Uruguay and Argentina.

originated with the voyage of John Cabot's son Sebastian. In 1508 the younger Cabot followed its coast northward until he encountered great ice floes and there was almost continuous daylight. Cabot was convinced that a passage could be found in that direction, but finding little support in England for further explorations, he went into the service of Spain in 1512, where he eventually rose to the position of Pilot Major overseeing the development of Spanish navigation.

The year following Cabot's arrival, Spain embarked on a decade of spectacular discoveries. In 1513 Vasco Nuñez de Balboa trekked from the shores of the Caribbean across the Isthmus of Panama and found a body of salt water that he concluded was a new ocean, distinct from the Atlantic. Then in 1519 Portuguese adventurer Ferdinand Magellan persuaded the Spanish king, Emperor Charles V, to furnish him with five ships for a voyage across Balboa's South Sea to Cathay.

Following the Atlantic coast of America southward, Magellan discovered the strait at its southern extremity, and after battling contrary winds in the tortuous narrows for five weeks, he emerged into the Pacific with three ships remaining. Setting off on what he reckoned would be a 2,000-mile crossing to the coast of Asia, Magellan and his men instead had to endure a ninety-eight-day voyage, sailing more than five times that distance before they reached the islands later known as the Philippines. They had discovered that the South Sea was a vast ocean spanning more than one-third of the globe. Magellan was killed in a fight with the islanders, but his Basque lieutenant, Juan Sebastián de Elcano, continued the voyage in the ship *Victoria*, finally bringing her home via the Cape of Good Hope in 1522.

Of the more than 250 men who had left Spain with Magellan three years before, 18 emaciated sailors had become the first circumnavigators of the globe. En route they had laid claim to the finest spice-growing islands in the East Indies: the Moluccas. Quickly, however, their accomplishment was overshadowed by news of another. In the same three years Spanish soldier-adventurer Hernán Cortés had discovered and conquered the Aztec civilization of Mexico.

It took six years of shipping to carry all of Cortés's Aztec plunder to Spain, and as one shipload after another arrived from the New World,

Emperor Charles V began to lose interest in the contest for the spice trade. In 1525 Garcia Jofre de Loaysa led a follow-up expedition through Magellan's Strait, but he died crossing the Pacific and only two of his seven vessels reached the Moluccas. Finding the Portuguese had occupied the islands, the Spaniards allied themselves with the Muslim Sultans in an effort to evict them. Only a handful of Spaniards survived two years of fighting, however, and they were compelled to surrender to the Portuguese. Three of them eventually reached Spain.

Between them, Magellan and Loaysa had taken a total of twelve ships to the South Sea, and only one had returned. Nor had either expedition succeeded in finding winds that would take them from the East Indies back to America. In 1527 Cortés sent three ships from Mexico to look for Loaysa, but the result was the same: Only one of them reached the Philippines, and it too was unable to find a way to return. Concluding that there was little prospect of Spain developing a viable spice trade, Emperor Charles sold his claim to the Moluccas to the Portuguese in 1529.

After Cortés's conquest of the great Aztec capital Tenochtitlán (Mexico City), the focus of Spanish exploration had shifted to a race by rival conquistadores to discover other wealthy kingdoms in the unknown reaches of the New World. By 1530 Cortés's lieutenant, Pedro de Alvarado, had plundered the civilizations of Central America southward to Panama. Then in 1531 Francisco Pizarro sailed from Panama to commence his remarkable and brutal conquest of the empire of the Incas, and within two years the flow of treasure from Peru rivaled that seized from the Aztecs.

Other adventurers added to Spain's New World dominions. In 1535 Juan de Ayolas ascended the Paraná and Paraguay Rivers from the River Plate and crossed the plains to Peru. In the same year another expedition followed the western slopes of the Andes southward into Chile and returned by the coast through the Atacama Desert. In the middle of the continent Gonzalo Pizarro crossed the eastern Andes, and his lieutenant, Francisco de Orellana, rafted 3,000 miles down the Amazon to the Atlantic. And from the Caribbean, Sebastián de Benalcázar ascended the Magdalena River and found the Indians of Colombia to be rich in gold and emeralds.

To the north of Mexico the Indians were found not to possess any great wealth. From the Pacific coast of Mexico, however, the long peninsula of lower California was discovered in 1533, and the Gulf of California was explored in 1539. Then in 1542 Juan Rodriguez Cabrillo battled the opposing wind northward on the outer coast of California possibly as far as latitude 43 degrees before turning back. Also that year Ruy Lõpez de Villalobos sailed from Mexico to the Philippines and named the islands for King Charles's son, Philip, but like the others before him he was unable to find a return route eastward, and eventually he too was obliged to surrender to the Portuguese. For the time being, Spanish colonization was limited to the Americas.

After conquest came organization of Spain's New World territories into two viceregal kingdoms: the Viceroyalty of New Spain, comprising Hispaniola, Cuba, Mexico, and most of Central America; and the Viceroyalty of Peru, encompassing Panama and all of Spain's South American territories. To obtain the labor needed to work their ranches and plantations, the Spaniards required every male Indian between the ages of fifteen and sixty to pay annual "tribute" in the form of money or labor.

By about 1545 all the treasures of gold and silver that had been accumulated by the native peoples had been seized and melted into bullion or made into jewelery, and a new era had begun, centered on mining by slave labor of huge deposits of silver in Mexico and Peru. The result was a dramatic increase in the value of bullion shipped to Spain. In the late 1520s the annual value of shipments, nearly all of it gold, averaged about 500,000 ducats. By the early 1570s, when Francis Drake was conducting his raids on the isthmus, the value of shipments had increased more than tenfold to over 5 million ducats per year, nearly all of it silver.[1] This did not include quantities smuggled into Spain as contraband, estimated to be equal to anywhere from 10 to 50 percent of the registered bullion. In comparison, the cost of maintaining the Duke of Alba's 45,000-man army in the Netherlands averaged just under 2 million ducats annually.*

In 1576 King Philip's colonial officials estimated that about 160,000 Spaniards were residing in the New World, along with 40,000 Negro slaves

---

*The ducat was worth about five shillings four pence of English money.

A Spanish silver mine

and large numbers of mulattoes and mestizos. By far the largest center was Mexico City, with a population of 15,000 Spaniards and 150,000 Indians. In comparison, there were only 13,500 Spanish households in all of South America. Not including tribes yet to be conquered, Philip's American colonies were reckoned to contain between 8,000 and 9,000 Indian villages inhabited by some 5 million Indians, of whom an estimated 1.5 million were males of tribute-paying age.[2]

To this point only France had challenged Spain's claimed monopoly of the New World. In 1534 Jacques Cartier had discovered the St. Lawrence River, disembarked, and claimed the land, which the Indians called Canada, for France. Cartier did not succeed in establishing a colony, however—the first permanent settlement came in 1608—and the French claim to this remote northern land posed no immediate threat to the Spanish, so they had largely ignored it.

In 1564, an expedition of French Huguenots set up a colony in the mouth of the St. Johns River in Florida. When word of the settlement reached King Philip, he dispatched Admiral Pedro Menéndez de Avilés to dispose of them. Embarking 2,000 soldiers in thirty ships, Menéndez reached Florida in 1565, and within a month he had rounded up and summarily executed more than 400 colonists—the same whom John Hawkins's stranded mariners had hoped to find in 1568. Menéndez then established a fort at St. Augustine to protect Florida from further intrusions.

Except for the African slave trade and the colonization of Brazil, where their policies were similar to those of the Spanish, the Portuguese had taken a different approach to exploiting their hemisphere. Rather than attempt large-scale conquests in Asia, they had established thriving trading centers at strategic locations: Goa on the southwest coast of India, Malacca in the narrow strait guarding access to the great Indonesian archipelago, and Macao at the mouth of the Pearl River on the coast of China.

To carry their rich cargoes on the long voyage across the Indian Ocean and home via the Cape of Good Hope, the Portuguese built progressively larger and more efficient ships. These armed merchantmen, called carracks, were the largest vessels afloat, ranging in size to well over 1,000 tons burden. While lowering the cost of oriental goods for Europeans, they took huge profits from the trade.

Soon after he succeeded to the throne of Spain, King Philip began to take an interest in the potential of his Philippine Islands. Under the Treaty of Tordesillas the islands, like the Moluccas, were actually located in the Portuguese hemisphere. In the absence of any agreed method of determining the eastern line separating the two empires, however, its position was disputed. To support his claim to the islands, Philip had his cartographers produce maps that understated the sailing distance across the Pacific, and argued that the line of demarcation actually cut through the Strait of Malacca, 1,000 miles farther west.

Philip persuaded Andrés de Urdaneta, one of the three survivors from the expedition of Loaysa, to come out of the monastery where he had taken Holy Orders to guide an expedition to the Philippines and solve the problem of the return voyage to America. The expedition, under the command

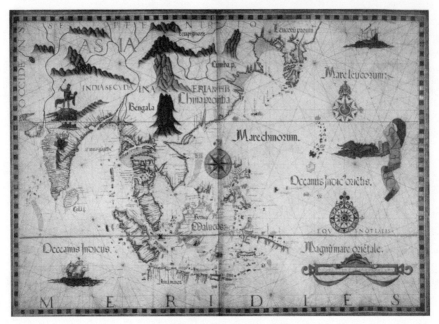

A Portuguese map of the East Indies,
by Diego Homem, 1558

of Miguel Lõpez de Legazpi, reached the Philippines from Mexico in April 1565. In June Urdaneta sailed far to the north, to the latitudes of Japan, where he picked up the prevailing westerlies and was carried back across the Pacific to the coast of upper California. Following the coast, that Cabrillo had previously discovered southward, he arrived in Mexico after a voyage of four months.

Thereafter one or more ships made the round-trip voyage from the port of Acapulco, Mexico, to the Philippines and back each year. The city of Manila was founded in 1571, and within three years Chinese traders were coming to meet the annual Manila galleon with silks, gold, gems, porcelain, and all manner of beautifully crafted items offered in exchange for New World silver. At last Spain had a share of the "China Trade." To protect their foothold in the Orient, the charts and sailing directions for the voyage were closely guarded. They were issued to the pilots only upon their departure and had to be given back to the authorities, along with the log of their just completed voyage, immediately upon their return.

Of growing concern to King Philip was the possibility of rivals intruding into his ocean via a northern passage from Europe. The theories of the northeast and northwest passages that were being promoted by cosmographers in the Netherlands and Germany were well known to Philip. At the heart of the possibility lay a fundamental question: Was America joined to Asia around the top of the Pacific, or were they separate continents? If they were joined, there would be no possibility of these supposed passages connecting to the Pacific. Based on the northward trend of the California coast, Friar Urdaneta believed that America was a separate continent, and had advised Philip that the northern strait separating it from Asia should be located and fortified against foreign use. However, development of the Manila trade had absorbed the available resources, and Urdaneta's recommendation had not been acted upon.[3]

After Sebastian Cabot's 1508 voyage in search of a passage around America, nearly half a century had passed before the English had undertaken another effort in oceanic exploration. In 1521 King Henry VIII had proposed that London merchants finance a company to pursue overseas ventures, but they had protested that such an initiative would imperil their existing trade with Portugal and Spain. A decade later Bristol merchant Roger Barlow had proposed a plan of exploration for a route to the Orient through northern waters, but this too had fallen on deaf ears. No one had bothered to preserve any information of the Cabot voyages or to translate into English the chronicles of Spanish achievements, which were eagerly being consumed by the literate classes on the continent, and no English cartographer had produced for his countrymen the new maps and globes that were revolutionizing concepts of the world.[4]

After the death of Henry VIII in 1547, the Privy Council had persuaded Sebastian Cabot to leave his position as Pilot Major for Spain and return to England to lead a national effort on the seas. Cabot, who was approaching seventy years of age, arrived in England intent on resurrecting his search for a passage around the north part of America, only to find that his sponsors preferred to look for a passage to the northeast, around Asia.[5]

In 1552 a group of London merchants formed a joint-stock company and recruited some 200 shareholders at twenty-five pounds per share. Styled the Merchants Adventurers of England for the Discovery of Lands,

Territories, Isles, Dominions, and Seignories (and later the Muscovy Company), they were granted a monopoly on all discoveries to the northeast, north, and northwest of England, and Cabot was appointed governor of the company for life.

The company's first expedition sailed in May 1553. After its three ships rounded Norway, two of them continued eastward until they discovered the coast of Nova Zembla at latitude 72 degrees, and then returned to the coast of Lapland to wait out the arctic winter. Although their crews had sufficient provisions, they were ill prepared for the intense cold, and they all froze to death. The third ship, commanded by Richard Chancellor, had become separated, and following the White Sea southward, he found the Russian village of Archangel. Journeying overland to Moscow, Chancellor managed to obtain a trade concession from Czar Ivan the Terrible, which thereafter became the company's principal enterprise.[6] Subsequent expeditions failed to advance the case for a northeast passage, and in 1557, having witnessed a quadrupling of the known world in his own lifetime, Sebastian Cabot died.

The following year, when Elizabeth ascended the throne, a new figure emerged as England's most influential cosmographer. Dr. John Dee, a brilliant Welsh mathematician, had studied at Cambridge and then at Louvain, a leading center of research in geography, astronomy, and navigational science, and was at the forefront of those fields. One of his mentors at Louvain, Gemma Frisius, was an advocate for discovery of a northern passage to the Pacific, and when he returned to England Dee had become a member of Sebastian Cabot's circle. Also, he had instructed young Robert Dudley, son of the late Lord Admiral of England, in geometry and cosmography, and through Dudley's friendship with Princess Elizabeth, had become her astrologer. Indeed, she had relied on a horoscope prepared by him to determine the most propitious date for her coronation. Having loyally served her through her darkest days, Dee was now a trusted adviser to the Queen on matters ranging from her ancient entitlements to geography and science.[7]

On the Continent growing demand for maps depicting the newly expanded world had transformed mapmaking into an industry as geographers recorded the latest discoveries and revised their concepts of what might be found in the still-unexplored regions of the globe. Because the Spanish continued to understate the breadth of the Pacific by thousands of miles, America was generally depicted as being joined to Asia somewhere to the

Dr. John Dee

north. In 1561, however, cartographer Giacomo Gastaldi published a new map on which he theorized that America was separated from Asia at the northern extremity of the Pacific by a so-called Strait of Anian. Three years later, Flemish geographer Abraham Ortelius, with whom John Dee was acquainted, incorporated Gastaldi's strait in his new, eight-sheet map of the world. This showed the supposed strait as beginning at latitude 40 degrees north in the Pacific and running northward between America and Asia for some 500 miles before joining with a broad sea extending across the top of North America to the Atlantic.

In 1566 English soldier-adventurer Sir Humphrey Gilbert, also an acquaintance of Dee, began circulating a crude copy of Ortelius's map together with a treatise advocating an effort to discover this passage. Titled *A Discourse of a Discoverie for a New Passage to Cathaia*, Gilbert's proposal laid out the case for a northwest passage being more likely and profitable than one to the northeast. Its discovery, he argued, would provide direct access to the richest region of the globe, thus eliminating Spanish or Portuguese middlemen. On his map Gilbert had copied Ortelius's notation "Sierra Nevada" on the northwest coast of America, near the Pacific outlet of the passage. To facilitate his project, Gilbert wrote, it would be desirable to inhabit "for our staple some place of America, about Sierra Nevada"; that is, to establish a colony on the far northwest coast of America to serve as a headquarters for English enterprise in the Pacific Ocean.[8]

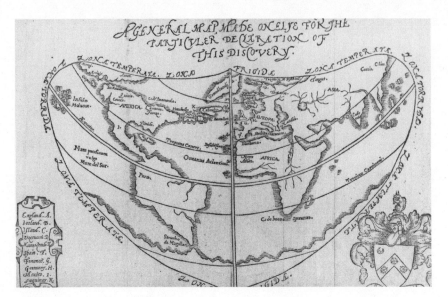

Sir Humphrey Gilbert's map illustrating the
supposed northwest passage around America

Gilbert had presented his proposal for the venture to Queen Elizabeth, but a counterpetition by the Muscovy Company pointed out that it had been granted a monopoly over all northern discoveries, whether to the northeast or northwest. After successfully blocking Gilbert's initiative, however, the company did nothing to advance exploration in any direction. Thus, the long-standing ambition to discover an English passage to the Orient had been stifled once again, and this was still the case when Francis Drake returned from the Caribbean in the summer of 1573.

❧ 5. ❧

The South Sea Project

*I*n December 1573 the complexion of Elizabeth's Privy Council was altered significantly by her appointment of Francis Walsingham as principal secretary of state for foreign affairs, replacing William Cecil. Lord Burghley, as Cecil was now titled, had served Henry VIII and then had guided the setting up of Elizabeth's government, and he remained her most senior minister. But he had always urged a conciliatory policy toward Spain, and Elizabeth had been persuaded by her close friend and confidant Robert Dudley, Earl of Leicester, to adopt a stronger approach.

Walsingham had already set up at his own expense a superbly effective network of spies to detect foreign plots against Elizabeth, and had served as her ambassador in Paris, where he had narrowly escaped the massacre of Protestants on St. Bartholomew's Eve the year before. Closely allied in their views and convinced that war with Spain was inevitable, Walsingham and Leicester became the leaders of a faction within Elizabeth's council that argued for more aggressive measures against King Philip. Also, both men were strong advocates for English maritime expansion and henceforth would play a central role in the planning of all overseas ventures.

As if on cue, in March 1574 the council received a proposal from Sir Humphrey Gilbert's cousin Richard Grenville, representing William Hawkins and a group of West Country adventurers, for a voyage to the South Sea. As presented, Grenville's proposal was to lead a peaceful expedition to explore and found settlements in the vicinity of the Río de la Plata and, after passing through Magellan's Strait, on the Pacific coast of America south of the territories occupied by Spain. Behind the scenes, Dr. John Dee wrote secret memoranda and spoke confidentially with the Queen and her councillors. The enterprise, it was said, would yield results comparable to those achieved by Portugal and Spain: new trade, discovery of gold and silver, and spreading of the Gospel.[1]

Grenville had gained notoriety as a sometime pirate, and it is highly doubtful that he and his fellow adventurers were bent on a peaceful expedition. Nevertheless, a license was granted for the venture, and in May 1574 a Spanish agent reported that Grenville was assembling an expedition of seven armed ships and 1,500 men at Plymouth. But then Elizabeth ordered a halt to his preparations, and it appears that Lord Burghley had convinced her that the enterprise was bound to incite hostilities with Spain and shatter the accord then being negotiated with the Duke of Alba.

Thereafter nothing more was heard of Grenville's South American project. Later that year, the Privy Council brought pressure to bear on the Muscovy Company to resume its northern explorations, and in February 1575, after some initial resistance, the company issued a license to its London agent, Michael Lok, and sea captain Martin Frobisher to carry out a search for a northwest passage around America.[2] Organization of the venture dragged, however, and Frobisher did not sail until the following year.

In the meantime Francis Drake reappeared. Early in 1575 a report from Walter Devereaux, Earl of Essex to the Privy Council, concerning his campaign against the rebels in Ireland mentioned Drake by name and referred to three frigates he had brought back from the Caribbean. From May through September Drake commanded a squadron of small ships in Ireland in the employ of Essex, ferrying troops and intercepting rebel shipping. Meanwhile, in July the Spanish agent in London, Antonio de Guaras, reported to King Philip that a ship had arrived at Plymouth laden with plunder that had been seized between Panama and Nombre de Dios with the help of the *cimarrones*. Drake had finally landed the spoils from his 1572–73 exploits in the Caribbean.[3] There is no indication where the treasure had been sequestered since his return from that voyage—whether in Ireland, perhaps, or on a ship.

Drake later said that when he left Ireland in the fall of 1575, the Earl of Essex gave him a letter commending his services to Secretary of State Walsingham. The recommendation, he recalled with some modesty, was "more than I was worthy, but belike I had deserved somewhat at his hands, and he thought me in his letters to be a fit man to serve against the

Lord Burghley, Queen Elizabeth, and Sir Francis Walsingham

Spaniards for my practise and experience that I had in that trade."[4] After he presented Essex's letter of introduction, Walsingham sent for him and, spreading a map out, asked him where he thought the King of Spain might be most annoyed by his activities. Drake said that he pointed to the place but told Walsingham that he would not sign his name to any such plan, explaining, "If it should please God to take Her Majesty away it might be that some prince might reign that might be in league with the King of Spain, and then will my own hand be a witness against myself."[5]

Some undated memoranda have survived, which evidently were prepared as notes for Walsingham to present the case for Drake's project to the Queen.[6] Sometime later the pages were singed by fire, but enough of the writing remains to make sense of their contents. The first page refers to Drake's ship as the *Francis*, and to six prefabricated pinnaces that were to be carried in her hold. The second page lists the participants in the venture, which was to be a joint-stock company, and credits Drake with a contribution of £1,000. The other investors were Walsingham, Leicester, and Christopher Hatton, captain of the Queen's bodyguard; the Earl of Lincoln, Lord Admiral of England; Sir William Winter, surveyor of the navy, and his brother George Winter, clerk of the Queen's ships; and John Hawkins, soon to be treasurer of the navy.

After the list of subscribers there is a note in which Walsingham was asked to see whether the Queen would lend her ship *Swallow* to the venture, and to ensure that she was "made privy to the truth of the voyage, and yet the colour [impression] to be given out [that it would be destined] for Alexandria [Egypt]." Evidently, then, these memoranda predated Elizabeth's consent for the enterprise.

Next in the surviving memoranda is a draft plan of the voyage. Some of the words have been lost on the burned edges of the page. However, it is quite apparent that this does not contain the "truth of the voyage" that Walsingham was to convey to the Queen. It is little more than a repetition of Grenville's original proposal for an expedition to explore the extremity of South America, stating that Drake would proceed north only as far as latitude 30 degrees south on the Pacific coast of South America. From subsequent events, however, it is abundantly clear that Drake was intent on raiding the coast of Peru, and he would not have dared to conceal this intention from such powerful associates. Walsingham knew that King Philip had spies at the court, and very likely the truth was not set down on paper for fear that one of them might get hold of the document.

The last note is a reminder to Walsingham that he should urge the Queen's approval with all possible speed, or the voyage "cannot take the good effect, as it is hoped for." Exactly when Drake hoped to sail was not indicated. However, he later said that soon after his meeting with Walsingham he was summoned by the Queen:

> [I] came not to Her Majesty that night for that it was too late. But the next day coming to her presense, these or the like words she said: "Drake! So it is that I would gladly be revenged on the King of Spain

for diverse injuries that I have received." And [she] said further that I was the only man who might do this exploit, and withal craved my advice therein; who told Her Majesty of the small good that was to be done in Spain but the only way was to annoy him by the Indies.[7]

After he explained his plan to her, Drake said, "Her Majesty did swear by her Crown that if any within her realm did give the King of Spain to understand hereof (as she suspected too well), they should lose their heads therefore."[8] And in particular, he stated, "Her Majesty gave me special commandment that of all men my Lord Treasurer [Burghley] should not know it."[9]

That these discussions took place sometime in the winter of 1575–76 seems fairly certain. They fit perfectly with the political situation that was developing at that time. By the fall of 1575 Walsingham's position was ascending and Burghley's was losing ground. The term of the peace negotiated with the Duke of Alba was nearing expiry, and there appeared to be little chance of its ratification as a permanent treaty by Philip. Elizabeth's chief complaints against Philip were his harboring of Mary Stuart's supporters, the Inquisition's harassment of the crews of English ships trading in Spanish ports, and his refusal to grant reasonable terms to his Protestant subjects in the Netherlands.[10]

A special ambassador had been sent to Madrid in an effort to resolve these issues, but in November he had returned empty-handed. The Inquisition continued to persecute Englishmen in Spain, and Elizabeth began to seriously consider accepting the sovereignty of the Netherlands, which Philip's rebel provinces were offering her. In the New Year tensions continued to mount as the Privy Council debated steps against Spain and acceptance of the Dutch proposal, and in March 1576 Parliament was summoned to provide for the defense of the realm. For these few months the political atmosphere, therefore, was well suited to Drake's project.[11]

Later in March, however, Elizabeth's disposition suddenly changed. She quarreled with her Parliament and the Dutch, and began turning her attention once more to securing peace with Spain.[12] In all probability, then, her approval for Drake's project was withdrawn sometime that spring.

* * *

In May 1576 Martin Frobisher and his pilot, Christopher Hall, received several days of instruction in geometry and the theory of oceanic navigation from Dr. John Dee. Then, after a farewell meeting with the Queen, Frobisher set sail from the Thames on June 12 with thirty-four men in two small barks and a pinnace to search for the northwest passage.

After calling at the Shetland Islands, Frobisher's vessels headed due west in latitude 60 degrees. On July 11 they made landfall at the southern tip of Greenland and briefly skirted its shores. Continuing westward, they met with a violent storm, and the pinnace sank with its crew of four. A few days later, with the storm still raging and huge icebergs looming out of the mists, Frobisher's consort, the *Michael*, turned back for England. Undaunted, Frobisher continued west and then northward in the *Gabriel*, skirting treacherous ice floes until the end of July, when he found between two headlands at latitude 62 degrees an entrance wider than the Strait of Dover and leading northwestward to the horizon.

To Frobisher, it appeared to be a continuous passage flanked by two long rows of mountainous islands. In reality he had sailed into the mouth of a large inlet in Baffin Island. Sailing some 100 miles into his supposed passage, he found it still open to the northwest. After a friendly exchange with the native Inuk people, five of Frobisher's men escorted one of them ashore but failed to return and were never seen again. With just thirteen men remaining, he turned for home to report his discovery of the long-hoped-for passage to the Pacific.

Frobisher reached Harwich Roads, north of the Thames, on October 2, 1576, and sent word of his discovery ahead to London. When he brought the *Gabriel* into the Thames four days later, a hero's welcome awaited him. Initially, the greatest interest was aroused by an Inuk man whom Frobisher had captured, hoisting him bodily aboard ship in his kayak. Within a few days, however, the unfortunate man sickened and died, and attention turned to a more sober assessment of Frobisher's discovery. The Privy Council appointed a commission headed by Sir William Winter of the navy board to examine Frobisher's claim.

Frobisher "vouched to them absolutely with vehement words, speeches and oaths that he had found and discovered the Straits and open passage by sea into the South Sea called Mar de Sur which goeth to Cathay."[13] Nevertheless, for all his assurances he had not provided the ultimate proof

Martin Frobisher

of his discovery by sailing through his strait to the South Sea, and behind the scenes there were doubts that such a voyage would be easily accomplished. The challenge as seen by the projectors was more candidly illustrated on a map subsequently produced by soldier-adventurer George Best, who accompanied Frobisher on his next voyage.[14] The map was a crude copy of another by the respected Flemish geographer Abraham Ortelius.

In 1570 Ortelius had created a revolution in mapmaking by publishing the first comprehensive atlas, titled *Theatrum Orbis Terrarum*. The concept of a book of maps covering all the regions of the globe won acclaim, and although very expensive, it had become the best-selling geographic work in Europe.[15] Through the popularity of his atlas, Ortelius's new map of the world had become the standard reference and was especially of interest to the proponents of a northwest passage. The map was based largely on the work of Ortelius's famous colleague Gerard Mercator, to which Ortelius had added whatever intelligence of distant regions he had been able to glean from ancient texts and heavily censored accounts of Portuguese and Spanish voyages.

Of particular interest to the projectors of the northern passage was the way that Mercator and Ortelius depicted America: While it was a separate continent from Asia, its northern part had a huge westward bulge, which filled much of the unexplored region of the North Pacific, making America equivalent in breadth to Asia. Ortelius placed the Strait of Anian, in longitude, 190

Abraham Ortelius's 1570 map of the world

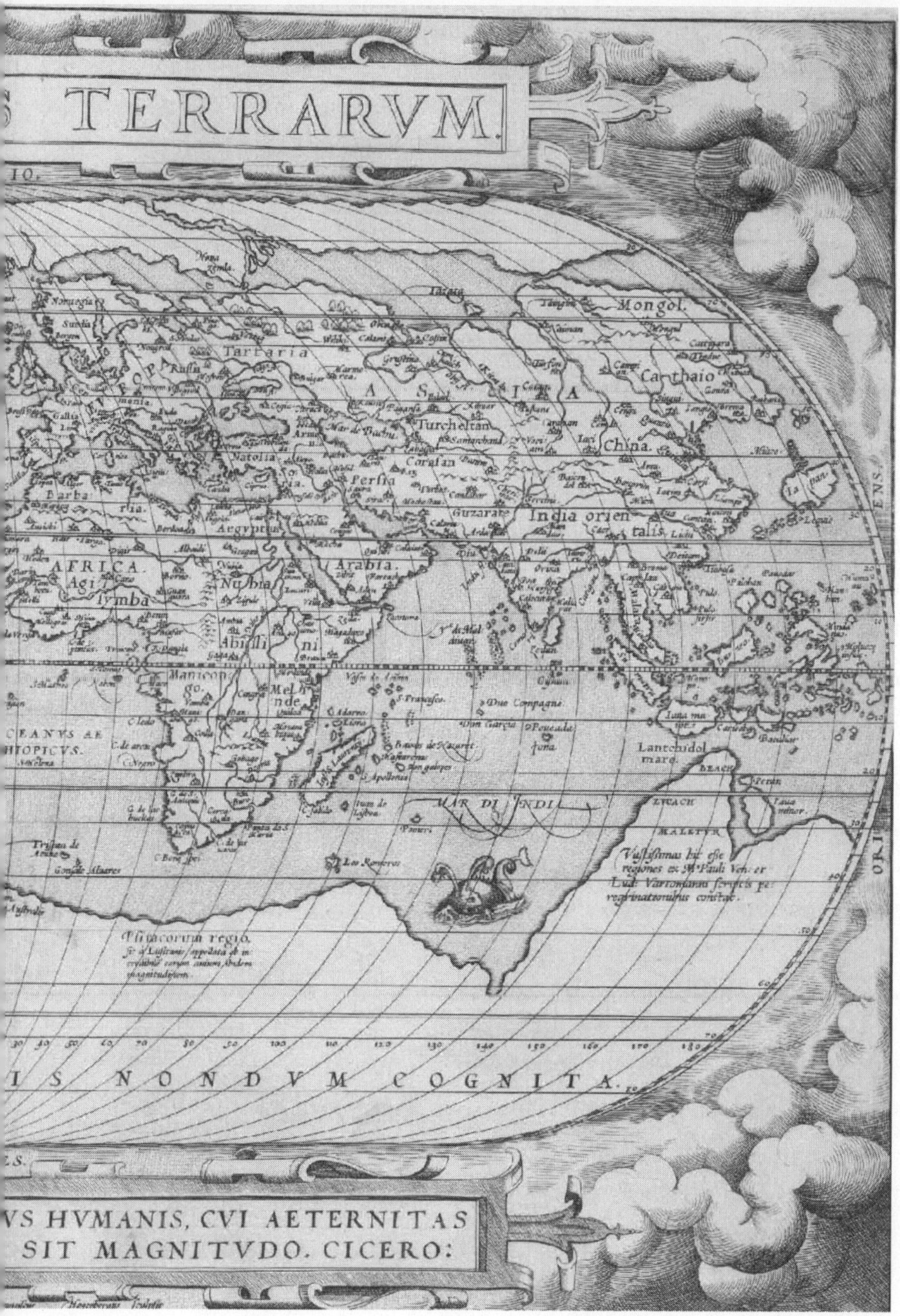

TERRARVM.

Norvegia

Tartaria

A   S   I   A

Mongol.

Canthaio

Turcheltan

China.

Coralan

Persia

Guzarate

India orien

talis

AFRICA

Arabia.

Nubia

Iymba

Abissini

Manico go.

Melinde

OCEANVS AE
TIOPICVS.

Lantchidol mare

MAR DI INDI.

ZVACH

MALETVR

BEACH

Vltimorum regió.

IS   NONDVM   COGNITA.

Vastissimas hic esse
regiones ex M. Pauli Ven: et
Lud: Vartomanni scriptis pa-
tet innotuerunt constat.

VS HVMANIS, CVI AETERNITAS
SIT MAGNITVDO. CICERO:

degrees west of England, where it began at latitude 60 degrees and ran north-ward between the two massive continents for some 360 miles before connect-ing to both a northeast and a northwest passage running around the globe above the Arctic Circle. The way was open in both directions, Ortelius's map suggested, but there was no certainty that the route to the northwest would prove any shorter or easier to navigate than that to the northeast.

On his copy of Ortelius's map, George Best optimistically showed Frobisher's strait extending westward across the top of North America, and then, far away on the opposite side of the globe, Ortelius's theoretical Strait of Anian connecting it with the South Sea. From a practical perspective, however, the question was obvious and the answer decidedly unappealing: What would Frobisher do if he sailed all the way across the top of this vast continent only to discover that the supposed Strait of Anian did not exist, that America and Asia were in fact joined, as many continued to believe? Very probably it would be too late in the season to get back to the Atlantic be-fore the arctic winter took them in its icy grip, and the expedition would suffer the same fate as the Muscovy Company's ships had in the northeast passage.

Frobisher's business partner, Michael Lok, was confronted with a serious financial predicament. Lok had committed the largest part of his personal resources to the first voyage, and to recover his outlay he had to enlist new backers to continue the venture with another voyage. His proposal for the new expedition called for Frobisher to take five ships with merchandise valued at £1,200 through his strait to Cathay, but there was little interest in the venture.

Upon his return, Frobisher had presented Lok with a piece of some unusually heavy rock that he had found on the shores of his "strait." Hoping that the rock might contain precious metal, Lok took samples of it to several assayers. Both the assay master at the Tower of London and George Needham of the Mines Royal declared the ore to be worthless. Others rendered similar opinions. In January 1577, however, Lok supplied a sample to a Venetian goldsmith then resident in London, Giovanni Baptista Angello, who succeeded in "finding" gold in the ore.[16]

Soon afterward, Elizabeth decided that she would invest in the follow-up voyage, and the Privy Council became involved in organization of the new venture. This time Frobisher was to take the Queen's ship *Ayde* as well

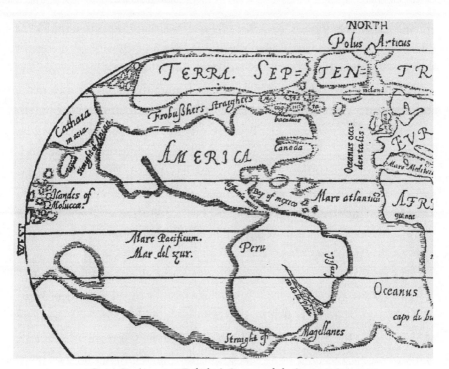

George Best's map of Frobisher's Straits and the Strait of Anian

as the barks *Gabriel* and *Michael*. Notwithstanding that he had reported finding the all-important strait, the priorities for his follow-up voyage had
shifted: His principal task was to gather more of the supposedly gold-
bearing ore.

Once his men had commenced extracting and loading the ore onto the
Ayde, Frobisher was to take the *Gabriel* and *Michael* and explore farther into his
strait. But only if the ore proved worthless in on-site testing (a nearly impossible technical requirement) was he to send the *Ayde* home and attempt
to reach Cathay with his two barks.[17] George Best, in his subsequent narrative of the voyage, put the decision in simpler terms. Frobisher's commission, he said, directed him "only for the searching of more of this gold ore,
and to defer discovery of the passage until another time."[18]

If this were the only decision that was taken in regard to the search for
the northwest passage, it would seem that the renewed interest in the subject was remarkably short-lived. However, at this same time another plan
was in the works.

* * *

After Frobisher's departure on his initial voyage of exploration, Richard Grenville had taken up the subject of the northwest passage in a new proposal, a copy of which he presented to Lord Burghley.[19] Frobisher, he wrote, was attempting to discover the passage from the wrong end. Rather than look for it from the Atlantic side, where its entrance lay at a high latitude in ice-filled waters, Grenville argued, it would be far better to explore for the passage via the salubrious climes of the South Sea: "[Where,] besides countries of most excellent temperature to be inhabited, if we think it necessary, and if we arrive too timely to enter the said strait of Anian, yet have we Cathay, and all the oriental Indies open unto us for traffic."[20] Thus, he wrote, even if the Strait of Anian were not found, there would still be ample opportunity to obtain a rich cargo before returning home.

Grenville proposed a voyage of fifteen months' duration. He would take three months to reach Magellan's Strait, three months to sail from there to latitude 50 degrees in the North Pacific, and three months to discover and map the entrance to the northern strait. Then, after spending three months locating and trading with Cathay, he would set sail for home through the northwest passage. Allowing that this final leg of the voyage would have to occur during the summer, it appears that he aimed to depart England by late spring of 1577.

Grenville's proposal avoided any suggestion of encroaching on King Philip's possessions, and it appears that in sharing it directly with Burghley he was attempting to assuage the ever-cautious minister's fears that his real aim in the South Sea was Spanish treasure. Evidently, Burghley was not persuaded, as this was the last that was heard from Grenville on the subject. But his proposal apparently did resonate with others.

In August 1576, before Frobisher's return from his initial voyage, John Dee began writing the first in what would become a series of four volumes on the potential for a "Brytish Impire."[21] It was a theme he had been pursuing with the Queen and some of her councillors, and from his evident excitement it appears that he had struck a positive chord. Remarkably, he completed the first volume, dedicated to Sir Christopher Hatton, in just six days. It would, he wrote, be advisable if funds were made available for the teaching of a number of foreign languages, including

the Chiny [Chinese] language, the Canadian, and the Islandish, etc. For that within these next few years following with men of all these countries, *and farther*, Great Affairs are by some of our countrymen to be handled: if God continue his gracious direction and aid thereto, as he hath very comfortably begun, and that *by means not yet published*.[22]

Dee's sudden burst of enthusiasm and his reference to foreign countries and great affairs comfortably begun, but not yet published, undoubtedly related to the renewed quest for a northern passage into the Pacific. Curiously, however, when Frobisher returned that fall to report his discovery, Dee did not add even an oblique mention of this news to his new work. Instead, he set to work on his second volume, which is now lost, but which appears from its title to have been concerned with the navigational science required for a long voyage.* Then that winter he wrote the third volume, but the manuscript disappeared, it is said for reasons of secrecy, soon after it was completed.[23]

As he continued to write, Dee received a number of important visitors at Mortlake, his house near London. On January 16, 1577, he was visited by the Earl of Leicester and Sir Christopher Hatton's associate Edward Dyer, and the same day Dee wrote to Abraham Ortelius at Antwerp querying his sources for the existence of the northern passage. A week later, on January 22, 1577, Dee received a visit from the earl of Bedford, Francis Drake's godfather. Then early in March Ortelius arrived in London, and on the twelfth he came to Mortlake to visit Dee.[24]

At the end of March Dee commenced writing his fourth book, titled *The Great Volume of Rich and Famous Discoveries*. He began with several chapters citing the evidence for wealthy lands lying beyond the shores of Asia and endeavoring to locate them in the South Sea according to his and Ortelius's interpretation of ancient accounts. Then Dee turned to his cardinal point, which was the need to settle the existence of the Strait of Anian, and after continuing at length on this theme, writing on May 15 he brought the discussion to a climax:

> Of how great importance then imagine you is that Attempt which is by a British Subject presently intended who (God sparing life & health) hath resolutely offered the employing of all his skill and talent, & the patient enduring of the great toil of his body to that place being the very end of the world from us to be reckoned to accomplish that

*The volume was titled *Queen Elizabeth Her Arithmetical Gubernatick: For Navigation by the Paradoxall Compass and Navigation in Great Circles*.

Abraham Ortelius

Discovery which of so many & so valiant captains by land & by sea hath been so often attempted in vain.[25]

In the margin of the page, Dee wrote, "A worthy attempt at Discovery, faithfully intended by a British Subject."

The following week Frobisher would embark on his second voyage to the northwest, but this could hardly be characterized as an expedition to "the very end of the world from us to be reckoned." The primary purpose of his voyage was to collect more of the supposedly gold-bearing ore, and there was little likelihood of his sailing any farther. Moreover, the context for Dee's guarded reference to "that Discovery" was his preceding discussion of efforts to discover the Strait of Anian.

Here was the basis for Dee's sudden burst of enthusiastic writing the previous August about "Great Affairs" not yet published, and the need for Englishmen to be schooled in numerous foreign languages. He could not have considered any plan to discover a northern passage "comfortably begun," as he wrote at that time, without a commitment to confirm the existence of the Strait of Anian; and the only practical means of doing so would be to send an expedition to the South Sea and northward "to the very end of the world from us"—as reckoned in sailing distance—just as Richard Grenville had proposed. And so after receiving some assurances to this effect the previous August, Dee had set about writing his great, four-volume work laying out the knowledge needed for the creation of a "Brytish Impire." However, Grenville was no longer in the picture, for another British subject had won approval to perform the voyage.[26]

PART TWO

Round About the Whole Globe of the Earth

⊰ 6. ⊱

The Preparations

*O*n *July 9, 1577, Francis Drake wrote to the government, claiming the royal bounty for construction of his new bark:* "The same Frances hath of late caused to be erected made and builded at his own expenses proper cost and charge one ship or vessel called the Pelican of Plymouth of the burden of one hundred and fifty tonnes."[1] Little more than 100 feet in length overall and perhaps 21 feet in beam, the *Pelican* was not a large ship by the standard of the day, especially considering the task she would be expected to perform. To the casual observer, she was a typical merchantman, a three-masted bark of the French type.[2]

However, from the outset her design had been conceived to suit Drake's purposes: Her hold was large enough to carry four prefabricated pinnaces as well as supplies and provisions, and her sturdy oak-timbered hull was specially double-planked to endure the stresses of the long voyage. Fully laden, she drew only thirteen feet of water, enabling her to operate in shallow coastal waters. Her mainmast rose to a height of about ninety feet, and she had double canvas sails, including special topgallants to make the most of a light wind and enhance her sailing speed.

Appearances aside, the *Pelican* was also much better armed than any merchantman. Above her hold, her gundeck, having about five feet of headroom, carried fourteen cannons mounted to fire from seven gunports on each side of the ship. The cannons were slender, long-range demi-culverins, each weighing about 3,400 pounds and capable of hurling a 9½-pound ball at an enemy well before it could come close enough to reply with its own guns.[3] In addition, there were four more of these mounted above deck to fire from her bow and stern, together with several smaller, breech-loading guns known as falconets. Altogether, the weight of the *Pelican*'s ordinance alone was more than thirty tons. She also carried a variety of incendiary devices that could be launched at the sails and rigging of an adversary to set them afire; and her armory contained ample numbers of harquebuses, crossbows, pikes, longbows, shields, helmets, corselets, swords, and pistols to equip her crew for a fight at sea or on land.

To accompany the *Pelican*, the queen provided the new eighty-ton bark *Elizabeth* with eleven guns instead of the *Swallow* as originally proposed. Rounding out Drake's squadron were the thirty-ton *Marigold*, the provision ship *Swan*, and the pinnace *Benedict*.

Tensions between England and Spain had recently escalated. In 1576 Dutch Catholics and Protestants had decided to unite under the leadership of William of Orange, elect their own assembly, and fight for independence from Spain. Philip had responded by appointing his half brother, Don John of Austria, hero of the victory over the Turks at Lepanto, to put down the rebellion. During the early months of 1577 Walsingham's spies had gradually exposed a plot by Don John and the Duke of Guise to invade England with 10,000 men, depose Elizabeth, and install Mary Stuart on the throne. Don John planned to wed Mary and rule England jointly with her. As Walsingham's agents gathered more evidence of the scheme, Elizabeth became infuriated.

Walsingham's reports of Don John's plot undoubtedly were what had cleared away the Queen's hesitation concerning Drake's venture. In late June as earlier proposed, John Hawkins drafted, for Walsingham to leak at the court, a fictitious plan to the effect that Drake was embarking on a trading voyage to Alexandria. However, it was not very long before Spanish suspicions were aroused. In late July Philip's representative in London, Antonio de Guaras, received a dispatch from one of his spies, warning: "Francis Drake is going to the Antilles, although they are spreading the rumour that they are going to Tripoli. . . . there is no doubt they are going where I say, and they will do much harm if your mercy does not take measures to keep

The bark Pelican, *later renamed the* Golden Hinde
(drawing of a replica constructed in 1974)

them from going."[4] Walsingham apparently succeeded in throwing de Guaras off the scent with another rumor, for on September 20 the latter wrote to Philip advising that Drake had undertaken for a large sum of money to abduct the Prince of Scotland.

The day after de Guaras painstakingly enciphered this dispatch, Captain John Winter arrived at Plymouth with the *Elizabeth* and the *Benedict*. They had been fitted out in the royal dockyard at Deptford on the Thames and were fully equipped and ready to sail. Winter was appalled by the state of the other ships, later complaining that they were "most untackled, most unballasted and unvictualled."[5]

Little is known of Drake's movements in the final months before the voyage, but there is good reason for believing that his itinerary included conferences with both John Dee and William Bourne, for uppermost in his mind would have been the enormous navigational challenge he faced. Certainly, Dee, because of his connections with the project's backers and his standing as England's foremost geographer and navigational scientist, must have been consulted by Drake. But Dee was a theorist, whereas Bourne was the practical innovator who devised methods of applying the theory. He was an instrument maker and the author of the first English handbook on navigation, *A Regiment for the Sea*, published in 1574. His book explained, in terms that a mariner could understand, the motions of the sun and moon, the methods of calculating tides, distances, and latitude, and the application of the available instruments.

In coastal waters a navigator relied on a simple magnetic compass to maintain his course, and the lead and line to sound for water depth. Together with the logbook, or "rutter,"* in which he recorded compass bearings, soundings, and other details for ready reference, these had long been the basic tools for navigating Europe's coasts, where a pilot could also rely on ancient lore and his knowledge of the principal landmarks. But the advent of ocean voyages, in which a ship sailed beyond sight of land for extended periods, had necessitated the development of the first instruments and techniques that enabled a navigator to estimate his position and progress without reference to familiar landmarks.

To ascertain his position in latitude—the distance north or south from the equator—a navigator used either a cross-staff or an astrolabe to measure the height of the midday sun. With the three-foot-long cross-staff, he held the butt to his cheek and sighted along it, moving the sliding crosspiece until its lower end touched the horizon and its upper end covered the disk of the sun, and then he read the corresponding elevation, marked in degrees where the crosspiece intersected the shaft. Alternatively, the astrolabe was a metal ring six to eight inches in diameter suspended from a thumb ring and had a movable dial along which one sighted until it was aligned with the sun, and then read its elevation from the scale of degrees marked around the circumference of the ring.

The observed elevation of the sun was then adjusted using printed tables setting out the sun's declination—its angular distance north or south of the equator—for each day of the year. William Bourne published tables covering several years at a time for English mariners in his *Almanac and*

---

*Short for "route book," from the French word *routier*.

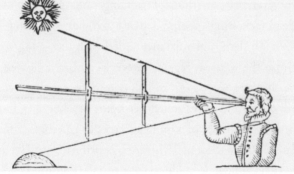

A cross-staff (top, left) and an astrolabe; using the cross-staff (above)

Prognostications. With these tables the true elevation of the sun was determined, and that number of degrees subtracted from ninety gave the navigator his position in degrees north or south of the equator, each degree representing sixty miles.[6] Under favorable conditions a skillful practitioner could determine his latitude to within a quarter of a degree or less.

While the practical means of determining one's latitude had been developed, however, there was no corresponding means of determining longitude—one's position east or west of a known point—from a ship at sea. Theoretically, as Bourne explained in *A Regiment for the Sea*, one could produce a book of *ephemerides* in which the moon's distance from the sun or a prominent star, viewed from a particular place, or "prime meridian," at a given hour could be predicted and tabulated, day by day, for several years to come. Then an observer in another location, finding the moon at a greater or lesser distance from that star, and knowing its rate of motion, could calculate the difference in local time between his position and the prime meridian. The time differential could then be converted to degrees of longitude—each four minutes being equal to one degree—and after adjusting for the observer's latitude* the degrees could be converted into miles east or west of the prime meridian.[7]

However, Bourne wrote, determining one's longitude by this means, known as the lunar distance method, entailed laborious calculations—too time-consuming to be attempted on a regular basis—and in any case required the use of a very precise instrument that would be rendered useless by the motion of a ship. Therefore, he advised, mariners should perfect their navigation by other means.[8]

The only alternative method of gauging one's position in longitude, known as "dead reckoning," required that a navigator combine several sets of observations. To determine distance sailed each day, a log attached to a line was cast into the water at regular intervals, and as it floated astern, the length of line that was played out in half a minute was measured and converted to sailing speed in miles sailed per hour, or "knots."† The navigator then combined this estimate of sailing speed with the ship's compass heading and his latest observation of latitude to continually update and plot his progress on a chart. Thus, he could make a rough reckoning of his position in longitude from his cumulative progress as plotted from his starting point.

Typically, in voyages to and from the New World, captains began by sailing north or south to the latitude of their intended landfall and then turned to cross the Atlantic, as Frobisher had done on his first voyage of exploration. Thus, by making the crossing with little deviation in latitude, the navigator had only to estimate the distance sailed each day to obtain a rough estimate of his position east or west of his starting point. Conversely, the farther north or south one sailed on an ocean crossing, the more unreliable dead reckoning became on account of unseen currents and the phenomenon of magnetic variation, which together could set one far off a reckoned course. This was precisely the problem Drake would face.

---

*As one moves north or south of the equator, each degree of longitude represents progressively fewer miles, as the longitudinal lines, called meridians, begin to converge toward the poles.

†For ease of calculation, the line was knotted at uniform intervals, each representing a sailing speed of one mile per hour; hence the origin of the term "knots" for a vessel's rate of travel.

To reach the Strait of Magellan, Drake had to sail south through more than 100 degrees of latitude—nearly one-third of the circumference of the globe. Then, when he entered the Pacific, he faced a voyage northward through another 100 degrees of latitude in order to reach the vicinity of the supposed Strait of Anian. Consequently, by the time he arrived at the far northwest tip of America, it would be impossible to determine its position in longitude by dead reckoning. Yet he needed to establish its longitude in order to determine the breadth of North America, and hence the sailing distance homeward through the northwest passage.

Most likely, the problem had first been referred to John Dee, but it appears William Bourne was consulted as well, and the result was two proposals.[9] To begin with, it was predicted that there would be a lunar eclipse in September 1578, by which time Drake should be in the Pacific. By careful calculation, it was possible to fix the hour that the eclipse would occur in England, and carrying this information with him, Drake would be able to compare it with the local time of the eclipse when it was observed in the Pacific. The difference in the local time of the eclipse could then be converted to degrees of longitude. However, Drake would not have reached the North Pacific by the time of the eclipse, and so it appears Bourne also devised a means for Drake to apply the lunar distance theorem, but on land rather than from the unstable deck of a ship at sea.

To calculate the sailing distance through the northwest passage, the position of Frobisher's eastern entrance to the passage was needed for comparison. Dee had become involved in the instructions to Frobisher's pilot, Christopher Hall, for their second expedition, which had sailed at the end of May 1577. Frobisher returned in late September, and by the second week of October he was in London. He and his men were warned not to divulge the navigational details of their voyage to anyone. However, it was recorded that they were able to report both the latitude and longitude of the entrance to Frobisher's strait.[10]

Before his return to Plymouth, Drake had a farewell meeting with the Queen. Elizabeth presented him with several gifts, including a sea cap and a green silk scarf on which her maids of honor had embroidered "The Lord guide and preserve thee until the end." She also gave him one of her swords, saying, as he later recalled, "We do account that he which striketh at thee, Drake, striketh at us."[11]

Drake was joined in the voyage by a dozen young gentlemen nominated by his backers. Among this group, Thomas Doughty was certainly the most ambitious. Highly educated, he had already served under the Earl of Essex in Ireland, where he had made Drake's acquaintance, and then after his return to London he had become secretary to Christopher Hatton. Doughty was accompanied by his younger brother John and their friend Leonard Vicary, a lawyer. Gregory Carey was a kinsmen of the Queen's favorite cousin, Lord Hunsdon, and John Chester was the son of the former Lord Mayor of London, while William Hawkins was John Hawkins's nephew, and George Fortescu was the son of the keeper of the royal wardrobe. Lawrence Eliot, whose sponsor is unknown, was a naturalist whose aim was to record the flora and fauna of the New World.

The captains of the other principal vessels were also connected to Drake's backers. John Winter, captain of the *Elizabeth*, was the son of Sir William Winter of the navy board; and Christopher Hatton, who had supplied the *Marigold*, had nominated John Thomas to command her. Appointed to serve as chaplain to the expedition was Cambridge-educated Francis Fletcher. The exuberant preacher was by his own account a veteran traveler, having previously sailed to Russia, Spain, and the Mediterranean, and would keep a journal of the voyage.*

When Drake returned to Plymouth, the provisioning of his ships was virtually completed. He had left James Stydye, one of the captains who had served with him in Ireland, in charge of lading the vessels. Aboard the *Pelican* it had been a tight fit. In addition to the pieces and equipage of the four prefabricated pinnaces, there were carpenters' stores for their assembly and for the repair of the *Pelican* herself, including extra spars, timbers, and planks; kegs of tar, pitch, and rosin; and spare anchors, canvas, and cordage as well as a portable blacksmith's forge accompanied by quantities of iron bars and plate and a supply of charcoal. Also, for construction of fortifications and other works on land, there

---

*Fletcher's original journal has been lost, but a copy of the first part has survived along with two narratives that are adapted from the second part, and these are the primary sources for many of the events of the voyage.

were a large number of axes, machetes, picks, and spades. All these items had to be fitted into the *Pelican*'s hold along with three tons of gunpowder and shot, sufficient water storage in casks to sustain the ship's company for sixty days, and as much food as could be carried.

For victuals Stydye had acquired the usual staples: biscuit, meal, pickled or dried beef, pork, and codfish; cheese, butter, rice, dried peas, raisins, salt, vinegar, sweet oil, mustard, and honey, and numerous casks of wine and beer.[12] Meals were cooked over a fire lit in an iron firebox, for which purpose quantities of firewood also had to be carried.

Then came the racks of arms and armor and a long list of miscellania, including lanterns, candles, buckets, fishnets, twine, hooks, needles and cloth, shoes, bedding, plates, bowls, and tankards. For trade with the native peoples he encountered, Drake's partners had supplied a variety of manufactured goods, probably including woolen cloth, copper kettles, basins and cups, knives, bracelets, looking glasses, and colored ribbons and beads.[13] And the Queen had given Drake an assortment of luxury items to be presented as gifts to the foreign potentates whom he met. These he kept in his cabin, which he had fitted out with finely crafted furnishings and decorations in order that "the civility and magnificence of his native country might, amongst all nations whithersoever he should come, be the more admired."[14]

Drake's personal retinue included his young cousin John, and Diego, his faithful Negro manservant from Nombre de Dios. John Drake, a lad of fifteen, had served as Drake's page in Ireland and was an exceptionally talented artist. He would later be referred to as a "painter"—the name given to one who sailed on maritime expeditions as an artist and mapmaker.* Also accompanying Drake were his youngest brother, Thomas, and several veterans of Nombre de Dios, including Thomas Moone, who commanded the *Benedict*.

Others had been recruited for specific skills: There were armorers, master gunners, cooks, carpenters, coopers, blacksmiths, a surgeon, an apothecary, a shoemaker, and a tailor. And, for entertainment, the *Pelican* carried

---

*It appears both Drake and his young cousin must have received instruction in the technique, probably by a French painter of the Dieppe or Le Havre school, as they would collaborate in the production of a richly illustrated journal of the voyage. Unfortunately, this precious work has been lost, although what appear to be copies of some of the illustrations have survived.

several musicians who formed a small orchestra. In addition to Englishmen, the company included a number of Scots, Danes, Flemings, Frenchmen, and even a Biscayan. In all, 164 men and boys sailed in the expedition's five vessels.

As Drake prepared to depart, in London fresh intelligence from the court had brought Spanish agent de Guaras to a new level of anxiety, and on November 14, 1577, he wrote an urgent directive to his spies. Drake's expedition, he warned, "is an enterprise of much importance to Spain. These are proceedings that promise to bring in a great deal of treasure. The queen is also involved, and others from the council, because they hope to gain much in this business. It is important for Spain to know the location in order to send them to the bottom of the sea."[15]

The next day Drake ordered his ships to weigh anchor, and at five o'clock in the afternoon they slipped out of Plymouth Sound in the closing darkness.

॰ 7. ॰

A Troubled Beginning

Through the night of November 15, Drake's squadron held its course southwest on a light offshore breeze. In the morning, though, the wind swung into their face and began to freshen into a strong gale. With the tempest growing in intensity, Drake gave the signal to turn and run into Falmouth Harbor, but even there they were not secure; within hours his ships were being pounded by the worst storm anyone could recall. Straining at anchor, they heeled so violently that it became necessary to cut down the mainmasts of the *Pelican* and *Marigold* to prevent them from capsizing. Even so, the *Marigold's* anchor cable parted, and she was driven ashore.

When the storm finally died out two days later, all of the ships had sustained significant damage. Drake managed to salvage the *Marigold* off the beach, and after a week spent in temporary repairs they returned to Plymouth. In the interval Drake inspected the ships' holds and found something to his disliking. When they reached Plymouth he promptly dismissed provisioner James Stydye from the expedition.[1]

One evening, as the repairs continued, Drake entertained the gentlemen who had joined the company together with some of the mariners at his house in Plymouth. No doubt his intention was to promote a spirit of fellowship between the two unfamiliar groups, but the occasion produced the first hint of a problem. The gentleman Thomas Doughty was agitated over the dismissal of Stydye. In Drake's garden, Doughty complained to one of the mariners, Edward Bright, that as he and Drake shared command of the expedition, he should have been consulted before Stydye was cashiered.

When Drake met him, Doughty had been employed by the Earl of

Essex as a courier carrying dispatches between Ireland and London. Impressed by Doughty's self-confident manner and claimed accessibility to men at the highest positions in the government, Drake had enlisted him to lobby for his South Sea project, promising him a part in the adventure. He did not know that Essex had discharged Doughty from his service for falsely inciting a serious incident. In an attempt to ingratiate himself to Essex, Doughty had returned from a trip to London reporting that the Earl of Leicester was Essex's enemy and was endeavoring to undermine his reputation at the court. The resultant rift between the two noblemen had only been repaired when Lord Burghley interceded to expose Doughty's charge as untrue.[2]

Doughty had, nonetheless, escaped this cloud and obtained employment as private secretary to Sir Christopher Hatton. Most likely, he had been instrumental in recruiting Hatton's support for Drake's project, as he appears to have been rewarded with his appointment as captain of the expedition's operations on land. In this capacity, however, he was simply one of several captains under Drake's overall command, and he had no grounds for claiming joint command with Drake of the whole enterprise.

Doughty had met several times with Lord Burghley, and he would later claim that Burghley was merely attempting to recruit him as his private secretary; yet it hardly seems credible that Burghley, having already taken Doughty's measure in the Essex affair, had any such intention. Most probably the shrewd Privy Councillor, being kept in the dark about Drake's plans, had simply exploited Doughty's ambition with flatteries designed to extract from him the details of the project, and given him to understand that his prospects for advancement might improve if Drake could somehow be diverted from his purpose.[3]

Drake evidently continued to regard Doughty as a trusted friend. Nonetheless, cornering Edward Bright in Drake's garden, Doughty alternately railed against Drake's dismissal of Stydye and bragged about his own part in obtaining approval for the expedition, claiming that he shared its command with Drake and should be consulted on all important matters.[4] Then, Bright later testified, he began speaking in dark abstracts, saying that he would choose twelve men "that should carry the bell away"; and promising Bright "that I should be one, and that he . . . would make me the richest man of all my kin if I would be ruled by him."[5]

Lord Burghley

Despite the ominous character of Doughty's remarks, it appears that Bright did not report them to Drake until some time later, most probably because he was intimidated by the prospect of bearing solitary witness against an articulate and apparently influential member of the privileged class. Word of his encounter with Doughty spread among the sailors, however, and soon there was growing unease in their ranks regarding all of the gentlemen. Doughty had successfully sown the first seeds of discontent.

Finally, after two weeks spent unlading, repairing, and relading the ships, all was in readiness. On December 13, 1577, Drake gave the order, and they stood out to sea again.

❧ 8. ❧

The Coast of Barbary

hen they were beyond sight of land, Drake signaled the other ships to come alongside the *Pelican* and gave them their sailing orders. There had been a change of plan, he explained, and they were not heading for the Mediterranean after all. They were to set their course for the Atlantic coast of Morocco, and if they became separated, they would rendezvous at the island of Mogador.[1] Some in the company probably had already guessed that Alexandria was not their true destination, and speculated that they were bound instead for the Caribbean.

Aboard the *Pelican* the men settled into their daily routine. The gentlemen were quartered in the stern-castle and dined with Drake in his great cabin, which was a picture of refinement. His table was laid with silver plate fringed with gold, and meals were served to the accompaniment of music from the viols of the ship's orchestra. No one sat until Drake insisted that they do so, and then they waited for him to lead the conversation, the topics ranging from cosmography to religion and inevitably to the oppressive regime of Spain.

The preacher Francis Fletcher was particularly impressed with Thomas Doughty, finding him "always desirous to edify others" and possessed of many excellent qualities: "a sweet orator, a pregnant philosopher, a good gift for the Greek tongue and a reasonable taste of Hebrew, a sufficient secretary to a noble personage of great place, and not behind many in the study of law."[2]

When he stepped on deck, however, Drake was truly in his element, for he was much closer in spirit to the simple mariners who were the backbone of the enterprise than he was to the highborn men who took their place at his table. The sailors, some fifty in number on the *Pelican*, slept below deck wherever they could find a niche between cannons and baggage. By Drake's order, gentlemen and mariners alike assembled twice a day for religious services, and often Drake himself led them in prayer, thus asserting his spiritual as well as temporal leadership.

The ships managed to stay together and make a fast passage, covering the 1,200 miles to the "land of Barbaria" in twelve days. En route they recorded their first casualty, a boy lost overboard from the supply ship *Swan*. On Christmas morning they made landfall at Cape Cantine, and that evening they reached the island of Mogador fifty miles down the barren coast. Lying about a mile offshore, the uninhabited island created a sheltered anchorage between it and the mainland.

After taking soundings, Drake moved the fleet into anchor on December 27 and ordered the pieces of one of his pinnaces lifted out of the *Pelican* and assembled on the island's beach. The next day a group of Berber tribesmen appeared on the mainland shore opposite and signaled that they wished to send a delegation out to the ships. Drake dispatched a boat that picked up two of them, leaving one of his crew as security for their return. When they came aboard, he entertained them with "a daintie banquet and such gifts as they seemed most glad of," and offered to trade with them for whatever commodities their country offered. The two emissaries accepted and indicated they would return with wares for exchange.[3]

The following day a group of tribesmen appeared, leading a caravan of thirty camels, and a boat was sent to meet them. One of the crew, John Fry, had visited Morocco before and understood a little of their language. When Fry walked up the beach to greet them, however, some of the tribesmen seized him and put a dagger to his throat, threatening to kill him if he did not accompany them. Lacking the means to rescue him, the boat crew withdrew. Fry's captors placed him on a horse, and within a few minutes the whole caravan disappeared from view over the brow of the escarpment. Incensed at their treachery, Drake led an armed company some distance inland the next day, hoping to recover Fry, but the tribesmen avoided contact and he was obliged to give up the search. After visiting the ruins of an old Portuguese fort and gathering some firewood, they returned to the ships and prepared to sail.

The incident, it turned out, was the result of a civil war then in progress in Morocco. The region was ruled from Fez and Marakesh by sultans of the Sa'dian dynasty, whose wealth was derived from the trans-Saharan trade with the African kingdoms to the south. Control of this lucrative commerce had long been coveted by the Ottoman Turks, and with their assistance the reigning sultan, Muhammad al Muttawakil, had recently been deposed by his uncle, Abdul-Malik. The deposed nephew had then appealed to King Sebastian of Portugal for help, and a Portuguese fleet was expected to arrive on the coast.

Consequently, Abdul-Malik had sent the men whom Drake had entertained as spies to find out if his ships were the vanguard of Sebastian's fleet. But they had been unable to do so because of the language barrier, and so Fry had been abducted and carried to Abdul-Malik's headquarters. When Fry explained to him that they were Englishmen, Abdul-Malik sent him back to Mogador with presents and an offer of friendship, but Drake had already departed. Eventually, Fry got back to England in a merchant ship.[4]

On January 7, Drake's squadron reached Cape de Guerre, where they intercepted three Spanish fishing vessels that Drake decided to bring with him. As they coasted southward, preacher Francis Fletcher marveled at one of the Atlas Mountains rising high above the hazy, sun-baked desert, its peak blanketed in snow,

> whereby as it is reported, the inhabitants of Morocco have singular benefit for from thence the people continually fetch snow and bring it to the city and other places to sell in the Markets, which they use for many things, but chiefly to mix with wines and other drinks which otherwise would (for the extreme heat of the Country) be unnatural and contagious to their bodies.[5]

At Río de Oro, just below the Tropic of Cancer, Drake captured a Portuguese caravel, and then at Cape Barbas he took another, bringing the number of vessels in his fleet to eleven. On January 16 they reached Cape Blanco, 900 miles southwest of Mogador, and that night had their first sight of the constellation of the Southern Cross, just above the horizon. Beyond the massive cape they found a spacious harbor, a popular refuge of the Portuguese because of its excellent protection from Atlantic storms. Riding at anchor was a Portuguese ship with just two occupants, the others having fled ashore with their valuables. Drake boarded her and removed several barrels of fish and four hundredweight of biscuit.

Aboard the English ships the gentlemen and some of the captains muttered among themselves that the expedition was degenerating into an exercise in petty piracy, but Drake had a reason for seizing so many vessels: The fleet was carrying only a portion of the provisions they would need on their long voyage, and they had to avail themselves of every opportunity to supplement them en route. The waters below the cape were teeming with fish, so Drake set the Spanish fishermen to work.

While they lay at anchor, Drake put his sailors to work as well, washing and trimming his ships, and then went ashore, where he was confronted with an appalling scene. The parched hinterland was devoid of drinking water, and the inhabitants clamored to trade anything, including their fellow human beings, to get some. It was a business in which the Portuguese prospered, bringing water from the Cape Verde Islands and exchanging it for gold, ambergris, and slaves. The natives "cared not at what price they bought it, so they might have to quench their thirst."[6] Some native men approached Drake with a woman

> with her little babe hanging upon her dry dugge [teat], having scarce life in herself, much less milk to nourish her child, to be sold as a horse, or a cow and calf by her side. . . . the circumstances whereof considered, our general would receive nothing of them for water, but freely gave it them that came to him, yea, and fed them also ordinarily with our victuals.[7]

Fletcher found the natives' manners and religion repugnant, writing that they performed the necessities of nature and even copulated in full view of bystanders, and offered the most loathsome sacrifices to their god, the sun. Still, he wrote, he preferred these primitive creatures of nature who worshiped the sun out of simple ignorance to the supposedly civilized papists, who professed to have the keys to all knowledge and power of heaven and hell, and yet venerated wooden idols.

After taking on a supply of fish, Drake released all of his prizes except for one of the fishing vessels, which he renamed the *Christopher*, giving her crew the *Benedict* in exchange, and then on January 21 they set sail on a southwesterly course for the Cape Verde Islands. With the trade winds at their back, they made an easy passage, reaching the first of the islands, Boa Vista, on the seventh day.

The Cape Verdes, comprising eight principal and several smaller islands, had been in Portuguese control for a century and were a vital way station on their sea routes to and from Africa, Brazil, and the East Indies. Employing slaves brought from the mainland, the colonists cultivated cotton and orchilla, a lichen from which dye is made, and indigo, hunted wild cattle and goats for their hides, and mined large reservoirs of salt. But the islands prospered primarily as the hub of the African slave trade. The merchants traded colorful cotton cloth, salt, and other goods to the Guinea coast chiefs in exchange for more slaves, who were then sold in their thriving markets to captains bound for the New World. This traffic also made the islands a favorite haunt of pirates seeking to waylay a richly laden merchantman.

On January 28 Drake halted at the island of Maio and sent Thomas Doughty and Captain Winter ashore with seventy men to forage. Excited by the opportunity to explore, preacher Fletcher joined them. Three miles from their anchorage they found a settlement with many houses, but all were in a ruinous state and the town's springs had been salted. The busiest port in the archipelago being located on the nearby island of Santiago, pirates found Maio a convenient place to lie in wait for their prey, and the frightened Portuguese inhabitants had abandoned their homes and withdrawn into the mountains. That evening Drake's men camped in the ruins of a church, making their meal of some goats and hens that inhabited its yard, and the next morning they set off inland.

Trekking through the valleys, they found cottages and pleasant vineyards but no people or storehouses, and the few springs they located proved too small and remote to be of any use. Nevertheless, Fletcher was enthralled with the quality and abundance of the island's produce: "We found . . . the fairest and most pleasant grapes I had seen in all my former travels in any kingdom."[8] Everywhere the trees were laden with fruit in all stages of ripening. There were fig trees and tall trees without any branches till the top, which bore "coco nuts"; and also "certain lower trees with long and broad leaves, bearing the fruit which they call *plantanes* in clusters together like puddings, a most dainty and wholesome fruit."[9]

Explaining in his journal that such perpetual abundance was the natural result of the sun's continued presence in the tropics, Fletcher bemoaned the ignorance of people in England, who, "boasting of their deep judgement of cosmography . . . do laugh and mock at and say it is a lie to report such things of God's great and marvellous works."[10] He therefore thought it unlikely that they would believe him when he told them that the beaches of Maio contained heaps of perfect salt, like drifts of snow, which were daily increased by the action of the sea and the sun. "It is a thing to be lamented," he concluded,

> that so sweet fruitful and profitable a land should either be possessed by so ungrateful ungratious a people as are the Portugals, or be so subject to such caterpillars of every kingdom and nation as are pirates and thieves of the sea, but that it should be inhabited by people fearing the Lord, to praise him for his benefits which he plentifully hath bestowed upon it.[11]

On January 30 they weighed anchor and made for Santiago, thirty miles to the west, where, they had heard, numbers of slaves had escaped into the mountains and were carrying on a guerrilla war against their former masters. On all of the island's headlands the Portuguese had set up large crucifixes bearing, Fletcher thought, an "evil faced" image of Christ, so he prevailed upon Drake to let him take some men ashore and tear one of them down. This accomplished, he returned to discover that some of the mariners, "being so much addicted to that opinion as the Portugals themselves," strongly objected to his doing so.[12]

As the ships rounded the southern cape of Santiago, the island's principal port came into view, its harbor guarded by cannons mounted in a stone fortress. Less than a league distant* a Portuguese ship was making for the harbor. Placing an armed contingent in the pinnace he had assembled at Mogador, Drake gave chase. As they drew nearer, the fort's cannon began to fire at them, but the shots fell short and Drake intercepted and boarded the vessel.

*One league was equivalent to three miles.

She was the *Santa Maria*, a ship of some 100 tons bound for Brazil with trade goods, and carrying several gentlemen and merchants. She had departed Lisbon with a cargo of linen, woolen cloth, canvas, tools, and implements, all of which Drake could put to good use, and she was also carrying 150 casks of wine and was fully provisioned and watered for the voyage.

Even more important to Drake was her captain, Nuño da Silva. A man in his fifties, da Silva had made his first voyage to Brazil as a boy and had returned many times as a seaman, pilot, and captain. Moreover, he was carrying a rutter and charts for the voyage, including soundings for that coast as far south as the Río de la Plata. Removing da Silva to the *Pelican*, Drake told him that he would be compensated for the loss of his ship. Fletcher recorded that when he heard they were bound for the South Sea, da Silva was eager to accompany them. It appears from this comment that Drake had by then informed the company of their true destination.

Drake placed Thomas Doughty in command of da Silva's ship, and they headed westward past the island of Fogo, whose volcano was erupting. Fletcher thought it rated as one of the great wonders of the world,

> reaching into the air about some 6 English miles or more as in form like a steeples' spire . . . out of the concavity whereof, the root being buried in the depth of the sea, riseth as out of a chimney first a most gross and thick smoke which filling the air at noon . . . that no palpable darkness in the night is to be compared to it. The smoke being gone, such abundance of flames immediately flash out with that force and violence that it seemeth to pierce the heavens, and the light thereof is so great that in the extremist darkness of the night it seemeth as noon day. . . . thirdly the flame being dispersed, there followeth in the tail of it such infinite numbers of pumice stones scattered abroad in the air that far off, falling down, they cover the water and are there to be taken up as sponges swimming upon the face of the seas.[13]

Beyond Fogo lay the last of the islands, lushly tropical Brava, its verdant hills plunging steeply into the sea. Ferrying the water casks ashore in the ships' boats, they refilled them under cascading streams of "sweet and wholesome" water and then gathered quantities of coconuts, plantains, figs, oranges, and lemons. Whether

Francis Fletcher's drawing of the volcano of Fogo

Drake realized the importance of the latter specifically for combating scurvy is uncertain, but he did make a practice of adding fresh fruit and other plants to his men's diet whenever possible. Then on February 1 he ordered sufficient food and drink placed in his new pinnace to see da Silva's passengers and crew safely to Santiago. As this was being done, a dispute arose among the men he had sent aboard da Silva's ship. There are two differing accounts of what transpired.

According to Fletcher, who was on the *Pelican*, Drake's trumpeter John Brewer, Edward Bright, and some other sailors who had been aboard the *Santa Maria* returned to complain that Thomas Doughty was pilfering from her. This may also have been the occasion when Bright finally told Drake about Doughty's remarks at Plymouth.

The charge of theft was a serious matter, for the one incentive the mariners had for enduring the risks and privations of a long voyage was the expectation that each would receive a fair share of any spoils. Fletcher wrote that upon receiving the complaint, Drake immediately went aboard the *Santa Maria* to investigate. But seaman John Cooke, who was on board at the time (and plainly was a Doughty sympathizer), later said it was Doughty himself who had sent for Drake, and that when he came aboard Doughty received him with an accusation of the same kind against Drake's brother Thomas. But Drake demanded to know if Doughty was in possession of anything from the ship, and Doughty produced some pairs of gloves, a ring, and some money which he said the passengers had given him in hope of favorable treatment.

Fletcher later wrote that Drake dismissed the matter as trivial but "in discretion" sent Doughty to the *Pelican* while he remained on the *Santa Maria*.[14] According to John Cooke, however, Drake flew into a rage and with "great oaths" charged Doughty with falsely accusing his brother in order to undermine his own credibility as Captain-General, and "swore by God's life" that he would not suffer it. However, Cooke said, "Master Doughty's very friend," Leonard Vicary, then intervened on his behalf, appealing for Drake to overlook the incident, "which in the end he yielded unto and, to the outward show, forgave and seemed to forget all that had passed."[15]

In any case Drake did send Doughty to take nominal command of the *Pelican*, which seems a strange thing for him to have done in the aftermath of the incident as described by Cooke. Perhaps he wanted to see what would happen if Doughty were placed in those circumstances. If so, he did not have to wait long to find out. When Doughty arrived on the *Pelican*, he ordered her master, Thomas Cuttill, to assemble her company and then delivered a speech to them. "My masters," he began,

> the cause why I call you together is for that I have somewhat to say unto you from the General. The matter is this, that whereas there hath been great travails, fallings out, and quarrels among you and that every one of you have been uncertain whom to obey . . . therefore hath the General by his wisdom and discretion, set down order that all things might be better done with peace and quietness.
>
> And for that he hath a special care of this place, being his admiral and chief ship. . . . he hath sent me as his friend whom he trusteth to take charge in his place, giving unto me the special commandment to signify unto you that all matters by-past are forgiven and foregotten; upon this condition, that we have no more of your evil dealing hereafter.
>
> And for the safer accomplishing hereof I am to tell you, that you are to obey one master in the absense of your General, who is to direct you in your business as touching navigation, which is Mr. Cuttill, whom you know to be a sufficient man.

To this point, Doughty's remarks were consistent with his place as titular commander of the ship, except that it is unlikely Drake would have

been pleased with his shifting the blame for the unrest onto the mariners.
But then Doughty continued:

> And for other matters, as the General has his authority from her high-
> ness the Queen's majesty and her Council such as hath not been com-
> mitted almost to any subject afore this time:—to punish at his
> discretion with death or other ways offenders; so he hath committed
> the same authority to me in his absense to execute upon those which
> are malefactors.[16]

Fletcher wrote in his journal that Doughty was thought to have exceeded his authority, "taking upon him too great of a command," and that
those who disliked him went to complain to Drake again, just as he was setting his Portuguese captives free in the pinnace.[17] For the time being, however, Drake did nothing further about Doughty.

❧ 9. ❧

Land of Giants

Seven hundred miles south of the Cape Verdes the trade winds died out, and on February 10 the fleet stood nearly motionless in the doldrums—the still, humid air and glassy calms straddling the equator. Light breezes came up and carried them for a few leagues and then subsided again, leaving them becalmed for long hours at a time under the intense tropical sun. To everyone's relief, the seemingly infinite numbers of lice that had plagued them perished en masse.

Sudden, drenching cloudbursts were a daily occurrence, enabling them to keep their water casks full. However, the sailors discovered that if they left their wet clothes in a heap, they soon moldered and disintegrated in the sultry heat. Violent lightning storms lit up the sky and issued tremendous claps of thunder but, apart from frightening the men, inflicted no damage on the ships. Harnessing every breath of air, they crossed the equator on February 17, and ten days later they finally found a steady wind and set their course southwest for Brazil.

Contrary to the dire warnings he had read in ancient Greek and Latin texts about the intolerable burning of the sun in the "torrid zone," Francis Fletcher found it to be an earthly paradise, "for God gave water from Heaven and provided health for us of body victuals and things necessary for the maintenance of our natural lives . . . as if we had been in the storehouse of his blessings."[1] The sailors' chief diversion was watching the remarkable flying fish, "of the length and bigness of a reasonable Pilchard, having two fins reaching from the pitch of the shoulder to the tip of the tail . . . whereof she flyeth as any feathered fowl in the air."[2] Among the fishes of the sea,

Flying fish and their predators, from the journal of Francis Fletcher

Fletcher thought none compared to them in freedom from corruption and slimy nature,

> the cause whereof I gather to be their continual exercise in water and air, for in the seas they are for the most part pursued by shoals of Dolphins and bonitos . . . whereof they are inforced to practise their flying in the air . . . whose flight is wonderful for swiftness and height, for it is equal to a pigeon in both, as also in distance or length; for its at least a quarter of a mile at a time.[3]

Numbers of them hit the sails and fell to the deck, where the sailors baited hooks with them and cast them over the stern to catch tuna and dolphin.

Equally fascinating was a species of large bird, "of bigness, Eagles' fellows," which came so far from land to prey on the flying fish yet never landed in the water. Snatching only fish that were airborne, they climbed far into the sky and then spiraled slowly downward devouring their meal.

The Portuguese pilot da Silva told the sailors that birds of this type could not abide to touch the water with their feet, and so they rested in the same manner, soaring to a great height and then gliding down, fast asleep until they came within a few feet of the water, where they awoke and flew up again to resume their slumber. However, Fletcher wrote, many of them came to rest on the ships, "taking them as it seemed for moving rocks," where they allowed themselves to be snared with lines put about their necks with poles, "without motion or removing away, as if they had been commanded of God to yield themselves to be meat for us."[4]

Drake had remained aboard Nuño da Silva's ship, which had been renamed the Mary, *with* his brother Thomas and the Portuguese captain, plotting their navigation. Language appears not to have been a serious impediment. Da Silva spoke Spanish and soon gained some grasp of English, while Drake had some facility, albeit unpolished, in Spanish and his manservant, Diego, spoke both languages.

Aboard the *Pelican* Thomas Doughty's antics continued. Approaching Master Cuttill and some of the mariners individually, he promised they would be rewarded if they did his bidding, and that he would use his influence to square whatever they did with the Queen and her council when they got back to England. It appears that Doughty's aim was to break away from Drake. At the same time Doughty's younger brother John allegedly boasted that the two of them possessed powers of witchcraft, claiming that they could call up the Devil in the form of a lion or bear, or poison their enemies by supernatural means. If the younger Doughty did make such claims, he was inviting serious trouble, because the Elizabethans commonly believed in and feared witchcraft, and nowhere was that dread more acute than among a group of superstitious sailors.

Finally, in midocean the situation came to a head when Drake sent his trumpeter, John Brewer, over to the *Pelican* on an errand. As Brewer stepped aboard the *Pelican*, Thomas Doughty had him seized and bent over a barrel, and under the pretext of an amusement, invited the assembled crew to join him in delivering a "cobbey"—a rough spanking to Brewer's naked buttocks. When Drake learned of this humiliating treatment of his messenger, he sent some men to fetch Doughty. The religious service was under way when they returned with him, and Drake was reading from the Bible.

As Doughty reached to climb aboard the *Mary*, Drake turned abruptly and shouted "stay there Thomas Doughty, for I must send you to another place," and then ordered that he be taken to the provision ship *Swan* and placed in the charge of Captain John Chester.[5] Fletcher recorded that Doughty was removed "in utter disgrace."[6]

Soon afterward Drake took da Silva over to the *Pelican*, leaving his

brother Thomas in command of the *Mary*. On March 9 they received the
sweet smell of land at latitude 13 degrees south, but learning from da Silva
that the Portuguese had swift galleys patrolling the coast, Drake decided to
remain offshore. The southernmost Portuguese settlement in Brazil was São
Vicente at latitude 24 degrees south, beyond which there was no European
habitation. Drake led his ships southward for another month before they
made landfall near latitude 32 degrees south.

Having been at sea for sixty-three days, they began to look for a sheltered harbor in which to rest and repair. As they moved inshore for a closer
look, however, they were suddenly engulfed in a dense fog, and moments
later the men handling the lead and line called out that the water depth was
rapidly diminishing. The shoals extended much farther to seaward than they
had expected. "If the Portuguese pilot had not been appointed of God to
do us good," Fletcher wrote, they would have been lost.[7] Quickly coming
about at da Silva's urging, they managed to avoid disaster, although not before one ship touched bottom.

Asked about the sudden appearance of fog, da Silva recounted a
Portuguese mariner's tale. The Indians, he said, had fled their natural soil
to escape the cruelty of the Portuguese colonists and had yielded themselves into the hands of devils as their patrons and protectors. When they
saw any ships on the coast, he said, they took up sand from the beach and
threw it into the air, causing such a haziness that the land could not be
seen, and increasing the shoals in the way of the ships. To this they added
such terrible winds, rains, and storms that there was no certainty of survival. Hence, this coast was known to Portuguese sailors as Terra
Demonum. Whether the Englishmen took this story seriously or not, it
proved to be prophetic.

No sooner had they extricated themselves from the shoals than they
were struck by a violent gale from the south. Thus far Drake had succeeded
in keeping the fleet together, but when the tempest subsided the *Christopher*
was missing. Searching the coast for her, they continued southward to their
planned rendezvous in the Río de la Plata, and on April 14 they came to anchor under a cape at the mouth of the great river. Two days later the
Christopher found them, and Drake named the place Cape Joy.

The next day they moved farther into the estuary, where they found a
rocky island inhabited by sea lions and killed a number of them to restore

their depleted larder. The sea lion oil, Fletcher noted, was so subtle that it "pierseth through any substance it is put on, and is a present help for outward inflammations in any members, whereof diverse of our men had good experience by my directions to their good comforts."[8] He soon had occasion to put his remedy to use.

Going ashore on the mainland, some of the sailors discovered a plant that bore a pleasant-tasting fruit, and they brought quantities of it back in their shirts and hats. The leaves proved to be covered with poisonous prickles that were impossible to remove from their clothes, and which worked their way into their pores, "raising red and fiery pimples with extreme itching and burning to the tormenting of the body in some extremity till they have consumed their poison, wherewith some of [the] men were mightily afflicted."[9] Fletcher found that the sea lion oil helped to relieve the sailors' discomfort.

On April 20 they sailed up the river until they stood in three fathoms of freshwater, and there filled their water casks while a party was sent ashore to forage. Fletcher had read the printed account that Drake carried of Ferdinand Magellan's great voyage, in which the natives of Patagonia were described as giants, and when the foraging party returned, he excitedly noted in his journal that they had news appearing to corroborate this story.

> For them who returned gave us to understand that the country was full of partridges and of most large bodies, bigger much than in England, as in like case they found the print of their feet in the soft ground, the breadth whereof was the length of one of our men's feet of largest size, which could be no other than the foot of a Giant, so that we conjectured that the Giants did possess some part of Brasilia on the north side of the River Plate.[10]*

Returning out of the river, Drake followed its south shore, looking for a safe anchorage in which to repair his ships, but found none, and on April 27 they rounded the south cape of the estuary and stood out to sea again. That night they were struck by heavy gales, and the next morning the *Mary* and the *Swan* were nowhere to be seen.

---

*The giant "partridges" that the men had seen were the South American ostrich, or rhea.

Searching for them "as diligently as contrary winds and sundry storms would permit," Drake continued southward for some 800 miles without sight of his missing ships and finally came to anchor on May 12 three leagues off a cape at latitude 47 degrees south.[11] Drake named it Cape Hope because they discovered a bay within the headland that offered promise of a good harbor, although its entrance was strewn with dangerous rocks. The next morning he set off with some men in a launch to investigate, but after they had rowed several miles the weather suddenly altered into "an extreme storm and tempest" accompanied by a thick mist in the bay.[12] Turning to head back to the ships, Drake discovered they were obscured by fog. Outside the bay the growing gale obliged the ships to weigh anchor and make for the open sea. Seeing Drake's plight, however, Captain Thomas threw caution aside and steered the *Marigold* among the rocks to rescue him, and they spent the night in the bay.

The following morning, May 14, the other ships having been scattered by the storm, Drake took some men ashore and lit signal fires to guide them back. There they saw two Indians and exchanged signs of friendship with them, but the Indians would not come near. By evening all of the ships were anchored in the bay except the still-missing *Mary* and *Swan*. The next morning Drake took another party ashore, and they found shelters in which the Indians were drying the carcasses of some rheas.

> The ostrich's thighs were in bigness equal to reasonable legs of mutton. They cannot fly at all, but they run so swiftly and take so long strides that it is not possible for a man in running by any means to take them . . .
>
> Among other means they use in betraying these ostriches, they have a great and large plume of feathers . . . bearing the likeness of the head, neck and bulk of an ostrich . . . to hide the most part of the body of a man. With this it seemeth they stalk, driving them into some strait or neck of land close to the sea-side.[13]

Thirty miles farther south Drake found a bay that was better suited to their purpose, and the following day they moved in to anchor, naming it Port Desire. Then he dispatched Captain Winter in the *Elizabeth* to the south and set off himself northward in the *Pelican* to search for their missing ships.

Within a few hours Drake found the *Swan*, but neither had any success locating the *Mary*.

On the Swan *relations between the gentlemen and the mariners had deteriorated to the* point of open hostility, and at the center of the problem, once again, was Thomas Doughty, backed by his brother, John. Also with them was Fletcher, who had joined the *Swan* in the Río de la Plata. Soon after Doughty came aboard, he had begun his familiar refrain, telling anyone who would listen that Drake owed his advancement to him, that he had a hold on Drake by reason of certain secrets, and that they had been given equal authority over the expedition. Doughty said his powerful friends in England would reward those who supported him and punish his enemies. Indeed, he told them, Lord Burghley had approached him to serve as his secretary.

One evening, as Doughty continued to agitate along these lines over dinner in Captain Chester's cabin, the master of the vessel, John Saracold, interrupted him. If there were traitors aboard, Saracold said, the general would do well to deal with them as Magellan had, which was to hang them as an example to the rest. Doughty's response was a direct contradiction of the speech he had made when he went aboard the *Pelican*: "Nay, softly," Doughty exclaimed, "his authority is none such as Magellan's was, for I know his authority so well as he himself does. And as for hanging it is for dogs and not for men." Infuriated by Doughty's arrogant reply, Saracold stormed out of the cabin, saying that he had heard enough of such talk and henceforth would take his meals in the company of honest seamen.[14]

Soon afterward Doughty accused Saracold of keeping the best victuals for the mariners, to which the master swore in reply that such rascals as he should be glad to eat the oar-pegs from the ship's boat. Blows were exchanged, and then Doughty attempted to persuade Chester to assert his authority over the master by force, saying that he would put the sword into Chester's hands to govern as he saw fit, after which, Doughty was heard to say that he would make the company cut one another's throats.[15]

On the evening of May 18, the Pelican *and* Swan *rejoined the fleet at Port Desire, and the* next day Drake ordered the *Swan* stripped of her provisions and everything usable and then burned. Trying to keep so many ships together was slowing him down, and he had determined to reduce their number.

As the men were beaching the *Swan*, some thirty Indians appeared on the hill overlooking the anchorage. Their leader put on a lengthy demonstration, exhorting them and pointing to the sun and moon, and then they arrayed themselves in a line along the ridge. When some of the sailors started up the hill to greet them, the Indians raised their bows, indicating that they should not come nearer.

Recalling his men, Drake tied some glass-beaded bracelets, knives, and other gifts to a rod and sent two of them to plant it at the bottom of the hill. After they had withdrawn, two Indians slowly descended, crisscrossing the face of the hill with bow and arrow at the ready as if stalking each other, until finally they retrieved the gifts, leaving in exchange some of their arrows and some ostrich feathers. The next day the Indians appeared again, and when Drake went ashore with a party, they all came down the hill to trade.

Naked except for animal skins draped over their shoulders, their bodies were painted from head to foot, some entirely black and others black on one side and white on the other, decorated with contrasting moons and suns. They had red circles painted around their eyes, and their noses and lips were pierced with pieces of polished bone or wood. They never cut their hair, instead knitting it with ostrich feathers to form a quiver for their arrows and a carryall for their possessions.

Among the items the natives offered in exchange were two pieces of wood, one round and the other flat, with which they made fire. Placing the flat piece on his knees, one of them demonstrated, drilling the round piece into it between the palms of his hands until a flame emerged. The weather was turning cold, and laying their infants on a bed of rushes next to the fire, they smeared their bodies with ostrich oil mixed with a chalklike substance to insulate them from the chill.

The men wore rattles on strings about their waists. Fletcher was astonished by the effect of the rattles, "which no sooner begin to make a noise but [the Indians] begin to dance, and the more they stir their stumps . . . the more their spirits are ravished with melody, in so much that they dance like madmen."[16] Seeing this, Drake brought the *Pelican*'s orchestra ashore to play for them, and led by Captain Winter, some of the sailors joined in the dance. "We thus using them with great kindness," Fletcher wrote, "they became more and more familiar with us, in so much that they would not absent themselves from our company."[17] After a short while, however, the Indians dispensed with the formalities of exchange and began stealing things that caught their fancy. One of them even snatched Drake's scarlet sea cap off his head and dashed away with it. But Drake "would suffer no man to hurt any of them."[18]

Toward the end of their two-week sojourn at Port Desire, Drake ran out of patience with Thomas Doughty. Initially, during the dismantling of the *Swan*, Doughty had the freedom of the *Pelican*. But Drake observed him closely and, after watching him engage in hushed conversations with several individuals, he confronted him. A heated exchange ensued, and then Drake struck Doughty and ordered him tied to the mainmast, where he remained for two days before being released. When the fleet was ready to sail, Drake ordered Doughty to go aboard the *Christopher*, which lay alongside the *Pelican*. But Doughty protested that there were men aboard the *Christopher* who would kill him, and flatly refused to go until, finally, Drake ordered him bound and swung onto her with the boat tackle.

With 200 freshly slaughtered sea lions to sustain them on the next leg of their journey, the company set sail on June 3. Drake had in mind to find his brother in the *Mary* and then make a dash for Magellan's Strait before the Southern Hemisphere winter took a firm hold. Again they were struck by a succession of gales, and on the third night the *Christopher* became separated from the fleet. After four days of searching, they found her and Drake led them into a bay, where he ordered her stripped and abandoned as well. While this was being done, Drake went aboard the *Elizabeth* and told her crew he was sending them a couple of "very bad men" whom he did not know how to carry along with him and still go through with the voyage. Thomas Doughty, he said, was a "conjuror" and a "seditious fellow," and his brother a "witch" and a "poisoner," and anyone who spoke with them would be regarded as enemies of the voyage.[19]

On June 14 they put to sea again and continued southward for three days until they met strong winds and came to anchor in a bay within 100 miles of Magellan's Strait, but still there was no sign of Drake's brother with the *Mary*. The following morning they turned back to search, and fi-

An Indian snatches Drake's cap, from Theodore de Bry's America Pars VIII, *1599*

nally on the evening of June 19 they sighted her. She had not touched land since leaving the Río de la Plata two months before. After becoming separated, Drake's brother had remained at sea for fear of missing the fleet. Da Silva's ship was leaking badly from the continual battering of the gales, and her crew were exhausted, many of them sick.

Winter was now upon them, and with the expedition in a vulnerable state there was no possibility of attempting the strait. A few leagues distant, behind a long, northward-pointing headland, stood a bay that Drake believed was Port St. Julian, where Magellan had waited out the winter, and it was there that he pointed his diminished fleet of four ships.

ᕤ 10. ᕥ

Island of Blood

ort St. Julian. The name must have evoked a sense of foreboding aboard
Drake's ships as they passed the somber gray cliffs guarding its
entrance on June 20, 1578. It was here, fifty-eight years before, that
Magellan had crushed a mutiny led by some of his Spanish officers and left
one of them hanging from a gibbet and two others marooned among the giants who were said to inhabit this land.

Drake chose an anchorage adjacent to a low sandy island where it was
feasible to careen the ships for repairs. The next day they landed and began
preparing an encampment, and Drake rowed with some men in one of the
ship's boats farther up the harbor to look for a source of freshwater. On the
possibility that they might find some game, surgeon Robert Winterhay
brought his longbow, and the master gunner, named Oliver, carried a harquebus. Some of the others took their swords and shields. Francis Fletcher
did not accompany them but recorded the event in his journal afterward, as
did mariner Edward Cliffe.

Going ashore on the mainland, Drake's party encountered two young
Indians armed with bows. They were exceptionally tall and well-muscled
but hardly the seven-foot giants that Magellan's chronicler had described.
Cliffe observed that there were taller men in England.[1] Drake presented
some gifts, and Winterhay engaged them in a friendly competition to see
who could shoot an arrow farthest. Winterhay easily won, and the Indians
were greatly impressed with his bow. On another attempt, however, the
string of Winterhay's bow broke, and the contest was suspended while he set
about repairing it. At this point an older Indian appeared and began ha-

Ferdinand Magellan

ranguing the young ones and making hostile gestures toward the Englishmen.[2]

As Drake's party turned to withdraw to their boat, one of the Indians, evidently believing that Winterhay's disabled bow was the only weapon they were carrying, suddenly shot an arrow through the surgeon's arm and quickly followed it with another that penetrated his lungs. The gunner Oliver took aim at Winterhay's assailant with his harquebus, but it failed to fire, and another Indian shot an arrow into Oliver's chest with such force that it passed through his heart and protruded from his back. At the same moment more Indians emerged from the woods on either side.[3]

Shouting orders, Drake told his men to keep moving and use their shields, and those who had none to shelter behind them and break any arrows that fell within reach, so that the Indians could not reuse them as they withdrew. Retrieving Oliver's harquebus, Drake reprimed, aimed, and fired it at the Indian who had started the fray. The gun being charged with both bullet and hail shot, the blast "tore out his belly and guts, with great torment as it seemed by his cry," and the others fled.[4] Finding Winterhay still alive, they rushed him back to the *Pelican*, but he was beyond recovery and died two days later. Oliver's body was later found stripped of his clothes and with an English arrow stuck in his left eye. They were buried side by side in a common grave near the camp.

As tragic as their loss was, the incident could have turned into a much graver calamity: But for Oliver's loaded harquebus and Drake's swift use of it, the entire party might have been slain. Considering the marked difference in behavior between these Indians and those they had met at Port Desire, Drake concluded that it had to stem from their memory, passed from one generation to the next, of cruelties inflicted on them by Magellan.[5] Drake had hoped to trade with them for food, and in an attempt at reconciliation gifts were left in various places, but they kept their distance.

Overarching all of Drake's other concerns was the problem of Thomas Doughty, whose attempts to undermine his command and disrupt the voyage at every turn had caused a great unease in the company. Many of the sailors had developed an intense dislike of him and, by association, several of the other gentlemen who sat idly about during the voyage.

By Drake's reckoning, however, Doughty did have a following, albeit loosely formed, of about thirty men, including a number of mariners who barely concealed their angst at being involved in such a perilous adventure, and would have welcomed any pretense to abandon the enterprise and return to England.[6] Even Captain Winter of the *Elizabeth*, although circumspect in his remarks, was less than enthusiastic about continuing the voyage. Moreover, they were soon to enter Magellan's Strait, which, one contemporary observed, "[was] counted so terrible in those days that the very thoughts of attempting it were dreadful."[7]

The potential for further dissension in the company leading to bloodshed, insurrection, or the desertion of one or more of the ships was therefore very real, and Thomas Doughty had amply demonstrated that, given the opportunity, he would gladly be the lightning rod for such an event. Yet there was little point in Drake charging him with mutiny unless he was prepared to execute him and put an end to the matter, and he was deeply worried about the repercussions when he got back to England.[8]

Although he had embarked on the voyage with the Queen's full knowledge and support, it is doubtful that she had put her name to a commission for the enterprise. Even if she had, Drake knew her reaction to Doughty's execution would depend in large measure on the views of her councillors, including Doughty's patron, Sir Christopher Hatton. Nonetheless, despite his reservations Drake decided to act. The proceedings were recorded by Doughty's friend John Cooke.[9]

On June 30 Drake had the entire company assembled on shore and stood before them with Captain John Thomas, also a Hatton appointment, at his side. After informing them that they were gathered to hear charges read against Thomas Doughty, Captain Thomas showed them a number of written statements taken from witnesses to Doughty's mutinous talk throughout the voyage. Then the accused was brought forward, and Drake addressed him:

> Thomas Doughty, you have here sought by diverse means, in as much as you may, to discredit me to the great hinderance and overthrow of this voyage, besides other great matters wherewith I have to charge you withal, the which if you can clear yourself of, you and I shall be very good friends, where to the contrary you have deserved death.[10]

Doughty denied any villainy toward him and said the allegations could not be proved. Drake then asked him how he wished to be tried. "Why, good General, let me live to come into my country, and I will there be tried by Her Majesty's laws," Doughty replied. "Nay, Thomas Doughty," Drake said, "I will here impanel a jury on you to inquire further of these matters that I have to charge you withal."[11]

Doughty then reached for his strongest card. "Why General, I hope you will see that your commission be good," he said, challenging Drake's authority to place him on trial. "I warrant you my commission is good enough," Drake replied. "I pray you let us then see it," Doughty countered, "it is necessary that it should be here showed."[12] It appears that he knew Drake did not have a written commission, and had reckoned all along that he would be powerless to prosecute him. But Drake would not allow him to turn the proceedings into an examination of the grounds for his authority, written or otherwise, and quickly brushed the issue aside. "Well, you shall not see it," he said, and then ordered Doughty's arms bound.[13]

As Doughty was being bound, Drake accused him of poisoning the Earl of Essex. It had been rumored that Essex's death, in September 1576, had been caused by poisoning, and conceivably Drake had come to suspect that Doughty was the culprit. This clearly was beyond proof, however, and it appears that Drake made the accusation in order to underscore his belief that Doughty was plotting to kill him. Doughty retorted that he had served the Earl well, and that it was he himself who had introduced Drake to Essex. Drake was indignant at this last assertion, exclaiming that Doughty had nothing to do with his coming into Essex's service.

A jury composed of forty gentlemen and mariners was sworn, and Captain Winter was appointed foreman. Then Captain Thomas read the statements of the various witnesses aloud, and one by one they came forward to certify them as true. "All of which," Cooke wrote, Doughty "did not greatly deny" until Edward Bright described his encounter with him in Drake's garden. Bright told of Doughty's remarks and how Doughty had later hinted that he wanted to break away from Drake and use the plunder he obtained to bribe the Queen and her councillors to smooth over his conduct when he got back to England. "Why, Ned Bright," Doughty protested, "what should move thee thus to belie me? Thou knowest that such familiarity was never between thee and me, but it may be I said if we brought home gold we should be the better welcome, but yet that is more than I do remember."[14]

Then Doughty let slip that Lord Burghley had obtained the "plot" of the voyage, and Drake jumped to his feet. "How?" he demanded. "He had it from me," Doughty replied. Apparently, Doughty had violated the Queen's injunction against revealing Drake's plan to anyone, and especially Burghley. It was the most damning evidence Drake could have hoped for. "Lo, my masters," he exclaimed, "what this fellow hath done! God will have his treacheries all known, for Her Majesty gave me special commandment that of all men my Lord Treasurer should not know it, but to see his own mouth hath betrayed him."[15]

Recognizing that he had made a potentially fatal admission, Doughty tried again to contest the legitimacy of the proceedings and said that he would sign anything if he would be allowed to live and answer the charges when they reached England. His friend lawyer Leonard Vicary joined in the appeal, declaring the trial to be illegal. But Drake would not hear of it. "I have not to do with you crafty lawyers," he said, "neither care I for the law, but I know what I will do."[16]

Vicary protested that he did not know how the jury could answer for taking Doughty's life when they got home. "You shall not have to do with his life," Drake replied, "let me alone for that. You are but to see whether he be guilty in these articles."[17] With the arguments thus concluded, Drake instructed the jury to consider the evidence and render a verdict.

After deliberating, the jury returned a verdict of guilty. Drake then walked down to the shore, calling everyone except Doughty and his brother to accompany him. There he rummaged through the bundle of letters and papers that he was carrying and then exclaimed: "God's will! I have left in my cabin that I should especially have had," inferring that he had forgotten to bring his commission.[18] But he showed them some of the letters, establishing that it was John Hawkins, not Doughty, who had introduced him to Essex, that Essex had then recommended him to Secretary of State Walsingham, and that the Queen had invested 1,000 crowns in the venture. Then he put the question of Doughty's fate to the whole company.

> And now, my masters, consider what a great voyage we are like to make. The like was never made out of England, for by the same the worst in this fleet shall become a gentleman. And if this voyage go not forward, which I cannot see how possible it should if this man live, what a reproach it will be, not only unto our country but especially unto us, the very simplest here may consider of. Therefore, my masters, they that think this man worthy to die, let them with me hold up their hands.[19]

There was no longer any room for equivocation, and the vote appears to have been nearly unanimous.

After pronouncing the sentence of death, Drake briefly wavered, offering to consider any practical means of sparing Doughty's life. Doughty requested that he be carried to the coast of Peru and put ashore there, but Drake refused, saying that he could not answer to the Queen for it. Then Captain Winter offered to take Doughty into his custody aboard the *Elizabeth* and guarantee his conduct until they reached England, but the prospect of turning back was met by a chorus of objections from Winter's men. Finally, Drake terminated the discussion and told Doughty to prepare for death two days hence, on July 2. Asked how he wished to meet his end, Doughty chose to die under the ax.

On the appointed day, the two bitter adversaries engaged in a remarkable display of chivalry. Doughty had asked to receive the sacrament from Chaplain Fletcher, and Drake offered to accompany him, "for the which Master Doughty gave hearty thanks, never once terming him other than 'my good captain.'" Then Drake invited Doughty to dine with him in his tent, and they did so, "each cheering up the other and taking their leave by drinking to each other."[20]

At the conclusion of the meal Doughty asked to speak privately with Drake, and they stood together for a few minutes before he was led away. The entire company was assembled to witness his execution. Doughty knelt and prayed for the Queen and for the success of the voyage, and then rose and asked forgiveness for himself and his associates. Then he knelt again and placed his neck on the block. After the ax had fallen, Drake commanded that Doughty's severed head be held up, and then cried out, "Lo! This is the end of traitors!"[21]

Before dismissing the company, Drake warned that if any other person should offend to a fraction of the extent Doughty had, he would die for it, and further, that if any of them struck a shipmate, he would lose a hand. The next day Fletcher read the funeral service as Doughty's remains were buried alongside those of Winterhay and Oliver. Notwithstanding that his testimony had helped to convict Doughty, Fletcher was horrified by the taking of his life. To reassure the preacher, Drake ordered the whole company to receive communion from him the following Sunday. After the service Drake commanded that all old quarrels between the men were to be forgiven, and warned that if anyone thereafter harassed another over past grievances, he would lay such a heavy punishment on him as to make him an example to the whole fleet.

In the interval the men had found, near the entrance to the harbor, the gibbet that Magellan had erected and, lying on the ground beneath, the bones of the Spanish mutineer Gaspar Quesada. Drake had them interred adjacent to the fallen Englishmen, and Fletcher inscribed a headstone in Latin, as he had done for the others. Then the *Pelican*'s cooper pulled the gibbet down and cut the timber into pieces to make into drinking tankards, as macabre souvenirs of their stay on what they called "the island of blood."

The work of careening the ships became the focus of daily activity. Cannons, equipment, and provisions were lifted out of each ship, and sails, cordage, and rigging were removed for repair. Then came the labor of removing the ship's ballast—the tons of stone or gravel laid in the bottom of the hull to lower her center of gravity in the water, so as to prevent her capsizing when lightly loaded.

When each ship was lightened, it was moved toward shore on the high tide until she became grounded, sideways to the beach, when the tide fell. Then lines were tied to her mast-tops and pulled shoreward, rolling the ship on her hull until her seaward side was exposed down to the keel at low tide.

With the ship tethered in this position, a team of men set to scraping off the barnacles and other sea growths that had attached themselves to her hull and slowed her sailing speed. They drilled and plugged wormholes and raked out the seams between the planks, wedging and hammering fresh caulking into them. The hull was then coated with a mixture of hot tar and brimstone carried in buckets from fires set up on the beach. When one side of the hull was finished, the ship was repositioned for work on the other.

On shore another team labored to repair sails and rigging, and the blacksmith set up his forge to replace broken fastenings. Aboard ship, a party bailed out the bilges and did their best to kill the rats that scuttered between their feet. John Hawkins had recommended careening as often as possible, believing that the filth and vermin that accumulated in the bilges were the chief cause of shipboard epidemics.

When these tasks were completed, the ship was floated off again and trimmed with new ballast. Some of the men set about rerigging her while others lifted her guns and equipment aboard. All her cannons were stowed deep in the hold for the next leg of the voyage.

First the *Pelican* and then the *Elizabeth* and the *Marigold* were careened, but Drake decided that da Silva's ship was too leaky and troublesome to warrant repair, and ordered her beached and used for firewood, reducing his fleet to three vessels.

While the work continued, the company slept ashore in tents. The nights were long and cold. It snowed several times, and the air and ground sent a constant, damp chill into their bodies. Port St. Julian was at nearly the same southern latitude as England was to the north, and Edward Cliffe considered the weather to be comparable, although "in the depth of winter, or rather colder."[22]

In fact, the winters at higher latitudes in both the Northern and Southern Hemispheres at this time frequently were colder than the oldest person could remember, because the middle of the century had marked the onset of one of the coldest periods in what modern scientists have called the Little Ice Age.* Around 1300 C.E., after 300 years of weather slightly warmer than the mid–twentieth century, global climate began to cool, and the glacial remnants of the last Great Ice Age had begun to grow once more.

For two centuries the effects of global cooling had been felt only sporadically. Around 1525, however, European chroniclers had begun to note an increase in the incidence of severe winters. Initially, the weather alternated between unusually cold and snowy versus mild and snowless winters. Then, in the 1560s, the cooling deepened, bringing greater accumulations of snow, which delayed spring and shortened the growing season.[23] By the 1570s the Thames River often froze over in winter, and even the lagoon of Venice sometimes did as well.[24] The climate had become significantly colder, and the winters of 1578–1580 appear to have been especially severe.[25]

Compounding the effects of the cold, Drake's men found that there was little fresh food to be had. Foraging parties reported the rookeries devoid of seal or bird, and attempts to hunt the elusive ostrich proved futile. They were forced to survive on wormy meal and biscuit, and an increasing number became too ill to work. Many were afflicted with scurvy. As the disease progressed, the victim's joints ached, his limbs and gums swelled, and he began to develop painful boils on his body. Then he grew steadily weaker and more listless, and his teeth began falling out. Ultimately, he became so racked with pain that he could not stand.

Drake found that a stew of mussels and seaweed restored some strength, and thereafter such quantities as could be obtained were fed to the sick. As the weeks passed, however, both the health and morale of the company continued to decline. Drake worried that if he did not get the fleet under way soon, he would never reach the South Sea.

Finally, on August 10, 1578, the ships stood ready, and the following day Drake called the company together. Although they were still in the grip of winter, he had resolved to attempt the strait without further delay. First, though, he had to

---

*From the mid–sixteenth century to the mid–nineteenth century, the global average temperature ranged from one to one and a half degrees Celsius (two to three degrees Fahrenheit) lower than that of the late twentieth century. At the peak of the last Great Ice Age 20,000 years ago, the global average temperature was only about five degrees Celsius (nine degrees Fahrenheit) cooler than in the late twentieth century. A drop of even a degree or two in global temperature therefore represented a very significant cooling, particularly in the mid- to high latitudes, where the temperature shift was greater than the global average.

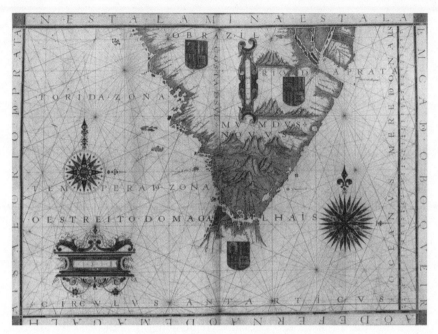

A Portuguese chart of Magellan's Strait

address the problem of low morale and, in particular, the ill feeling that still existed between the mariners and the gentlemen. The cold and misery had served only to accentuate their differences, as the latter continued to show little inclination to share in the hard work, considering it beneath their station and dignity to labor alongside common sailors.

When the men were assembled, Drake seated himself at a table under the flyleaf of his tent, flanked by Captains Winter and Thomas, and opened a large book. Once again John Cooke recorded the proceedings. "My masters," Drake began,

> I am a very bad orator, for my bringing up hath not been in learning, but what so I shall here speak let any man take good notice of what I shall say, and let him write it down, for I will speak nothing but I will answer it in England, yea and before Her Majesty, and I have here already set down.
>
> Thus it is, my masters, that we are very far from our country and friends. We are compassed in on every side with our enemys, wherefor we are not to make small reckoning of a man, for we can not have [another] man if we would give for him ten thousand pounds. Wherefor

we must have these mutinies and discords that are grown amongst us redressed, for by the life of God it doth even take my wits from me to think on it. Here is such controversy between the sailors and the gentleman, and such stomaching between the gentleman and the sailors, that it doth even make me mad to hear it.

But, my masters, I must have it left, for I must have the gentleman to haul and draw with the mariner, and the mariner with the gentleman. What, let us show ourselves all to be of a company, and let us not give occasion to the enemy to rejoice at our decay and overthrow. I would know him that would refuse to set his hand to a rope, but I know that there is not any such here. And as gentlemen are very necessary for government's sake in the voyage, so have I shipped them for that, and to some further intent, and yet though I know sailors to be the most envious people of the world, and so unruly without government, yet may I not be without them.[26]

This was a remarkable demand, challenging as it did the traditional boundaries of the privileged class, but Drake was determined that he would not sail with any man who did not accept these conditions. Therefore, he had reluctantly concluded that there should be an alternative for dissenters. If some wished to return home, he told them, he would spare the *Marigold*, but only for a homeward voyage, for he warned that if he found them in his way he would sink them. He gave them until the next day to respond. The offer proved unnecessary, however; to a man, they immediately voiced their wish to go forward on his terms.

He then asked them at whose hands they looked to receive their wages. "At yours," they replied. "Will you take wages or stand to my courtesy?" he asked. "At your courtesy," they replied, meaning that they preferred to receive a share of whatever plunder they obtained rather than straight wages.[27]

Then Drake turned to his captains and officers and relieved all of them of their commands. Startled, they protested, clamoring to know why they were being discharged. Could they give any reason why he should not do so? Drake asked. Ordering them to be silent, he proceeded to review again the grounds for his authority, this time quoting at length from his meetings with Walsingham and the Queen and stressing that command of the expedition was vested in himself alone, and that he alone would decide how it was to be delegated. "And now, my masters," he concluded, let us consider what we have done. We have now set together by the ears three mighty princes, as first Her Majesty, [and then] the Kings of Spain and Portugal. And if this voyage should not have good success, we should not only be a scorning or reproachful scoffing stock unto our enemies, but also a great blot to our whole country for ever. And what a great triumph would it be to Spain and Portugal, and again the like would never be attempted.[28]

Drake reinstated some of his officers, but replaced others, and then ordered the company to board their ships.

Into the South Sea

or several days the company waited in Port St. Julian for the south wind to slacken, and finally on August 17 it changed to a northerly and they put to sea. Three days later the cape marking the entrance to the strait, named by Magellan's sailors the Cape of the Eleven Thousand Virgins, came into view. At a distance the plumes of white sea spray rising from the base of its dark cliffs appeared to Drake's men like the spoutings of whales.[1] A strong westerly was blowing out of the strait, and that night they hove to in the lee of the cape. The next morning, August 21, 1578, Drake held a ceremony changing the name of his flagship from the *Pelican* to the *Golden Hinde* in honor of Sir Christopher Hatton.* Undoubtedly, it was a purposeful gesture, looking to the day when he would have to ask Hatton's forgiveness for executing his servant. Then, striking their topsails in salute to Her Majesty, they entered the strait.

Magellan had named the land on the south side of the strait Tierra del Fuego (land of fires) on account of the many fires the Indians lit along the shore as he passed by. The accepted view was that Tierra del Fuego was a single, unbroken landmass. The cosmographers believed that it was the northern extremity of a great, as yet unexplored continent they called Terra Australis, whose coastline, they theorized, circled the South Pole. Magellan's Strait therefore was thought to be the only passage into the Pacific between America and this vast southern continent.

No one aboard Drake's ships had any knowledge of the strait other

*Hatton's crest featured a hind, or female deer.

than what some had gleaned from the printed account of Magellan's voyage, which revealed that he had spent thirty-seven days picking his way through a twisting, narrow passage before finally emerging into the South Sea. Magellan had reckoned the distance through the strait at about 100 leagues, but beyond this the account gave few details of his navigation.*

Drake also carried a copy of the 1570 world map of Abraham Ortelius and a large chart that was said to have been obtained for him in Lisbon. Apart from approximating the latitude of the strait, however, the details on Ortelius's map were imaginary, and it is doubtful that the Portuguese chart contained anything more than a vague concept of the passage. But many aboard Drake's ships undoubtedly had heard old sailors' tales from Spain of the dreadful perils and hardships suffered by those who had attempted the strait.

After the survivors of Magellan's voyage returned to Spain in 1522, the follow-up expedition of Garcia Jofre de Loaysa had sailed into the strait in 1525 with seven ships bound for the Moluccas. One of Loaysa's ships was wrecked in the strait, and two others became separated and were never seen again. Enduring a four-month-long struggle against fierce winds and terrible privation, the others finally succeeded in reaching the South Sea only to be scattered by a great storm, after which they did not see each other again. Thereafter only a handful of captains had ventured this way.

In 1535 Simon de Alcazaba entered the strait with an expedition bound for southern Chile but was driven back by the winds. Alonso de Camargo sailed into the strait in 1540 with three ships bound for Peru, but he lost his own ship within two days and a second turned back. He pushed on in the third ship, finally reaching Peru a year later. In 1557 Juan Fernando de Ladrillero managed to sail from Chile to Spain via the strait, becoming the first to make the passage from west to east, but he encountered terrible storms and was forced to spend the winter in the strait. Since Ladrillero's voyage, no one had attempted the passage in either direction.

From the Atlantic, the strait squeezes through two narrows and then turns south and widens to about fifteen miles in Broad Reach. Initially the terrain on either side consists of low, rolling pampas, and Broad Reach afforded room for a square-rigged ship to maneuver in the face of a contrary

*The strait is in fact 363 miles from one end to the other.

wind. Still, there were hazards. The tides produce powerful currents, and the sea bottom is foul with jagged rocks. If a hemp anchor cable became snagged on one of these, it soon parted and the anchor was lost. Even if the ship was not driven ashore as a consequence, this was a serious mishap, for it was impractical to carry more than five or six anchors, and once they were gone a ship was helpless.

Partway down Broad Reach the strait begins to cut through the tail of the rugged spine of South America—the Andes—and beyond this point the conditions rapidly worsen. Sudden, violent squalls hurl down the mountain slopes with such force that a sailing ship could be knocked over on its beam ends in seconds. At the southern end of Broad Reach numerous channels branch off, and the squalls often converge from several directions, churning up chaotic seas and tornado-like waterspouts.

At Cape Froward the strait turns abruptly northwest and runs for 150 miles in a deep, narrow cut through the Andes before it reaches the Pacific, and it was here that sailors could be driven to despair. The currents created by the tides are swifter, the winds are even more boisterous, and for much of its length the channel is only two or three miles wide, leaving little room for a square-rigged ship to tack.* Often for days or weeks on end powerful headwinds funnel down the strait from the Pacific. Moreover, the flanking cliffs and mountains plunge steeply into the sea, and the seabed falls away to great depths, so there were few places a ship could anchor. Then, when the wind finally lightened, an exhausted crew might claw their way to within sight of the open sea only to meet a fresh headwind and be forced back down the strait, possibly all the way back to Cape Froward before they could get into a sheltered anchorage.

While he knew little about the specific difficulties, Drake was well aware of the fear that the strait aroused in his mariners, and his chief concern undoubtedly was that one of the captains might lose his nerve and turn back if they became separated. If he lost one of his ships, Drake knew he could find another when he reached Peru, but he could not replace English sailors. When they departed Port St. Julian, he had therefore taken his

---

*A ship could not sail directly into the wind. Instead, she had to turn, or "tack," obliquely to it until the wind filled her sails. To make headway against an opposing wind therefore necessitated continually "tacking" back and forth—otherwise known as "beating" into the wind—and the narrower a seaway became, the more frequently this laborious maneuver had to be performed.

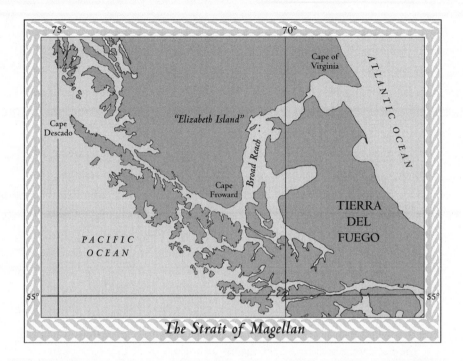

brother Thomas and most of the crew of the abandoned *Mary* aboard his ship. It is impossible to be certain of the exact numbers, but Drake was carrying about ninety of the company on the *Golden Hinde* and the remainder were divided between the *Elizabeth* and the *Marigold*.[2]

By the evening of August 22 they were forty miles into the mouth of the strait, and the next morning they passed the first narrows "with much wind, often turnings and many dangers."[3] The Portuguese pilot da Silva noted in his log that the Indians lit great fires on the shore as they passed. On August 24 they cleared the second narrows and came to anchor near three islands. Landing on the largest of them with the gentlemen and some of the mariners, Drake performed a ceremony and set up a monument taking possession of it for England. Naming it Elizabeth Island, he had one of its trees cut down and a section of the log placed in the hold of the *Golden Hinde* for presentation to the Queen.

The smaller islands he named St. George, for England's patron saint, and St. Bartholomew. The islands, they found, were teeming with a strange type of flightless bird, "bigger than a mallard, short and thick set together, having no feathers but instead thereof, a certain hard and matted down. . . . their feeding and provision is in the sea."[4] Magellan's men had referred to them as geese. The Welshmen in Drake's company dubbed them "pen gwinns," meaning white shirts, and that evening the company had a feast, finding them "a very good and wholesome victual."[5] After nightfall the red glow of an erupting volcano was observed far to the south.[6]

The next day they slaughtered 3,000 penguins, sufficient to sustain the company for about forty days, and then on August 26 they resumed their journey down Broad Reach.[7] On the twenty-ninth they rounded Cape Froward only to be driven back by a fierce headwind. Undaunted, Drake led the way in the *Golden Hinde* the next morning. "The mountains," Fletcher wrote,

> being very high and some reaching into the frozen region did every one send out their several winds; sometimes behind us to send us in our way, sometimes on the starboard side to drive us to the larboard and so the contrary; sometimes right against us to drive us further back in an hour than we could recover again in many. But of all others this was the worse: that sometime two or 3 of these winds would come together and meet as it was, in one body, whose forces being become one, did so violently fall into the sea, whirling, or as the Spaniard sayeth, a Tornado, that they would pierce into the very bowels of the sea and make it swell upwards on every side. The hollowness they made in the water and the winds breaking out again, did take the swelling banks so raised into the air, and being dispersed abroad it ran down again a mighty rain. Besides this, the sea is so deep in all this passage that upon life and death there is no coming to anchor.[8]

After three days of battling the whirling winds to make thirty miles' progress up the strait, Drake found a place shallow enough to anchor behind a cluster of islands. Magellan was right, he mused, there were many good harbors; the problem was, a ship needed to carry nothing but anchors and cables to find the bottom in any of them.[9]

Surveying the glacier-clad peaks towering above them, Fletcher was overawed.

> Neither may I omit the grisly sight of the cold and frozen mountains, reaching their heads, yea the greatest part of their bodies into the cold

Fletcher's drawing of a penguin

and frozen region, where the power of the reflection of the Sun never toucheth to dissolve the ice and snow, so that the ice and snow hang about the spire of the mountain circularwise as it were regions, by degrees one above another and one exceeding another in breadth, in a wonderful order.[10]

The mountains gave out such a "sharp breath" that the men suffered great discomfort. Even the trees seemed to stoop under the burden of the weather, although they kept their greenness. Three days farther up the strait Drake found another anchorage, and taking some men ashore, made a surprising discovery. From the continual weight of snow and freezing rain the boughs of the trees were tightly compacted, forming a natural arbor beneath which a variety of herbs, including thyme, marjoram, and Alexander's scurvy grass, grew in abundance on the forest floor. Other strange plants were fat with a gum that stuck to their hands and gave off a pleasant smell. Gathering as much of this bounty as they could, they carried it back to the ships, "whereby," Fletcher wrote, "we received great help both in our diet and physique, to the great relief of the lives of our men."[11]

Farther on, the sides of the strait appeared to merge, so Drake took some men in the *Golden Hinde*'s launch and rowed ahead to ensure that there was a way through. On the way back they met a party of Indians in a canoe. The people were "but naked men and women and children, whom we could not perceive to have either set places or dwellings, or any ordinary means of living."[12] They were wanderers, carrying shelters made of animal skins that they draped over a framework of poles. Their canoe was constructed of bark without any form of caulking, the stitching with thongs done so finely that it kept the water out. Inspecting their possessions, Drake found that their only tools were hatchets and knives fashioned from giant mussel shells. Yet their boxes and utensils were attractive in form and very finely made. Drake thought it quite remarkable that a people of such meager means were capable of making objects worthy of a prince.

Drake's reconnaissance of the strait had confirmed its continuation, and as soon as he returned he ordered his captains to get under way. Two days later, on September 6, 1578, they emerged joyously into the South Sea. Drake had brought them through the dreaded strait in just sixteen days. It was by far the fastest westward passage of the strait in that century, and probably for a long time afterward. Having a mind to posterity, Drake had asked Fletcher to engrave a metal plate recording the occasion, to be set up as a monument on Cape Deseado at the exit of the strait, which lies at latitude 53 degrees south. While they were looking for a place to anchor, however, the wind suddenly freshened, and they were obliged to make for the open sea.

As the maps he was carrying depicted the coastline as trending northwest from the strait, Drake steered a northwest course, which actually diverged from the coast. The wind was favorable, and they made good progress, sailing better than 150 miles in less than two days. But then the wind changed, and they were struck by a violent gale. It was the first in a series of storms that built up huge seas and drove them continually southwest under bare masts for the space of three weeks.

Evidently the skies cleared for a while, because on the evening of September 15 sometime after six o'clock—using their handheld instruments on a pitching deck, it would have been difficult to ascertain local time with any precision—they were able to observe the lunar eclipse that had been predicted before they left England. Since the eclipse had been projected to occur in England somewhat before one o'clock in the morning of September 16, a differential of about six hours in local time, they reckoned their longitude to be about 90 degrees west of the meridian of England.[13] Although it was a crude estimate of their position—an error of half an

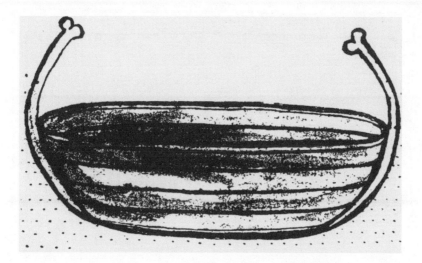

An Indian canoe in Magellan's Strait, as depicted by Fletcher

hour is equivalent to 7½ degrees of longitude—they appear to have been blown several hundred miles offshore.

Remarkably, the ships were able to stay within sight of one another as the storms raged on. However, when dawn broke on September 28, there were only two ships riding the monstrous waves. The *Marigold* had disappeared. Fletcher wrote that while standing the second watch during the night, he had heard the cries of her crew as she foundered, although considering the terrific noise that a storm makes in the rigging of a ship, this seems doubtful. Noting that the *Marigold's* master, Edward Bright, had been one of Doughty's accusers, Fletcher implied that her loss was God's retribution for what he regarded as the unjustified taking of Doughty's life, a sentiment he harbored for the remainder of the voyage.

By the time they were able to turn back for the coast on October 1, they were well offshore in latitude 57 degrees. A week later they had made their way back somewhat to the north of Cape Deseado when they were struck by another ferocious gale and Drake sought refuge on the forbidding coast. Fletcher recorded the terrifying moments as they drew nearer to what seemed to be certain catastrophe:

> Every mountain sent down upon us their several intolerable winds with that horror that they made the bottom of the seas to be dry land . . .

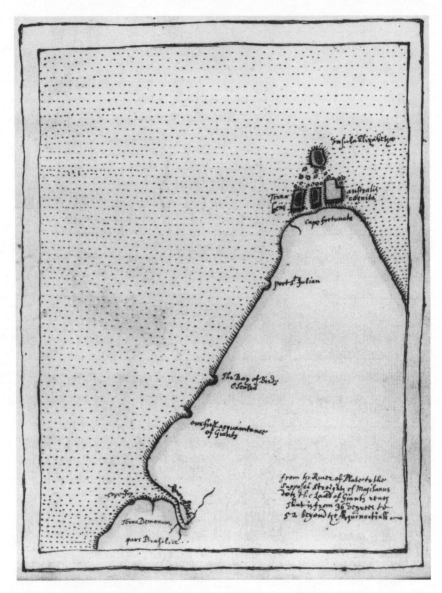

The extremity of South America (south at top) as drawn by Fletcher

sending us headlong upon the tops of the mounting and swelling waves of the seas over the rocks, the sight whereof at our going in was as fearful as death itself. At the last in this miserable state we were driven as through the eye of a needle into a great and large bay by a most narrow passage of rocks. . . . Where coming to anchor, within small time (being night) we had like entertainment from the hills as we

had before from the mountains, [and] with greater and more dangerous violence our cables broke, our anchors came home, our ships were
separated, and our spirits fainted as with the last gasp unto death.[14]

Within minutes the *Golden Hinde* was perilously close to being dashed to
pieces on the rocks, but somehow Drake succeeded in maneuvering her out
of the bay in the darkness and they escaped destruction.

The *Elizabeth*'s anchor held, and Captain Winter waited until morning
before attempting to leave the treacherous bay. When he emerged, the *Golden
Hinde* was beyond sight. It was the moment Winter had been waiting for.
Without bothering to look for Drake, he ordered the master to head back
into Magellan's Strait. That evening Winter anchored at the mouth of the
strait, and for two days he had big signal fires lit on the beach, probably hoping all the while that Drake would not see them. On the third day Winter ordered his crew to start back through the strait, and below Cape Froward they
found a sheltered inlet where they spent three weeks recuperating.

Undoubtedly, Winter was suffering from considerable stress after such
an ordeal, and Edward Cliffe, who was not a Winter sympathizer, said that
most of them were sick from the long watches, unrelenting misery, and evil
diet. However, Drake had instructed that in the event they did become separated, they would rendezvous at latitude 30 degrees on the coast of Chile,
and once they had recovered, most of Winter's crew were in favor of continuing the voyage. Indeed, as it turned out they would have had plenty of time
to rejoin Drake. But Winter had had enough. On November 1, "full sore
against the mariners' minds," Cliffe later wrote, they set sail for England.[15]

In the meantime the Golden Hinde *had once more been driven southward by a series of gales*,
this time to the southeast, paralleling the coast, and although this was not the
direction he wished to go, Drake was confirming an important observation.
Coming through the strait, he had suspected that the land on its south and
west sides was not an unbroken landmass but instead was composed of islands. There are in fact three other outlets from the strait into the Pacific, and
although they are narrow, Drake had passed within sight of all of them inside
the strait. Conceivably, he reconnoitered one or more of them in the ships'
boats; or perhaps he had simply observed the tide ebbing through them from

the strait. Whichever the case, it now became clear that the land south of Cape Deseado was indeed made up of islands, and he began looking for a place where he could shelter from the relentless gales.

Near latitude 55 degrees the storm died down, and on October 15 Drake took the *Golden Hinde* in among the islands, where he found the tides flowing as in Magellan's Strait. Probably, he was in Beagle Channel, which runs through to the Atlantic below the main island of Tierra del Fuego. Landing on one of the islands to take on water and firewood, he again found an abundance of herbs. Nearly all of the men were suffering from swollen legs and gums, and Drake thought one herb in particular, described as being similar to "pennyleaf," might relieve their condition. Ordering his men to gather as much of it as they could, he had the juice squeezed out of it and mixed with wine. Thereafter all began to recover except the two sickest, who soon died. After two days' respite, however, another storm blew up, and they were obliged to put to sea again.

When the tempest abated, they once more sought refuge among the islands, where they met some Indians in canoes and traded for chains of shells and other examples of their handiwork. For five days they lay at anchor resting, and then the gales returned with a sudden fury. The *Golden Hinde*'s cable parted, and they lost another anchor. Once again they were driven southeastward until at last, on October 24, the wind died out and the sea fell calm.

Scanning the horizon, Drake could see no more islands and no great southern continent. He had discovered the southernmost extremity of America, beyond which the Atlantic and Pacific Oceans meet and flow freely together. Taking the height of the sun, he determined that the southernmost island stood near latitude 56 degrees south. Landing on the island with a compass, Drake sought out its southernmost point, and there had Fletcher chisel on a rock Her Majesty's name, her kingdom, and the date. While Fletcher was doing so, Drake "cast himself down upon the point grovelling, and so reached out his body over it. Presently he embarked, and then recounted unto his people that he had been upon the southernmost known land in the world, and more further to the southwards upon it than anyone, yea, or any man as yet known."[16] Drake named the islands south of Magellan's Strait the Elizabethides.*

Fifty-two days had passed since they emerged from the strait, all but a few of them consumed by these great storms. With a calm sea and light winds, Drake was anxious to get to the appointed rendezvous with his other ships. At some nearby islands they spent two days replenishing their supply of penguin meat, and then, on the first day of November, Drake set their course northwest and north for the Kingdon of Peru.

*Cape Horn, which is the southernmost point of America, stands at latitude 55° 58′ S, but whether Drake actually discovered this cape is disputed. Credit for its discovery has generally been accorded to the Dutch navigators Jakob Le Maire and Willem Schouten, who sailed around it from the Atlantic in 1617. Some contend that Drake landed on Henderson Island, sixty-five miles to the west at the slightly lower latitude of 55° 39′ S. Regardless, he was the first European to discover the confluence of the two great oceans beyond Tierra del Fuego, and the passage bears his name to this day.

❧ 12. ❧

Chile

*A*fter the wild tempests of Tierra del Fuego, the voyage of the Golden Hinde northward was a happily benign experience. With favorable winds, Drake and his remaining company of eighty-some men and boys sailed 1,200 miles without stopping until, on November 25, they came to the island of Mocha, lying eighteen miles off the coast at latitude 38 degrees south.

Lowering the boat, Drake took a party of bowmen and harquebusiers ashore, where they were met by some Indians and traded with them for corn, potatoes, and two "sheep"—probably llamas. At the end of the exchange, communicating by signs and with the Spanish word *agua*, Drake indicated to them that he would land again the next day to get water from a nearby creek. The following morning he took ten men and some casks and headed ashore again. The Indians having greeted them cordially the previous day, they took only a few swords and shields with them.

Landing near the mouth of the creek, they began carrying the casks ashore while Thomas Brewer and Thomas Flood went ahead to look for a convenient place to fill them. Suddenly, some Indians leaped from hiding and charged them, and then 100 more jumped up from the reeds and loosed a hail of arrows at the men standing by the boat.

Scrambling back into the boat, all were struck by arrows. Drake was hit twice, one penetrating his face under his right eye and another creasing his scalp. Some of the Indians rushed the boat and seized hold of the oars and mooring line, but one of Drake's men had the presence of mind to cut the line with his knife, and somehow they struggled free. Leaving several of their oars in the hands of their attackers, they pulled desperately away from the beach in another shower of arrows. Fletcher was appalled at the scene.

> Not any one person escaped without some grievous wounds, and most had many so that their bodies were loaden with arrows from 2 to 3, 4, 5, 8, 10 and one had 21 in the several parts of their bodies; some in head and face as the General, some in the throat, breasts, arms, back, belly and where not . . . at whose departure arrows were sent to them so thick as gnats in the sun, and the sides of the boat within and without stuck so full of them . . . that a man might by the sight of the boat afar off judge what was the state of their bodies which were in it, who coming on shipboard the horror of their bloody state wounded the hearts of all men to behold them.[1]

Another party quickly armed and returned in the boat to rescue Brewer and Flood, but the multitude on the beach was too great and they watched helplessly as their unfortunate comrades were butchered. Aboard the *Golden Hinde* the master gunner Nele died of his wounds shortly afterward. Miraculously, the others survived. Fortunately, the arrowheads were small, and it was possible to pull them out. The crew was for raking the Indians with cannon shot, Fletcher wrote, "but the General would not for special causes consent to it."[2] The Indians had obviously mistaken them for Spaniards, Drake reasoned, and he would not add to the injuries they had already suffered at the Spaniards' hands.

Very likely, the Indians were members of the *Araucanian* tribe, whose territory extended to the Bío-Bío River, 100 miles to the north on the mainland. The *Araucanians* had been fighting the Spaniards for years, and the governor of Chile was presently in the field with a force endeavoring to quell another revolt by them.

The Spaniards had been pushing southward from Peru since 1535, conquering and enslaving Indians to work their gold and silver mines. After founding Santiago as the capital of the new province, they had established a number of outposts extending southward to Valdivia, on the coast eighty miles south of Mocha, where they had discovered rich deposits of gold. In 1551, however, the *Araucanians* had launched a major offensive and driven the Spaniards back, forcing them to abandon most of their forts and settlements south of Santiago. Adapting to European warfare, the Indians used

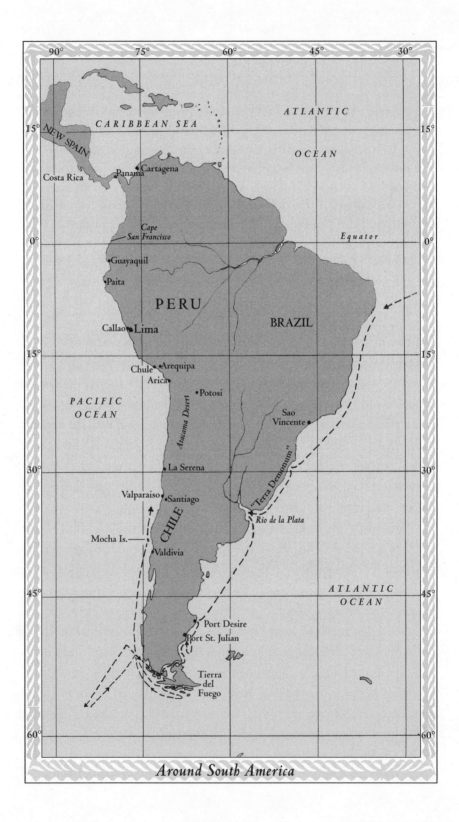

90°   75°   60°   45°   30°

CARIBBEAN SEA

ATLANTIC

NEW SPAIN

15°

OCEAN

Costa Rica

•Panama   •Cartagena

Cape
San Francisco

0°   *Equator*   0°

•Guayaquil

•Paita

PERU

BRAZIL

Callao• •Lima

15°

Chule• •Arequipa
Arica•

•Potosi

Sao
Vincente•

PACIFIC
OCEAN

Atacama Desert

30°   •La Serena   30°

Valparaiso• •Santiago

CHILE

"Terra Demonum"

Mocha Is.—

•Valdivia

•Rio de la Plata

45°   *ATLANTIC*
OCEAN   45°

•Port Desire
Port St. Julian

Tierra
del
Fuego

60°   60°

Around South America

captured horses and guns to defeat several Spanish columns, and by 1557 they were even threatening Santiago itself. Then they had in turn been pushed back and suffered a series of defeats at the hands of the conquistadores Pedro de Valdivia and Garcia Hurtado de Mendoza. Within a few years, though, the *Araucanians* had resumed their resistance, and the Spaniards' grip on their territory remained tenuous.

On the afternoon of the ambush, Drake ordered his men to set sail. A week later they came to anchor in the Bay of Quintero, 350 miles north of Mocha. They had missed Valparaiso, the port of Santiago, fifteen miles to the south, but they could see herds of cattle on the slopes behind the bay and knew they were in Spanish territory.

A lone Indian fisherman ventured near in his reed boat, and they lifted him "canoe and all" onto the deck of the ship. "A comely personage, and of goodly stature," the Indian "seemed very gentle, of mild and humble nature, being very tractable to learn the use of everything."[3] Presenting him with some gifts, they explained by signs that they needed food, and a few hours later he returned with several others carrying hens, eggs, and a fat hog. With them was an Indian named Felipe who spoke Spanish, and who said that there was a ship in the harbor of Valparaiso and offered to guide Drake there.

On Friday, December 5, Drake entered the roadstead of Valparaiso and found a solitary ship lying at anchor. She was the *Los Reyes*, employed in coastal trade, but nicknamed the *Capitana* because eleven years before she had served as the flagship for Alvaro de Medaña's and navigator Pedro Sarmiento de Gamboa's great voyage of discovery. Setting off from Peru, Medaña and Sarmiento had sailed due westward across the South Pacific, eventually discovering what they believed to be the fabled islands of Solomon, which they named accordingly. Then they had sailed north to pick up the return route from Manila back across the North Pacific to the Californias, and followed the coast to New Spain and finally Peru, completing a circuit of 18,000 miles in twenty-two months.

Seeing Drake's ship and not imagining her to be anything but Spanish, the *Capitana*'s crew brought out a drum and a butt of wine to welcome them. They remained unsuspecting up to the moment Thomas Moone led a boarding party onto her deck and struck one of them with his fist, crying,

"Go down dog!"[4] Much frightened, they quickly submitted, except one who jumped overboard and swam ashore to raise the alarm.

When the Spaniards were secured below deck, Drake manned both the *Capitana's* boat and his own with harquebusiers and went ashore, by which time the inhabitants had fled. Santiago was located sixty miles inland, and its port consisted of only nine or ten houses, a church, and a warehouse, the houses yielding quantities of bread, bacon, and preserves, and the warehouse containing a store of wine. They also carried away the church's bell, the chalice, and some silver ornaments, and Drake gave the priest's vestments and a missal to Fletcher.

Inspecting the *Capitana*, they found she was carrying 1,770 jars of wine, a quantity of cedar lumber, and four leather and iron–bound cases, each containing seventy-five pounds of gold—a substantial prize. Drake also gained a second ship to relieve the crowding on the *Golden Hinde*. Moreover, its Greek master John, or Juan Greco as he came to be called, was a veteran pilot of the coast, and his sea chart showed the locations of all the bays and ports from Valdivia to Lima. Putting all of her crew except the Greek and one other ashore, Drake installed twenty-five of his men on the *Capitana*, and the following day they departed.

When he returned his Indian guide Felipe to the Bay of Quintero, Drake gave him an assortment of gifts for the chiefs of his tribe and their neighbors, and asked him to convey a message to them: If the tribal leaders would agree to form an alliance with him, he would join them to eject the Spaniards from all the Indies.

Drake said he was going to his own country and would return with many harquebuses and swords and show them how to use them. "With a few people you can attack many and will always be the conqueror with many of us on your side," he said. "As it is necessary to fight while we are going and returning with all these arms, do so bravely and sustain yourselves the best way you can, and afterwards leave the burden to us and we will kill them and bring you liberty."[5] Undoubtedly, Drake was thinking of his alliance with the *cimarrones*, and, notably, this was the first indication that he was already formulating a follow-up voyage with a grander plan.

* * *

Two months had passed since they lost contact with the Elizabeth, *and three since the* Marigold *disappeared, but Drake was still hopeful of finding one or both at their agreed rendezvous. Five days out of Valparaiso, they came to the ap-pointed latitude of 30 degrees south, and for five more they searched the coast in vain.*

On December 19 they anchored in the Bay of La Herradura, and the next morning, after finding a stream, they began refilling their water casks. The Spanish town of La Serena was only eight miles away, however, and its inhabitants had been watching Drake's ships sailing back and forth along the coast for several days, during which word had come from Valparaiso that they were corsairs.

A dozen of Drake's men were working on shore when a lookout on the *Golden Hinde* saw a large body of Spanish horsemen with 200 Indians run-ning alongside on the ridge above the beach. Hearing the signal gun on the ship, and seeing the Spaniards, the sailors began wading out to a large rock where their boat could retrieve them. Richard Minivy, however, turned and stood in defiance of the onrushers and was promptly shot dead. After the others escaped, the Spaniards dragged Minivy's body up on the beach, where they beheaded it and cut out his heart, and then the Indians shot it full of arrows. When they had departed with their trophies stuck on spears, Drake took some men ashore and buried Minivy's remains.

The next morning some horsemen appeared with a flag of truce, but Drake ignored them and set sail. On the afternoon of the following day he entered the Bay of Salada, 100 miles farther north. The *Golden Hinde* was badly in need of repair after the battering she had taken off Tierra del Fuego, and the bay was suited for careening her. But first Drake wanted to rest his men and assemble one of his pinnaces. On December 23 they laid the frames of the pinnace out on the deck of the *Capitana* and began fitting it together in sections. Then Drake suspended work for the week of Christmas, which culminated with a "great feast" on New Year's Day 1579. It was just over a year since they had left England.

In the first week of January the pinnace was taken ashore and completed. Then, placing a small bronze cannon in her bow, Drake set off with Juan Greco and fifteen men southward to take one last look for his missing ships. But they were

The Golden Hinde, *from the Hondius Broadside map*

forced to give up the search on account of contrary winds, and returned two days later. In the meantime the *Golden Hinde*'s cannons were transferred to the deck of the *Capitana*, and then she was moved in to the beach for careening. By January 19 she stood ready with a freshly tarred hull and her cannons mounted, and that evening the company set sail again.

The immediate need after their layover was a supply of fresh water, as there had been none in the vicinity of the careenage. Taking the pinnace, Drake scouted the shoreline for streams while the ships followed, remaining two or three miles offshore.

After two days they came to a place the Greek pilot called Mormorena, where some Indians led them to a spring, but the flow was "scarcely so much as they had drunk wine on the passage thither."[6] As they continued northward the scarcity became more acute. They were skirting the great Atacama Desert, which stretches some 500 miles along the coast of northern Chile. The few rivers flowing from the desert were small and often drained into the ground before reaching the sea. It became necessary to send parties up into the country to look for springs, and two such forays resulted in amusement.

At a place called Tarapacá Drake's men came across a Spaniard lying asleep with thirteen large bars of silver stacked beside him. "We would not (could we have chosen), have awaked him of his nap; but seeing we against our wills did him that injury, we freed him of his charge, which otherwise would have kept him waking and so left him to take out (if it pleased him) the other part of his sleep in more security."[7] Nearby they met another Spaniard driving eight "Peruvian sheep" (llamas), each loaded with 100 pounds of silver. "We offered our service and became drovers; only his directions were not so perfect that we could keep the way which he intended, for almost as soon as he was parted from us we with our new kind of carriages were come unto our boats."[8] The Englishmen were fascinated by the llama:

> Their height and length was equal to a pretty cow, and their strength fully answerable. . . . Upon one of their backs did sit at one time three well grown and tall men, no mans foot touching the ground by a large foot in length, the beast nothing at all complaining of his burden in the mean time. These sheep have necks like camels, their heads bearing a reasonable resemblance of another sheep. The Spaniards use them to great profit. Their wool is exceeding fine, their flesh of good meat . . . yea they serve to carry over the mountains marvellous loads, for 300 leagues together, where no other carriage can be made but by them only.[9]

Each evening Drake returned to the *Golden Hinde* and worked late into the night recording his observations. "He carries a book in which he writes his log and paints birds, trees and seals," Nuño da Silva later recalled. "He is diligent in painting and carries along a boy, a relative of his [John Drake], who is a great painter. When they both shut themselves up in his cabin, they were always painting."[10]

Gradually, the strip of desert between the sea and the towering wall of mountains to the east narrowed, and toward late afternoon on February 6 they entered the harbor of Arica, a town of perhaps fifty houses nestled at the mouth of a valley filled with plantations and orchards. The port was the principal outlet for the silver extracted by thousands of enslaved Indians from the rich mines of Potosí, on the eastern slopes of the Andes, and then carried by llama train down to the coast for shipment by sea.

Drake had heard of Arica and hoped to find a valuable prize here. There were two barks in the harbor, their crews gone ashore. Boarding one, they found the owner, a Corsican, and a Flemish seaman named Nicolas Jorje in possession of a small amount of silver and coins. On the other ship, a Negro slave was the sole guardian of a small cargo of merchandise and wine. Drake ordered the wine brought over to the *Golden Hinde*, and that night several cannons were fired and the townspeople heard music and singing aboard the ships. In their drunken exuberance, two sailors posted to guard the ship containing merchandise set her on fire, and she burned through the night.

In the morning, suspecting that there was more silver stored in the town, Drake organized a landing party and started for shore. But the town magistrate was patrolling the beach with a body of armed horsemen, and Drake gave up the idea. The risk of casualties was too great, and he had discovered a more appealing opportunity. The Negro slave told him that a ship had departed there two days earlier carrying 500 bars of gold and 800 bars of silver, all of it registered to the King of Spain and bound for the port of Chule, fifty leagues to the north. Drake was furious with the Corsican and Nicolas Jorje, accusing them of concealing this fact and threatening to hang them for it. Taking them, the Negro, and the Corsican's ship with him, Drake set off after the treasure galleon.

Running ahead with some men in the pinnace, Drake reached Chule on the second day and found the treasure ship lying at anchor. Chule was a small port serving the town of Arequipa, forty miles inland, yet there was a large number of men gathered on shore. Approaching the ship, Drake saw that her sides were wet above the waterline: Her cargo had been removed. From shore the Spaniards jeered and shouted that he was too late. A rider had been sent from Arica to warn them, and they had just finished carrying the bullion ashore. In the distance Drake could see a long line of llamas ascending a hillside with the treasure. Placing a cable on the galleon, he towed her out of the harbor to join his ships, bringing the number in his fleet to five.

Drake was doubly concerned. Not only had a fortune eluded his grasp, but, more important, news of his presence had begun to precede him and he had not yet reached the main concentration of treasure in the shipping lanes between Peru and Panama. Up to this point it had been his policy to seize every ship he encountered to prevent the Spaniards from sending warning of his approach ahead by sea. But since they were now doing so overland, his increasingly cumbersome flotilla was slowing him needlessly. The next morning Drake had his men set all the sails on the *Capitana* and the other two prizes and let them go wherever they might without anyone on board. Then, with his company consolidated in the *Golden Hinde* and the pinnace, he urged them to make all possible speed, determined to reach his next objective unannounced.

༝ 13. ༅

Peru

*I*n five days Drake dashed 450 miles northward along the coast and on the afternoon of February 13 drew within sight of Callao, the port of Lima. Founded by Francisco Pizarro in 1535, Lima was the seat of the viceroyalty of the Kingdom of Peru, and the administrative capital of King Philip's South American dominions. Owing to the great distances over which communications had to be carried, the other provinces—Panama, New Grenada (Colombia), Ecuador, Río de la Plata, and Chile—each had their own governor. However, the viceroy of Peru, Don Francisco Alvarez de Toledo, was Philip's senior representative overseeing the affairs of the entire region.

Known as Los Reyes, or the City of Kings, Lima was located six miles inland from its harbor. With a population of 2,000 Spanish households, it was the second-largest European city in the New World, after Mexico City. The viceregal palace and the quarters of several hundred colonial officials, clergy, and soldiers formed the nucleus of the city. The Church was particularly prosperous, with five monasteries, two convents, and two hospitals.

As Lima was the center of Philip's southern colonial hierarchy, so its port town of Callao had become the principal entrepôt for the commerce of Peru and Chile. Here ships carrying gold and silver from Valdivia, Arica, and other southern ports were met by merchantmen from Panama and New Spain offering merchandise from Europe, native crafts, and silks and spices brought from Manila in trade. Those who had bullion from the smaller, privately owned mines often exchanged it for goods and returned southward. Others received additional consignments from the Viceroy and carried them northward to Panama or New Spain. While nearly all the gold was sent over the isthmus to Spain, a large portion of the silver was shipped to the Philippines, where it was eagerly acquired by Portuguese and Chinese traders to be turned into coin.

Thus, the port of Callao and the sea route between it and Panama regularly saw a flow of treasure exceeding even the amounts carried across the isthmus. Moreover, believing themselves insulated from attack by pirates, none of the shipowners bothered to arm their vessels with cannons; nor had the colonial government thought it necessary to patrol the coast or provide escorts for the shipments as they were obliged to do in the Caribbean. In the ten years that Toledo had served as Viceroy, Spanish commerce had been threatened only once, by the recent intrusion of Drake's friend and former lieutenant John Oxenham.

Oxenham had departed England for the Caribbean in April 1576 with fifty-seven men and two dismantled pinnaces, which he proposed to carry across the isthmus and use to raid shipping in the Gulf of Panama. Arriving at the isthmus, Oxenham left some men to guard his ship in a secluded bay and set off overland to enlist the aid of the *cimarrones*. While he was gone, the Spanish, acting on a warning received from their agent, de Guaras, in England, captured Oxenham's ship with his pinnaces and equipment. Undaunted, he built another pinnace, forty-five feet long with twelve oars on each side, and launched it on a river flowing into the Pacific.

Operating from the Pearl Islands near Panama, Oxenham and his men seized a vessel from Guayaquil carrying 60,000 pesos in gold, another from Lima with 100,000 pesos in silver, and narrowly missed capturing a third laden with a colossal 1.3 million pesos of bullion. They told one of the captured Spaniards, "This is nothing. Now we have come only to open the way. Presently you will see great things."[1] It appears Oxenham was expecting larger developments, most likely involving Drake. Conceivably, he had hoped to rendezvous with Drake and carry out a raid on Panama itself. While hiding his plunder up a river on the mainland, however, Oxenham and a number of his men were caught by the Spanish and forced to surrender. Of the eighteen Englishmen who were captured, fourteen were summarily executed at Panama, and Oxenham and three others were brought to Lima, where they were awaiting trial by the Inquisition.

Oxenham's intrusion had exposed the weakness of Toledo's defenses,

and he had responded by negotiating a peace with the *cimarrones* and ordering an armed galley constructed in Equador to patrol the coast between
Guayaquil and Panama. Yet no thought had been given to the possibility of
someone getting through Magellan's Strait, and although more than two
months had passed since Drake's raid on Valparaiso, no warning of his approach had been received at Lima.

When news of the raid had reached the governor of Chile, Rodrigo de
Quiroga, he was away in the south quelling another revolt by the
Araucanians. Hurrying back to Santiago, Quiroga had raised a small force
and ordered a ship prepared at Valparaiso to go in pursuit of Drake, but he
had fallen ill and the ship had sailed under the command of one of his soldiers while a second vessel was to have made all possible speed to Lima with
a report for the Viceroy. Inexplicably, neither had fulfilled its mission, and
the Indian runners sent overland from Arequipa were still days away from
Lima.

Eight leagues from Callao Drake intercepted a small trading bark and interrogated her captain
about the vessels in the harbor, learning that one carried much silver, and that
another was due to sail with 700 bars that had been brought down from
Lima. Also, the captain reported, the *Nuestra Señora de la Concepcion* had sailed
nine days earlier with a large consignment of silver belonging to King Philip.

Reducing sail, Drake waited until nightfall before entering the harbor.
The anchorage of Callao was on the north side of a point of land and protected by an elongated island lying just off the point. Approached from the
north, the bay offered a wide entrance, but from the south, as Drake chose,
there was only a narrow channel between the island and shoals extending
out from the point. With Juan the Greek serving as pilot and men taking
soundings on both sides, they groped for the channel in the dark. At one
point they nearly became grounded, and Drake threatened to hang the pilot
if they did, for they would have been easy prey for the Viceroy's troops. But
they slipped into the harbor and dropped anchor in the midst of seventeen
ships about ten o'clock at night.

Boarding each ship, Drake found most of them deserted, their crews
having gone ashore. None of them contained any treasure except one chest
of coins; the silver was still on shore, waiting to be loaded. On one of the

vessels, however, a Spaniard told Drake that four Englishmen, one of them named Oxenham, were imprisoned at Lima, and he began to improvise a scheme to rescue them. There was no possibility of reaching them in Lima, so he took the remaining Spaniards as hostages and sent his men around to all of the ships to cut their anchor cables, intending for the ships to drift to the mouth of the harbor, where he could corral them and negotiate an exchange for Oxenham and his men.

While they waited for this to happen, another ship, the *San Cristobal* out of Panama, entered the harbor and anchored nearby. Observing the light from her lamps, the harbormaster rowed out from shore to welcome her, then noticed the dark shape of the *Golden Hinde* silhouetted against the sky and altered his course to investigate. Discovering cannons protruding from her sides, he turned and rowed furiously for shore, shouting, "Frenchmen!" Hearing this, the captain of the *San Cristobal* cut his anchor cable and tried to escape. Drake sent some men in the pinnace to board her, but her crew discharged several harquebuses at them, killing one of the English sailors. Drake then fired one of his cannons, and the shot passed through both sides of the ship, after which her crew hurriedly climbed into their launch and abandoned her.

On shore, meanwhile, bells began to peal, and the streets of Callao came alive with torches and shouting men. Seeing that it was too late to effect his plan for Oxenham's rescue, Drake had his men cut down the masts of two of the largest ships so they could not be used to pursue him, and then installed some of his men on the *San Cristobal*, and they put out to sea.

At one o'clock in the morning the Viceroy was awakened at his palace in Lima and informed that a corsair was attacking Callao. Ordering the city's bells rung to sound the alarm, Toledo sent his officers to rouse the militia, and then he put on his armor and rode to the public square carrying the royal standard of Spain. In the meantime another messenger arrived, identifying the intruders as English. Toledo dispatched General Diego de Frias Trejo with 200 men on the double to apprehend them, but by the time they reached Callao, Drake was well beyond the harbor mouth, his ships' lamps flickering in the darkness.

After consulting his officers, General Diego sent to Lima for more troops and at first light set sail in two vessels. Emerging from the harbor,

The port of Callao

they saw Drake's ships about four leagues distant. Drake was becalmed, and seeing the Spaniards come out of Callao, he began transferring what he wanted out of the *San Cristobal* to the *Golden Hinde*.

As the morning progressed, Diego slowly closed in on Drake, who was still becalmed. In his rush to get under way, however, Diego had neglected to have his ships ballasted, and without any weight in their holds to stabilize them, they were pitching and rolling excessively, making most of the Spaniards seasick. When they were about a league from Drake, the wind picked up, and transferring his captives to the *San Cristobal*, Drake recalled his own men and set her free. Then, spreading the *Golden Hinde*'s topgallant sails, he stood off to the northwest.

When Diego came to the freed ship, the Greek pilot was among the released captives and explained that the corsairs had come through Magellan's Strait and taken his ship at Valparaiso, claiming to have sailed from England with five ships by order of their Queen. Their captain, he said, was a man named Francisco Draque, the same who had robbed much treasure from Nombre de Dios some years ago, and a great mariner and cosmographer. His ship, the Greek warned, was large and strong and carried eighty men and many pieces of artillery as well as incendiary devices to hurl at them.[2]

Diego managed to keep Drake in sight until nightfall and then halted to confer with his officers again. Most were for returning to Callao in order to reorganize—the unballasted ships were too slow to catch Drake, and many of the men were too sick to stand, let alone fight. This being the consensus, they turned back. When they arrived at Callao, however, the Viceroy was outraged that they had done so and ordered all of them confined to their vessels, where they remained for several days.

After listening to the accounts of Drake's released captives, Toledo convened an emergency meeting of his colonial council, the Audiencia. Toledo ordered that a ship be dispatched immediately to spread the alarm along the coast all the way to Panama: Any vessel carrying treasure was to land it under guard at the nearest port, and the newly completed galley at Guayaquil was to put to sea at once and search every bay and inlet from there to Panama for Drake. Further, a ship was to be sent north from Panama to warn shipping along the coasts of Nicaragua and Mexico, and to carry a report of the situation to the Viceroy of New Spain. Then Toledo ordered the casting of new artillery sufficient to arm the two ships that General Diego had used, and instructed the judges of the Inquisition at Lima to examine the Englishmen imprisoned there and find out everything they could about Drake.

On February 20 John Oxenham and his shipmates were brought individually before the inquisitors for questioning. The first, John Butler of Plymouth, told them no company of armed ships could possibly have sailed for the South Sea without the permission of their Queen. Oxenham was asked what he knew of such plans, and he told the court the Queen had granted a license for such a voyage to Richard Grenville but then revoked it. Oxenham said if she were to give a license to Drake, he would certainly come through the strait because he was a very good mariner and pilot, and there was no better person in England to perform the feat. Drake had often told him, Oxenham said, that if the Queen would allow it, "he would pass through the Strait of Magellan and found settlements over here in some good country."[3]

Questioned as to how many ships it would be possible for Drake to bring, Oxenham said, "With the aid of his relatives and companions he might be able to bring two or three vessels, but after discovering a good country they would be able to come with more ships."[4] Asked whether they had discussed how Drake would return to England, he said that some thought he would return by Magellan's Strait, "but others said that there was a route through another strait that passed into the North Sea, but nobody knows this for a certainty or has passed through it."[5]

Toledo's thoughts upon reading the prisoners' statements are not recorded, but the specter of Drake discovering the Strait of Bacallaos, as the Spanish called the northwest passage, and establishing a colony in the Pacific could only have added to his disquiet, for such a presence would have rendered insecure every Spanish ship and port from Peru to New Spain and the Philippines.

Toledo placed his son Don Luis in command of the force sent out to pursue Drake, though he would disembark at Panama and carry on to Spain to give a report of the situation directly to King Philip. General Diego was appointed admiral under Don Luis, and to advise them and serve as sergeant major of the expedition Toledo chose the great navigator and cosmographer Pedro Sarmiento de Gamboa, discoverer of the Solomon Islands. On the morning of February 27, with the newly cast artillery installed, 120 soldiers joined 80 sailors aboard the two ships, and they set sail in search of Drake.

After shaking off General Diego's pursuit outside Callao, Drake had set off on his own chase— of the treasure galleon *Nuestra Señora de la Concepcion,* otherwise less reverently called by the Spaniards the *Cacafuego.* Although she had a ten-day head start, Drake knew she would be calling at several ports en route to Panama, and reckoned that he could still catch her. Alternately sailing the *Golden Hinde* and pulling at the oars of the pinnace to tow her through the calms, Drake's men labored day and night to make up the distance, and on February 24 they reached the port of Paita, 500 miles north of Lima.

In the harbor was a bark laden with merchandise. Her crew fled in her boat, leaving the pilot and some slaves to deal with the pinnace full of armed men. Drake learned from the pilot that the *Cacafuego* had sailed from there two days earlier. He had the bark towed out of the harbor and set adrift, and then resumed the chase, taking the pilot with him, as was his custom. That evening they intercepted another ship but detained her only long enough to confirm that she was not carrying any treasure and to take from her a Negro named Francisco who said he had been a *cimarrone* on the isthmus.

On the morning of February 28 Drake overtook and boarded the bark of Benito Diaz Bravo, which was carrying a number of passengers and laden with rope, tackle, and provisions for the vessels being prepared at Panama to carry the new governor of the Philippines, Gonzollo Ronquillo de Peñalosa, to Manila. She also contained 18,000 pesos of gold and silver. Drake ordered the sails hoisted on Diaz Bravo's ship to test her speed. Satisfied with her performance, he told all the passengers and crew except Diaz Bravo, his clerk, and some Negroes to take whatever clothing and food they wanted and go ashore in their launch. Then he ordered two cannons lifted onto the deck of the bark and announced he was taking her with him, but would compensate Diaz Bravo in Valdivian gold.

While the passengers were waiting to be taken ashore, they told Drake the news from Europe. Six great personages had died in the past year, three of them on the same day. King Sebastian of Portugal, just twenty-one years of age, had landed in Morocco with an army to support Sultan Muhammed al Muttawakil in his fight with his uncle, Sultan Abdul-Malik, and all three rulers had perished in a single battle. Also, the Pope, the King of France, and King Philip's half brother, Don John of Austria, had died. When Drake told his men about the last three, they began to dance, and that evening he held a banquet in honor of the occasion. "My chickens and hams had to pay for it," Diaz Bravo later recalled wryly.[6]

That evening Drake recounted his voyage for Diaz Bravo and said that if God spared his life, he would return within two years with six or seven ships.[7] The next morning, however, he was in a different humor. He had decided not to take Diaz Bravo's ship after all and ordered his men to retrieve the cannons from her quickly as he was anxious to get under way. But then one of Diaz Bravo's slaves told Drake that there was more silver concealed aboard the Spaniard's ship. Furious, Drake ordered a rope placed around the neck of Diaz Bravo's purser and threatened to hang him if he did not divulge where it was hidden. Twice when the man exclaimed that there was none, Drake had him hoisted off the deck. The second time he was left dangling until he lost consciousness and then was swung out and dropped into the sea, where Drake's men lifted him into the pinnace and revived him. Then Drake had Diaz Bravo's sails wrapped around his anchor and heaved overboard, and at ten o'clock in the morning he departed, leaving the Spaniards thankful they were still alive.

Expecting they would soon overtake the *Cacafuego*, Drake offered a gold chain, which he had taken from one of Diaz Bravo's passengers, as a bounty to the first man to spot her. At noon they took the height of the sun and found they were directly on the equator. Shortly afterward a cry was heard from the crow's nest, and young John Drake descended to the deck to collect his reward; the galleon's sails were visible twelve miles to leeward.

To disguise the *Golden Hinde* as a heavily laden merchantman, Drake left all her sails up and trailed strings of wine jars filled with water behind her to slow her down. When he saw Drake's sails, the *Cacafuego*'s captain, San Juan de Anton, steered to converge with him. "About nine o'clock at night," Anton later recounted to Spanish authorities,

> the English ship crossed the stern of my ship, and shortly came alongside, abreast of the tack. I hailed her, but the Corsair did not answer. On asking what ship it was, the answer came that it was a ship from Chile, and believing this, I went to the side, the English ship having already run foul of me [taken the wind from his sails]. Some one said "Englishmen—strike sail," and another said "Strike sail, Señor San Juan de Anton! If not, see that we will send you to the bottom." I said, "What old tub is that to order me to strike sail? Come on board and do so yourself."
>
> When they heard this, a whistle sounded in the English ship and a trumpet responded. At once, they discharged what seemed to be about sixty arquebuses, and then many arrows which struck the side of my ship. Shortly, a heavy gun was fired with chainballs which carried away the mizzen-mast into the sea with the sail and the yard. Another heavy gun was fired, someone saying that I should strike. At this point, the launch came alongside on the portside with a matter of some forty arquebusiers, who climbed up the channels to which the shrouds are fastened and came aboard my ship. The English ship lay alongside on the starboard and thus they made me strike sail.

Drake capturing the treasure ship Cacafuego

They inquired of me for the pilot and captain as I was the only man on deck, and I denied being the man. However, as they saw no one else on deck they seized me and passed me on board the English ship, where I saw the Corsair, Francis Drake, armed with a coat of mail and a helmet, already disarming himself. He embraced me, saying "Have patience, such is the custom of war," and shortly ordered me shut up in [his] cabin.[8]

A bolt from one of the English crossbows had slashed Anton's face, and Drake attended to the wound himself. Then, with the *Cacafuego*'s passengers and crew secured under guard, he gave the order to sail northwest until they were well beyond sight of land to avoid any pursuers.

In the morning Drake went aboard the prize and remained until noon inspecting her cargo. When he returned, he told his men their labors had been rewarded. Anton's ship was carrying 1,300 bars of silver, weighing twenty-six tons, as well as thirteen chests full of silver coins and eighty pounds of gold. Anton later said in a deposition to the Spanish authorities that the value of the bars and coins together was 362,000 pesos, of which 106,000 belonged to King Philip. In addition, he said, there was some unregistered treasure aboard, the amount of which he claimed not to know, but which he estimated to have a value of about 40,000 pesos. However, the quantity of unregistered bullion was actually much larger than he admitted.

On March 3 Drake's men began to transfer the treasure across in the pinnace. It took three days to replace the *Golden Hinde*'s ballast with silver and restore her hold. As this work continued, Anton was kept aboard the English ship. He was seated at Drake's table for meals and the nightly performances of the ship's orchestra. Drake said he knew the Viceroy would send for Anton to get information: "Tell him that the Englishmen that he has killed are enough, and that he should not kill the four who are left [Oxenham and others imprisoned at Lima],* and if he does they will cost more than two thousand Spaniards, and in front of the Viceroy."[9]

Drake told Anton he was with John Hawkins at San Juan de Ulúa when the treachery of the Viceroy of New Spain cost the lives of 300 Englishmen, and said he had come to collect the money that was owed in compensation. He said the Queen of England had given him letters permitting him to make captures, and he had undertaken the labor of discovering a good route into the South Sea. If the King of Spain did not give Englishmen permission to trade on payment of the duties, he said, he would come back and carry off all the silver.[10]

Anton had a pair of silver drinking cups which Drake admired, and he took one of them as a memento, giving Anton in exchange a gilt silver bowl inscribed "Franciscus Draques" from his table service. He also gave Anton a gilded armor breastplate and a fine harquebus, which he said had been sent to him from Germany. Then, with everything in readiness to depart, Drake distributed an assortment of side arms and other gifts to Anton's

*John Oxenham, John Butler, and Thomas Xervel were subsequently hanged at Lima in November 1580. Only Butler's brother, a youth, was spared.

passengers and crew, and gave them each thirty or forty pesos in coins for their trouble.

While he was doing so, the Negro slave he had taken from Arica came to him and begged to be allowed to go with Anton as his master was old and needed him. Drake told him he had no desire to keep him against his wishes and asked Anton to return him to his master. All the other prisoners except Nuño da Silva were released to Anton as well, and they shoved off. As they hoisted sail, one of Anton's sailors called across, "Our ship shall no more be called the *Cacafuego* but the *Cacaplata*; your ship shall be called the *Cacafuego!*" and Drake's men gave out a roar of approval.[11]

Drake steered north by northwest for the coast of Nicaragua. The *Golden Hinde* was laboring, her hull fouled with barnacles and seaweed, and he had to careen her again as soon as possible. Anton had overheard talk of Nicaragua, and he kept her in sight for two days, to make sure that was where Drake was headed, before turning for Panama to report the seizure and everything he had learned.

❧ 14. ❧

New Spain

On March 16 Drake's pursuers passed Cape San Francisco, where he had captured Anton's galleon, and the following day they entered the port of Manta and found Benito Diaz Bravo repairing his ship. After hearing his story, navigator Pedro Sarmiento de Gamboa concluded that Drake must already have caught Anton, and proposed to Don Luis Toledo that they bypass the Gulf of Panama and cross over to New Spain at once. If his ship was already filled with treasure, Sarmiento argued, there was no point in Drake lingering on the immediate coast or entering the gulf, and their one chance of overtaking him was to head directly for the coast of Nicaragua, which he reckoned they could reach in about twelve days. However, Don Luis was anxious to get to Panama and carry on to Spain with his father's report, and ordered that they resume their voyage in that direction instead.

After releasing Anton, Drake completed the 600-mile crossing in nine days, arriving with the *Golden Hinde* and his pinnace on the shores of Costa Rica in the province of Nicaragua on the same day Toledo's ships reached Cape San Francisco. The next day they came to anchor near the island of Caño, and Drake sent a party with the pinnace into a river on the mainland to forage and refill some of the water casks. The dense tropical jungle was teeming with wildlife, and that evening they enjoyed fresh meat for the first time in nearly a month, including alligator and monkey. While they lay at anchor, they felt a violent earthquake, "the force whereof was such that our ship and pinnace, riding very near an English mile from the shore, were shaken and did quiver as if it had been laid on dry land."[1]

With his great treasure in hand, Drake determined to acquire a second ship to replace the pinnace and facilitate the long voyage to come. Thirty archers and harquebusiers were sent out in the pinnace to watch for a ship, and on March 20 they intercepted the bark of Rodrigo Tello, outbound from the Gulf of Nicoya with a cargo of sarsaparilla, lard, honey, and maize for delivery to Panama. At some forty tons she was well suited to Drake's purposes. Moreover, another stroke of luck attended her capture: Among her eleven passengers and crew were two pilots who had been sent by the Viceroy of New Spain to conduct the new governor of the Philippines, Gonzollo Ronquillo de Peñalosa, to Manila, and they were carrying the official navigation charts and sailing directions for the voyage to Manila and the return trip.

A search of the nearby coast failed to turn up a suitable beach where Drake could properly careen his ship, so he was obliged to settle for only a partial cleaning and repair of her hull. He ordered Tello's bark stripped of her cargo and then had his cannons lifted onto her deck and the treasure carried ashore. Then the *Golden Hinde* was moved into the mouth of the river, and when she became grounded at low tide, his men scraped and caulked her exposed sides down to the water. While this was being done, Drake had Tello's bark fitted with higher gunwales to suit an offshore voyage and enable her to carry more sail. Mindful of their vulnerable position, they worked swiftly, and on March 27, with the treasure reloaded and cannons remounted on the *Golden Hinde*, they set sail just after sunset and resumed their voyage along the coast of New Spain.

After studying the charts and other documents seized from the Manila pilots, Drake offered the senior of the two, Alonso Sanchez Colchero, 1,000 ducats if he would accompany them on the next leg of their voyage. Colchero pleaded with him not to be taken as he had a wife to care for, but Drake insisted that he must and gave him fifty pesos to send to his wife. Colchero then asked that he be allowed to write also to the Viceroy to explain that he was being taken against his will, and Drake granted his request but warned that he would check the letter's contents and if Colchero wrote anything to their disadvantage, he would hang him.

Two days up the coast Drake put Tello and all of his passengers and crew except Colchero in the pinnace with some water and food and released them. They later reported that Drake had treated them very well. However, it appears that he subsequently lost his patience with Colchero. Continuing northward, the *Golden Hinde* and her new consort reached the port of Realejo, where, Drake had learned, the Spaniards were constructing a galleon for the Manila route. According to Colchero, Drake wanted him to pilot them through the shoals at the entrance to the harbor so he could burn the new ship. When Colchero claimed that he was not familiar with this harbor, Drake had a rope placed around his neck and ordered him hoisted off the deck, as though to hang him. As Colchero described the incident, it closely resembled Drake's treatment of Diaz Bravo's purser.

Toward nightfall on April 3, a ship was seen on the horizon, and the following morning, just before dawn, Drake's men boarded her. She was coming from Acapulco laden with linen cloth and Oriental silks as well as chests full of dishes "very finely wrought of white earth in China." The principal passenger was a nobleman, Don Francisco de Zarate, who afterward wrote a long letter describing his encounter with Drake to Don Martin Enriquez, the Viceroy of New Spain and John Hawkins's old nemesis of San Juan de Ulúa.

When he was summoned to the *Golden Hinde*, Zarate said, he prepared himself for death. However, Drake greeted him courteously and then asked whether there was anyone aboard his ship who was related to the Viceroy of New Spain. When Zarate told him there was not, he replied: "Well, it would give me a greater joy to come across him than all the gold and silver of the Indies. You would see how the words of gentlemen should be kept."[2] He showed Zarate around his ship and then invited him to dinner.

> He ordered me to sit next to him and began to give me food from his own plate, telling me not to grieve, that my life and property were safe. I kissed his hands for this. . . .
>
> This general of the Englishmen is a nephew of John Hawkins, and is the same who, about five years ago, took the port of Nombre de Dios. He is called Francisco Drac, and is a man about 35 years of age, low of stature with a fair beard, and is one of the greatest mariners that sails the seas, both as a navigator and as a commander.
>
> His vessel is a galleon of nearly four hundred tons, and is a perfect sailer. She is manned with a hundred men, all of service and of an age for warfare, and all are as practised therein as old soldiers from Italy

could be. Each one takes particular care to keep his arquebus clean. He treats them with affection and they treat him with respect. He carries with him nine or ten cavaliers, cadets of English noblemen. These form a part of his council which he calls together for even the most trivial matter, although he takes advice from no one. But he enjoys hearing what they say and afterwards issues his orders. He has no favorite.

The aforesaid gentlemen sit at his table, as well as a Portuguese pilot whom he brought from England, who spoke not a word during all the time I was on board. He is served on silver dishes with gold borders and gilded garlands, in which are his arms. He carries all possible dainties and perfumed waters. He said that many of these had been given him by the Queen.

None of these gentlemen took a seat or covered his head before him until he repeatedly urged him to do so. . . . I managed to ascertain whether the General was well liked, and all said that they adored him.[3]

The next morning, a Sunday, Drake dressed "very finely" and had the *Golden Hinde* decorated with all its flags and banners, and then went over to inspect the contents of Zarate's ship. Zarate told Drake that his clothes were very costly and implored him not to take them from him. When Drake promised he would not, Zarate gave him a gold falcon with a large emerald set in its breast. After going through everything, Drake had his men remove several bales of linen and silks and four chests of China dishes, explaining to Zarate that he was taking the latter for his wife. Then he ordered all the passengers' trunks taken over to the *Golden Hinde*.

That evening Drake presented Zarate with a fine sword and a silver brazier and recounted his voyage, including the execution of Thomas Doughty. Zarate inquired whether any of the dead man's relatives remained on board and was told that there was one, who ate at Drake's table. "During all this time that I was on board, which was fifty-five hours, this youth [John Doughty] never left the ship, although all the others did so in turn. It was not that he was left to guard me. I think that they guarded him."[4]

The following morning Drake occupied himself with examining and returning the passengers' trunks, and after dinner he ordered Tello's bark brought alongside the *Golden Hinde* and had six cannons placed aboard her. Manning her with two dozen archers, he escorted Zarate back to his ship.

Drake had guessed from the outset that Zarate would relate everything he saw to Viceroy Enriquez, and this final display was the crowning touch in an effort designed to impress him.

Aboard Zarate's ship Drake lined up her crew and gave each a handful of coins, adding a few extra for those who appeared most in need. Then he released the Manila pilot Colchero and requested that one of Zarate's crew come with him to show him where he could obtain water. When all said that they did not know where it would be possible to land, Drake ordered the ship's pilot to accompany him, warning that he would hang him if he uttered a word of protest. Apparently it was at this point that Drake also took an interest in a member of Zarate's retinue, a young Negro woman, "a proper wench called Maria," who departed with him.[5]

A week later, at eleven o'clock on the morning of April 13, Drake entered the harbor of Guatulco, on the southern coast of Mexico, a small settlement serving as the port of the main town of the same name nine miles inland, and as a base for the pearl fishery. In the harbor was a trading bark taking on native products for shipment to Panama and Peru. On shore two Negroes were being tried for attempting to burn some of the buildings, and the curate and some Indians were decorating the church for Easter.

Gaspar de Vargas, the chief magistrate of the town, and Bernardino Lopez, lieutenant governor of the province, were visiting the port, and when they saw Drake's ships they went down to the shore to welcome them. After studying the boat full of armed men heading for shore, however, a Genoese sailor on the beach recognized them as Englishmen. Then one of the ships fired some of its cannons, and the Spaniards ran and hid in the woods behind the town.[6]

Leading twenty-five harquebusiers ashore, Thomas Moone caught merchant Francisco Gomez Rengifo fleeing his house with a gold chain and other valuables, and inside they found a large cache of coins and goods. The two Negroes on trial were freed, and one of them immediately volunteered to join Drake's company. Then Gomez Rengifo and the curate Simon de Miranda were taken out to the *Golden Hinde*. When they arrived, Drake was asleep in his cabin. Awakened, he reassured them that they would not be harmed and took them on a tour of the ship, then served them dinner. When the curate said that he could not eat meat during Holy Week, Drake ordered fish prepared for him instead.

After dinner a low table was placed on the poop deck with an embroidered cushion at its head. Kneeling on the cushion, Drake called for a large book and then tapped his hand, and nine others joined him around the table. Drake raised his eyes to heaven and remained in silent prayer for about a quarter of an hour, and then they began to recite the Psalms. When the onlooking Spaniards grew uneasy, he told them they could move to the bow of the ship if they did not wish to participate, but to remain quiet. Drake read aloud from his book for a while, and then four viol players accompanied them in the singing of hymns. At the conclusion of the religious service, which lasted about an hour, Drake ordered a boy to dance the hornpipe.

Afterward Gomez Rengifo asked Drake what book it was that he had read from, and he opened it to show him. It contained the stories of Protestants who were put to death by the Inquisition, and Drake showed him a picture of an Englishman being burned at the stake.[7]

That evening magistrate Gaspar de Vargas dispatched a runner with a letter warning the Viceroy about the arrival of a corsair.

All that I have been able to find out is that the men [on the Spanish trading bark] . . . think that the name of the pilot of the ship is Morera. An Indian who is ill and remained in the port recognized at first sight one or two men who used to frequent this port as sailors. I then came to this town of Guatulco and have just arrived here at ten o'clock at night, so as to send Your Excellency this dispatch by a suitable person who can reach Oaxaca in two and a half or three days and thence send another one [to Mexico City]. . . .

From this same place I sent another Spaniard to San Juan Acapulco, a hundred leagues from here, so that even if he has to kill horses in doing so, he should reach that port before the ship, so that the necessary precautions can be taken. Your Excellency might be served and an important expedition could be made there if, in all haste, four hundred men could be shipped in the large vessel belonging to Juan Diaz and in His Majesty's ship. . . . Doubtless they would obtain a certain victory over him.[8]

The next morning Drake's captives showed him where he could fill his water casks, and he set them free. The crew of the trading bark having fled ashore, Drake sent a message with Gomez Rengifo, ordering her captain to bring him a supply of firewood or he would burn his ship. His order was complied with the following morning. Through that day and evening Drake's men worked at stowing all their cannons in ballast and nailing the gunports shut and sealing them with caulking in preparation for the ocean voyage to come. Then, a couple of hours before daybreak on Good Friday, April 16, 1579, they raised their sails, and the *Golden Hinde* and her consort slipped out of the harbor. After sunrise the crew of the trading bark rowed out to inspect their vessel and discovered Drake's Portuguese pilot, Nuño da Silva, standing forlornly on her deck with his possessions, "the poor man very unwilling to have been left to ye Spaniard."[9]

❧ 15. ❧

News from the South Sea

y the time Drake departed Guatulco, colonial officials at Panama had formed a fairly complete picture of his raids along the coasts of Chile and Peru, and the alarming scope of his success was beginning to sink in. San Juan de Anton had reached Panama on March 15 to report the loss of the *Cacafuego*'s treasure, and the next day a judicial inquiry was convened to examine everyone who had come into contact with Drake. Anton and the others Drake had released with him gave depositions relating everything they had learned while held captive. On April 2 the ships of Don Luis Toledo arrived at Panama with Benito Diaz Bravo and others whom Drake had intercepted in the vicinity of Paita, and their accounts were added to the growing dossier concerning his raids.

After describing his encounter with Drake and what he knew of Drake's voyage to that point, each witness was asked for details regarding Drake's strength, and whether he had indicated the route by which he intended to return to England. San Juan de Anton estimated that there were 85 men in Drake's company, including 12 gentlemen, and gave a detailed description of his armaments, explaining that during the six days he had spent aboard his ship Drake had shown him everything.

Anton said that when asked how he proposed to get home, Drake replied that there were three possible routes. One was by the Strait of Magellan and another via India and the Cape of Good Hope, but Drake had not named the third, saying only that he expected to be back in England within six months. When Anton responded that he would not be able to return even in a year's time because he was in a "cul de sac," Drake told him that he was satisfied with his proposed route and was going to follow it.

Anton was convinced that Drake was leaving via the coast of New Spain because he had said that he was going to stop for water at the island of Caño. The other witnesses were of the same opinion and added another piece of information: Some of them had recognized a Portuguese pilot accompanying Drake, named Hernán Perez, who had worked as a pilot on the coast but had disappeared twenty years earlier, running off with 30,000 pesos of gold entrusted to him at Guayaquil.

After reviewing the witnesses' depositions and meeting with Anton, Pedro Sarmiento de Gamboa, navigator of the ships pursuing Drake, drafted a composite of all their testimony for Viceroy Toledo in Lima, enumerating for him the losses they had suffered. The total in registered gold and silver that Drake had seized between Valparaiso and Cape San Francisco, he wrote, amounted to 447,000 pesos, in addition to which there were unknown quantities of porcelain, jewels of gold and silver, and precious stones and pearls. Sarmiento reckoned the victuals, tackle, and merchandise he had taken and the damage he had inflicted on shipping amounted to a further 100,000 pesos.

As for the route Drake was most likely to take homeward, Sarmiento had no doubts. He would not dare return via the coast of Peru and Magellan's Strait because the whole country was up in arms against him. Nor would it be his preference to undertake the long and perilous route via the East Indies and Cape of Good Hope, where he would run the risk of being intercepted by the Portuguese. His preferred route, Sarmiento argued, surely would be to continue northward and return by the strait that was believed to exist around the northern extremity of America.

From the present month of March onwards, until September, summer and the hot season prevail as far north as the Cape Mendocino in forty-three degrees. That would be the shortest and quickest route for getting from this sea to his country, and while this route is not familiar to the pilots here, because they do not ordinarily navigate in that region, it is not unknown to the cosmographers and particularly to the English who navigate to Iceland, Bacallaos [Newfoundland], Labrador,

Totilan and Norway. For to them it is familiar and they are not afraid of navigating very far north.

As this corsair has, moreover, navigated in the aforesaid parts and is so well versed in all modes of navigation, it may be inferred and believed that he also must know about all this. A man who has the spirit to do what he has done will not be lacking in courage to persevere in his attempt, especially as he can take advantage, at present, of its being summer in the polar region.[1]

Sarmiento thought that by this time there was little chance of catching Drake. However, there was a new threat: Drake had told several of his captives that he had become separated from two of his ships after exiting the strait and was still hopeful of being reunited with them. He had even written out and signed a letter of safe conduct for Anton to carry in case he encountered them, telling him that their captain was a cruel man who would not leave one man alive, but that upon receipt of this letter he would allow them to go their way peaceably. Drake's ploy to divert his pursuers' attention had the desired effect. It was decided that Sarmiento should take the Viceroy's ships and search the coast back to Peru in the hope of intercepting the other Englishmen before they added to the damage already done.

Around the same date Don Francisco de Zarate's ship reached the port of Realejo in Nicaragua, and on April 16 he dispatched a letter to Viceroy Enriquez in Mexico City. Zarate made small mention of his losses, saying only that Drake had taken a few trifles from him, but he could barely contain his dismay at Drake's successful incursion into His Majesty's ocean.

I can assure Your Excellency that two or three of those who came in his service have already navigated where I have on this route of New Spain. ... He also carries painters who paint for him pictures of the coast in its exact colours. This I was most grieved to see, for each thing is so naturally depicted that no one who guides himself according to these paintings can possibly go astray. ...

I beseech Your Excellency to consider what encouragement it will be to those of his country if he returns thither. If up to the present they

*A "painting," or coastal profile, of the type Don Zarate was
alarmed to see in Drake's journal*

have sent cadets, henceforth they themselves will come after seeing how
the plans which this corsair had made in the dark, and all his promises,
have come true. He will give them as proofs of his venture great sums
of gold and silver.[2]

The first dispatch received by Enriquez, however, was the letter of
Gaspar de Vargas, the chief magistrate of Guatulco. It took ten days to
reach Mexico City, arriving on April 23. That day and the next Enriquez
wrote letters to King Philip, informing him of the raid on Guatulco, and
sent them posthaste to Vera Cruz, where a treasure fleet was due to sail for
Cuba and then Spain. Enriquez ordered a force of 200 soldiers to be sent
down to Acapulco to embark in the ships there and go in pursuit of the corsair. On April 26 he received a second dispatch from Vargas, identifying
Drake by name and relating that his ship was heavily laden with treasure,
which he said he had seized in Chile and Peru after passing through the
Strait of Magellan.

Enriquez anxiously dashed off another letter to Philip, enclosing
Vargas's second report but telling the King that he could not bring himself
to believe that Drake had come through Magellan's Strait. He was sure, he

said, that Drake must have crossed the isthmus as Oxenham had and seized the vessels now in his possession in the Gulf of Panama.

Then another letter arrived from Vargas advising that Drake had left behind a Portuguese pilot, Nuño da Silva, whose deposition he enclosed, and that he was sending the pilot to him under guard. While he waited, Enriquez dispatched a letter to Viceroy Toledo in Lima, informing him of the situation. "Up to the present," he told Toledo, "I have not seen the pilot. . . . I have had men stationed at intervals all along the road and am expecting him hourly. When he arrives I shall manage, by fair or foul means, to make a minute inquiry about this voyage."[3]

On May 21 Enriquez wrote to Toledo again to report the results of his initial examination of Nuño da Silva. In the meantime it appears he might have received Zarate's letter warning of the consequences of Drake reaching England, as his focus was on Drake's route out of the South Sea. "The said pilot arrived here yesterday morning, at eight o'clock and I spent the whole day . . . and this day until noon with him, examining him," Enriquez wrote. He said that although he had made every possible effort to ascertain from him the route Drake intended to take, da Silva insisted he knew nothing about this other than that he had heard several times that Drake was bound to go to look for the strait "de los Bacallaos," and that this could not be accomplished by keeping close to the coast. However, Enriquez was convinced that da Silva was deliberately covering up Drake's real plan of escape. Therefore, he wrote, he had handed da Silva over to the Inquisition so that they could obtain the information "by other means."[4]

Two days later da Silva was brought before a panel of judges. Under interrogation he gave a detailed account of everything that had happened since his capture at the Cape Verde Islands sixteen months earlier. Questioned about Drake's current strength, da Silva said he had departed Guatulco with not more than 88 men, among whom were Frenchmen, Scotsmen, Biscayans, and Flemings. For provisions,

> he took from Guatulco 25 kegs of water, besides some filled earthen jugs, many chests full of the flour which he had seized on the coast of Peru; besides another keg of flour and one hundred leather-covered

boxes of biscuit; also a quantity of maize. Of meat and fish he carried very little, not more than for thirty days' provision, also some oil and four kegs of wine. After fifty days he will be obliged to get a fresh supply of water.[5]

Then, questioned about Drake's plan for getting back to England, da Silva replied between interruptions:

While in Guatulco Drake took out a map and pointed out on it how he had to return by a strait which is in latitude 66 degrees north, and that if he did not find it, then by way of China [the Philippines]. . . .

He told all those he captured in the South Sea, after having robbed the rich galleon, that he came in the service of the Queen, whose instructions he carried by which to govern himself, and that further he came with another purpose than to capture ships. On the bronze cannon which he had in the pinnace there was engraved the round of the world with the Arctic Pole on it in an oblique manner, and he said that these were the arms which the Queen had given him, ordering him to make the round of the world. He told Don Francisco de Zarate that if the king would give the English license to trade in the Indies of the North Sea [Atlantic Ocean], they would be peaceable, but if not they would come and plunder in both seas.[6]

It was a remarkable statement. Da Silva had laid out Drake's mission and the underlying strategy with perfect clarity: Once he had found the short way back around the northern extremity of America, Drake would return that way to plunder again unless King Philip came to terms.

If the judges realized what an important revelation this was, however, there is no indication of it in the surviving documents. One of them interrupted da Silva to query whether Drake planned to raid Acapulco before he left the coast. After answering him, da Silva resumed his reply to the main question:

Many times [Drake] told me and some Spaniards whom he captured that he had to return by the Strait of Bacallaos, which he came to discover. . . . I believed this because if he had the intention of returning by the Strait of Magellan by which he came, there was no necessity to come as he did by the coast of New Spain, nor would he have taken the timber in the Strait to carry to the Queen if he had expected to return that way. He said that by August, 1579, he had to be back in his own country.[7]

From his candor it appears Drake was confident that even knowing his plans, the Spaniards would not catch him. That he expected to reach England in August, leaving himself just four months of sailing time from the date of his departure from Guatulco, was especially revealing. There was no possibility of him reaching England via Magellan's Strait or the Cape of Good Hope in that time. However, the judges apparently gave little credence to a search for the northern passage, as they then turned to questioning why Drake would not attempt to return via Magellan's Strait. In any case, the treasure fleet had sailed from Vera Cruz before the interrogation of da Silva began, and several months passed before his testimony was forwarded to Spain with the next fleet.

Ironically, the first reports to reach King Philip concerning Drake's presence in the South Sea came not from his colonial officials but from his new ambassador in London. In late 1577, around the time Drake was making his final preparations to sail from Plymouth, Philip's former agent, Antonio de Guaras, had been arrested in London and thrown into prison for plotting to free Mary, Queen of Scots, from confinement. Realizing he needed a formal representative at Elizabeth's court, Philip then appointed a nobleman, Don Bernardino de Mendoza, to serve as his ambassador to England. Upon his arrival in London in March 1578, four months after Drake's departure, Mendoza had immediately set to work expanding Philip's network of spies, and his informants soon included at least one member of Elizabeth's council, her Controller of the Household, Sir James Crofts.

Within a short time Mendoza had a good understanding of the forces at work in the council, as he reported to Philip:

During the few days I have been here, and in my conversations I have found her much opposed to your Majesty's interests, and most of her ministers are alienated from us, particularly those who are most important, as although there are seventeen councillors the bulk of the business really depends upon the Queen, Leicester, Walsingham and Cecil [Lord Burghley], the latter of whom, although he takes part in the resolution of them by virtue of his office, absents himself on many occasions as he is opposed to the Queen's helping the [Dutch] rebels so effectively. . . .

[Burghley] does not wish to break with Leicester and Walsingham. They urge the business under cloak of preserving their religion, which he cannot well oppose, nor can he afford to make enemies of them, as they are well disposed towards your Majesty, but Leicester, whose spirit is Walsingham, is so highly favored by the Queen that he centers in his hands and those of his friends most of the business of the country, and his creatures hold most of the ports on the coast, so that your Majesty's friends [in England] have had to sail with the stream.[8]

Soon after his arrival Mendoza had taken up his predecessor's concern about Drake's whereabouts, and in the same letter he reported that Drake's supposed voyage to Alexandria was a cover for another objective, although he assumed it was probably Nombre de Dios again. For his part, Philip had heard about Martin Frobisher's voyages of exploration for a northwest passage, and had made it a priority for Mendoza to find out all he could about them. By June Mendoza had managed to obtain a chart of Frobisher's second voyage into his strait the previous summer, and had reported on preparations for his forthcoming third voyage.[9] This was to be a major expedition employing twenty-five ships to carry home more of his supposed gold-bearing ore. But Frobisher's secret instructions from the Privy Council included other tasks as well.

Frobisher carried with him a prefabricated barracks to be set up in a fort that would be manned by 100 men with provisions to sustain them for eighteen months. Also, two ships would be left with them so that they could effectively guard the entrance to the passage. Then, once the mining operations and construction of the fort were under way, Frobisher was to explore 50 to 100 leagues farther into his strait and record the time of year when it was most free of ice. Fortunately for the men who were to remain through the arctic winter, as they likely would have perished, that part of the plan was abandoned when the ship carrying their barracks was crushed by ice floes and sank.

Frobisher returned to England in the second week of October 1578, and by the end of the year, after careful scrutiny of the manuscript by the

Robert Dudley, Earl of Leicester

official censor, the government allowed the publication of an account of his three voyages in search of the northwest passage written by his lieutenant, George Best. The book was printed by Henry Binnyman, "servant to the right Honourable Christopher Hatton." Binnyman prefaced the volume with a note in which he explained:

> I have in a few places somewhat altered from my copy, and wronged thereby the author, and have sought to conceal upon good causes some secrets not fit to be published or revealed to the world (as the degrees of longitude and latitude, the distance, the true position of places, and the variation of the compass) and which nevertheless, by a general and [a] particular map concerning the same, hereto annexed, is so sufficiently explained . . . [as] may sensibly be understood.[10]

In his introduction Best explained that one of the maps referred to by Binnyman had been drawn only "so far forth as the secrets of the voyage may permit." Indeed, neither of his maps indicated the location of Frobisher's discovery except in a crudely abstract fashion.[11] Thus, like the Spanish and Portuguese, the English had adopted a policy of eliminating or falsifying the information in their accounts and maps of exploratory voyages in order to conceal their most important discoveries.

Nevertheless by November 15, Mendoza was able to send Philip a detailed report on Frobisher's last voyage. Mendoza wrote that none of Frobisher's men dared to divulge anything about their navigation as they were "under threat of pain of death" if they did so. However, Mendoza explained, he was able to provide the details because he had a spy who had accompanied Frobisher. Mendoza's spy told him about the failed effort to leave men behind and accurately described the events of the voyage.[12]

For some months thereafter the principal topic in London maritime circles was the scandal that erupted when Frobisher's ore proved to be worthless. Stockholders in the venture refused to pay for their subscriptions, and soon Frobisher's business partner, Michael Lok, was headed for debtor's prison.

Then, on June 2, 1579, eight months after deserting Drake in the South Sea, John Winter arrived on the Devon coast with the *Elizabeth* and immediately dispatched a confidential report to the Privy Council, defending his decision to turn back. By June 10 and again ten days later Mendoza was able to write reports containing accurate accounts of Drake's voyage up to the point where Winter had become separated from him, including the trial and execution of Thomas Doughty, and to send Philip the first warning that Drake was loose in the South Sea.[13]

In the first week of August the treasure fleet arrived at Seville, and Philip began receiving the initial reports of Drake's raids from his colonial officials. From Nicaragua one official lamented, "It is a thing that terrifies one, this voyage and the boldness of this low man."[14] From Mexico City Don Martin Enriquez urged that Philip take immediate steps to prevent further intrusions. "Now Your Majesty will see how important it is that this sea should have security, and will give orders to safeguard that strait which affords a troublesome entrance to this country, Peru and China."[15] Don Antonio de Padilla, president of Philip's Council of the Indies, advised, "This matter much deserves great deliberation not only on account of the present case . . . but also in view of the future."[16]

After reading each letter and attached recommendations from Padilla, Philip penned his instructions in the margin. On August 6 he ordered that copies of all the reports were to be forwarded to Mendoza in London, but that Mendoza was not to raise the matter with the Queen until Drake reached England.

On August 11, after studying the opinion of the Audiencia of Panama that Drake intended to escape via the Moluccas and the Portuguese route around the Cape of Good Hope, Philip asked his uncle, King Henry of Portugal, to issue an order to intercept him in the East Indies. On August 16 another report raised the specter of other English corsairs following Drake through Magellan's Strait, and Philip instructed his officials to investigate the feasibility of fortifying the strait to prevent its use by foreigners. After issuing his instructions, Philip wrote on each letter "to be put with what relates to Drake."[17]

Within a week rumors of Drake's raids on shipping in the South Sea began circulating in Seville, where nervous English merchants dispatched a vessel to carry the news to London. It was said that Drake had taken 600,000 ducats, of which one-third belonged to the King. The news reached London on September 3, and on September 5 Mendoza reported, "The adventurers who provided money and ships for the voyage are beside themselves for joy, and I am told that there are some of the councillors amongst them."[18]

The merchants of London were anything but enthused by the news, however. Their prosperity depended in large measure on trade with Spain, and they were anxious about the potential repercussions. Upwards of 100 English merchant ships, 2,500 sailors, and £1 million in English property were in Spain in the weeks following the grain harvest, and if Philip had impounded them in retaliation for Drake's actions, many of the City's trading houses would have been ruined. However, Mendoza reported, when a delegation of them brought their concerns to the council, they were told not to worry; that Drake had undertaken a private voyage of discovery, and if he had plundered any Spanish ships, King Philip could hardly blame English merchants and seize their property.[19]

On September 29 Mendoza wrote that the members of the council who had money invested in the enterprise had sent word to officials at Plymouth instructing them to assist Drake in landing and guarding the treasure as soon as he arrived.[20] However, October and November passed without any sign of Drake, and at the end of December Mendoza reported that officials at every port in southwest England were still watching for him.[21] Then, in February 1580, he reported that Drake's backers had begun to believe that some mishap had befallen him and that if he did not arrive within the next two months they would have to give him up as lost.[22]

❧ 16. ❧

The Moluccas

While his countrymen were beginning to think he might be lost, and fully seven months after his departure from Guatulco, Drake was finally sighted again by Europeans. In November 1579 a Portuguese carrack was passing south of the Philippines bound for the Moluccas when her lookout saw a ship converging with them from the north. When they came closer, the captain of the carrack, thinking the other was a Spanish ship that had strayed off her intended course, sent his launch to offer assistance. His sailors rowed near and hailed her, but there were only two men on deck and they made signs with their hands warning the Portuguese to keep away. Frightened, the sailors returned to their ship, and their captain decided to continue on his way. That night the unknown vessel followed them, and at dawn she came toward them decked out with flags and pennants. As she drew nearer, someone on board shouted that they were English and ordered the Portuguese to strike their sails.

The galleon being a larger vessel and armed with cannons, her captain refused to submit and ordered his men to open her gunports and ready themselves for a fight. The corsairs fired seven or eight of their cannons and then turned their stern toward the carrack, leaving such a narrow target that the Portuguese gunners were unable to hit them. When the captain steered his ship in among some shoals, the corsairs veered off and headed southeast toward the Moluccas.[1]

Drake's aim in attempting to intercept the galleon had been to obtain food and capture a pilot who could guide him through the complex maze of waterways and islands comprising the vast archipelago of the East Indies.

The large Portuguese chart that he had obtained from Lisbon prior to the voyage probably gave him a valuable overview of the archipelago, but not sufficient detail with which to navigate around the myriad hazards he would inevitably encounter. His most pressing need, however, was to obtain a supply of food, as their provisions had been nearly exhausted during their crossing of the Pacific.

At their first landfall, among some unidentified islands, the natives had come out in 100 canoes, offering coconuts, fish, potatoes, and fruit in trade. The canoes had smooth and finely burnished hulls rising to inward-curving prows and sterns, and were fitted with outriggers on both sides. The people went naked, and their ears were pierced with ornaments that made them hang low on their cheeks. They chewed an herb that made their teeth "as black as pitch."[2] They were chewing betel nut, and based on these and other details that were recorded, a strong case has been made that they were inhabitants of the Palau Islands, some 500 miles east of the Philippines.[3]

In any case, after briefly pretending to be interested in trade, the islanders had swarmed aboard, stealing everything they could lay their hands on, including the sailors' knives from their belts, and it had taken all the energy Drake's men could muster to eject them from the ship. But hundreds more returned, and when prevented from climbing aboard, they unleashed a barrage of well-aimed stones with their slings. Finally, to drive them off, Drake had to resort to firing one of his cannons, killing about twenty of them.

Stopping next on the coast of Mindanao, the southernmost of the Philippine Islands, they had managed to refill their water casks, but they had departed the next day still in serious want of food, and thus had attempted to board the Portuguese ship. After seeing her armaments and counting the number of men aboard her, however, Drake had changed his mind. He still faced a voyage of more than 12,000 miles to reach England, and with his company reduced to 62 men and boys, he could ill afford to engage in any enterprise that carried a high risk of injury. Soon after breaking off their engagement with the galleon, they came to an island where two native fishermen agreed to guide them to the Moluccas, and a few days later they had their first view of the island of Ternate.

* * *

While the name Moluccas was sometimes used in reference to all of the spice islands of the East Indies, it specifically meant to the Portuguese the chain of four small islands near the equator that were the principal growers of the clove tree. The chain, comprising Ternate, Tidore, Motir, and Maquian, stretched only about forty miles but was the center of a larger kingdom of some seventy islands, spread over hundreds of miles, which had been ruled for centuries by sultans of the Muslim faith. In 1521 the Portuguese had built a fort on Tidore and commenced their subjugation of the sultans, later establishing a second fort on Ternate, in order to monopolize the enormously valuable clove trade. In 1575, however, Sultan Babu of Ternate had regained control of all the islands except Tidore, where the Portuguese remained entrenched.

When Drake's ship was sighted from Ternate, Babu sent two large war canoes out to ascertain whether he was Portuguese. Informed by Drake that he was not, and that he was not on friendly terms with them, the sultan's emissaries told him that the Portuguese had at Tidore a galleon and an armed galley that could do him much harm, and urged him to call at Ternate instead. Drake accepted the invitation and sent one of his gentlemen to present a velvet cloak to Babu as a token of friendship. When Babu learned that Drake was representing the Queen of England, he was delighted.[4]

The following day Babu came out in grand procession to welcome Drake. "The manner of his coming," Fletcher wrote, "as it was princely, so truly it seemed to us very strange and marvellous."[5] Leading the way were three great canoes called *caracoas*. On the sides of each were galleried outriggers seating three banks of rowers, their oars moving in unison to chanting and the beat of drums. Around the main deck of each stood rows of warriors, their weapons glistening. Behind them, on a raised platform covered by a canopy, sat ranks of dignitaries dressed in white linen. As each vessel glided swiftly by, all bowed very low in respect for Drake's Queen. Then they formed up side by side, prepared to tow the *Golden Hinde* into port, and the royal *caracoa* arrived, rowed by eighty slaves. Surrounded by seven brass cannons, Babu, a huge man, lay on a bed covered in cloth of gold, his servants fanning him with a large wing made of various colored feathers.

Not to be outdone for pageantry, Drake fired his cannons in salute and then had his orchestra strike up a tune. Babu was enthralled by the music and motioned for Drake to send the orchestra over in the *Golden Hinde*'s boat,

The Golden Hinde, *towed by Babu's* caracoas

which he then towed behind his barge while they entertained him. When they reached the harbor Drake explained through an interpreter that he wished to trade for supplies of food. Babu gave his consent, and shortly afterward canoes began arriving laden with rice, sugarcane, chickens, coconuts, and plantains. That evening the company enjoyed full stomachs for the first time in many days.

The next morning, as trade continued, Drake expressed an interest in acquiring a quantity of cloves. The merchants told him that he would have to pay an export duty levied by the Sultan, but Drake attempted to conclude a deal without paying the requisite tax, and when Babu learned of this he reportedly became enraged and began plotting to have him killed. Instead of coming aboard that afternoon as he had promised, Babu sent his brother with an invitation for Drake to come to his palace while his brother remained aboard ship as a hostage. Evidently fearful of the consequences for himself if Drake were assassinated, the brother "uttered certain words in secret conference with . . . [Drake] aboard his cabin, which bred no small suspicion of ill intent."[6] Drake's men prevailed on him not to go, and some of the gentlemen went in his place.

Drake sent some presents to the Sultan, and it appears that the rift was smoothed over. When his men arrived at Babu's royal compound, they were greeted by another of his brothers and conducted to a banquet attended by sixty noble personages. Babu entered with a rich canopy borne over him by his retainers and guarded by twelve warriors, dazzling Francis Fletcher with his personal opulence.

> From the waist to the ground was all cloth of gold, and that very rich; his legs bare, but on his feet a pair of shoes of cordivant [leather] died red; the attire of his head were finely wreathed in diverse rings of plated gold. . . . about his neck he had a chain of perfect gold, the links very great and one fold double; on his left hand was a Diamond, an Emerald, a Ruby and a Turky [turquoise], 4 very fair and perfect jewels; on his right hand, in one ring, a big and perfect Turky, and in another ring many Diamonds of a smaller size. . . . As thus he sat in his chair of state, at his right side there stood a page with a very costly fan (richly embroidered and beset with Saphires) breathing and gathering the air to refresh the king, the place being very hot.[7]

The next day Drake went ashore to meet with the Sultan. Although there presently was a truce between himself and the Portuguese, Babu knew it was only a matter of time before they organized a new force to reconquer his islands, and he was anxious to form an alliance with the Queen of England to prevent this. He said if the Queen would help him to expel them from his kingdom, he would concede to her the trade in cloves, which the Portuguese had previously enjoyed. Drake promised that within two years he would "decorate" this sea with English ships for whatever purpose might be necessary, and presented Babu with a coat of mail, a very fine helmet, and a gold ring set with a precious stone.[8] The Sultan in turn agreed to supply Drake with six tons of cloves and gave him a "rich ring" to present to Queen Elizabeth.

On the fourth day of Drake's visit, the commander of the Portuguese fort on Tidore, a few miles to the south, heard about the strange ship visiting Ternate. Thinking the men on board were Spaniards, he sent two of his men to invite them to call at his port for whatever they needed. When the

Drake being received by Babu

pair arrived, Drake politely informed them that he was English, and said that Babu had supplied all his wants.

Startled to find an English ship on this side of the globe, the Portuguese asked him where he was going and what he was looking for. Drake answered that he came to discover the world by order of his Queen. Asked how he had traversed such a long distance in such a small ship, Drake told them he had ten other ships, which he had sent to discover different places, and he was soon going to rendezvous with them. Then he told them about the death of their young king in Morocco. Astonished, the two Portuguese returned to Tidore to report the news to their commander. The following day they were sent back to obtain more information, but Drake was gone.[9]

Homeward

*F*rom Ternate Drake steered for the island of Java, 1,000 miles to the south-west on the edge of the Indian Ocean. His immediate priority was to find a secluded anchorage where he could careen the *Golden Hinde*. After their long voyage through warm tropical waters, her hull had once again accumulated a thick growth of seaweed, which would slow their progress homeward unless removed.

The second day out from Ternate they crossed the equator, and three days later came to anchor at a small, wooded island in the Banggai Archipelago. A campsite was cleared, and they ferried all the cannons ashore and placed them in defensive bulwarks around it. The more than twenty-six tons of treasure was unloaded, and the ship was pulled onto the beach for scraping, caulking, and a fresh coat of tar. The island, Fletcher wrote, was home to a strange kind of crab,

> of such a size that one was sufficient to satisfy four hungry men at a dinner, being a very good and restorative meat. . . . They are, as far as we could perceive, utter strangers to the sea, living always on the land, where they work themselves earths as do the conies, or rather they dig great and huge caves under the roots of the most huge and monstrous trees, where they lodge themselves by companies together. Of the same sort and kind we found in other places . . . some that, for want of other refuge when we came to take them, did climb up into trees to hide themselves, whither we were enforced to climb after them.[1]

As was his practice, Drake divided the company into two parties and assigned only light duties to one or the other on alternate days. Soon the inhabitants of nearby islands began supplying them with fish, fruit, and other fresh commodities, and they gradually regained their health.

While the ship was being readied to sail, it was decided that the Negro woman Maria and the two Negro men who had accompanied them from America would remain on the island, and they were given provisions, seeds, and other means to sustain themselves. Whether they wished to be left is difficult to discern from the limited mention of them in the written accounts. One account states that Maria was "gotten with child between the captain and his men pirates" and, "now being very great was left here on this island," implying that she was shared around as an object of pleasure and then ruthlessly abandoned when she became pregnant.[2] However, it is quite apparent elsewhere in this anonymous account that its source—possibly John Doughty—harbored considerable animosity toward Drake and his sailors, and the circumstances may have been quite different from what he implied.

Allowing that she had been in their company since the beginning of April, it appears that Maria's unborn child had been conceived aboard the *Golden Hinde*. It is unlikely, though, that she had promiscuous relations with the crew, for Drake would have known that nothing would lead to ill feeling and violence between sailors quicker than a contest among them for the affections of a woman. The only way he could have prevented such an eventuality would have been to have her sleep in his own cabin, and most probably it was he or his manservant, Diego, who had sired Maria's child.*

From mention that she was now "very great," it appears that Maria may have been close to giving birth, and for Drake to have taken her and a newborn infant on a long and taxing voyage would surely have diminished their prospects for survival. Quite possibly both she and her companions had been born into slavery and did not have homes to return to, in which case they may have welcomed the opportunity to found their own settlement. Drake named the island Francisco after one of the Negro men, and from this gesture it appears that he appointed him leader of the little colony.

*More likely Diego was the father, because neither of Drake's marriages produced any children.

✳ ✳ ✳

After twenty-eight days on the island Drake and his men resumed their voyage westward, emerging from the Banggai Archipelago within sight of the island of Celebes. Because of its long tentacles extending hundreds of miles to the northeast and south, the great island of Celebes had confounded the Portuguese navigators and was not accurately depicted on any chart or map at the time. Approached from the Banggai islands, however, its coast trends southwestward into the Bay of Towori, which then reaches westward some forty miles, giving the appearance of a passage between two islands. Arriving on the coast some distance to the north, they turned and followed it southwestward until January 9, "at which time," Fletcher wrote, "we supposed that we had at last attained a free passage, the lands turning evidently in our sight to westward."[3]

That afternoon the wind freshened into a light gale, and at eight o'clock in the evening the *Golden Hinde* was moving briskly along under full sails when she suddenly shuddered violently and came to a grinding halt. She had struck a submerged reef, and before the crew could haul in her sails the ship was driven hard aground. Rushing below to inspect her bilges, they were relieved to discover no new leaks. The ship had struck coral, not rock, yet her hull was intact. Thinking to carry an anchor out to deeper water and use it to pull themselves off the reef, Drake launched the ship's boat; but taking soundings, they could not find the bottom. The reef rose steeply from a great depth.

Darkness descended, leaving the ship's company in extreme peril. If the wind and waves grew stronger, she would have been driven farther onto the reef and there would have been no possibility of saving her. Moreover, the nearest land was six leagues away, and the ship's boat could carry only about twenty men, including the oarsmen. Four or five trips would have been necessary to ferry everyone ashore, and in the meantime the ship might have broken up. Even if everyone managed to get ashore, with little in the way of arms or provisions they would have been at the mercy of the natives.

The next morning they waited for the tide to lift them off, but high water came and went without any effect. Again they looked for someplace to set their anchor, but to no avail. Returning to the ship, Drake called the

The Golden Hinde *aground on the reef*

men together to pray for divine intervention, and Fletcher delivered a sermon and administered communion. Then Drake set all hands to work lightening the ship. Provisions, eight cannons, and three tons of cloves were heaved over the side, and at four o'clock in the afternoon the *Golden Hinde* suddenly heeled and slid off the reef into deep water.

Afterward Drake was furious with Parson Fletcher. It seems in his sermon Fletcher had suggested that the disaster was God's retribution for their piratical deeds, and may also have brought up Doughty's execution in the same vein. Denouncing Fletcher "to the devil and all his angels," Drake ordered him chained to a hatch in the forecastle wearing a sign that read "Francis Fletcher, ye falseth knave that liveth," and warned him if he once came before the mast he would be hanged.[4] How long Fletcher remained in Drake's bad graces is unknown.

There is a great deal of conflicting information concerning Drake's entire journey through the East Indies. The only date on which the accounts agree is that of his mishap on the reef, which occurred on January 9, 1580.[5] It is clear that the time he had taken to sail from his initial landfall in the western Pacific to this point was later inflated to conceal part of the time he had spent elsewhere since departing Guatulco, Mexico.[6] Then, after he got off the reef on Janu-

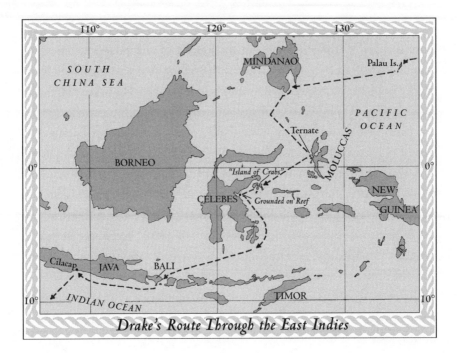

Drake's Route Through the East Indies

ary 9, the time consumed in reaching the south coast of Java was also exaggerated, but for a different purpose.

The anonymous account that reveals he left Maria and her companions at the island of crabs briefly states that after Drake escaped the reef, he continued his course westward toward Java. However, the most detailed account of the voyage, which was adapted from Fletcher's journal and then edited by Drake himself but suppressed and not finally published until many years after his death, presents a very different picture. According to this account, titled *The World Encompassed by Sir Francis Drake*, he met with contrary winds and was driven far to the east, toward Timor, before he was able to recover and head westward again, finally reaching Java after a voyage of two months. It describes numerous islands that were seen or visited along this route, including one called "Barativa," where he and his men received an especially hospitable welcome, and which the account places near the eastern end of Timor. But there are problems with this picture.

First, there were several alternate routes through the islands to the south coast of Java, all of them shorter than the one claimed in Drake's account. This was the monsoon season, when the prevailing winds are from the northwest, and with the wind thus on his beam or stern quarter, several of these passages lay open to him. Furthermore, the overall sailing distance from the Bay of Towori to Java via the longest of the alternate routes was only about 900 miles—not even a month's sailing. Most telling of all, it has proved impossible to trace Drake's travels based on the description of the islands in the account: In several instances there are simply no islands anywhere near the places indicated, and the obviously real island of Barativa has never been satisfactorily identified.

When Drake's account adds these wanderings to the journey from his initial landfall in the western Pacific—most probably in the Palau Islands— to the point where the *Golden Hinde* struck the reef, the entire voyage through the Indies until he departed the south coast of Java allegedly consumed an incredible six months. Not including time spent at various stops along the way, the account has him sailing for a total of 139 days to cover a distance, in the extreme, of perhaps 3,000 miles—an average of little more than 20 miles per day.* Yet Drake was a superb sailor who had already demonstrated how quickly he could move.

Although the identity of "Barativa" has never been established, *The World Encompassed* contains a revealing description of its populace:

> The people are Gentiles, of handsome body and comely stature, of civil demeanor, very just in dealing and courteous to strangers, of all which we had evident proof, they showing themselves most glad of our coming and cheeringly ready to relieve our wants with whatsoever their country could afford. The men all go naked save their heads and secret parts, every one having one thing or another hanging at his ears. Their women are covered from the middle to the foot, wearing upon their naked arms bracelets, and that in no small number, some having nine at least on each arm, made for the most part of horn or brass, whereof the lightest (by our estimation) would weight 2 ounces.
>
> With this people linen (whereof they make rolls for their heads and girdles to wear about their loins) is the best merchandise and of greatest estimation. They are also much delighted with *Margaretas* [pearls], which in their language they call *Saleta*, and such other like trifles. . . .

---

*By comparison, in the same season eight years later Thomas Cavendish made his initial landfall 600 miles farther out in the Pacific, in the Mariana Islands, and from there took a more northerly route, stopping in the Philippines, and yet still managed to reach the south coast of Java in a little over two months. He sailed from the Philippines to Java in just thirty-six days.

> We received of them whatsoever we desired for our need . . . so that
> in all our voyage (*Ternate* only excepted), from our departure out of our
> own country, hitherto we found not anywhere greater comfort and re-
> freshing than we did at this time and in this place.[7]

What is most revealing is the description of the people as "gentiles,"
because the word was used by the English to distinguish Hindus from
Muslims,[8] and by the time of Drake's voyage the islands of Bali and
Lombok, situated at the eastern end of Java, were the last strongholds of the
Hindu religion in Indonesia. Indeed, the description of the people and their
warm hospitality is a good portrait of the Balinese. And notably, when the
first Dutch expedition to the East Indies called at Bali in 1597, the officers
gained the distinct impression that the people had been visited by Drake.

According to the Dutch, the Balinese told them "a ship had anchored
in that same place with people who were in some respects like us [fair complexioned and bearded]."[9] The Dutchmen asked if they were sure of the
date, because Drake's countryman Thomas Cavendish had touched there in
1588, but the islanders were emphatic. They recalled the visit as being about
eighteen years before. "Among them," they told the Dutchmen, "were some
who knew how to divide a rope into five or six parts and then make the rope
whole again."[10] Thus it appears that Drake's men demonstrated the art of
splicing to the people of Bali.

The World Encompassed states that Drake found this island of "Barativa"
near the eastern end of Timor on February 8, a month after the grounding
on the reef, and then has him departing after a visit of two days and wandering for another month before he reached Java on March 11. Allowing,
however, that Bali is actually located only three miles from the eastern end
of Java, it appears that he must have taken a more direct route after all, and
reached his eventual anchorage on Java at least a month sooner than the account claims.[11]

The morning after coming to anchor at the port of Cilacap on the south coast of Java,
Drake sent some gifts to the local raja, who reciprocated by sending him rice,
coconuts, and some hens. The following day Drake took the ship's orchestra
ashore to entertain their host, and over the next two weeks they were visited
by a succession of chiefs from neighboring areas.

We had four a shipboard at once, and two or three often. They are wonderfully delighted in coloured clothes, as red and green; their upper parts of their bodies are naked, save their heads, whereupon they wear a Turkish roll, as do the Moluccans; from the middle downward they wear a pintado of silk, trailing upon the ground, in colours as they best like.

The Moluccans hate that their women should be seen of strangers, but these offer them of high courtesy, yea the kings themselves.

The people are of goodly stature and warlike, well provided of swords and targets [shields], with daggers, all being of their own work and most artificially done, both in tempering their metal as also in the form, whereof we bought reasonable store.[12]

While Drake visited the rajas ashore, his men brought the *Golden Hinde* into shallow water to inspect her hull for damage from the grounding and give it one more cleaning. With this task completed, they filled their water casks and took aboard hens, goats, quantities of fruit, coconuts, and sugarcane, and seven tons of rice. Then one day, as they were showing some visitors around the ship, they discovered two Portuguese spies among them taking careful note of their armaments. Afterward they learned from the villagers that there was a great ship like theirs approaching along the coast. The next morning Drake gave the order to set sail and steer southwest, across the Indian Ocean for the Cape of Good Hope, at the southern tip of Africa.

After Java the accounts provide very few details of the rest of Drake's passage home. The World Encompassed states that he sighted the east coast of Africa some 500 miles to the northeast of the Cape of Good Hope on the fifty-seventh day and then spent twenty-five days following it southward before rounding the cape. But here again there is conflicting information. John Drake later recalled that they did not touch land or anchor anywhere prior to rounding the cape. In any case, one of the sailors died, reducing the company to fifty-nine. With only three casks of freshwater remaining, they tried to find some in a large bay on the west side of the cape but narrowly escaped being wrecked and had to give up the search. Finally, spreading some sails on the deck, they were able to collect six or seven tons of rainwater.

The Golden Hinde *at Cilicap, Java*

A month later, after sailing another 3,000 miles, they sighted the coast of Sierra Leone seven degrees north of the equator, and Drake immediately dispensed the remaining water to his parched crew. John Drake said there was only one pint left for every three men, and if they had been delayed two or three days more, they would all have perished. Watering and resting at Sierra Leone for two days, they discovered that the mangroves were covered in delicious oysters, and Drake obtained a supply of lemons and other fruits from the natives.* Then, all of the accounts say, they set sail and did not touch land again until they finally landed at Plymouth. However, there are two letters that suggest there was more to their journey.

The letters were addressed to Dr. Gomez de Santillan, a member of King Philip's Council of the Indies, by a man named Pedro de Rada, residing at the harbor of Portugalete on the northern coast of Spain. In his first letter, dated July 29, 1580, de Rada wrote:

> *Very Illustrious Lord,*
> *Having, as was my duty, exerted vigilance in order to ascertain what success has been obtained by the Captain Francis, English Corsair, who entered the South Sea, I*

---

*Again it appears that Drake knew, intuitively at least, much more about the means of combating scurvy than is credited to anyone in that century, or indeed until the voyages of Captain James Cook two centuries later.

obtained the following from two inhabitants of this town, both masters of vessels and persons of credit who had arrived from Nantes in France.

There, two Frenchmen, whom I also knew to be reliable, who habitually come to this port and are now expected daily, told them and certified that the said Captain Francis, Englishman, with the same ship which had entered the South Sea, had come to Belle Isle in France, about 30 miles from la Rochelle in the mouth of the entrance to Nantes, and had brought a great quantity of treasure of gold and silver, a part of which he had unloaded secretly on the said Island and transported to the mainland of France.

After remaining there for about six days, he had gone to la Rochelle and Antioche which is in the same straits of la Rochelle, and there [the two Frenchmen] had learnt, from his own lips, how he had entered the self-same strait of Magellan and passed through it into the South Sea, and that he had not dared to go to England on account of having beheaded a noble gentleman whom he had carried in his company, and for other reasons.

Although I am now awaiting the arrival of these French shipmasters, in order to obtain from them the most authentic account possible, it seemed to me advisable to inform Your Grace of what has been related. . . .

Very Illustrious Sir, I kiss your hands,

Your Servant,
Pedro de Rada[13]

Notably, for this news to be true, Drake had to have arrived on the coast of France by the middle of July.

Then on August 19 de Rada wrote to Gomez de Santillan again with more information:

The French shipmasters whom I was expecting in order to obtain all the information I could, have arrived here. They state that an English ship of approximately 200 tons, with much artillery and a great quantity of silver and gold had arrived at Belle Isle de Saint Jean.

He had stayed at La Rochelle on his way, in search of some place where he could repair and clean his ship because it came covered with a superabundance of long seaweed, such as grows of its own accord on the vessels that navigate in the Indian Seas.

Therefore, without sailing much, he was searching for a suitable careening place in the islands of Houat which I myself have visited. They are uninhabited and situated between Morbihan in France and the entrance to the coast of Nantes.

When the Captains of the galleys of France heard of him, two of the galleys which patrol the coast attacked and fought him, not knowing who he was or what wealth he carried—but merely on the supposition that he was a Corsair.

He defended himself, however, and sailed for a second time towards la Rochelle.

It is believed that he was keeping about that coast, entertaining himself, until he received word from England, whither he had sent a message in order to ensure a safe return to that realm.[14]

De Rada's information was entirely consistent with Drake's mode of operation, and with his obvious concerns at that juncture. Once again he had returned with a ship full of plundered treasure unsure how the political environment had evolved in his absence, and whether he could safely land in England or would face censure for aggravating relations with Spain. Moreover, the uncertainty was compounded by his execution of Thomas Doughty. And so he had lain behind an island outside La Rochelle waiting for word from London that it was safe for him to return.

Evidently, then, Drake must have completed a much quicker passage home than any account of the voyage admits. Certainly he could not have spent six months wandering through the East Indies or departed Java any later than mid February. However, his reason for sequestering on the coast of France, involving as it did the Queen and the secret unloading of part of his plunder, was too sensitive to ever be publicly admitted. Thus, his eventual account of his voyage from the point of his mishap on the reef in the East Indies had to be fictitiously padded to cover up the true date of his arrival in home waters.

PART THREE

Celebrity amid Secrecy

❧ 18. ☙

"A Very Short Way"

here is a story in the folklore of southwest England about the return of Francis Drake from his voyage around the world. Legend has it that some fishermen tending their nets near the entrance to Plymouth Sound looked up and saw a weatherworn bark approaching from the southwest. As the bark passed them, someone aboard her called out an odd question: "Is the Queen still alive?" She was, and in good health, one of them replied. Afterward, the story goes, Drake rewarded the fisherman who had given him his first news of the Queen with a suit of white silk.

After coming to anchor in the harbor, the story continues, Drake sent ashore for his wife, and within a short time Mary arrived along with the mayor of Plymouth, John Blitheman. There were some awkward moments for Mary as Blitheman helped her explain that Drake had been gone so long that he had been given up for dead. Consequently, she had kept the company of a gentleman who proposed to wed her but then had died, leaving her a large legacy. At first Drake was "moved with great impatience," but "being persuaded by Master Hawkins and others he forgave her the offence and did receive her to his favour."[1]

A few years after their return, John Drake gave some of the same details in recalling the event.

> On reaching Plymouth they inquired from some fisherman "How was the Queen?" and learnt that she was in good health, but that there was much pestilence in Plymouth. So they did not land, but Captain Drake's wife and the Mayor of the port came to see him on the ship.

He dispatched a messenger to the Queen who was in London, which was sixty leagues distant, apprising her of his arrival, and he wrote to other persons at Court who informed him that he was in Her Majesty's bad graces because she had already heard, by way of Peru and Spain, of the robberies that he had committed. . . .

Thereupon [Drake] left the port of Plymouth with the ship and, lying behind an island, waited until the Queen sent him word.[2]

What was curious about both stories was Drake's inquiry about the Queen's health. He surely would have known from the message he received advising that it was safe to come out of hiding on the coast of France that she was alive and well. It appears, then, that these stories are glimpses of an earlier attempt to land at Plymouth, sometime in early July. From what John Drake said, it seems that Drake did sail straight home from Africa, but hearing upon his arrival that the Queen was upset by news of his return, he withdrew from Plymouth to the coast of France to await further word from his backers.

Undoubtedly, Elizabeth's displeasure at the time was rooted in her apprehension over ominous preparations in Spain for a major military venture. The previous winter Philip had begun to assemble a large army under the Duke of Alba and a fleet under the Marquis of Santa Cruz, the destination of which was unknown. The Spanish had given out that their purpose was to destroy the pirates' nest at Algiers and consolidate their control of the western Mediterranean after their defeat of the Turks at Lepanto, but few in England believed that explanation.

In January 1580 elderly King Henry of Portugal, successor to the young King Sebastian who had been slain in Morocco, had died, leaving no legitimate offspring to inherit the throne. The claimants included Henry's bastard son Don Antonio, the King of France, and Philip himself. Through the spring opinion in Elizabeth's council had been divided between the likelihood of Philip seizing the throne of Portugal or attempting an invasion of England. Consequently, when Elizabeth first received word of Drake's return, she may well have feared this was the final provocation Philip was waiting for to justify an assault on England.

In August, however, word reached London that Alba and Santa Cruz had invaded Portugal instead, easily routing Don Antonio's supporters and securing its throne for Philip. Although he would not be crowned until the following year, Philip was de facto King of Portugal and all its colonies, making him the first ruler in history who could claim an empire spanning the entire globe. Combining the riches that flowed into Lisbon with those of Spain gave him vastly increased revenues to fund his efforts to roll back Protestant advances in northern Europe. Moreover, with the crown of Portugal came control of a powerful fleet, including twelve great war galleons. Philip's expanded naval resources posed a serious threat to England.

To Elizabeth and her council, war appeared imminent.[3] There was an immediate need to strengthen England's defenses in preparation for the coming conflict, and to develop a strategy to distract Philip from his purpose in the meantime. Undoubtedly, Leicester and Walsingham seized the opportunity to point out to Elizabeth that the man who had demonstrated the strongest aptitude for the latter was presently awaiting word that it was safe to return home, and was carrying a large quantity of treasure that would also prove useful.

With the way for Drake's return thus cleared, he arrived at Plymouth on September 26, 1580. The next morning he sent trumpeter John Brewer, Hatton's man, to ride posthaste to London with word of his arrival. Brewer reached London on September 29, and within hours the city was buzzing with Drake's name.

Amid growing excitement, Elizabeth summoned the Privy Council. Of Drake's backers, only the Lord Admiral, the Earl of Lincoln attended. Led by Lord Burghley and the Earl of Sussex, the remainder of the council adopted the position that Drake's plunder might have to be restored to the owners, and proceeded to draw up an order that it be registered and brought to the Tower of London for safekeeping. When the order reached Walsingham, Leicester, and Hatton, however, they refused to sign it. After conferring with them, Elizabeth suspended the order and instructed that a rumor be spread that Drake had brought back very little treasure.

Almost as quickly as he had reached London, Brewer returned to Plymouth with a letter from Elizabeth telling Drake to bring some specimens of his labors and not to fear anything. The treasure was carried up to Saltash Castle and placed under guard, and Drake loaded some horses with gold and silver and set off with an armed escort for London.

The Spanish ambassador Mendoza had begun monitoring the proceedings the same day Brewer arrived in London. That evening he dashed off an urgent dispatch to Philip, relating the first details: From what he had heard of Brewer's story, he wrote, Drake had returned via the Portuguese Indies and the Cape of Good Hope.[4] The next day Mendoza requested an audience with the queen, but she refused to see him. Then, on October 16, Mendoza wrote another dispatch to Philip, reporting what his spies had learned about Drake's meeting with her.

Mendoza stated that Drake had spent more than six hours with Elizabeth and had presented her with "a diary of everything that had happened during the three years and a very large chart." Her councillors, he wrote,

> are very particular not to divulge the route by which Drake returned, and although, as I wrote to your Majesty, Hatton's trumpeter had said that the road home had been by the Portuguese Indies, Drake himself signifies to the contrary. . . . [His men] are not to disclose the route they took on pain of death. Drake affirms that he will be able to make the round trip in a year, as he has found a very short way.[5]

Mendoza was puzzled by the phrase "a very short way" but concluded that Drake might have returned by the Strait of Magellan. In spite of his diligent investigation of Frobisher's voyages, he failed to recognize a common thread in the injunction not to disclose any details "on pain of death," which was being imposed on Drake's men as it had been on Frobisher's. However, he was concerned with the emergence of a new threat: Drake was proposing to return to the South Sea immediately, he warned, and was offering his backers a return, in one year, of seven pounds for every pound invested.[6]

As it happened, Philip did not receive his ambassador's dispatch because Walsingham, no doubt anxious to find out what Mendoza had learned, had his agents intercept it.[7]

On October 23 two secretaries of the Privy Council were sent to see Mendoza. They told him the Queen had heard that Mendoza was complaining about Drake and the warm reception he had received at the court, and she wished to inform him that his complaints were groundless. She had inquired, and had been assured that Drake had done no damage either to King Philip's subjects or to his dominions. Further, she would not receive

Sir Francis Walsingham

Mendoza in his official capacity until she obtained satisfactory redress for his King having lately sent troops to Ireland in support of the rebellion there. Mendoza immediately replied with a letter accusing Drake of severing the cables of the ships at Callao and sinking others, of cutting off the hands of some Spaniards, and of robbing the King of Spain and his subjects of great quantities of bullion and pearls.

In his list of "proofs" against Drake, Mendoza said that San Juan de Anton had erred in stating that the bullion taken from the *Cacafuego* amounted to 360,000 pesos. According to the register, he said, the total was actually 693,000 pesos, in addition to which she was carrying 400,000 pesos "to be registered," which brought the total seized from the *Cacafuego* alone to more than 1 million pesos. From other ships, he said, Drake had taken another 136,000 pesos of unregistered gold in addition to 46,000 pesos that was registered.[8] Mendoza reckoned the total value of Drake's plunder at 1.5 million pesos. What he did not say was that he could only estimate the large portion of the total that various private parties had not registered in order to avoid the export tax. Drake knew that Mendoza could not prove the losses of contraband bullion, and advised his backers to deny any knowledge of such amounts.

On October 24 Elizabeth wrote to Edmund Tremayne, a clerk of the Privy Council appointed for the purpose of counting and registering treasure at Plymouth:

Trusty and wellbeloved we greet you well whereas by letters lately written unto you by our commandment from secretary Walsingham you
were willed in our name to give your assistance unto our wellbeloved
subject Francis Drake for the safe bestowing of certain bullion lately
by him brought into this our realm, which our pleasure is should now
be sent up [to London] as you shall further understand by the said
Drake.[9]

Drake returned to Plymouth at the end of October and went to Saltash
Castle with Tremayne. On Elizabeth's instructions, the sum of £14,000 was
set aside for Drake's crew, and Drake took £10,000 for himself. Then he
loaded a large train of packhorses with gold and silver and set off with an
armed escort for Elizabeth's palace at Richmond. Tremayne wrote to
Walsingham that he had not attempted to ascertain the amount of treasure
that had previously been "secretly landed" because he had seen a letter from
the Queen instructing Drake not to reveal the quantity of it to anyone.[10]

Tremayne was also asked to assist in refuting Mendoza's charges, and
with his dispatch to Walsingham he enclosed a deposition signed by the
forty-nine members of Drake's crew who remained in Plymouth. The men
said that although they had seized some ships, none had been sunk; and
while some gold and silver had been taken, the amounts were very small
compared with those claimed by the Spanish ambassador. As to injuries allegedly received by Spaniards, they said, only one man had been hurt (San
Juan de Anton), and Drake had not allowed him to depart until he had recovered from his wound.

Tremayne weighed and registered the remaining bullion, and when
Drake returned at the end of November, it was loaded back onto the *Golden
Hinde* for shipment to London. Drake brought the ship around to the
Thames in December, and on Christmas Eve 1580 the remaining treasure
was finally carried into the Tower of London and placed in a vault under the
Queen's jewel house.

How much of the treasure was siphoned off beforehand by Drake and his partners is
impossible to trace. To begin with, there were the unknown quantities of gold
and silver that the Spaniard de Rada's sea captains said he had secretly unloaded on the coast of France. Most likely, Drake had arranged for a ship to

come out from Plymouth to pick up this portion of the treasure separately. Notably, he had taken twenty-six tons of bullion from the *Cacafuego* alone, and the total plunder he brought back from the South Sea was likely closer to thirty tons.

At the end of October Mendoza's informant told him that the treasure that was being sent to the Tower of London for possible restitution to the owners consisted of "twenty of this country's tons of silver, each one 2,000 pounds; five boxes of gold, a foot and a half in length; and a huge quantity of pearls, some of great value."[11] It appears, then, that between six and ten tons of treasure had already been sequestered by that time. However, the amounts actually registered and delivered to the Tower of London in December were only ten and a half tons of silver and 101 pounds of gold—about half the sums Mendoza's informant had told him about. Moreover, the pearls, gems, and miscellaneous other precious items Drake had brought back had also disappeared.

Years later a man named Lewis Roberts wrote that he had seen an account in Drake's own hand showing that his partners received a return of forty-seven pounds sterling for each pound they had invested in the voyage. Assuming a cost of £4,000 to outfit the expedition, this suggests that they received in the vicinity of £200,000. Eventually, bullion and coins valued at £264,000 were deposited in the Tower of London, although this may have included the Queen's share of the profits. Even so, including whatever amount Drake took (certainly much more than £10,000), the gems, and other precious items, it appears the total value of the treasure was in excess of £500,000 — an enormous sum for the day.

By comparison, John Hawkins, who was treasurer of the Royal Navy, was managing all of its maintenance expenses as well as extensive modifications to its ships, creating a new class of sleek, efficient war galleons, with an annual budget of under £10,000.

Contemporary historian John Stow later wrote of the government's decision not to return the treasure: "If wars ensued, which the Spaniards long threatened, then the said Treasure of itself would fully defray the charge of seven years [of] wars, prevent and save the Common Subject from taxes, loans, Privy Seals, subsidies and fifteens, and give them good advantage against a daring adversary, the which said opinion strongly prevailed."[12]

* * *

Denied an audience with the Queen, Mendoza stirred up the Spanish merchants in London to agitate for restoration of Drake's plunder to its rightful owners, and told everyone he met that his King would surely retaliate if it was not returned. The already jittery mercantile powers in the City joined the chorus, again concerned that Philip might seize their assets in Spain.

As Mendoza continued to foment unrest with dire predictions of war, Burghley and Sussex led the doves on the council in an effort to persuade Elizabeth that the treasure had to be returned. At one point Drake's backers approached Mendoza and offered him 50,000 crowns to tone down his incendiary rhetoric, but the proud Spaniard refused to be bribed. At this point, however, Mendoza's position was abruptly undermined by King Philip himself.

Residing in London as agent for the merchant guild of Seville, many of whose members had suffered losses to Drake, was a man named Pedro de Zubiaure. Somehow, Drake's backers managed to convince Zubiaure that if he obtained the necessary authority from Philip, it would be possible to obtain restitution of the parts of the treasure belonging to Spanish merchants through private negotiations. Zubiaure wrote to Philip, who fell for the ruse, and on December 16 he advised Mendoza that Zubiaure would lead the effort to recover the treasure. Thereafter Mendoza's role in the matter was largely compromised, and the increasingly tangled negotiations dragged on for years with no appreciable results.

Especially galling for Mendoza were Drake's extravagant displays at the court. The New Year was the time for gift giving, and Drake made sure that 1581 was heralded with the richest presents anyone could remember. Mendoza lamented to Philip:

> Drake is squandering more money than any man in England, and proportionately, all those who came with him are doing the same. He gave to the Queen the crown which I described in a former letter as having been made here. She wore it on New Year's Day. It has in it five emeralds, three of them almost as long as a little finger, whilst the two round ones are valued at 20,000 crowns, coming, as they do, from Peru.
>
> He has also given the Queen a diamond cross as a New Year's gift, as is the custom here, of the value of 5,000 crowns. He offered to Burghley ten bars of fine gold worth 300 crowns each, which, however, he refused, saying that he did not know how his conscience would allow him to accept a present from Drake, who had stolen all he had. He

gave to Sussex eight hundred crowns in salvers and vases, but these also were refused in the same way. The Chancellor got eight hundred crowns worth of silver plate, and all the councillors and secretaries had a share in a similar form, Leicester getting most of all.[13]

The gifts had the desired effect. Drake found himself at the center of court life, moving among people of manner and station far different from those with whom he had previously associated. The hundreds of noblemen, foreign emissaries, promoters, and schemers jostling for a word or even a nod from the Queen were obliged to adjust to the fact that she had a new star.

Drake was daily singled out by Elizabeth to accompany her on walks in the garden or to withdraw for private conversation. One day she met with him an unprecedented nine times.[14] On New Year's Day she wore the crown he had given her and announced that in the spring she would go aboard the *Golden Hinde* and knight him, and that afterward his ship would be placed on permanent display in a specially built dry dock to commemorate his great voyage.

The reaction among the milling courtiers was a potent mixture. To the projectors of an English empire and the young gentlemen eagerly awaiting a chance for adventure in Her Majesty's service, Drake was an object of profound admiration. Although they knew none of the sensitive details, they knew that Drake had circled the globe, and they surrounded him at every opportunity to hear his stories of ostriches and Indians and besting the Spaniard. Others found him too boastful, however, and more than a few men of noble birth were taken aback by his extravagance and jealous of his preferential treatment by the Queen. Drake's seemingly boundless wealth, John Stow wrote, was "so far fetched twas marvellous strange, and of all men held impossible and incredible, but both proving true, it fortuned that many misliked it and reproached him; besides all this there were others that devised and divulged all possible disgraces against Drake and his followers, terming him the Master thief of the unknown world."[15]

Chief among his detractors were the mercantile leaders of the City, whose companies had not participated in the bountiful returns of the enterprise and who were outraged that their commerce with Spain should be jeopardized for the profit of a single corsair and a few people in high places. Outside these self-interested circles, however, Drake was met with unreserved affection. "In Court, Town and Country his name and fame became admirable in all places, the people swarming daily in the streets to behold him, vowing hatred for all who durst mislike him," wrote Stow.[16]

Within weeks of his return, the news of Drake's daring voyage around the world had created a sensation across Europe. From Antwerp, geographer Abraham Ortelius wrote at once to Dr. John Dee and other contacts in England, seeking the details of the voyage. Ortelius was anxious to incorporate Drake's discoveries in the next edition of his atlas, yet try as he might, he could not find out where Drake's travels had taken him. As he explained in a letter to his colleague Gerard Mercator in late November, the responses he received from England were frustratingly vague and contradictory. On December 12 Mercator wrote back.

> [Thank you for] the dispatch about the new English voyage on which you have previously sent me a report through Rumold [his son]. . . . I am persuaded that there can be no reason for so carefully concealing the course followed during this voyage, nor for putting out differing accounts of the route taken and the areas visited, other than they may have found very wealthy regions never yet discovered by Europeans, not even by those who have sailed the Ocean on the Indies voyages.[17]

Ortelius might as well have spared himself the effort. The information remained tightly wrapped in secrecy. Books, pictures, and ballads appeared in praise of Drake, but none gave out any information about the voyage.[18] A little pamphlet published in London early in the New Year "in commemoration of the valiant and virtuous minded gentleman, Master Francis Drake, with a rejoicing of his happy adventures" was probably typical of the genre. The closest its author, Nicholas Breton, could come to providing any particulars was to applaud that "our country man hath gone round about the whole world" and found "the land where treasure lies."[19]

Behind the scenes a new enterprise had been taking shape. In November 1580 Walsingham drafted a proposal for the incorporation of a company of adventurers modeled along the lines of the Muscovy Company and providing

that in consideration of the late notable discovery made by Francis Drake of such dominions as are situated beyond the said Equinoctal

line, if it may please her Majesty, that he may during his natural life supply the place of Governor of the said company, and in consideration of
his great travail and hazard of his person, the said discoverer to have
during his said life a tenth part of the profits of such commodities as
shall be brought into this realm from the parts above remembered.[20]

Drake was proposing to establish a colony—England's first overseas colony.
Alongside his 10 percent share as lifetime governor, the Queen was to receive 20 percent of the profits. Just where Drake's "late notable discovery"
was situated Walsingham's proposal did not say, although Elizabeth was no
doubt fully conversant with the details. The proposal said only that the
country in question was not lawfully possessed by any other Christian
prince. Most likely, Walsingham was by now alerted to the fact that
Mendoza had at least one informant on the council, and the location was
not put to paper for fear he might see the document.

Enough of the details were known, however, that Walsingham's proposal upset the stockholders of the Muscovy Company. On December 16
they presented a counterpetition, requesting that Elizabeth reaffirm their
exclusive entitlement to exploit all English discoveries of new lands to the
northeast and northwest. From their subsequent involvement with the project, it appears that this problem got worked out.

On January 9, 1581, Mendoza reported that Drake was to take ten
ships via the Cape of Good Hope and rendezvous in the Moluccas with
Leicester's brother-in-law, Francis Knollys, who was to bring six more ships
via Magellan's Strait.[21] Then on the sixteenth Mendoza wrote that Drake
had not yet settled accounts with his crew but was instead keeping them at
hand with small sums while attempting to persuade them to accompany
him on the new expedition.[22] Two and a half months passed before
Mendoza could find out anything more.

On April 4, 1581, Elizabeth led a procession from the court past throngs of Londoners to the
Golden Hinde, which stood in the Thames richly decorated for the occasion. As
she stepped aboard, one of her garters slipped down her leg, and the French
ambassador, the Seigneur de Marchaumont, darted forward to retrieve it. Slip-
ping it back on, Elizabeth promised that she would send it to him as a sou-
venir. A rickety bridge had been constructed from the shore, and about 100

onlookers had crowded onto it for a better view of the proceedings when it suddenly collapsed, tumbling them into the mud below. Apart from a few broken bones, there were no serious injuries.

Elizabeth brought with her a gilded sword and, ordering Drake to kneel before her, mused aloud that she might use it to strike off his head. But then she handed it to Marchaumont and asked him to administer the ritual taps on Drake's shoulders as she proclaimed him Sir Francis Drake, knight. The ploy was perfectly conceived to signal to King Philip the potential for a new alliance between England and France. Afterward Drake hosted the most lavish banquet anyone could remember since the days of King Henry VIII.

Two days after the ceremony Mendoza finally had fresh intelligence to report to Philip: "It is decided that Drake himself shall not go, although no doubt he has arranged the matter through other hands in order that he may not be too conspicuous."[23]

If Elizabeth had allowed him, Drake would have sailed again for the Pacific. Despite his showering her with riches and promising much more, however, she had decided against his going, and he had no choice but to obey. Elizabeth had been enthralled by everything he had told her, and certainly she understood the strategic potential of his plan, but unleashing him again, she must have felt, surely would have provoked Philip to war. Moreover, she had come to the realization that Drake was the most resourceful naval commander in her service, and if war were to come, she wanted him close at hand.

"Islands of Good Land"

The summer of 1581 saw little progress on Drake's plan for the Pacific venture. Leicester was to organize the investors and ships, and although Drake would not lead the expedition, he retained a proprietary interest in the enterprise and was to serve as principal adviser.

In June, Don Antonio, the ousted pretender to the throne of Portugal, arrived in England seeking to raise a private fleet to protect the island of Terceira in the Azores, whose inhabitants were refusing to swear allegiance to King Philip. Letters of marque from the "King" of Portugal gave legitimacy to the operation, and Walsingham, Leicester, Drake, and John Hawkins saw the project as an opportunity to set up a strategically located base from which to intercept Philip's treasure fleets returning from America. Part of the force was then to continue around Africa to secure the Portuguese Indies from Philip's grasp.

By midsummer twenty-five ships were hurriedly being fitted out for the expedition. On August 14 Philip instructed Mendoza to leave no doubt in Elizabeth's council that if Don Antonio sailed against him with its help, he would regard it as a declaration of war by England. Philip then wrote directly to Elizabeth, reiterating the threat. The prospect of an all-out war with Philip backed by his newly expanded naval strength proved too much for her to contemplate, and in September the project was abandoned.

In the meantime Drake had returned to Plymouth to take up residence with Mary in their newly acquired estate, Buckland Abbey. Built as a monastery by the Cistercian monks in the thirteenth century, the property had passed into the hands of the Grenville family in 1541, following Henry VIII's dissolution of Catholic monasteries. Sir Richard Grenville had devoted several years to converting the old Abbey into a stately home for himself, but in December 1580 he had accepted from Drake's agents the sizable sum of £3,400 for the abbey and 500 acres of land surrounding it. Located just four miles from Plymouth, its parks were full of deer, and the adjoining River Tavy, draining the valley where Drake had been born, was teeming with fish.

In September 1581 it was resolved that Martin Frobisher would command the expedition to follow up on Drake's discoveries, and the preparations got under way. Leicester purchased the 400-ton *Galleon Oughtred*, renaming it the *Galleon Leicester*, and soon afterward acquired the *Edward Bonaventure*. Leicester contributed £2,200 to the venture and solicited lesser sums from Walsingham, Hatton, the Earls of Warwick, Shrewsbury, Pembroke, and Lincoln, and Lords Hunsdon, Howard, and even Burghley. Drake was the second-largest investor, contributing £666 and the 40-ton bark *Francis*, and he promised to supply some of the men who had accompanied him around the world to guide the expedition.[1]

In the interval, King Philip had launched a new fleet for South America based on the recommendations of a veteran navigator and explorer. After assisting in the pursuit of Drake northward from Peru, Pedro Sarmiento de Gamboa had sailed from Callao in October 1579 with instructions from Viceroy Toledo to make a reconnaissance of Magellan's Strait and propose to the King a method of fortifying it to prevent further incursions into his ocean. Sarmiento entered the strait from the Pacific at the end of December and spent two months examining its shores and gathering information from the Indians before carrying on to Spain to report his findings.

Sarmiento reached King Philip, newly resident in Lisbon, in August 1580 and presented him with a report detailing the forts that would be necessary, the number of men and ships required, the proper time to leave Spain, and the route to be taken. Soon afterward Mendoza's dispatches from London advised of Drake's return and began warning of his proposal for a new voyage to the Pacific, and Philip decided to act. Through the spring and summer a fleet of twenty-three ships and 3,500 men was assembled under the command of Don Diego Flores de Valdez, and in September 1581 they set sail for Magellan's Strait to occupy and fortify it against use by foreigners.

* * *

In February 1582 Mendoza reported that Frobisher's expedition was to carry thirty carpenters and thirty bricklayers, leading him to the conclusion that its aim was to set up a colony.[2] But then Frobisher suddenly resigned or was relieved of his command for unknown reasons, and his place was taken by Edward Fenton, who had been vice admiral on his last voyage to the northwest. Serving as second-in-command to Fenton was one of Drake's trusted lieutenants, William Hawkins, nephew of John Hawkins. With him came a dozen more veterans of Drake's voyage, including pilots Thomas Hood and Thomas Blacoller, and John Drake, age twenty, serving as captain of the *Francis*.

On April 2 Fenton's commission was signed by Elizabeth. The purpose of the voyage, it read, was to be "for the discovery of Cathay and China as [well as] all other lands and islands already discovered," and Fenton was authorized to leave behind "to inhabit and dwell in and upon the same land" as many of his company as he thought advisable.[3] On April 11 Leicester wrote to Fenton, instructing him that Walsingham's stepson, Christopher Carleil, who already had been given responsibility for land operations, was to be put in charge of those who were to be left at the unnamed place.[4]

In the same week Fenton received his detailed instructions. Once in the South Sea, he was not to pass to the northeast of latitude 40 degrees south—meaning that he was to steer clear of King Philip's possessions— but was instead to take "your right course to the Iles of the Moluccas for the better discovery of the Northwest Passage."[5] The Moluccas being near the equator in the western Pacific, the instruction, taken literally, would hardly have been conducive to the better discovery of the northwest passage. However, "the Moluccas" was code for a different set of islands.

On April 20 Mendoza had important new intelligence to report to Philip. There were four ships preparing to sail from Southampton, he wrote.

> From what I have heard lately from persons who have been in communication with Drake and others, and have seen the secret chart of the voyage, I infer that their course is to be different from that which they originally intended, which was to go to the Cape of Good Hope and thence start for the Moluccas. The intention is now to run down the coast of Brazil to Port St. Julian and the Strait of Magellan, which Drake discovered not to be a strait at all, and that the land which in the maps is called Tierra del Fuego is not part of a continent, but only very large islands with channels between them. . . .

[Drake] has not explained the secret to anyone but some of the Councillors and the chief of this expedition, who placed before him the danger that would be run by sending these ships whilst your Majesty had so large a fleet in the Strait of Magellan. Drake replied: So much the better, as they were thus assured that your Majesty's vessels would stay there and keep guard to prevent anyone entering the South Sea; but after all they would find themselves deceived, as . . . there was open sea beyond Tierra del Fuego.

They are so confident about it that they are fitting out other ships for a similar voyage, and it would be very desirable that wherever these ships are encountered they and every man on board of them should be sent to the bottom and these expeditions stopped, as their effrontery has reached such a pitch that the Councillors say that they will send to these islands or wherever else they think proper, to trade and conquer.[6]

Thus alerted to Drake's southern discovery, Mendoza urged that a dispatch be forwarded to the fleet Philip had sent to the Strait of Magellan, ordering them to thoroughly explore the region to the south of them. However, his informants had failed to uncover Drake's northern discovery, and Mendoza advised Philip that, as he had "so often mentioned," the English expedition was bound for the Moluccas.

Around the same time hints of a northern exploit by Drake were put to paper by two English cosmographers. Not surprisingly, one of them was Dr. John Dee, who drew a remarkable map for his friend and longtime projector of a northwest passage, Sir Humphrey Gilbert.[7] The map was a view of the world centered on the North Pole, and on it Dee depicted a broad sea passage extending from Frobisher's entrance across the top of America into the Pacific. While this was not the first map to do so, what was remarkable was that whereas the famous map of Abraham Ortelius placed the Pacific coast of North America, in longitude, 190 degrees west of England, Dee's new map placed it just 140 degrees to the west—a reduction of some 1,500 miles in the supposed distance through the passage to the Pacific.

Also in the spring of 1582, an aspiring maritime chronicler named

A polar map drawn by Dr. John Dee, ca. 1582, placed the Pacific coast of North America (upper left) only 140 degrees west of England (lower right).

Richard Hakluyt printed his first compilation of voyages to the New World. It was a subject that had captivated the young Welshman from an early age. His cousin and mentor Richard Hakluyt the elder, a lawyer and member of the Middle Temple,* was deeply interested in geography and, in association with men such as Dee and Gilbert, had long advocated overseas exploration and colonization. In 1577 the elder Hakluyt had authored a treatise setting forth the considerations involved in selecting and laying out a site for England's first colony. The younger Hakluyt was, with his book, embarking on a career that would see him become England's foremost propagandist for overseas enterprise.

*The Middle Temple was one of London's Inns of Court—institutions that offered lodgings and instruction in a variety of disciplines to young courtiers.

Hakluyt's survey of voyages, titled *Diverse Voyages to America and the islands adjacent*, focused exclusively on North America. In his introduction, Hakluyt revealed that he had discussed with Drake a proposal to establish a program of lectures on the art of navigation and had obtained from him a promise of financial assistance. In his list of "names of certain late travellers" for the year 1578, Hakluyt placed "Francis Drake Englishman" and noted his discoveries "on the back side of America" as encouraging the hope of finding a northwest passage.[8]

Hakluyt also inserted into his book a map by Frobisher's former partner, Michael Lok, depicting the relationship of England to the Pacific coast of America in a different manner than that of Dee. On his map Lok cut northwest America off above California, leaving a vast inland sea between Frobisher's strait and the Pacific Ocean. On the Pacific coast he depicted a ship sailing into this sea at latitude 48 degrees, beyond a range of mountains labeled "Sierra Nevada," and above this he inscribed "Anglorum 1580." The clear inference was that both ends of the northwest passage had been reconnoitered by the English. And Lok's map did have one thing in common with Dee's: Again the Pacific coast of America was placed, in longitude, just 140 degrees west of England.

It seems that the subject of longitude was also of interest to some of the men who were preparing to embark with Fenton's expedition. The master of the *Galleon Leicester*, Christopher Hall, had been chief pilot on Frobisher's arctic voyages and had received instruction in mathematical navigation from Dee. Fenton's chaplain, appointed by the Earl of Leicester, was Richard Madox, a graduate of Oxford University. Madox kept a personal diary, much of it in cipher. In this, he made numerous entries and diagrams explaining such phenomena as the tides and light refraction, demonstrating a sophisticated knowledge of navigation and astronomy. On March 10, during the preparations for the voyage, he wrote a long entry explaining the lunar distance method of determining longitude, much as William Bourne had done in his *Regiment for the Sea*, published in 1574. Elsewhere Madox noted that he was carrying on the voyage a book of ephemerides and "a very precise instrument"—the two aids that Bourne cited as being essential for applying the method.[9]

Later, during the voyage, Madox evidently talked with Drake's men

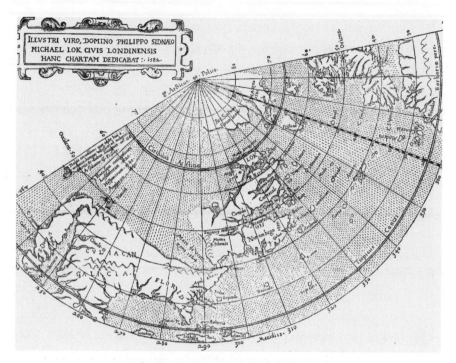

*Michael Lok's 1582 map also placed the Pacific coast
of America just 140 degrees west of England.*

about their South Sea exploits, as he noted in his diary that Drake had careened his ship "at 48 degrees to the north," on "the back side of Labrador,
and as Master [Christopher] Hall supposeth, nye thereunto."[10] The entry is
noteworthy not only as the earliest surviving mention of a latitude for
Drake on the northwest coast of America but also as an indication of confidence in the longitude of that coast, inferring that it was not as far west as
had previously been supposed.

Fenton's expedition finally sailed from Southampton on May 1, 1582. They were not long at
sea, however, before Drake's men began quarreling with Fenton, as it soon
became apparent that he was not at all enthusiastic about the long voyage to
the South Sea. The island of St. Helena in the South Atlantic was a way station for the great Portuguese carracks coming and going via the Cape of
Good Hope, and Fenton proposed instead to take over the island, seize some
ships, and send their cargoes to England. After the squadron became stalled

for a month on the coast of Guinea, however, his officers persuaded him to adhere to their instructions for the voyage, and they set sail for South America.

By the time they reached the coast of Brazil, it was the end of November. Continuing down the coast, they were within 300 miles of the Río de la Plata on December 19 when Fenton suddenly called his officers together to consider whether they should proceed farther. He was worried about encountering the Spanish fleet and argued that in any case they should return northward to the Portuguese settlement of São Vicente to obtain more provisions. The majority of Fenton's officers were for continuing the voyage, but during the next two days he persuaded several of them to change their minds, and on December 21 all but Drake's men agreed to turn back. Infuriated by the decision, John Drake deserted the expedition in the *Francis* the following night.

Returning north, Fenton reached São Vicente a month later. Shortly after their arrival three ships of the Spanish fleet entered the bay and commenced to attack them. The powerful guns of the *Galleon Leicester* promptly sank one of them and Fenton made good his escape, but he had no stomach for more and set his course homeward.

In the meantime John Drake stubbornly continued southward in the *Francis*. What he hoped to achieve with only seventeen men and a few provisions is unclear. Whatever his motivation, the decision soon led to disaster. When they reached the Río de la Plata, they sailed some distance up the river, as Francis Drake had done, in order to forage for food and refill their water casks. As they attempted to enter a smaller estuary, the ship was caught in the current and wrecked on some rocks. Scrambling ashore with only their clothes and a few weapons, they were soon captured and enslaved by the Indians.

One by one, the men died of wounds and sickness until finally, after thirteen months of privation, John Drake and two others managed to steal a canoe and escape across the river. On the south shore they met some Spaniards and were taken to the new settlement of Buenos Aires. Fearful of the consequences of revealing his identity, Drake assumed an alias. By coincidence, however, a man whom he had met aboard a vessel intercepted by Fenton on the coast of Brazil arrived three weeks later and immediately recognized him. Informed that he was the "nephew" of the infamous English corsair el Draque, the Spaniards took Drake and his companions inland to the colonial center of Sante Fe for questioning.

On March 24, 1584, John Drake was brought before a panel of Inquisition judges and interrogated for several hours about Francis Drake and their voyage around the world. Questioned where they had gone after departing New Spain, he answered (as recorded by the court scribe):

> He does not know what day they left Guatulco, only that it was in April and they went to seaward. They sailed continually to the north-west and north-north east. They travelled for the whole of April and May, until the middle of June. From the said Guatulco, which is in 15 degrees, they went to 48 degrees north. They met with great storms along the way. The whole sky was dark and full of mist. Along the route they saw five or six islands. Captain Francis gave one of them the name Saint Bartholomew and another one Saint James. These islands were in 46 and 48 degrees. To the land in 48 degrees Captain Francis gave the name New England. They remained there a month and a half, taking on water and wood and repairing their ship. . . . On account of the great cold they did not go further north than 48 degrees, and from the said New England they navigated to the southwest [across the Pacific][11]

When this deposition was forwarded to Lima, the Viceroy ordered that Drake be sent to him for further interrogation. A dispute then arose between the Viceroy and the Chief Inquisitor over which of them would have charge of him, and the matter was referred to King Philip for a decision.

For a year Drake and his companions languished in a hermitage, where they were permitted to speak only to the hermit and to an Englishman who had been in the country for forty years and had forgotten his native tongue. Finally, in the spring of 1586 the Viceroy sent for Drake, and he was taken on the long trek across the Andes and then carried by ship northward to Lima. There, in five sessions on January 8, 9, and 10, 1587, he was interrogated by the Inquisition once more. Questioned again about Francis Drake's northern voyage, he said:

> [From Guatulco] they left and sailed, always on a wind, in a north-west and north-northeasterly direction, for a thousand leagues [3,000

miles] until they reached forty-four degrees, when the wind changed and he went to the Californias, where he discovered land in forty-eight degrees. There he landed and built huts and remained for a month and a half caulking his vessel. The victuals they found were mussels and sealions.

During that time many Indians came there and when they saw the Englishmen they wept and scratched their faces with their nails until they drew blood, as though this were an act of homage or adoration. By signs Captain Francis told them not to do that, for the Englishmen were not God. These people were peaceful and did no harm to the English, but gave them no food. They are of the colour of the Indians here [Peru] and are comely. They carry bows and arrows and go naked.

The climate is temperate, more cold than hot. To all appearance it is a very good country. Here he caulked his large ship and left the ship he had taken in Nicaragua. He departed, leaving the Indians, to all appearance, sad. From here he went alone with the said ship [*Golden Hinde*], taking the route to the Moluccas.[12]

Besides querying again how far north Drake had gone, it appears the judges were particularly interested to know what became of the bark that he had seized from Rodrigo Tello on the coast of Nicaragua, which John Drake said they abandoned when they left northwest America for the Moluccas. Curiously, however, this transcript of John Drake's testimony at Lima omitted any mention of the islands previously described by him, or of New England. Nor did either of his surviving depositions mention the search for the northern passage alleged by Nuño da Silva in his testimony to the Inquisition in Mexico City in 1579.

In 1606 Spanish historian Antonio de Herrera published an account of Drake's voyage that was based on John Drake's testimony, but in this it appears that he must have had the use of another transcript that contained some additional information, as he wrote that after departing Guatulco, Drake sailed "with the purpose of seeking the strait which has been referred to," and "on this journey, saw five or six islands of good land. He called one Saint Bartholomew, one Saint James, and another which seemed to be the largest and the best, Nova Albion [New England]. Here he remained a month and a half, repairing the two ships which he had with him."[13]

Thus, it appears that John Drake must have been examined further at Lima and admitted the search for the northern passage and that they had repaired Tello's bark as well as the *Golden Hinde*. Here also was corroboration that Francis Drake's proposal for a colony was a direct outgrowth of his search for the northern passage, and that he gave the name New England to the largest and best of five or six islands "of good land," no doubt meaning islands of a size and character suitable for colonization.

"Seen and Corrected by Sir Drake"

*I*n the fall of 1582, as Fenton's ill-fated expedition was making its way southward in the Atlantic, the Privy Council drafted instructions for a
second expedition to the South Sea. Its objective was to seize the Moluccas
from Portugal and then probably to link up with Fenton. Five ships, two of
them owned by Drake, were fitted out, and in late November the expedition
sailed with sixty-three-year-old William Hawkins serving as Captain-
General. When they reached the Cape Verdes, however, they were attacked
by the Portuguese, and Hawkins lost a number of men, causing him to divert the expedition to the Caribbean, from whence he eventually returned
with a mysterious cargo of treasure, which Mendoza was sure he had seized
from a Spanish ship.

As the months passed, Drake divided his time between London and
Plymouth. In the class structure of the day ownership of land was the
foundation of power and privilege, and he soon acquired an impressive
array of holdings. In consideration for his services as a knight, Elizabeth
granted him title to the manor of Sherford, a former monastery near
Plymouth, and other manors and tracts of land in Dorset, Buckingham-
shire, Northamptonshire, and Yorkshire. In addition, he purchased the
manors of Yarcombe and Sampford Spiney in Devonshire. Then in October 1582 an investment of £1,500 made him the second-largest private
landowner (after the Hawkins family) in the town of Plymouth. The trans-
action brought him twenty-nine houses, some of which contained shops
and taverns, as well as a bake house, four gardens, two stables, and several
warehouses.[1]

In January 1583 Drake suffered a personal tragedy with the death of his wife, Mary. The cause of her death is not recorded. All that is known of Mary's last days is her burial on January 25, 1583, which is recorded in the register of St. Budeaux Church, where they had been wed fourteen years past. They probably had spent, in all, less than half of that time together, and the marriage was childless. To hold on to her memory, Drake took Mary's nephew Jonas Bodenham under his tutelage and assisted him generously through the remainder of his life.[2]

On May 29 the *Edward Bonaventure* reached Plymouth with news of the disintegration of Fenton's expedition and another personal blow for Drake. Coming so soon after Mary's death, the disappearance of young John Drake, whom he had treated like a son, must have been deeply disheartening. The lad's progress from pageboy to painter, seaman, and then captain of his first bark had been carefully managed by Drake to prepare him for a bright career. He had even presented him at the court. For many months Drake remained hopeful that he would return, but to no avail.*

Fenton arrived off Dover in the *Galleon Leicester* at the end of June 1583. He had placed the younger William Hawkins in irons following a violent argument in which Hawkins told him that he would have to answer to Drake for his actions. On July 6 Hawkins gave a deposition relating his version of the events and accused Fenton of having sold the expedition out to the Spanish ambassador before they left England. Soon afterward the Queen ordered Fenton arrested and imprisoned for failing to continue the voyage.

Not long after Fenton's return Drake began promoting a new expedition to the South Sea, and probably it was to further this cause that he began to present hand-drawn maps depicting his voyage to important people.

The earliest such map to survive is a print of the world map of Abraham Ortelius, on which Drake's route was drawn by hand with pen and ink. The manuscript additions to the map included, in cruder form, two of the features that later became common to all of Drake's commem-

---

*In 1587 it was learned from the pilot of a Portuguese ship that John Drake was alive and well in Peru, but had been sentenced to a lifetime of captivity. He never returned to England.

orative maps. Along with his route, two ships were drawn adjacent to Patagonia, representing the vessels that Drake had abandoned there. On subsequent maps the concept was enhanced by also depicting the number of vessels that remained, which eventually diminished to one as Drake's track continued into the Pacific. Below the extremity of South America a note was added about his discovery of the islands south of Magellan's strait. This note also was expanded on the subsequent maps. But what was most significant was Drake's track into the North Pacific, which continued northward past Ortelius's imaginary bulging coast all the way to latitude 57 degrees north—which, in reality, would have placed him well into the waters of southern Alaska. It appears, therefore, that this manuscript rendering of Drake's route was a precursor to his more elaborate maps, most probably drawn for an important person soon after Drake's return in 1580.[3]

The idea of producing a proper commemorative map of Drake's voyage may have resulted from his meeting a talented new immigrant to London. Jodocus Hondt, a native of Ghent in Flanders, had from an early age displayed an exceptional gift for drawing and calligraphy. Nurturing his potential, his architect father broadened his studies to include mathematics, Latin, and Greek, and arranged for him to apprentice as an engraver. However, the capture of Ghent by the Duke of Parma placed the Protestant Hondt family in jeopardy, and in 1583 twenty-year-old Jodocus and his sister Jacomina fled to England, where he latinized his surname by changing it to Hondius. In London Hondius set up as an engraver and illustrator, and it appears soon afterward he met Drake. It was the beginning of a decadelong relationship in which he produced many maps for Drake.[4]

In order to depict his voyage for persons outside the immediate circle who were privy to the details, it appears Drake had to consult Walsingham, who was still enforcing the official secrecy surrounding the subject, as it is very clear from close examination of the maps that some rules were adopted governing what could be revealed. Since the maps concerned her dominions, it is possible the Queen was also involved in the deliberations.

Chief among the rules was that there could be no hint of a northwest passage, and Nova Albion was to be placed, in latitude, ten degrees (600 miles) south of its true position. No doubt the reason was to guard against the possibility that one of Mendoza's informants might see one of the maps

An early depiction of Drake's voyage drawn on a print of Ortelius's world map showed him reaching latitude 57 degrees.

and realize Nova Albion's strategic relationship to the possibility of a northern passage around America. As a result of these and other strictures, on each map the depiction of Drake's route and Nova Albion formed a cryptograph—a carefully conceived representation that was fully intelligible only to those who knew the rules designed to conceal the true location of his northern discoveries.[5]

It is recorded that Drake presented one of his maps, described as "richly decorated with coloured and gilded designs," to the Archbishop of Canterbury, though it has unfortunately been lost.[6] However, a surviving manuscript map drawn with pen, ink, and watercolor on vellum almost certainly was another in the series.[7] In the upper-left corner of the map its title, in Latin, reads:

A true description of the naval expedition of Francis Drake, Englishman and Knight, who with five ships departed from the western part of England on 13 December 1577, circumnavigated the globe and returned on 26 September 1580 with one ship remaining, the others having been destroyed by waves or fire.[8]

This and the scenes in the lower corners of the map, which depict events that occurred on the voyage, make clear that its original purpose was

The Drake Mellon map, ca. 1584, is an example of the hand-drawn maps Drake gave out privately to commemorate his voyage around the world (the route of his 1585–86 Caribbean expedition was added later).

solely to commemorate Drake's voyage around the world. The scene in the lower-left corner shows the *Golden Hinde* being towed into Ternate by Sultan Babu's *caracoas*, and the one at the lower right depicts his ship aground on the reef near Celebes. Then sometime later the route of Drake's 1585–86 Caribbean expedition was added to the map along with the flag and inscription marking the founding of Virginia, and probably also the bound-

ary separating North America from New Spain.* As these additions were likely made soon after Drake's return from the Caribbean, it appears the map was drawn in its original state sometime before he sailed on that voyage in September 1585, and possibly as early as 1583 or 1584. Indeed, it may have been Hondius's prototype.

*This is one of the two earliest known maps to depict a boundary line separating North America from New Spain, thereby marking the conception of a British North America. The other is the so-called French Drake map, which is reproduced later in this chapter.

The cryptograph of Drake's northern voyage on the Drake Mellon map placed Nova Albion at latitude 40 degrees, behind a peninsula where he made his initial landfall.

On the map, Ortelius's great westward bulge in northwest America was eliminated, but the continent was still excessively broad; except for a flag and a small opening denoting the entrance to Frobisher's strait, there was no suggestion of a northwest passage. In the Pacific, Drake's track continued northward to a landfall at precisely latitude 40 degrees on the northwest coast of America before heading southwest across the Pacific. His landfall was depicted as being on the outer coast of a southward-pointing peninsula. Nearby, an English flag was planted, again at 40 degrees, but at the head of the inlet behind the peninsula, and an inscription explained that Drake discovered this place and named it Nova Albion in the year 1579.

If Drake had hopes of an early commitment from the Queen to a new South Sea expedition, he was to be disappointed. Amid increasing signs of aggressive intent on King Philip's part, Elizabeth was preoccupied in using every device at her disposal to forestall open hostilities. To counter the growing menace from Spain, she had reopened negotiations to marry the Duke of Anjou, brother of King

Henry III of France, and form a new alliance with the French.

In November 1583, Walsingham uncovered efforts by Ambassador Mendoza to organize an uprising of English Catholics in support of an invasion of England that would have replaced Elizabeth with her cousin Mary Stuart and returned the country to Catholicism. In January 1584, armed with compelling evidence against him, Elizabeth expelled Mendoza from England. However, the situation continued to deteriorate.

In June 1584 Elizabeth's continuing hopes for a strategic marriage were dashed when the Duke of Anjou suddenly died of a fever. The following month brought more bad news: William of Orange, the leader of the Dutch liberation forces, had been killed by an assassin's bullet. Resistance to the Duke of Parma's army of occupation was severely shaken, and it was feared that it might collapse altogether and leave England standing alone against Spain.

In July Leicester and Walsingham persuaded Elizabeth that she had to put on a show of force, and Drake's project, which undoubtedly had been under discussion for months, finally received her approval. On July 19 she agreed to invest £17,000 toward equipping Drake's proposed expedition to "the Moluccas." By November the plan called for eleven ships, four barks, twenty pinnaces, and 1,600 men.[9] Undoubtedly this was the same scheme Drake had proposed in 1580, and once again his aim was to halt the flow of Peruvian silver with which Philip was financing his military adventures in Europe. Probably, he was intent on sacking Lima and Panama City before continuing north to complete the discovery of the northwest passage. Then, with a fleet resupplied via the passage and based at Nova Albion, he could have continued to interdict Philip's South Sea commerce until he came to terms.

Elizabeth signed Drake's commission for the new South Sea expedition on Christmas Eve 1584.[10] Soon afterward, though, it became apparent that she had changed her mind. Most probably, she felt uneasy about Drake taking so many ships and experienced men away to the Pacific when she feared a Spanish invasion fleet might soon appear off England's shores. She likely already had these concerns when she signed Drake's commission, but it was in her nature to approach problems in this manner, for she had a way of shaping men's ambitions to her purpose by degrees. Thus, once Drake had begun assembling his fleet, his objective was changed to the Caribbean.

No doubt Elizabeth's reasoning was that Drake could sail at the end of the summer, sack Philip's Caribbean possessions and possibly even seize his gold fleet, yet still be home in time to help defend against any invasion attempt the following summer. Eager for action, Drake embraced the plan, although he must have been disappointed that he was unable to prosecute his grand scheme for the South Sea.

In the meantime, at the beginning of 1585 Drake married again. His bride, Elizabeth Sydenham, was in her early twenties and by accounts a beautiful and virtuous lady. Her father, Sir George Sydenham, was a sometime sheriff of Somerset, and her mother's father had served as attorney general to Henry VIII. Elizabeth stood to inherit extensive landholdings in her own right. Nevertheless, in the marriage agreement, signed February 9, 1585, Drake—obviously taken with her—granted his manors of Yarcombe, Sherford, and Sampford Spiney as well as Buckland Abbey to Elizabeth and their heirs in perpetuity.[11]

While Drake was assembling his fleet, Walsingham was scrambling to round up allies for the coming fight with Spain. Still of the greatest importance was the posture France would adopt in the conflict. Working in Paris, ostensibly as secretary to English ambassador Sir Edward Stafford, but also gathering intelligence about French and Spanish activities in the New World for Walsingham, was the younger Richard Hakluyt. There Hakluyt found much curiosity and speculation about Drake's great voyage. On October 16, 1584, Ambassador Stafford had written to Walsingham: "I find from Mr. Hakluyt that Drake's journey is kept very secret in England, but here is in everyone's mouth. When questioned about it, I have answered as an ignorant body, as indeed I am, except for what I find by their speeches here. It may [be] they hit not all right, but they guess in great part."[12]

In March 1585, perhaps coincidentally but conveniently so, Walsingham received a letter from Henry of Navarre, the next in line to the throne of France, and notably a Protestant, requesting the chart and a "discourse" of Drake's voyage.[13] Henry's request could not have been more fortuitous, as it gave Walsingham the opportunity to open a dialogue with the future king around the possibility of an alliance. It is therefore possible that

The altered latitude of Drake's northern reach in the Anonymous Narrative. The writer originally noted 50 degrees, then changed this to 53 degrees, and finally to 48 degrees.

Walsingham had Stafford plant the idea of Henry making the request in order to provide this opening.

In any case, receipt of a map "many coloured and gilded" was soon acknowledged by Henry, and with it presumably he received the discourse of Drake's voyage he had requested, because later in the year an account of the voyage was also sent to another Protestant prince, William of Hesse.[14] No doubt the intended message was the same: If the Protestant princes of Europe were prepared to join the fight against Spain, England had the man who would lead them to victory on any sea. Thus, it was no longer a question of no details of Drake's voyage being given out, but rather what information would be provided and to whom.

Neither the account sent to Henry of Navarre nor the one subsequently given to William of Hesse has survived. However, the early manuscript account known as the "Anonymous Narrative" may have been the first draft of both. Titled "A discourse of Sir Francis Drake's journey and exploits . . . into Mare de Sur," it appears to have been adapted from a deposition taken from one of Drake's company shortly after their return.[15] In the narrative, Drake's northern exploit in particular was carefully abridged.

After devoting some 2,000 words to Drake's voyage from southern Chile to Guatulco, the manuscript offered fewer than 200 words about his journey from Guatulco to northwest America and then on to the Moluccas. But what was most significant was that when he came to state the northern limit of Drake's travels, the writer changed the latitude twice.[16] First he wrote 50 degrees north, and then he changed this to 53 degrees, and finally he altered it a second time, to 48 degrees—the latitude previously given by Fenton's chaplain Madox and John Drake as the northern limit of Drake's explorations.

Evidently, while adapting his narrative from the original document, the writer had been noting Drake's progress northward when he remembered that 48 degrees was the official cutoff point for information about the voyage.[17] This was as far as anyone was allowed to say that Drake had gone. Moreover, the narrative made no mention of the islands John Drake spoke of in his deposition, or of Nova Albion, and said that after turning back, Drake followed the coast southward until he found a harbor at latitude 44 degrees, where he careened his ship before setting sail across the Pacific.

Elizabeth's hope of avoiding hostilities with Spain reached a new low in June 1585 when word came that Philip had ordered all English merchant shipping in Spanish ports arrested and stripped of everything useful to equip his fleets at Seville and Lisbon. Drake's commission and letters of reprisal were signed on July 1, and on September 14 he put to sea with twenty-five ships, eight pinnaces, and 2,300 men. What followed seemed to the Spaniards like a whirlwind of fear and destruction.

Two weeks later Drake brazenly sailed into the northern Spanish port of Vigo, demanding to know whether Spain was at war with England and why King Philip had impounded English ships. Confronted by Drake's formidable fleet, the Spanish governor denied knowing anything about a war and quickly undertook to release the English merchantmen and supply whatever provisions he needed.

After threatening the Spanish coast for three weeks and narrowly missing a returning treasure fleet, Drake made for the Cape Verde Islands. At first sight of the English fleet, the inhabitants of the island of Santiago fled into the mountains, and when they refused to pay a ransom to recover their towns, Drake ordered them put to the torch. Then he set sail for the Caribbean. Drake reached the island of Hispaniola* on December 29, and on New

---

*Now Haiti and the Dominican Republic.

Year's Day he captured the city of Santo Domingo, the oldest Spanish settlement in the New World. The governor made the mistake of trying to drag
out the negotiations for a ransom, and before it was paid one-third of the
city's buildings had been systematically destroyed by Drake's men.[18]

Next Drake headed south across the Caribbean to Cartagena, sailing
boldly into its outer harbor on February 9. That night he landed 1,000
men and, although outnumbered by the defenders, including 400 Indians
armed with poison-tipped arrows, they captured the city the following day.
As usual, Drake treated his Spanish captives with the utmost courtesy.
When he learned that the wife of the governor was gravely ill, Drake
granted him leave to be at her side; and when she subsequently died, Drake
attended her funeral. Again the Spaniards were slow to come to terms, however, and by the time a ransom of 107,000 ducats was agreed upon in early
March, Drake's men had already demolished or burned 248 of the city's
buildings.[19]

There had been some prior thought of leaving an occupying force at
Cartagena, but during the Atlantic crossing an outbreak of disease had
killed upwards of 300 men—more than the number lost in battle—and the
pestilence returned at Cartegena, killing or incapacitating hundreds more.
With only 700 men fit for service and the appointed time for his return to
England looming, Drake departed Cartagena in mid-April. Returning
homeward through the Yucatán Channel and Florida Strait, he stopped
briefly on the coast of Cuba for water and joined his sailors in the labor,
"into the water to his armpits, fully clothed and shod, carrying barrels and
demijohns of water."[20]

Skirting the coast of Florida, the fleet arrived at the Spanish settlement
of St. Augustine on May 27. The previous summer, before Drake left
England, an expedition sponsored by Sir Walter Raleigh and commanded
by Sir Richard Grenville had sailed from Plymouth to set up the new colony
of Virginia at Roanoke Island, off what is now North Carolina. Drake regarded the Spanish presence in Florida as a threat to Raleigh's fledgling
colony and proceeded to raze the fort and town of St. Augustine while the
Spaniards sniped at his men from the surrounding woods.

On June 9 they arrived at Roanoke and found the colonists in poor circumstances. They had not planted any crops, instead depending on the
Indians for food, and Grenville had failed to return at Easter with more pro-

visions as promised. After conferring with Drake, they decided to abandon the settlement and return with him to England.

By the time Drake reached Portsmouth on July 27, 1586, the news of his sacking of Santo Domingo and Cartagena, carried home by fast dispatch boats, had already begun rippling through Europe. Once again he had laid bare, for all to see, the weakness of Philip's colonial defenses. In Spain, national morale plummeted. Rumors that Philip would soon be bankrupt led to a financial panic, and the bank of Seville was forced to close its doors. In Rome the Pope's dismay was tinged with grudging admiration for Drake's audacity. "God only knows what he may succeed in doing," he exclaimed.[21] In England church bells pealed at the news of Drake's latest triumph over the King of Spain, and across Protestant Europe he was proclaimed the greatest naval genius of the age. A foreign visitor to Elizabeth's court shortly after Drake's return wrote:

> The whole Court . . . is resounding with praise for Drake; and although mine is more modest, I of course believe in the truth of what I have reported about him. I have met him, and if I am any judge of a man's character he seems destined by the Good Lord to achieve great things: perceptive and intelligent by nature, his practical abilities astonishing, his memory acute, his skill in managing a fleet virtually unique, his general manner moderate and restrained, so that individuals are won over and gripped by affection for him. He easily evokes obedience from soldiers and sailors, and consequently if he is compelled to be severe, such is the fairness with which he acts that all resentment or even hatred soon dies away. I say nothing about his magnanimity; and about his learning, experience and technique in navigation, which events themselves have made abundantly clear.[22]

Allowing that he had been absent for less than a year, Drake must have been surprised to hear upon his return that a new expedition had departed for the Pacific under the command of Thomas Cavendish just a few days prior. Indeed, considering that everyone knew Drake was due to arrive very shortly, and that he undoubtedly would have liked to be consulted regarding the plan of the expedition, Cavendish seems to have departed in almost unseemly haste, as though he wished to avoid meeting with Drake. Very possibly, he was under instructions to do so.

No doubt because of the continued secrecy surrounding the South Sea project, little is known about the planning of Cavendish's voyage. When Drake sailed for the Caribbean the previous September, Cavendish was at sea as a member of Grenville's expedition to found Virginia. It seems doubtful that Drake knew him as more than a passing acquaintance.

Just twenty-six years of age, Cavendish had been educated at Cambridge and the Inns of Court, and he was related to many of the prominent men at the court. Leicester had been at the head of an army in the Netherlands since December, and in his absence Lord Hunsdon, the Queen's favorite cousin, appears to have had a hand in recruiting Cavendish's backers, who would of course have included Elizabeth.

If he had not already been told prior to his departure in 1585, Drake must have realized on his return that Elizabeth had no intention of allowing him to embark on another long voyage to the South Sea while there was any threat of a Spanish invasion of England. She could spare a young adventurer like Cavendish, but not the one man whom the King of Spain feared most. Drake's attentions were to remain focused on strategies and actions to distract Philip from his grand design, and this was a challenge he took up energetically.

By September Drake was busy with a new scheme to help Don Antonio liberate the Azores. The Queen agreed to support the project if the Dutch would share the expense, and so on October 14, 1586, Drake sailed for Rotterdam carrying reinforcements and money for Leicester's brigade and a proposal for the creation of a combined Dutch and English fleet. After visiting with Leicester and meeting representatives of the Dutch Estates General, Drake returned to London in mid-November with offers from Holland and Zeeland to contribute to the project.

It appears that during his visit to the Netherlands or shortly after his return, Drake met someone who was deeply interested in his South Sea voyage and showed him a familiar map.[23] The map was a rough copy of one of the commemorative maps that Jodocus Hondius had produced for Drake—undoubtedly the one

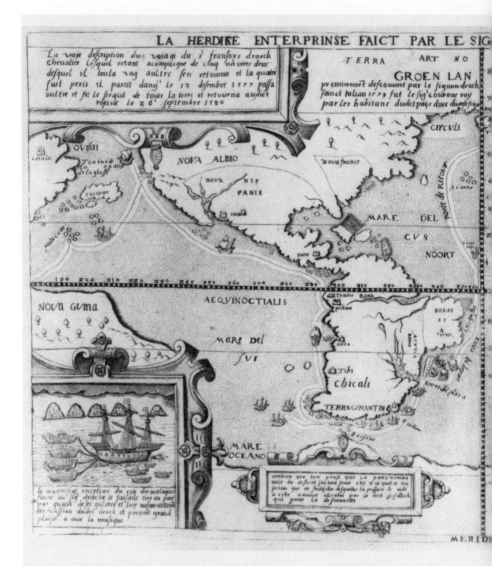

The French Drake map depicts Drake's landing, again placed at latitude 40 degrees, as an island. In the bottom margin a note states in French "carte vouee et corige par le dict siegneur drack" (map seen and corrected by the aforementioned Sir Drake).

Walsingham had sent to Henry of Navarre.[24] On the original, Drake had made a significant alteration to the cryptograph of his northern voyage. From Central America his track continued northward past four coastal islands to latitude 48 degrees, where an inscription in French read "turned

back because of the ice." Then it returned southward to a stopping place at precisely latitude 40 degrees, on the second-to-last island, before heading across the Pacific.

Thus, the southward-pointing peninsula that Drake's previous maps had depicted as his stopping place had become an island, one of a chain of four stretching, according to the scale of the map, some 500 miles along the northwest coast of America, recalling the testimony of John Drake to the Inquisition at Lima. Drake must, therefore, have planted his

The cryptograph on the French copy of Drake's map (left) showed him stopping at the smallest of four islands. On the subsequent Dutch edition of his map, the island where Drake stopped was redrawn to become the largest in the chain.

flag not at the head of an inlet but on the back side of this island, on the shores of the strait separating it from the mainland; except, where John Drake testified that they had given the name Nova Albion to "the largest and best" of the islands, Drake's revised cryptograph showed him stopping at the smallest in the chain.

After discussing his copy of the map with Drake, the visitor wrote along its bottom margin in French "map seen and corrected by the aforesaid Sir Drake." A year later, a finished rendition of the map with the inscriptions changed to Dutch was printed in the Netherlands and inserted, somewhat incongruously, in a book about Drake's 1585–86 Caribbean expedition.[25] However, in this finished version, now known as the Dutch Drake map, there were two significant changes from the rough copy of Drake's original map. One was the introduction of a broad sea passage reaching across the top of America, implying a junction with the Pacific somewhere beneath the scrollwork in the upper-left corner of the map. The second change was more subtle: In Drake's cryptograph, the island where his track stopped after he "turned back on account of the ice" had been carefully redrawn to become the largest of the four.[26]

The identity of the person who obtained these corrections from Drake has never been determined. Not long after his visit to the Netherlands, however, Drake set Jodocus Hondius to work adding some information to Abraham Ortelius's popular atlas maps of the world and America, and in 1587 Ortelius had new editions of these maps engraved to incorporate

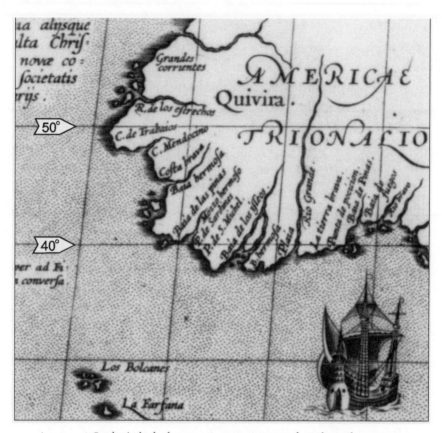

A section of Ortelius's third atlas map copying information about the northwest coast of America exactly as supplied by Drake.

Drake's information. It appears that the visitor who showed Drake his copy of Henry of Navarre's map may have been an associate of Ortelius, and that after correcting that map, Drake had agreed to supply more information by way of revisions to Ortelius's atlas maps.[27]

In the revisions, Hondius retained Ortelius's westward-bulging coastline in northwest America but added new information to it. On Ortelius's world map he added Drake's chain of coastal islands, but about ten degrees higher in latitude than they appeared on Henry of Navarre's map. Farther north, near latitude 57 degrees, Hondius added a "River of the straits." Then far to the south, at precisely 40 degrees—the same latitude where Drake had placed Nova Albion on his private commemorative maps pursuant to the ten-degree rule—Hondius placed an island and noted a "Bay of small ships." On Ortelius's map of America he added "strong currents" at latitude 54 degrees, another "River of the straits" at 49 degrees, a "Cape of worries" at 48 degrees, and farther down the coast, a "great river."[28]

There was not sufficient space on the two maps for all the information that Drake wished to include, however, so he subsequently had Hondius create a third, entirely new map for Ortelius containing still more details.[29] Altogether, on the three maps Drake named more than twenty distinct places—capes, rivers, and bays—along the northwest coast of America, albeit arrayed along Ortelius's imaginary coastline. Whether he had any sort of official approval to give these particulars out, much less publish them in the famous atlas of Abraham Ortelius, seems highly doubtful. No such information had so far been allowed to be published in England, and all of the place-names were given to Ortelius in Spanish, probably to disguise the fact that they were leaked to him by an English source.[30]

Early in 1587 Drake's plan to assist Don Antonio was dropped in favor of more urgent action. Intelligence from Lisbon indicated that Philip's Admiral of the Ocean Sea, the Marquis of Santa Cruz, was assembling his grand Armada in earnest with a view to launching the long-feared invasion of England later that year.

On March 15 Drake's new commission was signed. His instructions were to impede the flow of ships and supplies to Santa Cruz and to distress the enemy fleet within its own harbors if possible. As with his Caribbean expedition, the mobilization was organized by way of a joint-stock company, and as an inducement for the London merchants to invest, Drake was expected to intercept treasure ships returning from the West and East Indies. If he discovered that the Armada had already sailed, he was to cut off as many of its ships as he could to prevent them from reaching England.

By the end of the month twenty-four ships and 3,000 men were assembled at Plymouth, and on April 2 Drake wrote to Walsingham: "The wind commands us away. Our ship is under sail. God grant we may live in His fear as the enemy may have cause to say that God doth fight for Her Majesty as well abroad as at home."[31]

What followed was Drake's most brilliant raid. When he arrived off Cadiz on April 19, part of his fleet was trailing well behind, but Drake

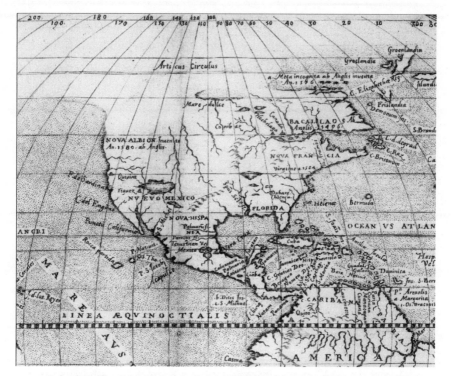

Richard Hakluyt's 1587 map of the New World placed Nova Albion at latitude 50 degrees and depicted the trend of the coast to the north with remarkable accuracy.

headed straight into the harbor. After a brisk fight he sank a 1,000-ton Genoese ship and then began stripping others of their cargoes and burning them. By the time the remainder of his fleet arrived the following day, Drake had already led a flotilla of boarding parties into the inner harbor, setting ablaze a 1,500-ton warship belonging to Santa Cruz himself and dozens of merchantmen carrying supplies and provisions for the Armada. Some 6,000 Spaniards rushed to the defense of Cadiz but could only watch in dismay. "With the pitch and tar they had, smoke and flames rose up so that it seemed like a huge volcano, or something out of hell," one lamented.[32]

In two days at Cadiz Drake sank or brought away thirty-eight ships. Next he positioned his fleet off Cape St. Vincent, at Portugal's southwest tip, seizing forty-seven merchantmen laden with supplies for the Armada and destroying two forts that guarded the coast. From Madrid, the Venetian ambassador wrote, "The English are masters of the sea, and hold it at their discretion. Lisbon and the whole coast is, as it were, blockaded."[33]

Then, as swiftly as he had appeared, Drake was gone again. On June 8 he reached the Azores, and the following day he overtook and captured a huge Portuguese carrack, the *San Felipe*, reputably among the greatest in the East Indies fleet. She was carrying 659 passengers and a huge cargo of spices, silk, jewels, china, ebony, and indigo as well as gold and silver. Drake reached Plymouth with the great prize on June 26. Fearing just such a loss, Santa Cruz was forced to put to sea with as much of his fleet as was ready and spend the summer patrolling the Azores to protect the homecoming Indies fleets rather than prosecuting the invasion of England.

Richard Hakluyt was still residing in Paris, although he returned to London at frequent intervals carrying secret dispatches to Walsingham.[34] In April 1587, as Drake was assaulting Cadiz, he printed in Paris a new edition of Peter Martyr's celebrated history of Spain's American empire, *Decades of the New World*. Then in May, before the book was bound, he inserted in it an extraordinary map of the New World.[35] On it were noted Frobisher's Meta Incognita in the far northeast, Raleigh's Virginia on the east coast, Drake's Elizabeth islands at the southern extremity of the continent, and then, far away in northwest America, Nova Albion. As it was the first printed map to do so, it appears that Walsingham had decided to announce England's territorial claims in the New World. Certainly, Hakluyt could not have published the map without Walsingham's permission.[36]

What was most remarkable about the map, however, was the detail of the northwest coast of America. As on the earlier maps of Dee and Lok, the coast lay, in longitude, just 140 degrees west of England, in sharp contrast to Abraham Ortelius's popularly accepted notion. And on the coast, Nova Albion was placed at its true latitude of 50 degrees north. From Nova Albion the coastline continued northwest and north to 55 degrees and then began to curl westward toward Asia, just as the coast of Alaska does, so that the map bore a closer resemblance to the actual trend of the coastline than any that would be produced for two centuries thereafter.

"That Posterity Be Not Deprived"

*W*ith word out of Lisbon that Philip's grand Armada was nearly ready to sail, Drake wrote to the Privy Council from Plymouth on March 30, 1588, requesting that his fleet be strengthened in order to launch another preemptive strike. As this entailed moving the largest part of the Queen's navy to Plymouth, the Privy Council decided that the Lord Admiral, Lord Howard of Effingham, should lead the combined force, with Drake serving as his vice admiral. Drake accepted Howard's command gracefully and quickly convinced him of his plan, but three times they set sail for Spain only to be driven back by southwesterly gales. Then, on July 19, the news came that the Armada had been seen off The Lizard and would soon be nearing Plymouth. The English sailors labored through the night and next morning towing their ships out against the wind, and in the afternoon the Spanish fleet emerged from the misty weather.

It was a formidable sight, 130 ships tightly arrayed in a two-mile-wide crescent formation and flying the banners of all the noble houses of Spain. Ironically, after working for two years to assemble Philip's great invasion fleet, the Marquis of Santa Cruz had died in February. In his place, Philip had appointed the Duke of Medina Sidonia to command its 8,000 mariners and 19,000 soldiers. Medina Sidonia's instructions, written by Philip himself, were to avoid breaking formation to engage the English fleet and continue on directly to the Flemish coast, where the Duke of Parma was waiting to join him with 27,000 soldiers. Then he was to escort the vessels carrying Parma's troops across the Channel and land their combined armies in Kent, where Parma would lead the march on London.

During the night Drake and Howard worked their way to windward with fifty-four ships, and the next morning Medina Sidonia discovered them at his rear. With the Spanish fleet to leeward, the English were able to maneuver close enough to use their cannons against the Armada's flanks, but they dared not attempt to penetrate Medina Sidonia's densely packed formation, where his much bigger ships were waiting to grapple onto them and overwhelm them with masses of soldiers.

Despite nearly exhausting their ammunition, the English guns inflicted little damage on the big Spanish galleons at long range. After sending ashore for more powder and shot, the English fleet, grown to ninety ships, renewed its attack off Portland Bill on July 23. With half the fleet Drake vigorously pounded Medina Sidonia's right flank but did not succeed in breaking it.

The battle continued, with sharp clashes off the Isle of Wight on July 24 and 25 having little effect on the slow but steady progress of the Spanish juggernaut eastward toward its rendezvous with Parma. However, Medina Sidonia still had not heard from Parma exactly where he was embarking his army, so he made for the French coast with the English still nipping at his heels, and came to anchor in the Bay of Calais on July 27. The next day he finally received a dispatch from Parma, and the news was disheartening: Parma's troops at Dunkirk and Nieuport would not be ready to embark for another week. Medina Sidonia was faced with a dilemma. His pilots warned that there was no suitable anchorage for the Armada beyond Calais, and that if he arrived before Parma was ready, the strong northward current would carry them past their rendezvous into the North Sea.

On July 28 Howard held a council with Drake, Frobisher, and John Hawkins, and they resolved to send fire ships into the Spaniards' midst that evening in an effort to dislodge them from the bay. The tactic worked: When they saw the fire ships bearing down on them, most of the Spanish captains cut their anchor cables and ran for open water. The next morning Medina Sidonia's carefully shepherded fleet was scattered in disarray along the coast toward Gravelines. Moving in among them, the English kept up their attack for nine hours, inflicting heavy damage on many of Medina Sidonia's ships and preventing him from re-forming his battle order. In the evening the weather turned foul, and by the following day the Spaniards were being carried by wind and current toward the North Sea. Drake shadowed them as far as Scotland and then turned back.

For Medina Sidonia's men, the worst was yet to come. Rounding the Orkney Islands, they ran into a series of violent storms, and one-third of their number were wrecked and perished on the coasts of Scotland and Ireland. News of their fate began to reach London in the middle of August, and on the twentieth a special religious service was held at St. Paul's Cathedral to give thanks for England's deliverance.

Soon thereafter, in the space of six days, two events occurred that affected Drake considerably. On September 4 the Earl of Leicester suddenly collapsed and died. Leicester's death was a great loss for Drake, for he had benefited many times from his influence with the Queen. Thereafter he had to depend in such matters entirely upon Walsingham, whose support he certainly enjoyed, but whose acerbic manner frequently aroused her ire. Moreover, without Leicester's backing of Walsingham, the balance of support in the Privy Council soon swung back to Burghley.

Then, on September 9, Thomas Cavendish arrived at Plymouth, having duplicated Drake's feat of circumnavigating the globe, and carrying a fabulous load of plunder seized from a Manila galleon off the Pacific coast of Mexico. However, Cavendish's second ship had not returned, and he had an important report to deliver. From Plymouth he wrote to Walsingham:

> There be some things which I have kept from their [officials'] sight for special causes which I mean to make known to your honour at my coming to London, for I protest before God that I will not hide any one thing from you, neither concerning the quantity of my goods nor the secrets of the voyage, which in many things shall not be known but unto your honour for they be matters of great importance.[1]

When Cavendish reached London, the whole story came out behind the usual cloak of official secrecy. He had entered Magellan's Strait in January 1587 and found the Spanish fortifications abandoned: All of the garrison but a solitary survivor had succumbed to starvation and disease. After battling fierce winds for forty-nine days, Cavendish reached the South Sea in late February. By September he was at the entrance to the Gulf of California with his two remaining ships and a captured bark, having sunk nineteen Spanish ships and burned Acapulco. Near Cape San Lucas at the southern tip of the Baja Peninsula, they lay in wait for the returning Manila galleon. On November 4 the 700-ton *Santa Ana* was sighted, and after a six-hour fight she surrendered. Besides 122,000 pesos of gold, she was carrying a rich cargo of spices, pearls, silks, and brocades. The total value of her cargo was estimated to be more than 1 million pesos.

Putting the galleon's passengers and crew ashore with some provisions, Cavendish took as much of the cargo as his ships could carry and then set fire to the galleon, after which the two English ships parted company as planned. The 60-ton bark *Content* and the captured Spanish bark remained behind to commence their northern mission, while Cavendish in the 120-ton *Desire* set his course across the Pacific and home via the Cape of Good Hope.[2]

From Cape San Lucas, Cavendish reached the Mariana Islands—a distance of 6,600 miles—in forty-two days, and the Philippines on the fifty-sixth day. There a troubling incident occurred. Cavendish had brought with him one of the pilots of the *Santa Ana*, named Ersola. While riding at anchor in the Philippines, Ersola was caught trying to smuggle a letter through the natives to the Spanish governor at Manila, urging him to come after Cavendish. Ersola wrote that Cavendish had only one ship, the other having "gone for the North-west passage, standing in 55 degrees." Somehow he had learned the latitude of Drake's strategically vital discovery. Cavendish promptly ordered Ersola hanged and then made for the Indian Ocean.[3] Notably, he did not bother stopping in the oft-mentioned Moluccas, and his voyage from the Pacific coast of Mexico to England took less than ten months in contrast to Drake's seventeen months.

From Mexico in November the *Content* had ample time to locate Drake's Strait of Anian and get through the northern passage the next summer, and she should have reached England by the time Cavendish arrived home. But she had not returned, leaving the existence of the passage in doubt. Moreover, Cavendish said that he had seen nothing to support Drake's claim that Tierra del Fuego was composed of islands. The inference was obvious: If that discovery was a figment of Drake's imagination, then perhaps his supposed discovery of the Strait of Anian was as well.

In November 1588 Cavendish brought his bark Desire, *fitted with sails of blue damask* and her crew wearing chains of gold, into the Thames, where they were

Thomas Cavendish

greeted by throngs of Londoners much as Drake had been eight years before. Drake would have been less than human not to have been annoyed by the attention given to Cavendish. However, it appears that he had lately received assurances from Walsingham that publication of an account of his own great voyage would at last be permitted.

Some time earlier Drake had enlisted his friend Philip Nichols, who had served as chaplain and secretary on his 1585–86 Caribbean expedition and his raid on Cadiz, to adapt a narrative of his voyage around the world from the journal of Francis Fletcher. It appears Drake had seized the journal from Fletcher prior to their return in 1580.[4] This was the second volume that Philip Nichols had undertaken to write for Drake, the first being a narrative of his exploits on the isthmus in 1572–73, and it appears that they were planning to publish the volumes as a set.

However, Walsingham had a different project in mind. For the past several years Richard Hakluyt had been gathering material for a monumental new work. To be titled *The Principall Navigations, Voyages and Discoveries of the English Nation*, the volume would be sponsored by and dedicated to Walsingham, and would be a masterpiece of propaganda for English maritime enterprise.[5]

In December Hakluyt began packing his papers in Paris, and by the New Year he was back in London gathering more material for his book, which would eventually run to more than 800 pages.[6] For Drake's voyage he

already had the use of the anonymous narrative containing the altered latitude of Drake's northern reach, but this compressed Drake's northern exploit into fewer words than Hakluyt hoped to offer his readers.[7] The chief
inadequacy in the narrative was the absence of any information about Nova
Albion—its discovery, its resources, climate, and people, and Drake's taking
possession of it for England. However, editing Fletcher's journal, Nichols
had produced a more fulsome account of the voyage, including a description of Nova Albion, and Hakluyt was able to borrow Nichols's draft account to enhance his narrative.[8]

In the spring of 1589, as Hakluyt continued writing and editing,
George Bishop and Ralph Newberie, deputies to the Queen's printer, began
printing the first sections of his book, including the title page containing
the long-awaited announcement. The third part of the volume, it promised,
would contain an account of a voyage to the South Sea and "*Nova Albion*
upon the backside of *Canada*, further than ever any Christian hitherto hath
pierced."

Around the same time a special silver medallion was issued to commemorate Drake's voyage. Commissioned with a subsidy from Parliament
funds, the medal contained a map depicting Drake's route around the
world—the first such map known to have been published in England. Just
6.8 centimeters (2½ inches) in diameter, it was engraved by Michael
Mercator, grandson of the famous geographer, who was then residing in
London.[9] On the map, the configuration of the continents was taken
from the map that Hakluyt had printed in Paris in 1587 with one notable
exception: Whereas Hakluyt's map had placed the northwest coast of
America, in longitude, 140 degrees west of England, this medallion map
moved it 30 degrees farther west, substantially fattening North America,
no doubt to discourage any attention to the possibility of a northwest
passage.

In the Pacific, Drake's track continued north to latitude 48 degrees,
where "Nova Albion" was inscribed. Then, pursuant to the ten-degree
cover-up rule, it reversed southward to the mouth of an inlet in the coast,
implying a stopping place there before heading across the Pacific. The inlet
extended northward from 38 to 40 degrees, as in Drake's early private maps,
except that the medallion did not display a flag at its head. Apparently, the
inlet detail was preferred to the chain of islands Drake had revealed in his

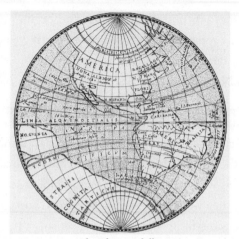

*A paper impression from the Silver Medallion map of Drake's voyage,
issued in London in 1589.*

1585 map for Henry of Navarre, and these details in the medallion were intended to conform to the narrative that Hakluyt was preparing.

In late February 1589, Drake, Elizabeth, and the Privy Council agreed on a plan to deliver
a crippling blow to King Philip. Drake would lead the largest naval force ever
to sail from England: 180 ships and 17,000 men. Elizabeth placed the highest priority on destruction of the remainder of Philip's Armada, which was being repaired at the ports of Santander and Corunna in northern Spain. After
disposing of the Spanish fleet, Drake was to land an army commanded by Sir
John Norris, then support his attempt to occupy Lisbon and install Don Antonio on the throne of Portugal. Then he was to continue on to the Azores
and seize the islands and any treasure ships he encountered there.

It was an impossibly ambitious plan, and the unwieldy expedition was
troubled from the start. The government was slow with the money required
for provisioning, and when the fleet put to sea on April 18, there were only
five weeks' victuals aboard. The ships were soon scattered by a series of violent gales, and some thirty turned back. When the fleet regrouped on the
north coast of Spain, the wind prevented it from reaching Santander, so
Drake headed for Corunna instead. Entering the harbor where Medina
Sidonia's entire Armada had assembled the year before, they found only a
handful of ships. Worse, onshore winds pinned them there for two weeks,

and by the time they got under way, disease had begun to ravage the fleet. Drake's council of captains was opposed to attempting Santander again, so Drake and Norris decided to get on with the Lisbon project.

On May 18 Norris and Don Antonio landed with 6,000 men on the coast north of Lisbon, and then Drake took the fleet around to the first of three forts guarding the Tagus River, leading to the city's harbor. Don Antonio was certain that word of his return would quickly bring a popular uprising against the city's Spanish garrison. If this occurred, Drake was to attempt to force his way into the harbor. When Norris reached the walls of the city, however, they were lined with hostile Portuguese militia, and after several days there was still no sign of a revolt in support of Don Antonio. All the while the English soldiers and sailors continued to sicken and die by the hundreds. By the time Norris rejoined the fleet in the first week of June, he had lost 2,000 men and as many more had died aboard the ships.

Drake managed to salvage some of the expedition's expenses by seizing a fleet of sixty merchantmen laden with naval stores. However, several attempts to reach the Azores were defeated by contrary winds, and after sacking the town of Vigo on Spain's northwest coast, Drake pointed the fleet homeward. As the exhausted force staggered into ports along the south coast of England, the enormity of the human toll became appallingly clear. Of the 17,000 men who had embarked in the fleet less than three months previously, nearly half had died, due almost entirely to malnutrition and disease. Moreover, the expedition had failed to achieve any of its objectives, including the destruction of the remainder of Philip's Armada so earnestly desired by Elizabeth.

It has been suggested that the failure of the expedition was the cause of an apparent falling-out between Drake and Elizabeth later that year, but this is hard to certify. On July 7 she wrote to Drake and Norris, "There hath been as much performed by you as true valour and good conduct could yield."[10] The Privy Council inquired of them what new enterprise they could recommend using the resources that remained "for the greatest annoyance of the enemy."[11] Drake and Norris responded that neither ships nor men would be fit for another campaign that summer. In October the Privy Council held an inquiry into the conduct of the expedition, but Drake and Norris gave reasonable explanations for their decisions and the matter appeared to have been concluded. Within a year Norris was back at the head of an army.

In November, however, Drake left the court and thereafter did not become active in naval affairs again for nearly three years. Some have suggested that he was sent away in disgrace, although this is disputed. Then, at the end of November, with his book printed and awaiting binding, Richard Hakluyt was obliged to insert in it a note to the reader explaining that he was unable to provide his promised account of Drake's voyage after all.

> I must confess to have taken more than ordinary pains, meaning to have inserted it in this work; but being of late (contrary to my expectation) seriously dealt withal not to anticipate or prevent another man's pains and charge in drawing all the services of that worthy Knight into one volume, I have yielded unto those of my friends which pressed me in the matter, referring the further knowledge of his proceedings to those intended discourses.[12]

The inference in the note was that Drake had withdrawn his permission for Hakluyt to use Philip Nichols's draft narrative, preferring to publish the full account independently. Allowing, however, that Walsingham was his most powerful ally and had a personal financial stake in Hakluyt's book, this hardly seems likely. Besides, Hakluyt still had the option of using the earlier narrative, that he possessed. Clearly, his excuse was a fabrication, and the only logical explanation is that the matter was by then out of Walsingham's hands, that the account had been withheld on the Queen's order.

Conceivably, Elizabeth *had* sent Drake away from the court in disgrace over the dismal performance of his expedition, and to punish him further, she had ordered the story of his great voyage withdrawn. Certainly, she was capable of being vindictive when she turned on someone. However, there is no evidence that this is what occurred, and indeed there are good reasons for believing that Drake's fall from favor actually came about in reverse order to this scenario.

It was no coincidence that a globe or map was a prominent feature in many portraits of Elizabeth. Since her early tutoring by John Dee she had been deeply interested in geography and maps, and very little such material escaped her close scrutiny. From the great chart and illustrated journal that

Drake had presented to her upon his return from the Pacific, as well as the hours he had spent discussing with her his vision for Nova Albion, there can be no doubt that she had a keen grasp of its location and defining features.

In her meetings with Drake after his return from the Pacific, it had been agreed that Nova Albion had to remain a closely guarded secret until the discovery of the northwest passage was completed and the colony was securely established, lest the Spanish discover its location and move to prevent these developments. Indeed, it undoubtedly was by her order that the ban on publication had been imposed in the first instance. Therefore, there is reason to believe that she may have been displeased when she learned Walsingham was sponsoring publication of an account of Drake's voyage, including a description of Nova Albion, in spite of the fact that Cavendish's second ship had failed to return and the discovery of the northwest passage had yet to be completed.

Probably, there had been hope that the *Content* with its load of treasure might yet return in the summer of 1589 when the ice again cleared from the supposed northwest passage, or via the Cape of Good Hope as Drake had done. By the fall of 1589, however, there still was no sign of her, and when Hakluyt delivered the last part of his book to the printers, Drake's voyage was not included. Instead, the word *instructions* was printed at the end of page 643, indicating where the account was to be inserted if permission was received for its release.

What transpired in November to put Drake in Elizabeth's bad graces is a matter for conjecture, as there is no hint in the contemporary record. There can be little doubt that he was dismayed to learn she had ordered his account withheld from publication. Very possibly, he exacerbated the problem by proposing that he lead a new expedition to the Pacific and complete the discovery of the passage himself. It would certainly have been in character for him to do so after Cavendish questioned the reliability of his discoveries, and he had always advocated taking the war to the Pacific in any case. Indeed, Elizabeth may well have held out that he would finally be permitted to do so once he had conclusively disposed of Philip's invasion fleet. However, his recent expedition had failed to put an end to her fears, and a suggestion that he be allowed to go off to the Pacific might well have infuriated her.

In any case, early in 1590 Hakluyt's magnificent compendium of

English voyages and discoveries was released without an account of the greatest voyage of all, but recommending in his note to the reader that his account of Cavendish's voyage (which omitted the disappearance of the *Content*) would satisfy their curiosity about the South Sea.

Then, on April 6, 1590, after a lengthy decline in health due to overwork, Sir Francis Walsingham died. With the loss of his last great friend on the Privy Council, Drake's prospects of an early reconciliation with the Queen were dashed. He was effectively grounded.

In private circles curiosity about Drake's voyage remained strong, and one project in particular served to stimulate new interest in his discoveries. Hakluyt had mentioned it in the introduction to *Principall Navigations*, explaining:

> I have contented my self with inserting into the work one of the best general maps of the world only, until the coming out of a very large and most exact terrestrial Globe collected and reformed according to the newest, secretest and latest discoveries, both Spanish, Portugal, and English, composed by M. Emmerie Molyneux of Lambeth, a rare Gentleman in his profession, being therein for divers years, greatly supported by the purse and liberality of the worshipful merchant, M. William Sanderson.[13]

Emery Molyneux's terrestrial globe-map and its celestial counterpart were to be the first globes produced in England, and with a diameter of twenty-five inches, the largest and most detailed yet made anywhere.[14]

Molyneux's patron, William Sanderson, had sponsored the three voyages of John Davis in 1585, 1586, and 1587, during which Davis had explored the strait running north between Greenland and Baffin Island. On his third voyage, Davis had sailed a twenty-ton pinnace across the Atlantic and northward in his strait to latitude 73 degrees, 400 miles above the Arctic Circle. There he saw the sea extending northwestward free of ice, but a hard opposing wind repeatedly drove him back until his provisions ran dangerously low.

On his return, Davis had introduced Sanderson to Molyneux, a mathematician and instrument maker, who proposed to make a globe to illustrate as realistically as possible Drake's voyage and the relationship of his discoveries to Davis's strait.[15] Walsingham had sanctioned the project, and Jodocus Hondius was enlisted to engrave the globe-map.

The design of the globes was assisted also by an exchange of information with Dutch mapmaker Peter Plancius,* who had recently produced a pair of globes for his patron, Jacob Van Langeren.[16] On his celestial globe Molyneux copied some of the constellations from Plancius's celestial globe design, and in return Plancius obtained some new information about the far northwest coast of America, which he incorporated in his new map of the world.[17] Like Ortelius, Plancius evidently was given the information only by latitude, as his coastline was imaginary; but on it he inscribed a new set of place-names, including "Cape of storms" at 50 degrees, "frozen land" at 53 degrees, and a "white cape" at 55 degrees.

Molyneux's globe project provided details concerning Drake's discoveries that Davis could not otherwise obtain, and with this information in 1590 he set sail for the Pacific with a ship and a pinnace. Near the Canary Islands, however, his ship suffered heavy damage in a fight with a Spanish galleon, and he was compelled to return to England. Then, toward the end of the year, plans began to be laid for Thomas Cavendish to lead a new expedition out to the Pacific. This time he was to take five ships, including the *Desire* under the command of Davis. Cavendish would escort Davis to the Californias, and from there Davis was to continue northward with the aim of returning via the northwest passage.[18]

In late July 1591, prior to their departure, Molyneux presented his much-anticipated terrestrial globe, beautifully engraved and colored, to Elizabeth at Greenwich Palace. Soon afterward it was seen covered down to the floor by a taffeta curtain.[19] Molyneux's plan had been to produce more copies of the globe for sale to persons of importance in England and abroad, but it had been deemed appropriate for viewing only by a privileged few. Consequently, he was obliged to produce a less revealing edition for wider consumption.

In his second attempt, completed in 1592, Molyneux removed Drake's island of Nova Albion and cut off the coast to the north at latitude 54 degrees. However, he retained the inscription "Nova Albion" straddling the

---

*Plancius later became one of the founders of the Dutch East Indies Company and served as its chief geographer.

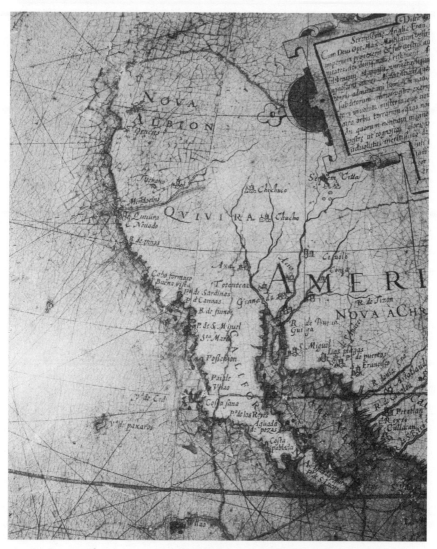

On Emery Molyneux's suppressed 1592 globe, Nova Albion was inscribed straddling the 50th parallel of latitude.

50th parallel of latitude, so this edition also was apparently deemed too re-vealing.[20]

In his third edition, also engraved in 1592, Molyneux was obliged to thrust the northwest coast of America, in longitude, some 1,500 miles far-ther west and to move the inscription "Nova Albion" from latitude 50 de-grees southward to 46 degrees.[21] This edition of the globe was approved for public viewing and became famous.* Contemporary playwright William Shakespeare's comparison of a kitchen maid to a terrestrial globe in *The Comedy of Errors* is an allusion to it.[22]

Thomas Blundeville, an instructor in mathematics at the Inns of Court, wrote a treatise on the globe in which he described Drake's track around the world and calculated that from England to Nova Albion and home again Drake had sailed 12,010 leagues (36,030 miles). But Blundeville knew there was more to the voyage than this, and he concluded his treatise with a thinly veiled appeal to the Queen to allow Drake to provide a detailed account of his whole voyage—"of all which things I doubt not that he hath already written."[23]

By April 1592 Cavendish and Davis had made their way partway through Magellan's Strait, but finding they could get no farther due to violent headwinds, they retreated to Patagonia for repairs. However, Cavendish's ship became separated from the others, and he fell ill and died at sea in June. His men then turned back for England.

Davis made three more attempts to get through the strait, and on the third he succeeded in reaching the open Pacific, but with his sails in tatters and his men dying from scurvy, he was compelled to turn back. It took his exhausted crew two months to gather enough penguin meat for the voyage home. On the Brazilian coast he lost thirteen of his men to attacks by the Portuguese and Indians. In the tropics the meat turned into a mass of maggots, and eleven more men died. When Davis finally reached the coast of Ireland on June 11, 1593, only fifteen out of his original company of seventy-six men remained alive. The news of Cavendish's death and the disintegration of the expedition had already reached England in late 1592.

After his falling-out with Elizabeth in 1589, Drake had returned to Plymouth, where he was appointed Deputy Lord Lieutenant of Devon with responsibility for shoring up its defenses, preserving the peace, and overseeing the judiciary. For his

---

*By the time Molyneux completed this third edition of the globe, the project had cost his sponsor, William Sanderson, the astonishing sum of £1,000.

London visits, he leased a large old house, "The Herber," on Dowgate Street, near the church of St. Mary Bothaw.[24] For three years, however, he spent most of his time in residence at Buckland Abbey, attending to projects such as the expansion of Plymouth's fortifications and construction of a new water supply for the town. There he also spent long hours editing and revising Philip Nichols's narratives toward the day when he finally would be permitted to publish them.[25]

With Christmas of 1592 approaching, Drake was invited to the court and received warmly by Elizabeth, and it appears that all was forgiven. Perhaps her treasury was running low, as there was soon talk of a new expedition to the Caribbean. Drake wasted no time submitting his revised memoirs for her approval. On New Year's Day 1593 he wrote to Elizabeth:

Madam

Seeing diverse [others] have diversely reported and written of these voyages and actions which I have attempted and made, every one endeavouring to bring to light whatsoever inklings of conjectures they have had; whereby many untruths have been published, and the certain truth concealed as I have thought it necessary myself . . . so I have accounted it to present this discourse to Your Majesty . . . being the first fruits of thy servant's pen.

Drake said he was not apologizing for anything he had done, but merely trying to set the record straight so that he would not be excluded from consideration for like actions in the future. Also, he said, he had written for the ages, "that posterity be not deprived of such help as may happily be gained hereby, and our present age at least may be satisfied in the rightfulness of these actions, which hitherto have been silenced."[26]

Drake added that he hoped his labor both in performing his mission and in writing his report of it, which he found no less troublesome, would not be lost. Although Elizabeth was at last favorably disposed toward publication of an account of his Pacific voyage, Drake's hopes of seeing his own story of the voyage in print were once more in vain.

Drake's account stated that from Guatulco he sailed northward to a landfall at latitude 48 degrees, where contrary winds and bitterly cold weather obliged him to turn back, and he returned southward without landing until he found a harbor at 38° 30' and named that place Nova Albion.[27] No doubt reluctantly, he had substituted Fletcher's account of events at the harbor where they careened the *Golden Hinde* for his description of Nova Albion. However, the narrative still maintained that the purpose of the voyage was to discover a passage around the northern extremity of America. Above all, it was his extraordinary effort to discover the passage that he wished to have remembered by posterity, even if he had to say that he did not succeed in the quest. And so the narrative said that he concluded after a vigorous search that there was no strait. Nevertheless, even the admission that this was his purpose was unacceptable.

Instead, it was decided that Richard Hakluyt's still-unpublished short narrative, which had been abridged from Philip Nichols's original adaptation of Fletcher's journal and also retained some of the same offending information, would be revised and printed, and that would be the end of the matter. Reworking his narrative, Hakluyt eliminated all mention of a search for the northern strait and said that upon departing Guatulco, Drake had taken a "somewhat northerly" course for the Moluccas, but after encountering bitterly cold winds at latitude 42 degrees, he turned back toward land and found the harbor he called Nova Albion at 38 degrees. Ironically, however, Hakluyt neglected to instruct the printers to remove the note in the margin of the old page which read "the purpose of Sir Francis to return by the Northwest passage," and this incongruous statement was printed alongside the carefully expurgated account.[28]

Exactly when Hakluyt's narrative, titled *The Famous Voyage of Sir Francis Drake*, was finally released has been the subject of much debate among historians.[29] One document in particular testifies to its release sometime after Drake's letter of January 1, 1593, submitting his revised narrative to Elizabeth. The document is a splendid map of the world designed and engraved by Hondius.[30] Clearly, this was the ultimate rendition of Drake's commemorative map, produced to accompany his own account of the voyage. In the lower corners of the map are the same scenes depicted on the private maps that Hondius began making for Drake nearly a decade before. In the upper corners Hondius had added two more scenes, one of them depicting the bay in northwest America where Drake careened his ships, now relabeled "Portus Nova Albionis."

Like Molyneux's globe, Hondius's commemorative map had undergone

On Jodocus Hondius's Broadside map, Nova Albion was placed back at latitude 40 degrees and a smudged area shows where the map's engraved plate was scrubbed to erase Drake's track northward down to 42 degrees.

numerous revisions. At some point he had been obliged to extend the northwest tip of America, in longitude, nearly 200 degrees west of England. Then, undoubtedly to Drake's annoyance, Hondius had been instructed to include Cavendish's voyage on the map, together with a note stating that Cavendish did not find Tierra del Fuego to be composed of islands as Drake had claimed.*

After these revisions, however, the engraved plate for Hondius's map still showed Drake reaching northward to latitude 48 degrees before he

---

*At the same time, Hakluyt had been obliged to omit any mention of Drake's discovery of the passage below Tierra del Fuego from his narrative, so it appears that a decision had been made, somewhat belatedly, to try to cover up or deny this discovery as well.

turned back, which was consistent with Drake's revised account of the voyage as presented to Elizabeth on New Year's Day 1593. But then the plate was altered by a not entirely successful attempt to erase Drake's northward track from 48 degrees back to 42 degrees, so that the map conformed to Hakluyt's published account.

If Drake's track beyond 42 degrees was erased by Hondius himself, it seems likely that Hakluyt's account was finally released sometime in 1593, as Hondius emigrated to Amsterdam before the end of the year. However, it is possible that he departed before the account was finally approved, and someone else altered the plate and printed the first copies of the map. Drake visited Amsterdam in 1594 and may have returned the altered plate to him at that time.

In 1595 Hondius reissued the map in the Netherlands, where it was pasted on a broadsheet containing accounts of Drake's and Cavendish's voyages. The accounts were taken from Hakluyt's published narratives except for one passage. Where Hakluyt stated that Drake gave the name Nova Albion to "this country," the broadsheet stated that

> [Drake named] this Island *Nova Albion*, on account of its white cliffs, and that it would have some similarity with England, the which in former times was so called. On this island . . . as a memento that he had been there, as also especially from weight of right and title, which he had taken over in the name of her Majesty, he erected on a post, a plate of silver, on which were engraved the name of her Majesty, as also the voluntary yielding of the country to her Majesty, and below the same plate of silver he fastened her Majesty's picture and coat of arms, being a half of an English shilling, under which he wrote his own name.[31]

From its reference to Nova Albion as an island, it appears that the account had been adapted from a different rendition of Hakluyt's narrative than was eventually allowed to be published in England.

ঀ 22. ঁ

A Forgotten Secret

On June 12, 1593, *another expedition sailed from Plymouth for the Pacific* Ocean. It was commanded by thirty-four-year-old Richard Hawkins, the only son of Sir John Hawkins. The younger Hawkins had built his ship, the 350-ton *Dainty*, expressly for the voyage at the end of 1588, following Cavendish's return, but he had been persuaded "to desist from the enterprise."[1] However, since Cavendish was dead and Davis was believed to be, Hawkins, with the aid of his father, had obtained the Privy Council's consent for his voyage. Its purpose was discovery, and there were hints that a great empire-building enterprise was to be launched as soon as Hawkins returned.[2] Years later Hawkins wrote that his voyage was intended "for the Islands of Japan, of the Philippines and Moluccas, the kingdoms of China and the East Indies, by way of the Straits of Magellan and the South Sea."[3] Undoubtedly, however, his real plan was to raid the coast of Peru and then continue northward to Drake's Strait of Anian.[4]

Hawkins lost nearly half his company to scurvy and to desertion by his second ship, the *Fancy*, before he entered Magellan's strait in February 1594. Three weeks later he was within sight of the South Sea, but a powerful westerly suddenly came up and drove him seventy miles back into the strait. A few days later he again reached the mouth of the strait only to be blown back eighty-five miles. Then the *Dainty* ran hard aground on a submerged pinnacle of rock in the middle of the strait. She was stuck amidship, and her bow and stern sagged under their own weight as the tide fell until it appeared her back would be broken. Miraculously, Hawkins got her off the reef intact, and at the end of March, forty-six days after entering the strait, he emerged into the Pacific.

After Drake's raid, the Spaniards had set up a chain of outposts to relay warnings along the coast, and there was no possibility of maintaining surprise beyond the first place where Hawkins made contact with the inhabitants. Hawkins knew of this from Cavendish's men and had planned to remain offshore until he got north of Callao, where he hoped to snatch a good prize and escape to the Californias before the Spaniards could mount a pursuit. But his men clamored for a raid on Valparaiso, and Hawkins relented.

In a short time news of his presence reached Lima, and the viceroy dispatched his brother-in-law, Don Beltran de Castro, with upwards of 1,000 men in six heavily armed ships to intercept him. When Hawkins encountered them 300 miles south of Callao in the middle of May, they chased him for twelve hours before he escaped by running to seaward after nightfall.

Determined to leave the coast as quickly as possible, Hawkins made a last stop on June 10 in the Bay of Atacames, just north of the equator, to effect some hasty repairs and fill his water casks. Just as he was weighing anchor to depart, Don Beltran entered the bay with three of his armed ships. The *Dainty* was a sturdy fighting ship, but with only seventy-five men Hawkins was hopelessly outnumbered and outgunned. Nevertheless, the battle continued through that day and the next. Finally, on the third day—with nineteen men dead, nearly forty wounded, and Hawkins himself lying incapacitated with six wounds—the *Dainty* surrendered.

Don Beltran so admired the valor of the Englishmen that he refused to turn them over to the Inquisition, and eventually most of them were sent back to England. Although a prisoner, Hawkins was treated as a respected guest of Don Beltran until he was sent to Spain in 1597.* It was during his detention at Lima that Hawkins learned of the deaths of his father and Sir Francis Drake at sea in the Caribbean.

Discussion of another raid on King Philip's Caribbean possessions had begun shortly after Drake's return to the court at Christmas 1592. The original plan put forward by Drake and John Hawkins had been to land a small army at Nombre de

---

*In Spain Hawkins was put in a dungeon and remained there until his mother-in-law purchased his freedom in 1603.

Dios and march across the isthmus to capture Panama, thereby cutting off Philip's supply of bullion from Peru. Conceivably their aim was to link up with Richard Hawkins. However, Elizabeth had vacillated, and the preparations did not finally get under way until December 1594. Humiliatingly for Drake, her consent was conditional on his acceptance that command of the expedition would be divided equally between him and Hawkins. Hawkins, who had not been in the Caribbean for twenty-six years, was appointed to ensure that Drake did not stray from the agreed plan.

By the beginning of August 1595 Drake and Hawkins were ready to sail with twenty-seven ships and 2,500 men, but again the Queen delayed. A small Spanish force from Brittany had landed in Cornwall and burned three villages. Already concerned about rumors that Philip was assembling a new invasion fleet, Elizabeth began thinking of redirecting the expedition to reconnoiter the Spanish ports. Drake and Hawkins protested that their force was ill suited to the purpose. Then word came that the flagship of Philip's treasure fleet had been heavily damaged in a storm and had put into San Juan de Porto Rico, where she was lying without rigging or guns but still laden with 2.5 million ducats' worth of bullion. Finally, after extracting a firm commitment that they would return before the end of April 1596 to help defend England's shores, Elizabeth gave her consent, and they sailed from Plymouth on August 28, 1595.

En route the English fleet suffered many delays, and by the time they reached Puerto Rico on November 12, the Spanish had received ample warning of their coming. San Juan's defenses had been reinforced, and the treasure had been taken from the crippled galleon and stored safely ashore. In the meantime John Hawkins had fallen ill with an unknown ailment and, after lying in his cabin for a week, died on the evening of their arrival at age sixty-three. His death cast a pall over the fleet. The following night Drake attempted an assault on the harbor but was repulsed.

Concluding that there was no possibility of penetrating the city's defenses, Drake decided to move on to their second objective, Nombre de Dios and Panama. Inexplicably, he then spent a month wandering the South American coast in search of plunder, and when he finally came to anchor at Nombre de Dios on December 27, the Spaniards were well prepared for him. They had evacuated Nombre de Dios and entrenched themselves in a fortification straddling the road to Panama. A force of 800 English soldiers suffered heavy casualties attempting to breach the barricade and was compelled to retire. Drake's officers saw that he was becoming deeply depressed.[5]

Withdrawing the fleet to a nearby island for rest and repair, Drake briefly contemplated raiding Nicaragua. In the middle of January, his men began dying of the fever, and Drake himself fell ill with dysentery, then known as the "bloody flux." After lying in a steadily deteriorating condition for a week, Drake gathered enough strength to rise and, with help, buckle on his armor, after which he lay down again and died within an hour, at four o'clock in the morning on January 28, 1596. The fleet anchored off Porto Bello, and there Drake's body, encased in a lead coffin, was lowered into the sea while trumpets sounded and cannons thundered a final salute.

The news of Drake's death was carried to England and Spain by their respective fleets. From Panama Don Alonso de Sotomayor, commander of the Spanish troops on the isthmus, reflected the view of many Spaniards who had served against Drake. He was, Sotomayor wrote, "one of the most famous men of his profession that have existed in the world, very courteous and honourable with those who surrendered, of great humanity and gentleness, virtues which must be praised even in an enemy."[6] The reaction in Spain was decidedly less magnanimous, however. When word reached Seville in April, its merchants rejoiced in the streets, and the jubilant citizenry illuminated the city with torchlight celebrations. King Philip was lying ill in bed when he was informed. His expression turned to delight, and he exclaimed, "It is good news, and now I will get well."[7]

The first ships of the English fleet reached Plymouth toward the end of April, and the announcement of Drake's death swept the country into sorrow. Tributes to the nation's fallen hero poured forth in verse, prose, and song. The most common medium was the broadside—forerunner of the newspaper—which was printed and pasted up in public places. One began:

> *He who wars at sea such hazards underwent,*
> *Through love of his Country ever led;*
> *Drake now at length the eternal shores had reached*
> *Of Peace, and for his reward eternal Peace.*[8]

In the most elaborate epitaph, a book of verse, Charles Fitz-Geffrey recounted many of Drake's achievements but was most eloquent on the subject of his voyage around the world.

> *A Golden Hind, led by his art and might,*
> *Bare him about the earth's sea-walled round*
> *With the unresisted Roe outrunning flight,*
> *While Fame (the harbinger) a trumpe did sound.*
> *That heaven and earth with echos did abound;*
> *Echo of Drake a high praise of his name,*
> *Name royaliz'd by worth, worth raised by fame.*
> *Tell how he bare the round world a ship,*
> *A ship, which round the world he bare.*
> *Whose sail did winged Euru's flight outstrip,*
> *Scorning tempestuous Borea's stormy dare,*
> *Descrying uncouth coasts, and countries rare:*
> *And people which no eye had ever seen,*
> *Save day's fair golden eye, & Night's bright Queen.*[9]

Reciting the many places Drake had been, Fitz-Geffrey saved the most important for last:

> *He that the rich Moluccas had seen*
> *He that a new found Albion descried*
> *And safely home again his bark did guide.*[10]

On the Continent the news of Drake's death caused a sensation, and demand for pictures of him and accounts of his exploits soared. In Germany Crispin van de Passe engraved a portrait of Drake and added the inscription:

> *Had Ovid know my life as well*
> *True tales there would have been to tell:*
> *How Neptune's son had spread his wing*
> *And around the Oceans drawn a ring;*
> *Then into Drake, this Dragon-Knight,*
> *Transformed was he (amazing sight!)*
> *Thus was I always armed for wars*
> *With tail and talons, wings and jaws.*[11]

In Spain playwright Felix Lope de Vega Carpio countered with *La Dragontea*, a long work in verse celebrating Drake's demise. Vega could not entirely conceal his admiration for Drake, however, and ironically in one stanza paid him the tribute he had wanted most:

> *Well did thy Queen know thy great valour,*
> *Which might cause the depths of the sea to tremble,*
> *When she gave thee the three vessels,*
> *Which in a single voyage saw the Earth's two poles.*[12]

With the capture of Richard Hawkins, the effort to complete the discovery of the northwest passage via Drake's Strait of Anian came to an end. After recovering from his ordeal, John Davis published a book in which he argued that the passage truly existed and urged that its discovery was of the utmost importance to England.[13] But all of the powerful men who had backed Drake's scheme were gone, and there were no new patrons for the enterprise. Nevertheless, the cloak of secrecy continued.

In 1596 John Blagrave, a member of Emery Molyneux's circle, produced an extraordinary map based on Molyneux's 1592 globe, which had been suppressed as too revealing.[14] On his map, a view of the world centered on the North Pole, Blagrave reproduced the coastlines of America and Asia exactly as positioned on Molyneux's globe. Then at latitude 60 degrees, between the two continents, he depicted a ship emerging into the Pacific from the northwest passage after a short voyage from England, in sharp contrast to the long journey Drake and Cavendish had to take around South America. Near the outlet of the passage, on the Pacific coast of America, an indentation in the coast and the inscription "Nova Albion" promised a safe haven for the English sailors.

Blagrave had intended to insert the map in a book he published in the same year, but when the book appeared, it did not include the map. Like Molyneux's globe, Blagrave's map had apparently been suppressed.[15]

In 1598 Richard Hakluyt began printing his second edition of *Principall Navigations*, expanded to three volumes. The third volume, dedicated to Burghley's son Sir Robert Cecil, was published in 1600 and contained two accounts of Drake's voyage. The result, however, was more inconsistencies. First Hakluyt revised his previous narrative, *The Famous Voyage*, removing mention of the northern coast being covered in snow as well as his note in the margin of the page referring to Drake's intended return via the northwest passage. Also he altered the latitude where Drake turned back on account of the cold from 42 to 43 degrees, although he retained the sailing distance northward from Guatulco as "600 leagues at the least." Apparently to emphasize England's claim to the region, he added a second account devoted exclusively to Drake's northern voyage. In this account Hakluyt repeated the latitude of 43 degrees for Drake's northern reach but changed the sailing distance to "800 leagues at the least."[16]

In Amsterdam in 1597, Jodocus Hondius published the "Christian Knight" map of the world, and on its northwest coast of America he laid out the same place-names that had been given to his fellow countryman Peter Plancius during Molyneux's globe project. Then in 1598 Hondius commenced work on a new globe, on which he introduced yet another set of place-names for the northwest coast of America. Hondius's coastline was imaginary, but on it he inscribed a rich new nomenclature, including a "Coast of objections" at latitude 53 degrees, an "Inlet of the islands" at 54 degrees, and a "Cape of good fortune" at 55 degrees, as well as a "long inlet" at 51 degrees, a river and "mountainous land" at 49 degrees, and a "Cape of snowcapped mountains" at 48 degrees.[17]

In 1597 Emery Molyneux emigrated to Amsterdam, taking with him the engraved plates for his suppressed 1592 globe. There, assisted by Hondius, he produced a new copy of the globe and then Molyneux died. Sometime after his death, the date on the globe was altered from 1592 to 1603—the year of Queen Elizabeth's death—and it was sent to London to be preserved at Drake's favorite institution, the Middle Temple, Inns of Court.[18]

The globe contains a feature that is compelling proof of the location of Nova Albion: At latitude 48 degrees Molyneux's coastline turns sharply eastward into a large indentation that unmistakably matches the mainland coast behind the largest island on the Pacific shores of North America.* The existence of this hidden inner coastline could not have been guessed at, let alone depicted with such accuracy, unless Drake had passed through the straits separating the island from it. And on the mainland opposite the

*The globe can still be viewed by appointment in the Library of the Middle Temple.

On Molyneux's globe, the indentation of the coastline beginning at latitude 48 degrees matches the mainland coast behind Vancouver Island. Cape Mendocino was placed at 43 degrees, and just below it a boundary line follows a river inland. From there, Drake's track heads across the Pacific.

missing island, Molyneux retained the inscription "Nova Albion" straddling the 50th parallel of latitude, and beneath it, "F. Dracus."[19]

The death of Elizabeth effectively brought the long war with Spain to an end. King Philip had died in 1598, and with her passing both nations sought a resolution to the conflict, which was concluded with the signing of the Treaty of Westminster by Philip III and Elizabeth's successor, James I, in 1604. A new English search for the northwest passage commenced soon afterward, but henceforth the effort focused on discovery of the passage from its Atlantic entrance.

Richard Hakluyt's expanded edition of *Principall Navigations* was his last great work of propaganda for English overseas exploration and colonization. After his death in 1616, most of his papers came into the possession of historian Samuel Purchas. In 1625 Purchas published the next great collection of journeys, titled *Purchas, His Pilgrimes,* and in his second volume he reprinted Hakluyt's account of Drake's northern voyage word for word.

Purchas also included in his book an account that Hakluyt had obtained, but never published, of a Greek pilot named Juan de Fuca, who claimed to have discovered the Strait of Anian in 1592 while in the service of Spain. In the narrative that Hakluyt had prepared, de Fuca told of finding an opening in the northwest coast of America near latitude 48 degrees, and through it an inland sea which he claimed would lead to the Atlantic Ocean. However, de Fuca's account and his offer to complete the discovery of the passage for England appear to have caused a stir when they were sent to Lord Burghley and Hakluyt from Venice in 1596, and after due consideration it apparently was decided that they should be omitted from *Principall Navigations.*[20]

In the same year that Purchas's work was published, England and Spain went to war once again, and the hostilities soon led to a renewed interest in the heroes of the previous war, particularly Sir Francis Drake. The following year a book devoted to Drake's early exploits on the Isthmus of Panama was printed. Titled *Sir Francis Drake Revived,* it was the first of the two volumes written by Drake's chaplain Philip Nichols many years earlier, and then edited by Drake before he submitted them for Elizabeth's approval. In 1628 the second volume, "offered now at last to public view," was published under the title *The World Encompassed by Sir Francis Drake,* "being his next voyage to that to Nombre de Dios formerly imprinted, carefully collected out of the notes of Master Francis Fletcher in this employment, and diverse others his followers in the same." Forty years after Hakluyt had borrowed Nichols's first draft of the account, Drake's own narrative of his voyage had finally come to print.

By the time Drake's much-amended account appeared, nearly everyone who had been privy to the true extent of his voyage was dead. However, two men who had known Drake and some of the details of his voyage were still alive and did subsequently leave some additional information.

In 1573 the Earl of Leicester had secretly married the widowed Lady Sheffield, and the following year she bore him a son, who was given his father's name, Robert Dudley. When Elizabeth learned of the secret union, she was enraged and refused to accept the legitimacy of either the marriage or their child as Leicester's heir. In time young Dudley was accepted at the court, however, and there he met both Drake and Thomas Cavendish, the latter recently returned from his voyage around the world. In 1591 Dudley married Cavendish's sister, Anne, and following Cavendish's death, he served as executor of his estate. Coming into possession of two of Cavendish's ships, he proposed to lead his own expedition to the South Sea but was dissuaded from doing so and sailed instead to the Caribbean in 1594 at age twenty. After Leicester's death Dudley petitioned for recognition that he was his father's rightful heir, but was unsuccessful. Embittered, he emigrated to Italy in 1605 and spent the remainder of his life there.

Around 1630 Dudley began work on an atlas of sea charts, which was eventually published in 1647, after his death. Beautifully engraved in Florence, the atlas included two charts of the Pacific coast of North America. Both charts depicted imaginary coastlines but incorporated specific details of the coast, which appear to have been copied from a rutter, or illustrated journal.

Two of the details are recognizable as real features of the coast.[21] The first, a distinctive headland which Dudley called "Cape of Storms" and placed at latitude 50 degrees, at the northern extremity of his coastline, was actually a very good likeness of Cape Flattery, which is located at latitude 48° 23'. The second feature, a large bay that Dudley placed between latitudes 49 and 50 degrees, is easily recognizable as Grays Harbor, actually located near latitude 47 degrees.[22] It appears that Dudley knew of a "Cape of Storms" at 50 degrees and an important bay between 49 and 50 degrees and mistakenly assumed that these details represented those places.

Sir William Monson was another member of the generation who went to sea in Drake's later years. He joined Elizabeth's navy around 1585 and was a captain by 1589, thereafter rising to the rank of admiral. A few years prior to his death in 1643, Monson organized the papers, knowledge, and opinions that he had accumulated over his lifetime into a volume that ran to more than 400 pages.[23] Several of Monson's tracts contained comments about Drake, with whom he had been acquainted, about his great voyage, and about the search for the northwest passage.

Monson gave only a brief account of Drake's voyage, but one comment

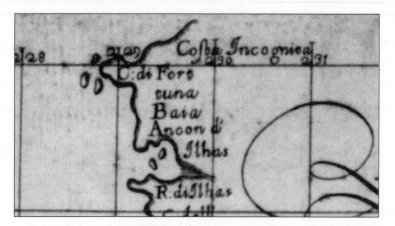

At its northern extremity, Robert Dudley's imaginary coastline contained two recognizable features—Cape Flattery and Grays Harbor—although Dudley placed them in the wrong latitudes.

in particular suggests that he knew more about it than he felt able to reveal.[24] In his introduction to the voyage he examined Drake's career, comparing his imperfections to his perfections. Regarding Drake's perfections, Monson cited his determined conquest of the dreaded Strait of Magellan, and "lastly and principally, that after so many miseries and extremities he endured, and almost two years spent in unpractised seas, when reason would have bid him sought home for his rest, he left his known course and ventured upon an unknown sea in 48 degrees, which sea or passage we know had been attempted by our seas but never discovered."[25] Monson's reference to "an unknown sea in 48 degrees" as the beginning of the passage bore a striking resemblance to the account of Juan de Fuca. However, Monson had heard about de Fuca's claim and seemed to have little confidence in its veracity.[26]

Monson also included in his memoirs *A Discourse Concerning the North-West Passage*, written by him in 1610, in which he reviewed the arguments for its existence and explained the optimum organization of an expedition for its discovery. This, he said, was best undertaken with three vessels: a ship to transport the equipment and supplies, and two small barks to carry out the explorations. "The two barks," he wrote, "must be strong and short because of their aptness to stay and tack if they come into a narrow strait, shoal water, or amongst ice."[27]

The captains of these small vessels, he went on, would have to be skillful mariners and good cosmographers; men of great resolution not to be daunted by any disaster. In the event that the vessels should separate, they would "appoint a place of meeting," and "upon either of their returns, they [would] appoint a certain place on shore where to leave their letters wrapped in a box of lead, and in those letters to make relation of their success."[28] And most important, "The masters must take an oath to use their best efforts to advance the voyage, and to keep secret the journal, the plate and cards [charts and sea cards], and all other writings that concern their navigation, [which] must be taken from them at their coming home and sealed up to present to his Majesty."[29]

From Monson's reference to an oath of secrecy and to the journals and charts still being turned over to the Crown in his day, it seems likely that all such materials beginning with Frobisher's and Drake's explorations were still sequestered in the guarded precinct of the Privy Chamber. The palace of Whitehall, which was one of Elizabeth's favorite residences, was destroyed by fire in 1698, and possibly that was when they were lost.[30] Or conceivably, the collection was sealed up in some forgotten hiding place during the civil war that ravaged England not long after Monson's death. In any case, the journals and charts of Drake's voyage appear to have been lost sometime before the end of the seventeenth century.

Despite the passing of generations, virtually every new map of the hemisphere recorded Drake's visit to an imaginary northwest coast of America. One in particular exemplifies the abiding sense of curiosity and mystery that surrounded his northern voyage. In 1726 satirist Jonathan Swift even included in his first edition of *Gulliver's Travels* a map locating his fictional kingdom of *Brobdingnag* in relation to Drake's storied exploit. Swift's fanciful kingdom aside, the map was a typical representation of the coast in that day, suggesting a tantalizing connection between Porto Sir Francis Drake, Nova Albion, and the Strait of Anian.

In 1741 a Russian expedition under the command of Vitus Bering sailed eastward from the Siberian port of Petropavlovsk and discovered the Aleutian Islands. Following the 1,200-mile-long string of islands eastward, Bering's two ships became separated. Captain Alexi Chirikov reached the coast of southern Alaska, where he lost two parties of men to ambushes by Indians and turned back.

Bering reached the northern coast of the Gulf of Alaska and followed it back westward. On his return voyage, however, Bering's ship was wrecked, and he and his men were marooned on a remote island. That winter Bering and more than half his men perished. The following summer, the survivors managed to build a boat from the ship's timbers and reach Siberia carrying a number of valuable furs.

By 1760 Russian fur hunters had worked their way along the Aleutian Islands into southwestern Alaska and were sending back increasingly precious cargoes of furs. For some years the Russian government managed to keep these developments secret in order to prevent rival powers from becoming interested in the region. Eventually, though, word reached the Spanish through their ambassador in Moscow, and their old fears of a northern intrusion into their colonial sphere were reawakened.

In 1774 pilot Juan Perez sailed from Mexico with instructions to reconnoiter the northwest coast of America as far as latitude 60 degrees. Making his landfall near 54 degrees, Perez was met by some 200 Indians who came out in very large canoes from a broad, eastward-trending opening in the coast. Perez did not explore further, however. Returning southward, he met more Indians in canoes and attempted to land a party for water, but a squall forced him to abandon the effort and stand away from the coast, after which he continued on to Mexico.

The following year a second expedition was dispatched northward from Mexico to continue these explorations, and one of the ships succeeded in reaching latitude 57 degrees north. However, like Perez, the members of this expedition did not realize that the coast they saw was composed of large islands.

In the meantime the English had heard of Bering's strait, and in 1776 the British Admiralty decided to send Captain James Cook on his third great voyage of exploration to settle once and for all the possible existence of a northwest passage. Cook's secret instructions, issued two days before he sailed in July 1776, were to

> Proceed in as direct a course as you can to the coast of Nova Albion, endeavouring to fall in with it in the latitude of 45° 0' North. . . .
> Upon your arrival on the coast of Nova Albion you are . . . to proceed northward along the coast, as far as the latitude of 65°, or farther

. . . and to explore such rivers or inlets as may appear to be of a considerable extent and pointing towards Hudsons or Baffins Bays.[31]

From their reference to Nova Albion, it is likely the Admiralty staff had
made some effort to find the log and charts of Drake's voyage. Perhaps they
found one or two of his old commemorative maps and examined the
Molyneux globe preserved at the Middle Temple. Beyond this, however,
they apparently knew nothing of Drake's discoveries other than that Nova
Albion lay to the north of 45 degrees.

After a voyage of eighteen months via the Cape of Good Hope, Cook
discovered the Hawaiian Islands in January 1778 and then made his initial
landfall on the coast of northwest America, at latitude 44 degrees, on
March 6. In his journal Cook wrote "the long-looked-for coast of Nova
Albion." A storm soon blew up, and he was obliged to move offshore. After
briefly sighting Cape Flattery, but not the opening in the coast immediately
to the north, he noted in his journal that the supposed strait of Juan de
Fuca seemed highly improbable. Cook's next landfall, on March 29, was a
rugged, storm-swept headland protruding some eight miles to seaward at
latitude 50 degrees, and the following day his ships entered an inlet a little
to the south, which he named Nootka from the language of the Indians.

Cook spent nearly a month in Nootka Sound repairing his ships and
conversing with the Indians by signs without learning that the sound was located on a large island. Then, resuming the voyage northward on April 26,
he stood well out to sea and did not see the coast again until he was above
latitude 56 degrees a week later. Consequently, he missed two more openings in the coast. Cook continued his voyage around the shores of Alaska
and eventually charted Bering Strait through to the Arctic Ocean before returning south to winter in the Hawaiian Islands. In February 1779 he was
killed in a dispute with the natives on the island of Hawaii.

After Cook's death his ships returned northward to complete the survey of Bering Strait and then called at China on their way home. There a
number of the company discovered that some sea otter furs that they had
acquired in trade with the Indians at Nootka Sound were worth a small fortune to the Chinese. An account and chart of Cook's voyage were published
in 1784, and within two years there were several ships on the northwest
coast trading with the Indians for the valuable sea otter pelts. As they

probed the coast for more villages to trade with, its complexity began to be revealed.

In 1786 an opening to the eastward was discovered between 51 and 52 degrees, and the following year Captain George Dixon rediscovered the broad entrance that Perez had seen at 54 degrees, and found that the outer coast between the two openings was a large cluster of islands, which he named the Queen Charlottes. Also that year, Captain Charles Barkley discovered a long opening just above 48 degrees and named it after the Greek pilot Juan de Fuca, whose long-ago claim now appeared to be substantiated.

In the meantime the Spanish had become increasingly concerned about rumors of the growing activity on their northern flank, and in 1789 the Viceroy of Mexico sent an expedition to occupy Nootka Sound, which had become the principal summer haven of the predominantly English fur traders. At Nootka they began impounding the traders' ships and sending them to Mexico. When a report of these actions was carried to London by one of the traders, the resultant furor escalated to a threat of war between England and Spain. Saner heads ultimately prevailed, and it was agreed that Captain George Vancouver, who had served as a midshipman on Cook's last voyage, would go to Nootka to negotiate a resolution to the dispute with Spain's representative, Juan Francisco de la Bodega y Quadra. While there, Vancouver was to systematically explore and chart the entire coast between latitudes 30 and 60 degrees.

Vancouver arrived on the coast of California with two ships, HMS *Discovery* and HMS *Chatham*, in April 1792 and commenced his survey northward. On his approach to Nootka he located the entrance to the Strait of Juan de Fuca and sailed in to investigate. At the eastern end of the strait he turned southward into a long maze of inlets, which he explored to its extremities and named Puget Sound. Then returning northward past an archipelago of small islands, he found a broad sea stretching northwestward to the horizon. There he encountered two small Spanish vessels that had come from Nootka under the command of Dionisio Alcala Galiano to explore this newly discovered inland sea, and they agreed to cooperate in their investigations.

Vancouver believed that these waters were an enclosed gulf accessible only through de Fuca's strait. However, Galiano had been told by the Indians that there was another passage leading back into the Pacific, and

George Vancouver

when they reached the northern end of the gulf, at latitude 50 degrees, they found the tide draining northward through several narrow channels. Working their way through the treacherous channels, Vancouver and Galiano found that they converged into a narrow, sixty-mile-long strait leading almost due westward toward the Pacific. History records that they were the first Europeans to sail through the narrow strait and chart the mainland coast behind the largest island on the Pacific coast of North America.

At Nootka Vancouver was received graciously by Quadra, and during their negotiations they developed a warm friendship. It was suggested that both their names be given to some feature of the coast, so the newly discovered island was named Quadra and Vancouver Island. Eventually, following the Spanish withdrawal from the region, Quadra's name was dropped, and it became known simply as Vancouver Island. After their initial negotiations, however, Vancouver and Quadra found it necessary to seek further direction from their respective governments, and while they waited for their instructions Vancouver continued his task of exploring and charting the coast. For two more years he worked his way up the coast, methodically surveying every channel and inlet.

In October 1794, with the Nootka crisis moving toward a final settlement between Britain and Spain, Vancouver sailed for England, carrying the first detailed chart of the entire Pacific coast of North America. From latitude 30 degrees northward to Cape Flattery at 48 degrees, he had found the coast to be singularly exposed and unremitting, with no islands of any consequence and few sheltered harbors besides the Bay of San Francisco and Grays Harbor. The one great river on this stretch of coast, discovered by American captain Robert Gray in 1792 and named after his ship *Columbia*, had a treacherous shoal across its mouth and had to be approached with extreme caution.

At Cape Flattery, however, the character of the coast changed suddenly and dramatically. Beginning with 275-mile-long Quadra and Vancouver Island, a chain of large islands screened a complex mainland coast containing innumerable inlets and fjords. Between the islands and the mainland a series of connecting straits ran northwest and north for a distance of some 800 miles, from Puget Sound nearly to latitude 60 degrees. Into the straits, although perhaps for reasons of secrecy Vancouver did not depict them on his chart, drained three major rivers—at latitudes 49, 54, and 56 degrees—which were as yet unexplored and unnamed by Europeans. However, Vancouver had explored every strait and inlet to its end and there was no remaining possibility of a passage through this coast to the Arctic Ocean. The only seaway between the Pacific and Arctic Oceans, the Bering Strait, lay 2,000 miles west and then north around the great Peninsula of Alaska.

PART FOUR

The Northern Voyage,
April to September
1579

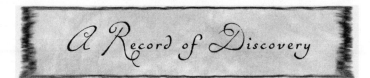

A Record of Discovery

Despite the shroud of secrecy imposed around Drake's northern explorations, and the loss of the original journals and charts of the voyage, a remarkably rich record of his discoveries has survived due to his efforts to preserve the information for posterity.

In the earliest surviving depiction of his route around the world, drawn with pen and ink on a print of Abraham Ortelius's map of the world, Drake's track reaches northward to latitude 57 degrees, which places him in the waters of southern Alaska. Presumably, then, this was where he "turned back on account of the ice," as noted on the hand-drawn maps that he gave out to important friends. On those maps he was obliged to place Nova Albion at latitude 40 degrees, ten degrees south of its true location. The earliest of them indicated that he made his initial landfall on the outer coast of a southward-pointing peninsula and then chose a site for Nova Albion at the same latitude, in the inlet behind the peninsula.

As his cryptograph evolved in subsequent maps, Drake revealed that this "peninsula" was actually an island—the largest in a chain of four islands stretching some 500 miles along the coast. Adding back the ten degrees subtracted to conceal its true location places the island at 50 degrees, and so it must have been Vancouver Island. This is confirmed by Emery Molyneux's suppressed globe, which omitted the island but accurately depicted the mainland coast behind it and retained the inscription "Nova Albion" straddling the 50th parallel of latitude. It follows, then, that Drake must have made his landfall on the outer coast of Vancouver Island, and then selected a site for the future colony very near 50 degrees on the east coast of the island.

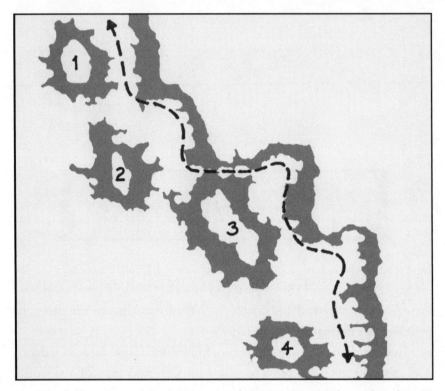

The islands on the Dutch Drake map magnified for comparison with the actual coastline on the opposite page (numerals and dotted lines added by the author; gray represents the ink on the original map).

What is striking about Drake's long chain of islands is that he appears to have formed a comprehension of the great coastal archipelago extending northward from Cape Flattery that the later, eighteenth-century explorers acquired only after numerous expeditions. Granted, Captain Vancouver and his Spanish contemporaries worked their way methodically up the coast, surveying and charting every inlet to its end, whereas Drake could have conducted a fast-paced reconnaissance, following the general trend of the coast instead. Even so, Drake's identification of these islands as such would have been an astonishing feat of exploration, for it is clear that to have done so he would have to have discovered and sailed the length of the straits separating all of them from the mainland. Nonetheless, this is what his maps and the information he leaked to Ortelius and others reveal.

It was the change Drake made to his cryptograph for the Dutch Drake

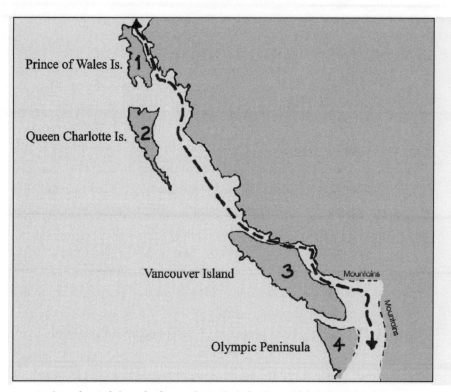

To have identified these islands as such, Drake had to have sailed the length of the straits separating them from the mainland (dotted lines).

map that opened the way to this appreciation. The key is the island where his track stops, which he redrew to become the largest in the chain. The details were engraved at a very small scale, so they are bound to appear crude and somewhat distorted when magnified. However, the islands fit the coast in a particular way that suggests firsthand knowledge of its complexity. Placing Drake's coastline alongside a modern map, one sees at once that he took pains to illustrate the narrow, eastward-trending strait separating Vancouver Island from the mainland to the north—the same narrow strait that Vancouver and the Spanish discovered two centuries later in their circumnavigation of the island. It appears that Drake was describing his probes into the coast as he redrew the island and the mainland behind it.

Then the two islands to the north are offset to the west and aligned as they should be to represent the Queen Charlotte Islands, undoubtedly seen as a single island, and farther north, Prince of Wales Island. Thus, it appears that Drake must have sailed the length of the straits at least as far as the

northern extremity of Prince of Wales Island, at latitude 56° 20'. And since
the straits were trending northward toward the Arctic sea, he could well have
believed that he had found the Strait of Anian.

This explains why 48 degrees was originally chosen as the cutoff point
for information about the voyage—to conceal the existence of the islands
and straits extending northward from Cape Flattery. No doubt, too, this
was why Hondius was obliged to revert to the inlet cryptograph in his
splendid broadside map. However, Drake did manage to insert on that map
one more clue to his journey: His track continues northward past the inlet
and then reappears emerging from its mouth, indicating that he passed behind the island of Nova Albion on his return southward.

Yet what accounts for the southernmost island in Drake's chain, where,
in reality, there is no island? Coming down the straits from the north and
seeing the mountainous Olympic Peninsula widely separated from the
mainland, he probably thought, initially at least, that it was another in this
long chain of islands. But he would not have found a way around this "island," so this would account for John Drake's reference to five or six "islands
of good land." Since there are no other comparably large islands south of
Prince of Wales Island, the two islands that are not depicted most probably
were farther north.

The evidence in Drake's maps and the Molyneux globe, by itself, is compelling. At the same time, Drake also gave Hondius, Ortelius, and other
mapmakers a great many descriptive place-names—capes, bays, and rivers—
along the coast as far north as latitude 57 degrees. His capes at 48, 50, and
54 degrees correspond to three of the most prominent capes on the coast:
Cape Flattery (also realistically depicted in Robert Dudley's 1647 chart),
Cape Cook on the outer coast of Vancouver Island, and Cape Knox at the
northwest tip of the Queen Charlotte Islands. And Drake's rivers "of the
straits," at 49, 53, and 57 degrees, respectively, match within one degree the
three largest rivers that flow into the straits: the Fraser, the Skeena, and the
Stikine. Other names such as "Coast of objections" and "frozen land" correspond to events described in *The World Encompassed*. Clearly, then, these were
the highlights of Drake's journey along the coast. But there was one other set
of information.

On the third map that he had Hondius prepare for Ortelius, at precisely 40 degrees, where he placed his landing on his own maps pursuant

The place-names on the underside of Ortelius's bulging northwest coast are highlights of Drake's journey from Nova Albion southward to the bay where he careened his ships.

to the ten-degree rule, Drake noted a "Bay of small ships" and "beautiful maidens," no doubt referring to the site of his future colony. Then several more place-names and features follow, including a "Bay of islands" which is also the outlet of a large, double-channeled river; farther down the coast a "great river"; and second from last, another "Bay of small ships," also labeled "Bay of fires." Unfortunately, the latitudes of these places are nonsensical because they are arrayed along the underside of Ortelius's great continental bulge. However, *The World Encompassed* describes the Indians lighting fires on the occasion of Drake's departure from the bay where he stopped to careen his ships, so this set of place-names represents the highlights of his journey from Nova Albion down the coast to that bay, which the "Anonymous Narrative" states they found at latitude 44 degrees. Therefore, these names relate to places between latitudes 50 and 44 degrees.

Combining all of this information, a surprisingly detailed picture emerges, and it becomes possible to reconstruct Drake's explorations with remarkable clarity.

INFORMATION FROM DRAKE'S NORTHERN VOYAGE

Latitude North	Place-name or Feature	Source
57°	"River of the straits"	Hondius, Ortelius
55°	"Northwest Passage"	Hakluyt
	"White cape"	Hondius, Plancius
	"Cape of good fortune"	Hondius
54°	"Cape Mendocino"	Hondius, Ortelius
	"Strong currents"	Hondius, Ortelius
	"Inlet of the islands"	Hondius
53°	2nd latitude written over	Anonymous Narrative
	"Frozen land"	Hondius, Plancius
	"Coast of objections"	Hondius
	"River of the straits"	Hondius, Ortelius
52°	"Rugged coast"	Hondius
51°	"Long Inlet"	Hondius
50°	1st latitude written over	Anonymous Narrative
	"Cape of worries"	Hondius, Ortelius
	"Cape of storms"	Hondius, Plancius
	Drake's landing (flag)*	Hondius
	"Nova Albion"	Molyneux
	"Bay of small ships,"	
	also "beautiful maidens"*	Hondius, Ortelius
49°	"Mountainous land"	Hondius
	"Point of small fish"*	Hondius, Ortelius
	"Point St. Michael"*	Hondius, Ortelius
	"Bay of islands"*	Hondius, Ortelius
	"River of the straits"	Hondius, Ortelius
	Double channel river (detail)*	Hondius, Ortelius
	"Beautiful bay"*	Hondius, Ortelius

48°	3rd latitude written	*Anonymous Narrative*
	"Cape of snowcapped mountains"	*Hondius*
	Cape Flattery (detail)	*Molyneux*
	Cape Flattery (detail)	*Dudley*
47°	Grays Harbour (detail)	*Dudley*
46°	"Beach"*	*Hondius, Ortelius*
	"Great river"*	*Hondius, Ortelius*
	"Rugged coast"	*Hondius, Ortelius*
	"Point of position"*	*Hondius, Ortelius*
44°	Drake's careenage	*Anonymous Narrative*
	"Bay of small ships," also "Bay of fires"*	*Hondius, Ortelius*
	Whale Cove (detail)	*Hondius*
43°	Cape Arago (detail)	*Molyneux*
	Coquille River (detail)	*Molyneux*
	Drake's point of departure from North America	*Molyneux*

*Placed after adjusting the latitude to compensate for the ten-degree rule. For further details, see Bawlf, *Secret Voyage* (2001), 56–66.

Drake's Strait of Anian

*B*efore first light on *Good Friday, April 16, 1579, the* Golden Hinde *and its* consort, the small bark seized from Rodrigo Tello, slipped out of the bay of Guatulco, New Spain, and steered southwest. Drake had put his last captives ashore, and aboard the two ships his company numbered about eighty-five, including the Negro woman Maria and the two Negro men who had joined them.[1] They had seen their last of the Spaniards. The time of year was approaching when Drake had to get through the northern passage or face a very long voyage home.

When he entered the Pacific, Drake had no clear idea of the prevailing winds across this vast ocean. The Spanish carefully guarded the information they had pieced together from their explorations to prevent it from falling into foreign hands. The coastal traders kept their own rutters and charts, however, and Drake's men were under orders whenever they boarded a ship to seize the pilot and his documents as a first priority. Consequently, Drake had interrogated numerous pilots and collected a great deal of information about navigation on the coast of Chile and Peru. Also, he had with him a pilot named Morera who appears to have been familiar with the coast of New Spain.[2] However, Drake had not only to navigate along the Spaniards' coasts but also to find a wind that would carry him to the as yet undiscovered northwest tip of America.

Part of the answer had come from what he had learned about the development of navigation between Peru and Chile. The problem the Spanish discovered when they began pushing southward into Chile was that the wind and current came up from the south. Whereas sailing northward from

Chile was easy, the voyage southward from Peru against the wind and current could take months.

In 1563 the problem was solved by pilot Juan Fernandez, who stood well out to sea instead of following the coast. From Callao, latitude 12 degrees south, Fernandez sailed several hundred miles offshore on the trade winds and then worked his way southward until he picked up the westerlies, which carried him back onto the coast, arriving at Valparaiso, latitude 33 degrees, after a voyage of just twenty days. Thus, Fernandez had discovered that the circulation of winds off the coast of South America is counterclockwise, and Drake had learned all about this.[3]

He then had the extraordinary good fortune to intercept, on the bark of Rodrigo Tello, the two pilots carrying the secret charts and sailing directions for the voyage to the Philippines and back. These revealed that the circulation of winds north of the equator was the reverse to that off South America—clockwise rather than counterclockwise. From the port of Acapulco in New Spain, the Manila galleons sailed southwest to between latitudes 12 and 14 degrees north, where they picked up the trade winds, and then continued due westward across the Pacific to the Mariana Islands, and then on to the Philippines. On the return voyage, they sailed northward until they found the westerlies between latitudes 35 and 40 degrees, which brought them back to the coast of North America, where the wind swung southward and carried them down the coast to Acapulco.[4]

Thus, along the Pacific coast of North as well as South America the winds blow from the higher latitudes toward the equator. For Drake to have attempted to sail from New Spain northward following the coast would have meant an exhausting and time-consuming struggle against the prevailing wind. The fastest route, he had concluded, was to follow the example of Spanish navigation from Callao to Valparaiso, sailing with rather than against the circulation of winds.

Southwest of Guatulco Drake's ships picked up the trade winds and then continued due westward for 1,500 miles before turning northward. From that point they sailed northwest and then north by northeast for another 3,000 miles until, in latitude 44 degrees, the wind changed and Drake altered their course to east by northeast. He had deduced and harnessed the circulation brilliantly, sailing efficiently around the vortex of

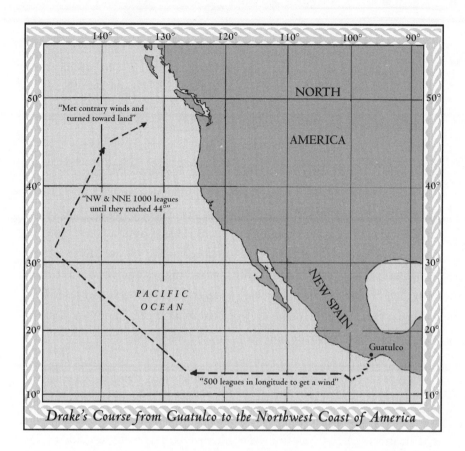

Drake's Course from Guatulco to the Northwest Coast of America

Map labels:
- 140° 130° 120° 110° 100° 90°
- 50° 50°
- NORTH
- "Met contrary winds and turned toward land"
- AMERICA
- 40° 40°
- "NW & NNE 1000 leagues until they reached 44°"
- 30° 30°
- PACIFIC OCEAN
- NEW SPAIN
- 20° 20°
- Guatulco
- "500 leagues in longitude to get a wind"
- 10° 10°

winds that would be discovered and named Fleurieu's Whirlpool two centuries later.[5] In all, they traveled nearly 5,000 miles in forty-eight days.

On the morning of June 3, with a gale blowing out of the northwest, they made landfall on a rugged, steeply mountainous coast near latitude 50 degrees north.[6] Ahead, the seas collided with rock-strewn beaches and high bluffs. Here and there gaps between the mountains suggested inlets, but their entrances were difficult to see due to mists blowing down the coast. A short distance to the north a headland extended several miles to seaward, offering some shelter from the wind, and Drake brought his ships to anchor in its lee.

[It was] a bad bay, the best road we could for the present meet with, where we were not without some danger by reason of the many extreme gusts and flows that beat upon us, which if they ceased and were still at any time, immediately upon their intermission there followed most vile, thick, and stinking fogs, against which the sea prevailed nothing till the gusts of wind again removed them, which brought with them such extremity and violence when they came, that there was no dealing or resisting against them.[7]

Drake subsequently referred to the headland at latitude 50 degrees as the "Cape of storms" and "Cape of worries," and it is indeed one of the stormiest and most treacherous capes on the outer coast of Vancouver Island. It has since been named Cape Cook, after Captain Cook, and the bay on its south side where Drake anchored is Checleset Bay. It was at best a temporary refuge, good only for so long as the wind continued from the northwest. The bay is wide open to the southwest and southeast, and had a gale suddenly come up from either of those directions, Drake's ships would have been in imminent danger of being driven ashore and wrecked.

There are several streams at the back of the bay, and it is possible that they managed to refill some of their water casks and obtain firewood. It appears also that some Indians came out to meet them in their canoes. They were members of the *Nuu-chah-nulth* tribe, whose territories extended from Cape Cook down the coast to the Strait of Juan de Fuca. Their oral history contains many vivid and detailed accounts of the visits of Captain Cook and the Spanish two centuries ago. However, one band who resided near Checleset Bay has a tradition that the first Europeans visited them many generations earlier.

As with all the tribes of the northwest coast, the *Nuu-chah-nulth* observe the elaborate traditions of the potlatch, or gift-giving feast. By custom, the first gift is presented to the most honored guest, usually a visiting chief. Yet the Checleset people have a different custom than other *Nuu-cha-nulth* bands: They carry the first gift down to the sea and dedicate it to the "great chief" of the bearded men who visited them in his "floating house" long before Cook and the Spanish came.[8] It is doubtful that Drake saw their village, but they were whale hunters, and he would have been impressed by the size and quality of their seagoing canoes. Probably, he presented them with some gifts.

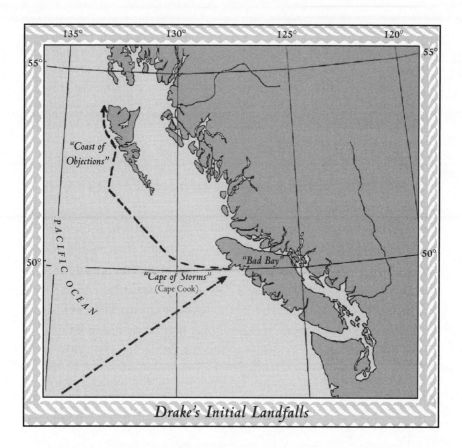

Drake's Initial Landfalls

When the wind died down, the ships were engulfed by thick, "stinking" fogs,* and Drake spent some anxious hours awaiting an opportunity to escape the bay. Finally, a fresh wind cleared the fog away but also probably obliged him to quickly weigh anchor and put to sea before they were driven against the cape.[9]

After moving some distance to seaward, they turned and made rapid headway to the northwest. By the afternoon of June 4 they were in latitude 52 degrees.

> [But] in the night following we found such alteration of heat into extreme and nipping cold that our men in general did grievously complain thereof, some of them feeling their healths much impaired thereby; nei-

---

*The northwest winds cause the upwelling of deep, cold water along the west coast of Vancouver Island, creating dense fogs whenever the wind subsides. The upwelling water is rich with decaying sea life—hence the stink.

ther was it that this chanced in the night alone, but the day following carried with it not only the marks, but the stings and force of the night going before, to the great admiration of us all; for besides that the pinching and biting air was nothing altered, the very ropes of our ship were stiff and the rain which fell was an unnatural congealed and frozen substance, so that we seemed rather to be in the frozen zone.[10]

They had met and crossed a weather front drawing freezing air from the coastal mountains to the east and northeast.

In the afternoon of June 5 the wind backed around to the north, and they were obliged to alter their course eastward, where they made their second landfall, at latitude 53 degrees, sooner than expected.[11] The outer coast of the Queen Charlotte Islands lies 150 miles farther west than Cape Cook, and finding the land so far west was a disappointment. They were as far north of the equator as Magellan's Strait was south of it, and still there was no indication of the coast turning eastward. Moreover, the farther they went, the colder the weather became.

> Neither did this happen for the time only . . . for it came to that extremity in sailing but 2 deg. farther to the northward in our course that though sea-men lack not good stomachs, yet it seemed a question to many amongst us whether their hands should feed their mouths, or rather keep themselves within their covers from the pinching cold that did benumb them. Neither could we impute it to the tenderness of our bodies. . . . our meat, as soon as it was removed from the fire, would presently in a manner be frozen up, and our ropes and tackling in a few days were grown to that stiffness that what 3 men afore were able with them to perform, now 6 men with their best strength and uttermost endeavour were hardly able to accomplish; whereby a great discouragement seized upon the minds of our men and they were possessed with a great mislike and doubting of any good to be done that way.[12]

Drake later referred to the coast at latitude 53 degrees as the "Frozen land" and "Coast of objections." Indeed, it was exceptionally cold in comparison to the modern era. The latest date that freezing weather was recorded at this latitude in the twentieth century was in early May. But the

1570s were one of the coldest decades at the beginning of the Little Ice Age, and it appears that the coast from the Queen Charlotte Islands northward was still immersed in a stubbornly protracted winter. Most probably, the colder temperatures combined with the flow of moist air off the Pacific had produced a deep accumulation of snow, which was retarding the onset of spring. Drake prevailed upon his men to continue their quest.

> Yet would not our General be discouraged, but as well by comfortable speeches of the divine providence, and of God's loving care over his children, out of the Scriptures, as also by other good and profitable persuasions, adding thereto his own cheerful example, he so stirred them up to put on a good courage, and to quit themselves like men, to endure some short extremity to have the speedier comfort, and a little trouble to obtain the greater glory.[13]

At latitude 54 degrees they came to a cape. Rounding it, they were confronted with a stunning panorama: Beginning thirty-five miles to the northeast a long line of shimmering white mountains extended northward over the horizon. Between the cape and the mountains a broad passage led due eastward. Drake later referred to the cape at 54 degrees, "strong currents," and "Inlet of the islands." The passage is now called Dixon Entrance, and the mountains to the northeast are the islands of southern Alaska.

Immediately adjacent to the cape an island offered shelter from the icy wind. When the Spanish expedition of Juan Perez arrived there in 1774, about 200 Indians came out to meet them in twenty-one big dugout canoes, some of which exceeded forty feet in length. Clothed in furs and woven capes, the Indians traded finely carved spoons and bowls and brightly painted wooden boxes for ribbons, beads, and especially iron. These were *Haida* Indians, whose forefathers had resided on the shores of narrow Parry Passage, between the island and the cape, for countless centuries.* Given their inclination to trade and Drake's efforts to befriend the native peoples wherever he went, it is possible that he met the Haida, and even that he visited their village, although there is no record of these events.

* * *

*Human occupation of the Queen Charlotte Islands dates from at least 7000 B.C.E.

If Drake did meet the Haida *of Parry Passage, this was just one of many encounters* he was bound to have had with the Indians of this northwest coast as he penetrated it further. In the late eighteenth century, before European diseases began to decimate the population, ships calling at their villages were often met by hundreds of people in canoes. They were fierce, war-like people and frequently embarked on raiding expeditions against rival tribes, descending swiftly on their villages to plunder and carry away slaves. During the maritime fur trade several ships were attacked and some crews massacred. Such incidents were usually provoked by an insult from the traders, however, and the first recorded contacts with Europeans were generally friendly.

The *Haida* were one of three major tribal groups that inhabited the northern region of the coast, each with numerous villages. *Haida* territories included the whole of the Queen Charlotte Islands as well as parts of the islands on the north side of Dixon Entrance; the *Tsimshian* occupied the mainland coast opposite; and the *Tlingit* controlled the remainder of the islands and mainland northward to the end of the archipelago. Their combined population was likely in the range of 30,000.[14] Although each major group was linguistically distinct from the others, their social organization, technology, and methods were very similar. All constructed massive post-and-beam houses and traveled widely on the coast in fleets of large dugout canoes; and all had shared in the development of one of the most sophisticated aboriginal cultures in the world.

Among the many manifestations of their elaborate mythology and art, the one most frequently remarked upon by early visitors was the totem pole—the tall timber posts that the Indians carved with strange human and animal figures and set up in front of their houses. There were fewer of these prior to the arrival of the fur traders in the late eighteenth century with a plentiful supply of iron blades, but the totem pole undoubtedly was a long-established part of the culture by that time. A trader who visited Parry Passage in 1791 wrote of the experience:

> After the vessel was fast, I went in the boat accompanied by Cow [Haida] to view two pillars which were situated in the front of a village about a quarter of a mile distant.... They were about 40 feet in height, carved in a very curious manner indeed—representing men, toads, etc., the whole of which I thought did great credit to the natural genius of these people.

Photograph of a Haida *village (1878)*

In one of the houses of this village the door was through the mouth of one of the before-mentioned images. In another was a large, square pit with seats all round it sufficient to contain a great number of people.[15]

The journal of Francis Fletcher most probably contained similar notes about the villages that they saw and visited, much as he had described the aboriginal peoples they had met on their voyage around South America. Unfortunately, when Drake's narrative was adapted from the journal, everything concerning the voyage north of 48 degrees was omitted except for the passages concerning the cold weather. Drake managed to retain these by altering the latitude of the weather ten degrees to the south to explain his turning back at 48 degrees. Two of the passages make fleeting reference to the Indians he met in the "frozen zone," but this is all that remains from what would have been fascinating observations of the people and their culture two centuries earlier than any other written record.

Turning into Dixon Entrance, Drake worked his ships eastward. If he *had* visited the *Haida* village in Parry Passage, a short distance along the shore after emerging from the passage he would have come to an unforgettable landmark in the form of a massive pillar of stone rising straight up from the shore to a height of 100 feet. It is now called Pillar Rock.

Fifty miles farther east Drake would have seen that this low-lying land ended in a long sand spit, and recognized that the "Coast of objections" was an island. On the north side of Dixon Entrance the mountains and hills of Prince of Wales Island were cloaked in snow. With the sun so near the summer solstice, Fletcher was perplexed that it seemed powerless to remove the snow.*

> The chiefest [cause] of which we conceive to be the large spreading of the Asian and American continent, which (somewhat Northward of these parts) if they be not fully joined, yet seem they to come very near one to the other. From whose high and snow-covered mountains, the North and North-west winds . . . send abroad their frozen nymphs to the infecting [of] the whole air with this insufferable sharpness: not permitting the sun, no, not in the pride of his heat, to dissolve that congealed matter and snow, which they have breathed out so nigh the sun and so many degrees distant from themselves.[16]

As long as the coast was overlain with a blanket of cold air, the rate of melting would have been slow. Ultimately, if snow remains through the summer and compacts under the weight of subsequent years' snowfall, the result is glaciation. Such was the case with the coastal mountains on the mainland of southern Alaska, which through countless millennia had accumulated immense glacial fields, many of which crept like monstrous, slow-moving rivers down to the sea.

During the warmer climate of 1000 to 1300 C.E. the coastal glaciers had retreated; then, with the onset of global cooling, they had begun to grow once more. Local high-pressure systems became established over the ice fields and sent out severe *catabatic* winds—cold air outflows such as Drake encountered—and when these collided with the moist storms blowing in off the Pacific, huge snowfalls accelerated the aggregation of ice.[17]

---

*The Elizabethans did not understand the principle of solar radiation. They believed that the sun warmed the air, which in turn melted the snow and brought on spring. However, it is the absorption of the sun's radiation by the Earth's surface that generates warming in the first instance, and nearly all of the radiation that reaches ground covered in snow is reflected back into space.

Pillar Rock

The oral history of the *Tlingit* Indians who resided in Glacier Bay, 200 miles north of Dixon Entrance, tells of their villages being swept away by the rapidly advancing walls of ice,* and of the great hardships they suffered when they were forced to resettle on the shores of adjacent Icy Strait.[18]

The glaciers reached their farthest point of advance within two or three decades of Drake's voyage and remained there for another century or more.[19] When the eighteenth-century explorers arrived, they found them "calving" large numbers of icebergs into the straits. Since the end of the Little Ice Age in the middle of the nineteenth century, the glaciers have been

*From the *Tlingit* account it appears that the glaciers advanced very rapidly, and this accords with the European experience. In the mid–seventeenth century the de Bois Glacier, near Chamonix in France, was reported to be advancing, in distance, "over a musket shot every day, even in August" (Fagan, *The Little Ice Age*, 124).

retreating—more than fifty miles in the case of Glacier Bay—but even people born in the early years of the twentieth century recall icebergs larger than a house drifting down the straits.

Prince of Wales Island comes to a southerly headland just below 55 degrees, and beyond it a second mountainous coast becomes visible. Drake later referred to the "white cape" and "Cape of good fortune" at 55 degrees. The southern tip of the island is now called Cape Chacon. Rounding the cape, Drake found a large opening leading northward. This is Clarence Strait, which extends northwest for some ninety miles between the island and the continental mainland.

Clarence Strait is intersected by long inlets that cut deep into the mainland to the foot of the towering coastal mountain range. In the winter and early spring cold air intermittently pours down from the high snowfields and out through the inlets into the strait, where it lies trapped by long Prince of Wales Island, as in a trough. When this occurs, the inlets and strait are overlain with cold air and icy fogs until they are flushed out by a fresh wind.* Fletcher was again perplexed by the sun's inability to do its work.

> For the sun striving to perform his natural office, in elevating the vapors out of these inferior bodies, draweth necessarily abundance of moisture out of the sea; but the nipping cold . . . meeting and opposing the sun's endeavour, forces him to give over his work imperfect; and instead of higher elevation, to leave in the lowest region wandering upon the face of the earth and waters as it were, a second sea through which its own beams cannot possibly pierce, unless sometimes when the sudden violence of the winds doth help to scatter and break through it.[20]

Alternately becalmed in fog and sailing on the cold gusts coming from the inlets, Drake's ships made their way northward past the end of Prince of Wales Island and then, following a northeastward turn of the strait, they abruptly met an impassable barrier. Drake later noted a "River of the straits," at 57 degrees, and there is only one river to which he could have

*This was a regular phenomenon until the early twentieth century but now occurs infrequently.

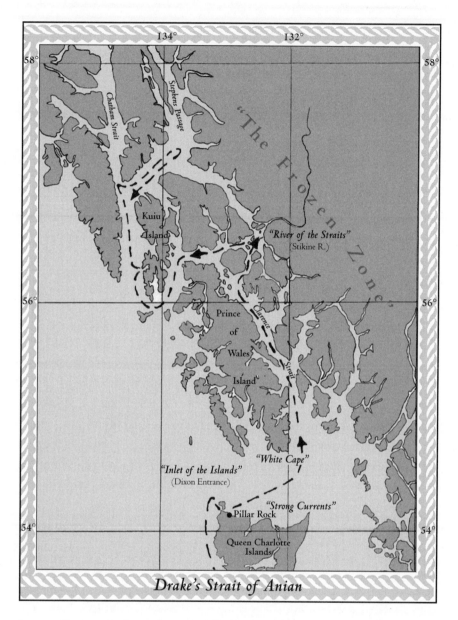

Drake's Strait of Anian

been referring. At latitude 56° 30′, the shallow delta of the Stikine River extends across the strait, all but blocking it. Only a narrow, nine-mile-long channel, now called Dry Strait, connects along the outer edge of the delta to the straits beyond, and as the name implies, the channel virtually drains at low tide.

Drake probably took a boat far enough up Dry Strait to see for himself that there was no possibility of the *Golden Hinde* getting through. They would have had to tow her, and with only their small launches to do the work, she would have become grounded on the falling tide before they got clear of the channel, and potentially become stuck there. However, Drake would have seen the continuation of the straits to the north, thereby confirming that the land on the west side of the blocked strait likely was another island. Just prior to their reaching the delta, the strait had come to a junction with a passage leading westward past the end of Prince of Wales Island, and Drake would have returned to it with the aim of finding a way around the barrier.

The land on the north side of what is now called Sumner Strait is actually composed of three islands, the westernmost being Kuiu Island, but the passages separating them are obscure and tortuous. Forty miles to the west the strait turns southward between Prince of Wales Island and Kuiu Island. Then they would have rounded the southern tip of Kuiu Island at latitude 56 degrees and discovered a twelve-mile-wide passage leading northward. Captain Vancouver later named it Chatham Strait.

It would have been difficult for Drake to conceive of a better match for Abraham Ortelius's theoretical strait than Chatham Strait. Its western shore, now called Baranof Island, presents an uninterrupted line of snow-covered mountains marching due northward over the horizon. Moreover, there undoubtedly were icebergs drifting down the strait. With the passage heading directly for the Arctic sea, here surely, Drake must have thought, was the Strait of Anian. Ortelius had placed the strait's junction with the northwest passage at 66 degrees, but with the bitterly cold wind and the icebergs, Drake may well have believed that it was nearer.

To be certain this was the Strait of Anian, he would have wished to probe farther, which would have meant laboriously beating to and fro against a brisk north wind that was blowing down the strait. Compounding their travails would have been the problem of maneuvering their ships safely around the icebergs that lay strewn in their path, many of which would have been of a sufficient size to sink one of them in a collision under sail. To save the risk and time maneuvering his ships, Drake would have wanted to assemble one of his two remaining pinnaces, which he had reserved for this stage of the voyage.

Seventeen miles up Chatham Strait an inlet, now called Port Malmesbury, penetrates the rugged coast of Kuiu Island. In 1954 a prospector named Donald Mac-

Donald spent the summer exploring the geology of the inlet. During the course of his explorations, MacDonald later recounted, he became curious about a cave he could see partway up a high vertical cliff at the mouth of the inlet, so he climbed up to investigate.[21] Inside the cave, he said, he found some ancient *Tlingit* burial boxes and artifacts, which he left undisturbed.* From the floor of the cave, he picked up a small, rectangular piece of metal, and carrying it out into the daylight, found in its corners holes containing rust, indicating that it had once been nailed to something. When he brushed some dust off the plate, he said, he found that it was inscribed with a writing that he could not read. In 1956 MacDonald called at the Smithsonian Institution to report his discovery, and a staff member requested a photo of the plate.[22]

MacDonald said that the plate was too dark to be photographed, so he supplied the Smithsonian with a rubbing of the plate, which was found to be inscribed in Latin. The inscription, he said, stated that Francis Drake had named some place "Port Discovery" and had taken possession of the surrounding country in the name of Queen Elizabeth. However, MacDonald said that he was told the plate must be a hoax, as there was no record of Drake being anywhere near Alaska. Not wishing to become involved in a controversy, he said, he put the plate away in a trunk containing his papers, but some years later thieves ransacked the trunk, and its contents were never recovered.[23]

Nevertheless, there is mention of Drake leaving such plates at several important points on the voyage. Francis Fletcher refers to one that he inscribed for Drake to leave at Cape Deseado upon their exiting Magellan's Strait; the broadside account of Jodocus Hondius states that Drake had inscribed and "erected on a post" on the "Island" of Nova Albion a plate of silver; and all of the accounts describe Drake having a plate nailed to a "great post" at the bay where he subsequently careened the *Golden Hinde*. It stands to reason, then, that he would have left another at the entrance to the all-important Strait of Anian, and herewith arises an intriguing question: What was the inspiration for him nailing these plates up to "great posts" if not to draw attention to them by imitating the totem poles that he first saw in the northern Indian villages he visited?

Tlingit chiefs and shamen were often buried with their possessions in caves. Unknown to MacDonald at the time, three of the burial boxes had already been removed from the cave by looters. They were subsequently recovered by U.S. Forest Service archaeologists, and one proved to be 600 years old. Unfortunately, the remainder of the contents of the cave has disappeared without a trace.

In the passages that Drake retained in his narrative describing the freezing weather he encountered, there are two references to the inhabitants of the "frozen zone." In the first, discussing the depth of the cold they experienced, the narrative observes:

> And that it was not our tenderness, but the very extremity of the cold itself that caused this sensibleness in us, may the rather appear, in that the natural inhabitants . . . to whom the country air and climate was proper, and in whom custom of cold was as it were a second nature; yet used to come shivering to us in their warm furs, crowding together, body to body, to receive heat one of another, and sheltering themselves under a lee bank if it were possible.[24]

This passage suggests more than a fleeting visit with one particular band of Indians, in what Fletcher referred to as the "frozen zone." Then, in an obvious reference to their village, the narrative states, "Hence comes it that in the middest of their summer the snow hardly departeth even from their very doors, but is never taken away from their hills at all."[25] The match between the description and the climatic conditions in the coastal archipelago of southern Alaska at that time is simply too compelling to be any sort of contrivance on Fletcher's or Drake's part.

Conceivably, then, Drake had chosen to assemble his pinnace in Port Malmesbury, for which purpose he would have remained four or five days.[26] Although there is ample evidence of native activity in the inlet through many centuries, it has not been determined whether it was inhabited at the time of Drake's voyage.[27] Just three miles to the north by trail, however, was large Tebenkof Bay, which contained several *Tlingit* villages.[28]

When the pinnace was ready, Drake would have headed up the strait, maneuvering more easily around the icebergs, to see what lay beyond the horizon.* According to the earliest surviving rendering of his route, in pen and ink on a copy of Ortelius's world map, Drake's farthest point of advance northward was 57 degrees, which would have placed him at the southern extremity of Admiralty Island, around which the strait forks. Here Chatham Strait narrows to a width

---

*Optically, objects at sea level begin to dip below the horizon at a distance of about eleven miles.

of six miles, but Drake would have seen the mountains on its west side still continuing due northward over the horizon. However, he would also have found the number of icebergs in the strait increasing, because sixty miles farther north it connects to Icy Strait, which was the outlet for all the ice then being calved by the massive glaciers that had consumed Glacier Bay.

The eastern branch of the straits passes through Frederick Sound to the north side of the Stikine River delta and also continues northward beyond the horizon, and Drake would have seen more ice calved by the numerous glaciers along the mainland coast to the east and north. By the time they returned to his ships Drake and his men would have probably traveled about 150 miles. But the reconnaissance had proved crucial, for from everything that transpired thereafter there can be no doubt that he was convinced he had discovered the Strait of Anian.

Before he could proceed farther, however, he had to find a site for the future colony of New England and a secure haven in which to careen his ships. Moreover, time was of the essence. He had to be back in the strait by the beginning of September in order to reach the Atlantic Ocean before the arctic winter closed the passage.

Nova Albion

$\mathcal{E}$merging out of the strait, Drake likely followed the outer coast southward, as there would have been no point in retracing his former route through Clarence Strait. There are numerous small islands along the outside of Prince of Wales Island where Drake and his men would have found sea lion and seabird rookeries from which to replenish their depleted victuals.* Then it appears they turned into Dixon Entrance once again.

Although Hondius misplaced it slightly at latitude 53 degrees on the map he prepared for Ortelius, the second "river of the straits" that Drake later referred to could only have been the Skeena River.[1] To have found the mouth of the Skeena, he must have been curious about the eastern end of Dixon Entrance and the possibility of a passage eastward through the continent as an alternative to the Strait of Anian and the northwest passage. This alternate concept was popular with the cosmographers and mapmakers of the day, including Dr. John Dee, and it probably appealed to Drake after he saw the ice in the strait. Approaching the Skeena, he would have encountered the large population of *Tsimshian* Indians residing near the river because of its huge salmon runs. However, he would soon have found that there were no promising openings eastward, and would not have lingered.

Turning southward, they would have followed the mainland coast in what is now called Hecate Strait, which separates the Queen Charlotte

---

*It appears Drake gave the name St. James to Prince of Wales Island. If so, it is likely that he called these adjacent islands the Isles of St. James.

Islands from the mainland. For 180 miles this coast takes on the character of the outer coast, with dangerous shoals often shrouded in fog, and high bluffs worn smooth by the Pacific storms blowing through the wide gap between the Queen Charlotte Islands and Vancouver Island. There are several openings to a maze of channels and inlets behind this facade, but these openings are often shrouded in fog, and from Drake's reference to a "rugged coast" at 52 degrees it appears that he made no attempt to probe them.[2] With the wind at their backs they would have passed down this coast in a couple of days at most.

Then at latitude 51 degrees they entered a ten-mile-wide opening behind a great headland stretching far to the west of them. The headland was the northern end of Vancouver Island, and the opening was Queen Charlotte Strait, leading southeastward for sixty miles. This was the territory of the *Kwakwaka'wakw** people, who resided in numerous villages around the strait and adjoining inlets, and Drake could not have avoided meeting them. They were fierce, head-hunting warriors. When Spanish explorers entered these waters in 1792, one of their boats was pursued by a large number of them in war canoes, although the incident ended peaceably.

From his mention of strong currents at the "Inlet of the islands," it is clear that Drake observed the tidal flows closely as an indication of whether an opening held promise. At its eastern end Queen Charlotte Strait dissolves into an archipelago of smaller islands, and rounding the first of these, he would have found powerful tides ebbing and flooding through a narrow passage that led eastward along the shore of the great headland. It is possible, too, that he learned by signs from the Indians that the passage connected to a large body of water somewhere to the east, and that he recruited some of them to guide him, as he sometimes did elsewhere on the voyage. Drake afterward called it the "long inlet."[3] It was the same narrow passage now called Johnstone Strait that Galiano and Vancouver discovered in their 1792 circumnavigation of Vancouver Island.

The strait, which rarely exceeds two miles in width, continues nearly due eastward for fifty miles with several channels and inlets branching

---

*Otherwise known as the *Kwakiutl*, their loosely allied tribes controlled most of northern Vancouver Island and the mainland opposite.

Kwakiutl *warriors confronting a party of eighteenth-century explorers*

northeast before it comes to a final fork. One branch of this last fork follows the coast of Vancouver Island southward; the other goes eastward. Both branches lead to treacherous outlets. The key to the route taken by Drake is found in the corrections he made to the copy of Henry of Navarre's map. From the emphasis that he gave to the large embayment of the mainland coast at the eastern extremity of the strait, it appears that he was again looking for a passage through the continent and thus chose the branch of the strait leading in that direction, away from Vancouver Island.[4]

Soon Drake and his men would have heard the low roar of rushing water, and he likely anchored the ships while he went in the pinnace to investigate. A short distance ahead was a swirling cauldron of eddies, overfalls, and whirlpools known as the Yuculta Rapids, the result of large tidal flows being forced through three narrows at rates of up to ten knots. Four times a day they reverse direction with the tide changes, the water falls slack for only a few minutes, and then the current begins building in the opposite direction, soon reaching a velocity at which it is impossible to steer a sailing vessel.

When the Spanish explorer Galiano arrived with his vessels *Sutil* and *Mexicana* at the eastern end of the rapids in 1792, the Indians came out from a nearby village to warn him of the hazards.

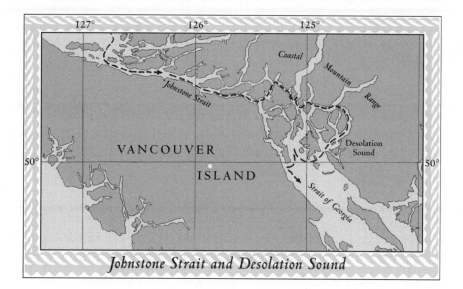

Johnstone Strait and Desolation Sound

The Indians, indicating the course of the sun, signed to us that the favourable moment for which we longed [slack water] would come when the sun was near the peak of a high mountain on the continent. The time passed quickly with the entertainment afforded by watching the rush of waters, the many trees which were washed down by its violence, the continual passage of the birds, and the play of the fish which made lovely colours on the shingle where we were anchored. . . .

The Indians came and accompanied us in their canoes, serving as pilots. We seized the opportune moment and were shortly beyond the most critical point, but the tide, which had not stopped except for a moment, began to acquire force and reached the *Sutil*. It took away her steerage way and began to carry her along.[5]

Hurling through the rapids, the forty-five-ton *Sutil* was caught in a whirlpool and spun around three times so quickly that the men became dizzy before she broke free. The *Mexicana's* sailors used oars as poles to fend their ship off the rocks until they reached a small cove partway through the rapids, where they managed to get some lines ashore and anchor for the night.

Much later the wind increased in strength, so that we heard it whistling through the plants above us and through the trees on the mountains.

> At the same time the violent flow of the waters in the channel caused
> a horrible roaring and a notable echo, this producing an awe-inspiring
> situation, so that we had so far met with nothing so terrible.[6]

A westerly wind generally blows through here, and Drake would have
had this to carry him through the first narrows at slack water. However, he
would have begun to lose steerage in the rapidly building turbulence, and
most likely he ran lines to the pinnace and had his men row furiously to tow
each ship through.

Just to the east of the rapids, a deep fjord, now called Bute Inlet, cuts a
twisting course forty miles northeastward into the mainland between towering mountain walls. Drake may have taken the pinnace some distance into
the inlet before concluding that it was not a passage. Then, following the
mainland coast that led first eastward and then southwest through what is
called Desolation Sound, they emerged quite suddenly into a broad expanse
of water that was quite unlike anything they had seen before. Captain
Vancouver later named it the Gulf of Georgia, but because it is in fact a
strait, it has since been renamed the Strait of Georgia.

Drake would have been struck by how suddenly the tortuous labyrinth
had given way to a beautiful inland sea. To the west the long headland that
they had followed through the narrow strait continued southeastward beyond the horizon, its mountains shielding this sea from the Pacific storms.
Although the mountain peaks were still covered in snow, the air and water
would have been noticeably warmer, and there would have been an immediate sense of greater life and abundance.

Indeed, the Strait of Georgia was a scene of almost unimaginable natural abundance prior to the advent of Euro-American settlement and industry in the nineteenth century. Each year upwards of 100 million salmon
devoured their last sustenance in its waters before returning up its rivers and
streams to spawn and die. Pursued by the ravenous salmon, enormous
schools of herring were driven to the surface, where flocks of circling gulls
descended to join the feast. Countless other species from cod to halibut and
great, forty-foot basking sharks thrived in these waters year-round. Seals
and sea lions abounded, and a variety of whales, including orca, gray, hump-
back, and pilot, frequented the strait in large numbers. When Captain
Vancouver reached the same area, he noted in his journal that "numberless

whales, enjoying the season, were playing about the ship in every direction."[7]
Surrounding all—from the shores of the strait to the white peaks of the
mountains—stood vast, deeply verdant forests.

It is not difficult to imagine Drake's thoughts: What better place than
this bountiful oasis for the colony that would be essential for the future ex-
ploitation of the northwest passage? Ships would be able to come and go
between this sea and the Strait of Anian with little chance of detection by
the Spaniards, crops could be grown and the abundance of the sea harvested
to reprovision them, and with a limitless supply of timber the colonists
could build a fleet of new ships to pursue his vision for a great enterprise.
From a base in this hidden inland sea, a month's sailing would see an
English squadron lying in wait at the southern tip of California for the returning Manila galleon, or two months would take it into the port of
Panama to seize the gold and silver of Peru.

They were at 50 degrees, the same latitude as the cape of storms where
they had made their first landfall on the outer coast. If he had not already
concluded or been informed in signs by the Indians that the land to the west
was an island, Drake soon had other evidence to the effect. To this point the
tides had ebbed north and westward through the narrow strait. But a mile or
two to the south, the tide fell with little current, and a short distance beyond it ebbed southward rather than northward, indicating another outlet
into the Pacific somewhere to the south. The land to the west was indeed an
island, and in virtually the same latitude as England. Here was the perfect
embodiment of the colony so fervently advocated by Sir Humphrey Gilbert
and Dr. John Dee to serve as the headquarters of English commerce in the
Pacific.

The evidence in Drake's maps is compelling: He gave the name Nova Albion to Vancouver
Island and chose a site at or very near latitude 50 degrees on its east coast for
his future colony. Drake later referred to this place as the "Bay of small ships"
with the added allure of "beautiful maidens."[8] Due to the cloak of official secrecy there is no surviving description of this bay, or of the events that transpired there except for Jodocus Hondius's account of Drake setting up a
"post" and nailing to it an inscribed silver plate and a sixpence. Yet there is

only one place near 50 degrees that would have met the practical needs that Drake had to take into consideration for the establishment of his colony.

He would first have crossed the Strait of Georgia to get a look at the other outlet of the narrow strait, now called Discovery Passage, which he had previously bypassed in favor of continuing eastward through the Yucultas. At the outlet of Discovery Passage, however, he would have encountered violent tidal rips, and he certainly would not have considered locating the colony in such a treacherous place. Then he would have turned and followed the coast of Vancouver Island southward.

For some distance there is no sheltered anchorage, but twenty miles to the south the coast dips behind a headland, now called Cape Lazo, and two islands. As Drake's ships drew abreast of these features, the arrangement of the coast beyond would have come into view. Tucked inside the cape is a bay two miles wide at the mouth and extending northward about three miles. It is open to the southeast, but a spit extending from the cape partway across its mouth creates a harbor that is protected from the weather that periodically batters the cape from that direction. Reaching southward behind the island below the cape is a long, sheltered sound. All along its far shore the forest inclined gradually for several miles before ascending the slopes of the mountains.

Between the cape and the north point of the island a line of roiling water warned of dangerous shoals. Taking soundings, they would have found a channel deep enough for the *Golden Hinde*, and after waiting for high water, they would have entered the bay. It is now called Comox, which is an Indian word meaning "plenty." Very likely, they were accompanied by a large number of Indians who had come out in canoes to meet them. From Drake's later reference to "beautiful maidens," it appears the reception was friendly.

The Indians were members of the *Pentlatch* tribe, a branch of the *Salishan*-speaking peoples whose territories extended down both sides of the Strait of Georgia. Their village, composed of rectangular, plank-covered houses, stretched along the beach in the lee of the cape. In front of the village there was a harbor sufficient for a sizable fleet of ships. Applying his customary diplomacy and gifts, Drake would likely have been invited to the village with much ceremony and then conducted on a tour of the surrounding country.

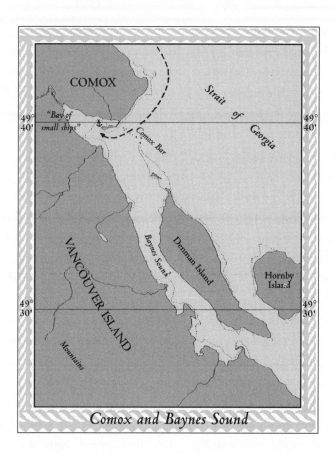

Comox and Baynes Sound

At the head of the bay is the estuary of a substantial river. Its tidal marshes at that time teemed with waterfowl. In the river the Indians constructed ingenious weirs to trap the returning salmon, which were then hung on racks and dried, or cured over smoking fires. Drake would have been staggered by the numbers and size of the salmon in comparison to those of Devon. One of the species native to this river averaged seventy pounds in weight.

More astonishing still for the Englishmen would have been the girth of the firs and cedars in the surrounding forest, many of which six or eight men linking hands would not have been able to reach around. Two or three of these trees would have supplied ample timber to build an entire ship. The experience, with shafts of light passing between the towering trunks to the thick carpet of moss on the forest floor, would have felt like walking through a huge, dimly lit cathedral.

Exploring the sound to the south, now called Baynes Sound, they would find several more sheltered anchorages and careenages along its four-teen-mile length, including a fine bay adjacent to its southern entrance. In many ways Baynes Sound would have reminded Drake of Plymouth Sound. On its beaches, the receding tide would have revealed rich beds of clams and oysters. Along its west side, six creeks drain into the sound, and Drake could have envisioned numerous estates extending inland from this shore. The island enclosing the sound, now called Denman Island, was quite dry but would have been seen as excellent grazing for livestock.

The lamps in Drake's cabin must have burned late into the night as he and his young cousin worked to compress his observations into illustrations and notes in his journal. He could not have hoped for a more commodious place in which to establish a colony. Nor would he subsequently find any-where nearby a place offering better natural defenses against an intervention by the Spaniards.

Undoubtedly, Drake would have been keenly interested in the potential for an alliance with the Indians such as he had enjoyed with the *cimarrones* on the Isthmus of Panama and subsequently proposed to the *Araucanian* Indians of Chile. He would have seen their intimate knowledge of the land and its resources, their numbers, and above all their ready mobility on the water as being invaluable for the defense and sustenance of the colony. Ironically, however, it would have been the latter attributes—their numbers and their mobility—that caused him to leave the bay of Nova Albion within a few days.

To this point Drake had passed fairly quickly through the territories of several distinct tribal groups. But he had entered a densely populated region in which all the tribes were loosely allied. The total *Salish* population inhabiting the shores of the strait at this time was probably in excess of 30,000.[9] Moreover, their vil-lages were located at intervals of no more than twenty or thirty miles—a distance easily covered by a well-manned canoe in a few hours. The Salish were a warlike people, sometimes fighting among themselves, but espe-cially vigilant for intruders from the north—*Haida* and *Kwakwaka'wakw* raids were a regular occurrence. Taking advantage of the comparatively be-nign seas in the strait, their long, slim war canoes were designed for man-power and speed.

The combined population of the *Pentlatch* villages in Comox Harbor and Baynes Sound when Drake arrived likely was in the range of 1,500 to 2,000.[10] However, word of the strange men visiting Comox in great, winged canoes, and of the wondrous things that they possessed would have traveled down the coast very quickly. Within two or three days the population would have begun to swell by hundreds with the arrival of large parties led by the chiefs of other villages who were eager to meet the strangers and share in the distribution of gifts.

Although the approaches made by the chiefs would have been formal and dignified, with much speech making, Drake would have viewed the growing assemblage of warriors with increasing concern. If he were suddenly attacked by such numbers, he would have been obliged to resort to the use of his cannons, and the resultant slaughter would surely have created a legacy of bitterness and hostility which would have seriously undermined his plan for the colony. Most probably, it was on the third or fourth day that Drake set up his great post with Fletcher's carefully engraved plate of silver proclaiming Nova Albion, and then gave the order to set sail.[11]

Following the coast of Nova Albion closely for another forty miles, Drake would have met many more Indians and passed several villages, but he would not have seen anything to change his opinion that he had found an excellent place for the future colony.[12] However, the details on the Dutch Drake map and the third map given to Ortelius make it clear that he was intrigued by the mainland opposite, where the mountains turned eastward, leaving a large gap in the coast. The gap was the valley and estuary of the Fraser River. Crossing the strait to investigate, Drake found what he at first thought was a "Bay of islands." He was not alone in this misconception. Two centuries later the first Spanish explorers thought the same. But Drake also referred to a "river of the straits" at latitude 49 degrees, which could only have been the Fraser River, and the river's unmistakable double-channeled configuration is depicted in the third map Drake had Hondius prepare for Ortelius.[13]

A little to the north of the river he noted on the map "Point of sardines" and "Point St. Michael," which most probably would be Point Atkinson and Point Grey, flanking Burrard Inlet—a great natural harbor and the site of the future city of Vancouver. Having initially conceived of the lowlands south of Burrard Inlet as a bay of islands, Drake probably took his pinnace some distance into the inlet in an attempt to follow the mountains eastward. Then, from the detail of the river on the map, it appears that he might have ventured into both the north and south arms of the Fraser River with the same object in mind.

At its mouth, the estuary contained many small islands. There Drake would have met a great concentration of *Salish* Indians at this time of year because of the huge runs of salmon entering the river to return to their spawning grounds. What is particularly intriguing about the detail of the river that was given to Ortelius is that it shows the junction of the river's two arms, which is located about fifteen miles inland. Conceivably Drake was met by the *Musqueam* people, who had a very large village near the mouth of the north arm, and was conducted by them on a tour upriver. As tidewater reached beyond the junction, he could have taken the pinnace and possibly also the Spanish bark up the north arm of the river on the rising tide and then returned down its south arm on the falling tide.

Continuing southward from the river's mouth, they would round a headland and find Boundary Bay—undoubtedly the "beautiful bay" referred to by Drake. At the head of the bay was a vast tidal marsh, one of the principal refuges for countless millions of waterfowl on their annual migrations along the Pacific coast. Immediately to the east a towering volcano stood cloaked in snow.* Then, looking to the southwest beyond some islands, they would have caught their first glimpse of a long bank of snow-capped mountains marching westward.

Sailing clear of the islands, they found the southern tip of Nova Albion and a broad strait leading westward toward the Pacific—the strait later named after the Greek pilot Juan de Fuca. From the evidence of the southernmost island in Drake's islands cryptograph, it appears that he initially thought that the snowcapped mountains lining the south shore of the strait were part of another large island, as there is a wide gap between them and the mountains on the mainland to the east.

This "island" was actually the Olympic Peninsula, and the gap to the

---

*Mount Baker, elevation 10,778 feet.

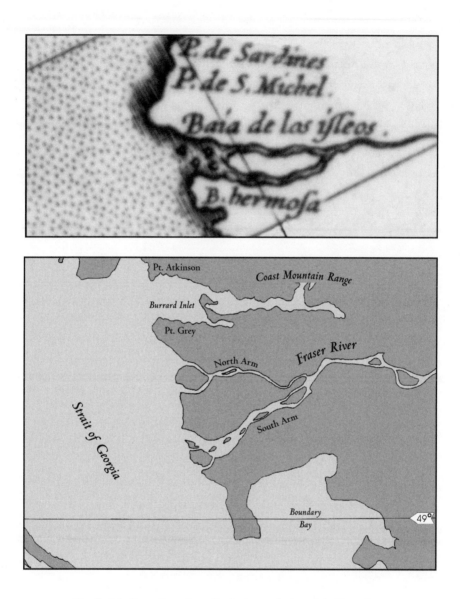

Detail of the Fraser River from Ortelius's map (top), and the Fraser River delta today (above)

east was Puget Sound. For the future defense of the colony, it would have been important to know whether there was another opening to the Pacific somewhere farther south, and it appears that Drake sailed some distance into Puget Sound with the aim of finding the answer to this question. It is uncertain how far he went, but one map suggests that he may have gone, as far as Tacoma Narrows, past the site of the future city of Seattle, before he turned back.* Then, again with future defensive arrangements in mind, he would have returned to the southern tip of Nova Albion and followed its coast into the Pacific, noting the positions of its harbors.

*See the map of Father Ascension in the postscript of this book.

Point of Position

*B*efore he even saw it, the outermost extremity of the majestic mountains to the south of Nova Albion had become a pivotal feature of Drake's reconnaissance. Unless he subsequently found another opening from the Pacific farther south, this "cape of snowcapped mountains" a little north of 48 degrees marked the southernmost entrance to the straits, and would be the crucial landmark that would guide ships safely to the future colony. From its southern tip, the coast of Vancouver Island runs continually northwest into the open Pacific and becomes increasingly rugged and forbidding. The mouth of the strait separating it from the Olympic Peninsula is only twelve miles across, and Drake would have seen that a ship approaching from the southwest in a storm would be in imminent danger of being wrecked on this shore if its captain failed to locate the cape and round it sharply eastward.*

The cape is now called Cape Flattery, and its native inhabitants were the *Makah*. Like their *Nuu-chah-nulth* neighbors on the outer coast of Nova Albion, they spoke a *Wakashan* dialect and were whale hunters. From the accuracy of the drawing Robert Dudley copied years later, it appears Drake made a careful study of the cape, probably including paintings of its profile from both the northwest and the southwest. The bay that he depicted on its north side is Neah Bay, which was the site of a large *Makah* village. As the guardians of the cape, they would potentially have been the most valuable

---

*It was for precisely this reason that the west coast of Vancouver Island was the scene of many shipwrecks in the nineteenth century and gained a reputation as "the graveyard of the Pacific."

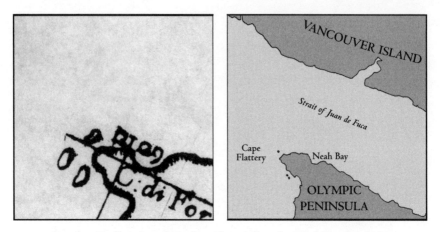

Detail on Dudley's chart (left); Cape Flattery (latitude 48° 23') today (right)

sentinels for the future colony, and Drake likely took special pains to be-friend them.

Fourteen miles to the south on the Pacific coast of the Olympic Peninsula another Makah village was buried in a mudslide sometime early in the century following Drake's explorations. Because the slide was composed of wet clay, which ad-mitted very little oxygen, the collapsed houses and their contents were pre-served with minimal decay. When archaeologists excavated the site in the 1970s, they found thousands of artifacts that were used in everyday life by the Indians of the northwest coast, but which had long since decomposed at other village sites.

As with the natives Drake met in the Strait of Magellan, the most common cutting edges—knives, adzes, and other blades—used by the *Makah* were made from mussel shells. However, the archaeologists also un-earthed in the houses twenty-eight iron blades fitted to native-designed handles, and fourteen other hafts with ferrous stains where iron blades had once been fitted. The articles were knives fashioned from flat plate, chisels hammered from rectangular bars, and square nails used by the Indians as drill bits. All were made from high-carbon steel.[1] The Indians of the northwest coast extracted and used limited amounts of native cop-per, but the processes for smelting iron and hardening it into steel were

Grays Harbor on Dudley's chart

unknown to them. The archaeologists therefore theorized that the *Makah* had salvaged the iron from the wreck of a Japanese junk that had become disabled and drifted across the Pacific. However, it is more likely that it came from Drake.[2]

Allowing that practically everything the Indians' way of life depended upon—houses, canoes, and implements of all types—was laboriously fashioned from wood, they must have clamored for pieces of the hard, smooth metal they saw aboard Drake's ships, for use as woodworking tools. With so many tribes to placate in his travels along the coast, Drake may well have exhausted his supply of trade items. However, he appears to have been carrying a considerable amount of German steel, as he gave 600 pounds of it to San Juan de Anton, captain of the treasure galleon *Cacafuego*, when they parted.[3] Perhaps he had the *Golden Hinde*'s forge set up at some point to produce more knives as well as chisels.

On Dudley's chart, the next detail he copied is unmistakably Grays Harbor, cutting into the coast at the base of the Olympic Peninsula ninety miles south of Cape Flattery. To have drawn its shape so accurately, Drake must have taken the pinnace right to the mouth of the Chehalis River, fifteen miles from the coast at the head of the inlet, no doubt probing for a more southerly entrance to his straits.

As he followed the coast southward, Grays Harbor was the first of three large openings that Drake would have encountered in a span of fifty miles. The next is Willapa Bay, which lies behind a low, twenty-mile-long spit of beach; and the third is the mouth of the Columbia River. To the south of the Columbia the coast becomes an unyielding line of headlands and beaches in front of mountainous terrain. There is no evidence that Drake entered Willapa Bay. However, on the third map that he had Hondius produce for Ortelius, the place-names after the cluster of information describing the Fraser River were "beach" followed by "great river" and then "rugged land."

The only river south of the Fraser worthy of the title "great river" is the mighty Columbia, and Drake's description of the coast on either side fits perfectly.[4] Although it was noted as the "Rio de San Roque" by the Spanish in 1775, several captains subsequently mistook the waves churning over the bar at its mouth for surf breaking into a large bay until American captain Robert Gray crossed the treacherous bar in 1792 and claimed discovery of the river. To have identified it as a great river, then, Drake may well have taken his pinnace across the bar and some distance into its mouth.

After "rugged land" Drake had Hondius note "Point of position" on his map, which was an odd name for him to give to a place. To an Elizabethan mariner, the reference would normally have meant a place where latitude had been established, since the problem of fixing one's longitude from a ship at sea was unsolved. Allowing, however, that Drake clearly had determined his latitude at frequent intervals along the coast, it is improbable that he would have singled out a solitary place for this designation based on an observation of latitude there.

When settlers began arriving in Oregon in the mid–nineteenth century, the *Tillamook* Indians told them of a place on the coast where strange men in ships had landed many generations before and left some things on a mountainside. The place was Nehalem Bay, thirty miles south of the Columbia, and the mountain, which rose directly from the back of the beach, was called Neahkahnie by the *Tillamook*. For centuries they had regularly burned off its seaward slope to create new forage for game. The settlers found rocks on the mountainside inscribed with compass bearings, arrows, and other symbols, and by 1890 a hunt for buried treasure was under way.[5]

The digging continued sporadically for more than half a century without turning up any treasure, although a storm exposed an

Elizabethan coin on the beach below. Then in 1968 local historian Wayne Jensen undertook to locate and systematically chart all of the cairns and markings on the mountainside. At the foot of the mountain was a circular platform of stones about ten feet in diameter and two feet high, and nearby a rock inscribed with the numerals 1632 inside a triangle, which some thought was the date of the unknown visitors. Almost a mile up the mountainside, however, Jensen and a friend found another circular platform, and nearby a squared stone with a groove cut into it that was exactly an English yard in length, possibly for the purpose of measuring out cordage.[6]

Realizing that they had found some sort of archaic survey, Jensen enlisted the help of surveyors to locate the cairns and connecting lines precisely. The number 1632, it turned out, did not represent the year of the survey but rather the distance, measured in English yards, between the centers of the two circular platforms. Beneath the stones comprising the platforms they found charcoal residue, indicating that fires had been lit on top of them. The line connecting the platforms was the base of a large triangle. More than a mile to the west on the mountainside, the third corner of the triangle was inscribed with the words *deos* and *augur*, which are Latin for "the gods" or "heavens," and for "predict."[7] Also converging at this point between the sides of the triangle were several other lines, and on a flat rock within the triangle were etched a number of lines radiating outward to different points on the compass.

Searching through examples of archaic survey methods, Jensen and the surveyors came upon one that appeared to be too close a match to be a coincidence: a drawing by William Bourne, contemporary of Francis Drake and author of *A Regiment for the Sea*, of a survey that he set up near his home in Gravesend on the Thames River.[8] This particular survey by Bourne may have been for the purpose of demonstrating the use of triangulation to measure the distances to several prominent landmarks. Like the survey on Neahkahnie Mountain, however, it was constructed from a meridian of longitude that was aligned to magnetic north.[9]

Given the similarities in the layout of the two schemes, Jensen and the surveyors came to the conclusion that the one on Neahkahnie Mountain was probably set up by Francis Drake to establish some sort of boundary.

However, it surely was Drake's attempt, employing the lunar distance method, to determine the longitude of the Pacific coast and hence the sailing distance through the northwest passage.

Although Bourne's drawing of his survey at Gravesend does not appear to relate to the lunar distance method, the general principles involved in the method are evident in the layout of the survey on Neahkahnie Mountain. In England, Bourne would have set up a "prime meridian" where he calculated his ephemerides—his tables predicting the angular distance between the moon and one or more prominent stars at a given hour each day for several years to come. When Drake reached the northwest coast of America, he would have had to lay out another meridian and replicate Bourne's method in order to determine the angular distance between the same objects at the same time of the day, local time.[10] This would differ from the angular distance predicted for the prime meridian in England at that hour, and theoretically, armed with a formula based on the rate of motion of the moon, Drake would have been able to translate that difference into hours and minutes of time. Once he knew the difference in local time between England and his "point of position," this in turn could have been converted to difference in longitude.*

However, the challenge came in applying the method. A small error in the observations on the Pacific coast of America would have resulted in a substantial alteration of the time difference and longitude calculated. Moreover, this was before the use of telescopes, and the observations had to be made with the naked eye. To address this problem, Bourne had created for Drake the geometric equivalent of a very large cross-staff laid out on the ground. Evidently, an hour was chosen for the observations when the moon and star were relatively low in the eastern sky. Thus, projecting long sight lines through widely separate points on the meridian made for greater accuracy.[11] One side of the triangle was aligned to the moon and the other to the sun or a designated star, and the angle of the western vertex marked "heavens" and "predict" represented the angular distance between them for comparison with that predicted by Bourne for the same date and hour, local time, in England.[12]

*Since the Earth rotates fifteen degrees every hour, every four minutes of difference in local time represents one degree of longitude.

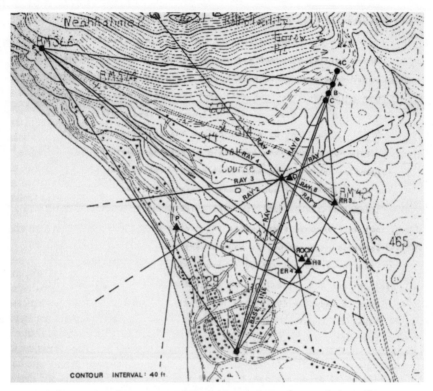

The layout of Drake's astronomical observations for longitude using the lunar distance method (reconstruction by a modern survey)

No matter how accurate the observations were, however, the longitude calculated from Bourne's method was bound to contain a substantial error because he and his contemporaries were unaware of the irregularity of the moon's motion, which would not be discovered until after the introduction of the telescope to astronomy by Galileo thirty years later. Consequently, Bourne's formula for converting differences in lunar distance to time and longitude would have been flawed.[13]

Notably, the actual longitude of Neahkahnie Mountain is about 124 degrees west of Greenwich—the modern prime meridian, very near Gravesend. By contrast, Drake evidently came to the conclusion that he was about 140 degrees west of England, as shown in the maps drawn by Dee and Lok following his return to England. If he did so on the basis of the survey on Neahkahnie Mountain, the cumulative error in the calculation of difference in local time was slightly more than an hour. Still, the result was a huge correction from the prognostications of Ortelius and Mercator, and Drake would now have reckoned that the sailing distance from his Strait of Anian to Frobisher's eastern entrance to the northwest passage was no more than 3,000 miles.[14]

⤞ 26. ⤝

A Sorrowful Farewell

*W*hen the observations for longitude were completed, Drake likely again led the way down the coast in the pinnace, sailing close inshore while the ships followed to seaward. Time was growing short. It was already mid-July, and if the northwest passage was to be attempted, they had to be back in the Strait of Anian by early September. Moreover, they had come 700 miles southward, and he had to allow for the time required to get back to the strait. But first he had to repair his ships, and everywhere they had gone they had encountered large bands of warlike Indians whose ready mobility along the coast made beaching the ships anywhere near them a decidedly risky proposition.

Below the Columbia River, however, the number and size of native contingents traveling the coast had diminished, and Drake was anxious to find a sheltered anchorage without further delay. For many miles there was none, as the coast is an unremitting line of exposed beaches. Here and there a river cut through the dunes, but in each case its mouth was blocked by a treacherous sandbar. Finally, sixty miles below their "Point of position" Drake came upon a small bay on the north side of a headland. It was barely half a mile across and lined with steep bluffs, but inside the bay was a sandy beach protected by a long spit of rock extending to seaward on its north side. Taking soundings, he found that there was sufficient depth in the bay to admit the *Golden Hinde*.

Drake made a detailed drawing of the bay and its sheltering spit. Initially, he drew the spit at low water. Then as the tide rose, the neck of the spit became inundated and it separated slightly from the shore, so he added a sketch of it in this state alongside, probably as a ready reference point to gauge high water in the bay. Afterward he added his fortified encampment to the drawing, along with a ship and groups of people lighting fires and looking out to sea.[1]

The lighting of fires by the Indians was described in *The World Encompassed* as occurring when Drake departed the bay, and he apparently attached some sentimental importance to the event. On the third map he had Hondius produce for Ortelius, he referred to this second "bay of small ships" also as the "Bay of fires." It was the next place noted down the coast from "Point of position."[2] Later, to conform with the official cover-up, Drake labeled his drawing of the bay "Portus Nova Albionis" and gave it to Hondius to insert in the upper-left corner of his broadside map as a surrogate for the real bay of Nova Albion.

The identity of the bay depicted in Drake's drawing has been the subject of intense debate in northern California for more than a century, despite the fact that the earliest surviving account of the voyage, the "Anonymous Narrative," plainly states that Drake careened his ship at latitude 44 degrees, which would be on the coast of Oregon. However, the published accounts placed his careenage at or near 38 degrees, and when the California gold rush brought the city of San Francisco to life, its citizens eagerly embraced the story that Drake had landed somewhere nearby, and they began looking for the harbor where he had set up his camp among the Indians and repaired the *Golden Hinde*.

Some opined that Drake had landed in the very bay of San Francisco, while others favored one of the bays a short distance to the north: Bodega Bay, Bolinas Bay, or the bay that the Spanish named Drake's Bay when they arrived in the area at the end of the eighteenth century.[3] Interest reached a zenith in 1937 when a brass plate that appeared to be inscribed with Drake's proclamation of Nova Albion was brought to the University of California at Berkeley by a man who said he had found it in a field north of the Golden Gate.[4] Caught up in the excitement, one noted anthropologist concluded that a handful of Indian words and phrases recorded by Francis Fletcher and others positively identified the natives as members of the Miwok tribe who inhabited the area in Drake's time.[5]

Eventually, groups formed in support of virtually every bay in northern California as the place where Drake had landed. However, none of the

A drawing of Drake's "bay of fires" in the corner of the Hondius Broadside map

contending bays even remotely resembled the careful drawing Drake made of his careenage, and efforts to find remnants of his fortified camp proved fruitless. Then, with the quadricentennial of Drake's voyage approaching, the plate of brass was sent for metallurgical testing, and it was found to be a piece of modern rolled brass. The plate supposedly inscribed with Drake's proclamation of Nova Albion in California was a twentieth-century hoax.[6]

In 1980 an English engineer named Bob Ward resolved to investigate the assertion in the "Anonymous Narrative" that Drake's careenage was situated at 44 degrees. Examining the coast at that latitude, Ward found a small bay—indeed, it is the only one on the entire coast—that matches Drake's drawing, including his alternate depiction of the shape of the tidal spit at high water, perfectly. Then, reviewing old newspaper and archaeological reports for the area, he discovered that several European artifacts predating the eighteenth-century explorers, including a cutlass with sixteenth-century English armory markings, had been unearthed in the vicinity.[7] The bay is

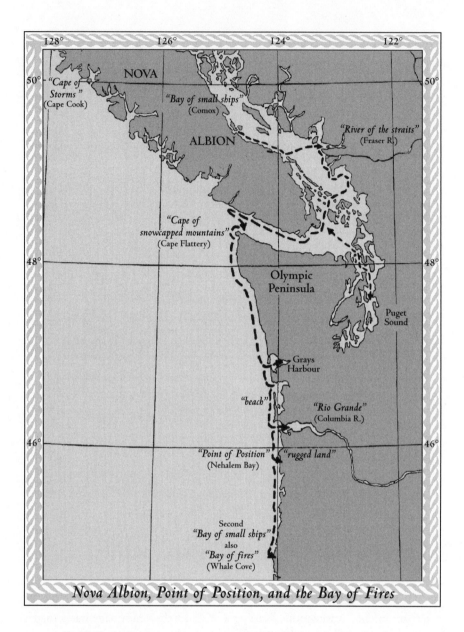

Nova Albion, Point of Position, and the Bay of Fires

now called Whale Cove, and it is situated at latitude 44° 45' on the coast of Oregon.

On July 17 Drake brought his ships to anchor in the bay.[8] *The following morning the people* of the country appeared and sent a lone spokesman out in a small canoe.

Stopping some distance from the ships, the Indian delivered a long speech accompanied by many gestures and then returned to shore. Repeating the exercise, on his third approach he left a bundle of feathers and a basket filled with an herb, which he called *Tobah*, in one of the boats lying alongside the *Golden Hinde*. Drake attempted to reciprocate with an assortment of gifts, but the Indian would not come near enough to receive anything except a hat that was cast into the water from the ship.[9]

Landing, Drake chose a campsite on top of the bluffs immediately adjacent to the beach where he proposed to careen the ships, and set his men to clearing the ground and building a defensive bulwark.

> When the people of the country perceived us doing, as men set on fire to war in defence of their country, in great haste and companies, with such weapons as they had, they came down unto us, and yet with no hostile meaning or intent to hurt us; standing, when they drew near, as men ravished in their minds with the sight of such things as they never had seen or heard of before that time; their errand being rather with submission and fear to worship us as Gods, than to have any war with us as mortal men. . . . At this time, being willed to lay from them their bows and arrows, they did as they were directed, and so did all the rest, as they came more and more by companies unto them, growing in a little while to a great number, both of men and women.[10]

The men were mostly naked; the women wore aprons woven from bulrushes and deerskins draped over their shoulders. Drake distributed shirts and linen cloth, entreating them to cover their nakedness, and made a display of eating and drinking to show that he and his men were not gods but mere mortals like themselves. After exchanging gifts, the Indians returned to their village, about three-quarters of a mile distant, where "a kind of most lamentable weeping and crying out" was heard, "the women especially extending their voices in a most miserable and doleful manner of shrieking."[11]

Drake's men completed their fortifications and set up the camp, and on July 21, having transferred her guns to the deck of the Spanish bark, they moved the *Golden Hinde* closer to the beach and began ferrying her precious cargo ashore.[12] Two days later a large assembly of native men, women, and children—"invited by the report of them that first saw us"—appeared at the top of a hill overlooking the camp. After a long oration by their leader, the men laid down their weapons and descended the hill bearing gifts. At the same time,

> the women, as if they had been desperate, used unnatural violence against themselves, crying and shrieking pitifully, tearing their flesh with their nails from their cheeks in a monstrous manner, the blood streaming down along their breasts. . . . [They] with fury cast themselves upon the ground, never respecting whether it were clean or soft, but dashed themselves in this manner on hard stones, knobby hillocks, stocks of wood, and pricking bushes, or whatever else lay in their way, iterating the same course again and again. . . .
>
> This bloody sacrifice (against our wills) being thus performed our General with his company in the presence of those strangers fell to prayers; and by signs in lifting up our eyes and hands to heaven, signified that the God whom we did serve and whom they ought to worship was above. . . . In the time of which prayers, singing of Psalms and reading of certain chapters of the Bible, they sat very attentively; and observing the end at every pause, with one voice still cried, *Oh*, greatly rejoicing in our exercises.[13]

After the Indians retired the last of the treasure was brought ashore, and the *Golden Hinde* was pulled onto the beach for careening.

On July 26 two native emissaries arrived at the camp, informing Drake by signs that their *Hioh*, or "king," was coming, and requesting that he send some token that he might do so in peace. Drake obliged, and then as a precaution he gathered his men and drilled them noisily around the camp to discourage any thoughts the Indians might have had of attacking them. Shortly, there

> were assembled the greatest number of people which we could reasonably imagine to dwell within any convenient distance round about. Amongst the rest the king himself, a man of goodly stature and comely personage, attended with his guard of about 100 tall and warlike men. . . .
>
> After these, in their order, did follow the naked sort of common people, whose hair being long, was gathered into a bunch behind, in

which stuck plumes of feathers; but in the forepart only single feathers like horns. . . . every one had his face painted, some with white, some black, and some with other colours, every man also bringing in his hand one thing or another for a gift or present. Their train or last part of their company consisted of women and children, each woman bearing against her breast a round basket or two having with them diverse things, as bags of *Tobah*, a root called *Petah*, whereof they make a kind of meal and either bake it into bread, or eat it raw; broiled fishes like a pilchard; the seed and down aforenamed, with such like.[14]

Partway down the hill they stopped, and the scepter bearer gave an oration that lasted for more than half an hour. He then began chanting a song, and the whole multitude began to dance, moving gradually toward the camp. Seeing that their intentions were harmless, Drake gave the order to allow them into the compound. When the dance concluded, they made signs for Drake to sit down, and the chief and several others gave speeches.

> Or rather, indeed, if we had understood them, [these were] supplications that [Drake] would take the Province and kingdom into his hand and become their king and patron, making signs that they would resign unto him their right and title in the whole land, and become his vassals in themselves and their posterity;* which that they might make us indeed believe that it was their true meaning and intent, the king himself, with all the rest, with one consent and with great reverence, joyfully singing a song, set the crown upon his head, enriched his neck with all their chains and offering unto him many other things, honoured him by the name of *Hyoh*.[15]

After Drake's "coronation" the Indians visited the camp almost daily. Some who were suffering from disease, cankers, or old wounds sought healing from Drake and his men, believing they could cure them by simply blowing on their afflictions. "But that . . . they might understand that we were but men and no gods, we used ordinary means, as lotions, emplasters

---

*This interpretation of the Indians' intentions was of course completely unfounded, as they would not willingly have surrendered their country to Drake. Most likely, they were simply bestowing on him the honors of a chief and inviting him to visit in peace.

and unguents most fitly (as far as our skills could guess) agreeing to their griefs."[16] Often the Indians neglected to bring food for themselves, and Drake was obliged to share with them the sea lions and mussels his foraging parties brought back.

When the *Golden Hinde* was repaired and refitted, the Spanish bark was careened as well. Then, with the ships ready, Drake led a large party of men up into the country to acquaint himself with its resources and the manner in which the Indians lived on the land. The natives' dwellings, they discovered, were entirely different from the rectangular, plank-covered houses of the Indians to the north. Indeed, they were low and cone-shaped,

> digged round within the earth, and have from the uppermost brims of the circle clefts of wood set up and joined close together at the top, like our spires on the steeple of a Church; which being covered with earth, suffer no water to enter and are very warm; the door in the most of them performs the office also of a chimney to let out the smoke.* . . .[17]
>
> Their houses were all such as . . . described, and being many of them in one place, made several villages here and there. The inland we found to be far different from the shore. . . . infinite was the company of very large and fat Deer which we saw by the thousands, as we supposed in a herd; besides a strange kind of Conies [rodents], by far exceeding them in number: their heads and bodies . . . are but small, his tail like the tail of a rat, exceeding long; and his feet like the paws of a Want or mole; under his chin, on either side, he hath a bag into which he gathereth his meat. . . . the people eat their bodies, and make great account of their skins, for their king's holydays coat was made of them.[18]

The "very large and fat Deer" undoubtedly were Roosevelt Elk, and to have seen them in such numbers, Drake may well have trekked through the coastal mountains into the uplands of the lush Willamette River valley, some twenty-five miles to the east. The strange "conies" described were muskrat, whose habitat extended over most of North America except coastal California below Cape Mendocino.[19] Drake's party was after venison, however, and found hunting in the company of their native friends a fascinating experience.

---

*The house type, known as a *kekuli*, or pit house, was widely used in the interior of Oregon, Washington, and British Columbia, but very few examples have been found on the coast (see note 20 to this chapter).

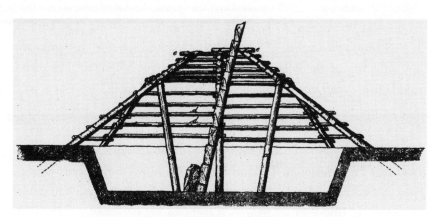

A kekuli was framed with poles and then covered with earth.

They are a people of a tractable, free, and loving nature, without guile or treachery; their bows and arrows (their only weapons, and almost all their wealth) they use very skilfully. . . . the men commonly [are] so strong of body that that which 2 or 3 of our men could hardly bear, one of them would take upon his back, and without grudging carry it easily away, up hill and down hill an English mile together; they are also exceeding swift in running, and of long continuance, the use whereof is so familiar with them that they seldom go, but for the most part run. One thing we observed in them with admiration, that if at any time they chanced to see a fish so near the shore that they might reach the place without swimming, they would never, or very seldom, miss to take it.[20]

With the use of their English longbows and the help of the Indians to carry the meat, the hunting party probably returned to the bay with a substantial and heartily welcomed supply of venison. Before departing, Drake had another "great and firm" post set up and nailed to it a plate.

[On this] plate of brass . . . is engraven her grace's name, and the day and year of our arrival there, and of the free giving up of the province and kingdome both by the king and the people, into her majesty's hands; together with her highness' picture and arms in a piece of sixpence current English money, showing itself by a hole of purpose made through the plate; underneath was likewise engraven the name of our General, etc.[21]

Finally, on August 23 Drake gave the order to set sail. The Indians "took a sorrowful farewell of us, but being loath to leave us, they presently ran to the top of the hills to keep us in their sight as long as they could, making fires before and behind, and on each side of them."[22]

In the course of his work for Drake, it appears Jodocus Hondius prepared some illustrations of the voyage for inclusion in *The World Encompassed*. When the account was suppressed, Drake or Hondius apparently gave them to maritime chronicler Theodore de Bry, who incorporated them in his book *America Pars VIII*, published in Frankfurt in 1599. One of them is the only surviving contemporary illustration of Drake and his men on the northwest coast of America.[23] It is a compressed view of the events at Whale Cove. In the foreground, Drake is receiving his "crown" from the "king" of the Indians, who are emerging from Hondius's fanciful *kekulis*. In the background Drake's men are setting up a rather anemic-looking "great post." Beyond, in the bay, are four ships. As was often the case in illustrations of the period, the ships are generic, but they could only represent the *Golden Hinde*, the Spanish bark, and the remaining two pinnaces. Evidently, Drake had by this point assembled the last remaining pinnace.

In the drawing that Drake made of the anchorage, on the other hand, the details of the Indians lighting fires upon his departure were obviously added thereafter. Also in this drawing is a "ship"—possibly a pinnace— that appears to have been left at anchor. Conceivably, the last pinnace that Drake had assembled and taken with him had been specially designed for the final leg of his journey; perhaps, like the *Golden Hinde*, specially double- planked to reinforce her against the menacing ice floes that Frobisher had warned him to expect in the northwest passage.

The World Encompassed *states that the prevailing wind along the coast in August and* September was from the north.[24] Consequently, to return to the Strait of An- ian, Drake would have had to steer a similar, though much shorter, course to that which had brought him north from New Spain. In this instance he would only have had to sail about 300 miles offshore before he would have found the wind backing around to the west and then begun his turn north-

Barbaræ cujusdam Regionis Incolæ, Draconem Anglum, Regem sibi eligere cupiunt.
Pars· VIII· p·12·

Drake's crowning by the Indians at his careenage, from Theodore de Bry's
America Pars VIII, *1599*

ward. In all, the sailing distance was about 1,000 miles, and if he did not
meet a major weather disturbance, he would likely have reached the entrance
to the strait toward the end of the first week of September.[25] There is no surviving account of Drake's return northward, or of what transpired between
him and his men when they reached the strait. However, the situation that
would have confronted him surely must have been one of the most difficult
in his life.

In all probability Drake expected to find that the ice he had encountered in the strait would have dissipated by the end of summer. But this
would not have been the case, as summer warming actually accelerates the
discharge from Alaska's coastal glaciers. He would have found even more
icebergs in the strait than when he first explored it. And undoubtedly, the
wind was still blowing from the north, which meant they would have had to

tack back and forth continually to get up the strait, all the while—day and night—exercising great care not to collide with a massive piece of ice. To maneuver the *Golden Hinde* under these conditions would have consumed a great deal of time, and the time Drake had available had grown critically short.

Some of Drake's men had sailed for the Muscovy Company on the Arctic sea route to Russia, and he would have learned from them that it remained navigable only until late October. Assuming the same for the northwest passage, Drake would have calculated that this left him about forty-five days to reach the North Atlantic before the Arctic winter took hold.

They had reckoned that the North American continent was about 3,000 miles wide. In the simplistic view of the day, it was assumed that the arctic coastline of America ran in more or less a straight east-west line, and the prevailing wind in the northwest passage was from the west. Allowing that the wind would be at his back, Drake had probably calculated that they could sail on average at least four miles per hour (100 miles per day) and therefore could sail the breadth of the continent in about thirty days. However, that left them, at most, fifteen days to work their way northward against the wind and hazardous icebergs to the junction of his strait with the passage, and according to the map of Ortelius, this final cape could be as much as 600 miles farther north.

The alternative Drake faced was a voyage of some 20,000 miles across the Pacific and homeward via the Indian Ocean. But he had to bring the *Golden Hinde* with her great load of plunder safely home, and without it slowing them down he would have reckoned there was a good chance of the smaller, nimbler Spanish bark and the pinnace making a successful dash through the passage. Having come all this way, it had to be attempted.

How the men were selected for this mission will never be known. Even their names were subsequently lost to memory except for one man: the pilot named Morera. However, it is a fact that some twenty of Drake's men were unaccounted for when he left this coast.* No doubt Drake offered

---

*When he departed Guatulco, Drake's company numbered about eighty-five. When he arrived in the Moluccas, however, it numbered only sixty-three, including Maria.

"profitable persuasions" such as he had first promised in June.[26]

Most likely, they were instructed to proceed to the junction of the strait with the passage eastward, and then to continue only if the seaway clearly was open. If not, they would have had to return down the coast to their former camp at Whale Cove, which alone offered a secure relationship with the Indians, and await rescue. There certainly would not have been any thought of them trying to return to England via Magellan's Strait or crossing the Pacific in such small vessels. But Drake would have assured them that with the great cargo of treasure he was bringing back, the Queen would allow him to return for them if need be, and to fulfill his plan for Nova Albion.

They likely sheltered for a day or two in the same anchorage where they had assembled the first pinnace in June while Drake explained his decision and saw to the preparedness of the expedition. Then, no doubt after speeches of encouragement and prayers for a safe voyage, they parted, the men of the little vessels, hopeful of reaching the North Atlantic in six weeks, starting up the strait while Drake and his remaining company aboard the *Golden Hinde* "turned back on account of the ice,"[27] to face a much longer journey.

With the wind at his back, Drake would have made a swift passage down the outer coast, likely passing Nova Albion and the "Bay of fires" within a week. Before departing the coast, however, he had set himself one more task: to locate the Cape Mendocino that was indicated in his captured documents as the northern limit of Spanish navigation. At 43 degrees he found what he believed to be the Spanish cape, now called Cape Arago.* Ten miles south of the cape they found the mouth of the Coquille River and topped up their water casks and firewood. Later, on Molyneux's 1592 globe, the river was designated as the boundary separating Elizabeth's dominions on the northwest coast of America from New Spain. From there, the globe shows Drake's track heading south by southwest across the Pacific.[28]

In the five months since he departed Guatulco, Drake had journeyed 9,000 miles through unknown seas and along forbidding shores to perform his mission.[29] This accomplished, he would join his discoveries, south and north, to the coastline on the Spanish charts to produce, for presentation to

---

*Cape Arago is depicted on Emery Molyneux's suppressed 1592 globe, but is labeled "C. Mendocino."

the Queen, a grand chart of the entire Pacific coast of America, from its southern extremity at latitude 56 degrees all the way to his Strait of Anian at latitude 57 degrees north. He had undertaken and performed the most important voyage in the history of his nation, and in consideration of his labors, he must have thought, he surely would be given command of the great enterprise he envisioned being founded on his discoveries.[30]

POSTSCRIPT

An Old Sailor's Yarn

Not long after the news of Drake's death at sea reached England in April 1596, the government received a curious new proposal for discovery of the northwest passage. Martin Frobisher's former associate Michael Lok was residing in Venice at the time, and in April he was introduced to an "ancient pilot of ships," a Greek named Juan de Fuca, who told him a remarkable story of his own discovery of the passage.[1]

De Fuca, whose real name was Apostolos Valerianos, was returning to his homeland after forty years' service with the Spaniards in the New World. He told Lok that he was aboard the Manila galleon *Santa Ana* when she was captured by Thomas Cavendish in 1587, and that he had lost goods of his own worth 60,000 ducats in the raid. Then, he said, he was the pilot of three ships that the Viceroy of New Spain sent out with 100 soldiers to discover the Strait of Anian and fortify it to prevent its use by the English, but the voyage was cut short on account of a threatened mutiny. However, the surviving account states,

> he said that shortly after the said voyage was so ill ended, the said Viceroy of Mexico sent him out again, Anno 1592, with a small Caravela and a pinnace armed with mariners only . . . and that he followed his course in that voyage West and Northwest in the South Sea, all alongst the coast of New Spain and California and the Indies, now called North America (all which voyage he signified to me in a great Map, and a sea-card of mine own, which I laid before him), until he came to the latitude of forty seven degrees, and that there finding . . . a broad Inlet of Sea between 47 and 48 degrees of latitude, he entered thereinto, sailing therein for more than twenty days . . .

And also he said, that being entered thus far into the said strait . . . and finding the sea wide enough everywhere . . . he therefore set sail and returned homeward again toward New Spain, where he arrived at Acapulco, Anno 1592.[2]

De Fuca told Lok that when he returned, the Viceroy promised to reward him for his discovery. After two years, however, he still had not been paid, so he went to Spain. There, he said, he was received at the court, but again no reward was forthcoming. The reason, he concluded, was that the Spanish understood the English had given up their quest for the discovery of the northwest passage, and therefore his information was no longer of any importance. Yet if the Queen of England restored to him the value of the goods that Cavendish had seized from him, and furnished him with "one ship of forty tons burden and a pinnace," he offered to complete the discovery of the northwest passage "in thirty days time, from one end to the other of the straits."[3]

After Lok wrote down de Fuca's description of his voyage and his proposal to complete the discovery of the northwest passage, de Fuca continued his journey home to the island of Cefalonia. Lok exchanged letters with him while writing to Burghley and Hakluyt for the money to bring him to England, but then he learned that de Fuca had died.

In England, Hakluyt apparently contemplated including de Fuca's story in his second edition of *Principall Navigations*, as he organized Lok's letters into this narrative, but the account did not appear in his volumes, and was not finally published until Samuel Purchas found it among Hakluyt's papers and included it in his great book of travels, *Purchas, His Pilgrimes*, in 1625.

Although the strait at the southern end of Vancouver Island was subsequently named after him, historians have tended to view Juan de Fuca's account as purely apocryphal. There is no record of the voyage that he claimed to have undertaken at the Viceroy's behest in 1592, or of him being received at the royal court of Spain. Moreover, the earlier voyage on which he claimed to have served as pilot, which he did accurately describe regarding the threat of a mutiny, actually occurred in 1594. The suspicion therefore is that de Fuca's story was nothing more than a fabrication designed to extract money from the English government.

When de Fuca's story reached Hakluyt, however, he must have recognized at once that it was actually an account of Drake's northern explorations. Lok's original correspondence containing de Fuca's story has not survived, but all one need do is substitute 54 and 55 degrees respectively for the latitudes given in the published version and follow the details of de Fuca's story to see that they match Drake's voyage [inserted in brackets] perfectly:

> he followed his course in that voyage west and northwest in the South Sea [around *Fleurieu's Whirlpool,* and] all alongst the coast . . . now called North America . . . until he came to the latitude of 54 degrees [the northwest tip of the Queen Charlotte Islands], and that there finding that the land trended north and northeast [the southern Alaska archipelago], with a broad Inlet of Sea between 54 and 55 degrees [Dixon Entrance], he entered thereinto, sailing therein more than twenty days, and found the land trending sometime northwest [in Clarence Strait] and northeast [into the Stikine River delta] and north [in Chatham Strait], and also east [in Johnstone Strait] and southeastward [in Georgia Strait], and a very much broader sea [behind Nova Albion] than was at the said entrance, and that he passed by diverse islands in that sailing. And that at the entrance to this said Strait, there is on the north-west coast thereof, a great headland or island [the Queen Charlotte Islands] with an exceeding high pinnacle, or spired rock like a pillar thereon [Pillar Rock].
>
> Also he said that he went on land in diverse places, and that he saw some people on land clad in beasts skins . . . And also . . . that he not being armed to resist the force of the savage people that might happen [in Georgia Strait], he therefore set sail [into the Pacific] . . .[4]

It appears, then, that Hakluyt, in the course of preparing his draft narrative from Lok's letters, must have altered the latitudes given by de Fuca to conceal the location of the Strait of Anian. Then a decision apparently was taken to omit the account altogether. Still to be resolved, however, is the question of how de Fuca learned the details of Drake's secret explorations. Notably, Drake did capture a pilot his men called Juan Greco, or "Juan the Greek," at Valparaiso, Chile, in 1578, but he set him free at Callao, long before he sailed into the north Pacific. Then in 1587 Cavendish too captured a Greek pilot on the coast of Chile, and in all probability these Greeks were one and the same Juan de Fuca.

The accounts of Cavendish's voyage do not say where he left the Greek pilot, but it is possible he put him ashore at Cape San Lucas after he captured the Manila galleon. If so, de Fuca would have met Juan Sebastián Vízcaino, a Spanish merchant-adventurer who was among the passengers left there from the *Santa Ana*.[5] And if de Fuca sailed on the first expedition that he described to Lok—the 1594 voyage that was cut short because of a threatened mutiny—then he must have met Vízcaino again, because Vízcaino commanded that expedition. Its real purpose was to establish a military outpost near the southern end of the Baja Peninsula to protect the returning Manila galleons against English pirates, who were believed to have discovered a secret route into the Gulf of California from the north.[6] However, de Fuca must have left the New World shortly after this voyage.

In 1602 the Viceroy sent Vízcaino out again, and on this expedition, which sailed up the outer coast of California, possibly as far as latitude 43 degrees north, Vízcaino was accompanied on the voyage by a Friar, Antonio de la Ascension, who later wrote that their secret purpose was to discover the Strait of Anian.[7] Behind this quest lay a remarkable story that Ascension told to a colleague, who published a memoir about it in 1626.[8] Ascension recounted that a foreign pilot named Morena had accompanied Drake on his voyage—no doubt the same pilot identified during Drake's raid on Guatulco by the name Morera.[9] According to Ascension's colleague:

> When the Captain Francisco Draque returned to his country, this pi-
> lot—who had come emerging from the Strait [of Anian] in his com-
> pany—was very sick . . . and to see if the airs of the land would give
> him life, as a dead thing they put him ashore. The which [pilot] in a
> few days recovered health and walked through the land for a space of
> four years. He came forth to New Mexico and from there to Santa
> Barbara [in the province of Chihuahua], and then passed to the mines
> of Sombrerete . . .
> he had travelled . . . more than 500 leagues of mainland, until he
> came far enough to catch sight of an arm of the sea . . . The pilot told
> how this arm of the sea runs from north to south, and that it seemed
> to him that it went on to the northward to connect with the harbour
> where the Englishman had put him ashore. And that on the sea coast

he had seen many good harbours and great inlets; and that from the
point where they put him ashore he would venture to get to Spain in
40 days in a good ships-tender, and that he must go to get acquainted
with the Court of England.[10]

Morera's story must have been extracted under interrogation by the
Spanish authorities, for anyone who even hinted that he wanted to go to the
court of the heretic Elizabeth, much less had been with Drake, would have
attracted intense scrutiny. However, it appears that Morera also drew a map
for his interrogators, because Father Ascension produced one that obviously
is related to the pilot's story. The map, published in Spain in 1622, was the
first to depict California as an island, which it then became on most maps
for a century or more thereafter.[11]

From the top of the Gulf of California, Ascension's map shows a long,
narrow sea passage reaching northward and emerging into a broader opening behind a great square headland clearly resembling the Olympic
Peninsula, except that it is placed a little below its true latitude.
Undoubtedly this was the arm of sea described by Morera, and also the origin of Spanish fears that the English had found a way into the Gulf of
California from the north; hence Vízcaino's first expedition in 1594, on
which de Fuca appears to have served as pilot.

At latitude 49 degrees Morera evidently drew a river—obviously the
Fraser—although either he or Ascension omitted the island of Nova
Albion and the Queen Charlotte Islands. At 55 degrees, however, Morera
evidently drew a long, southward-pointing headland that would be Prince
of Wales Island, and there running northward from the headland to a junction with the northwest passage is Drake's Strait of Anian, albeit somewhat
simplified. Clearly Morera had been with Drake when he discovered the
strait, and the Spanish had heard all about the voyage, or at least what
Morera had been persuaded to tell them, sometime around 1584.

Here, undoubtedly, was the basis of Juan de Fuca's story. Most probably both he and Ascension had read Morera's account and copied his map
when each was in the service of Juan Sebastián Vízcaino. Although their accounts were given from different perspectives, there was nevertheless a common theme: that the Strait of Anian had been discovered, and that one or
two small vessels could get through the northwest passage, for which there

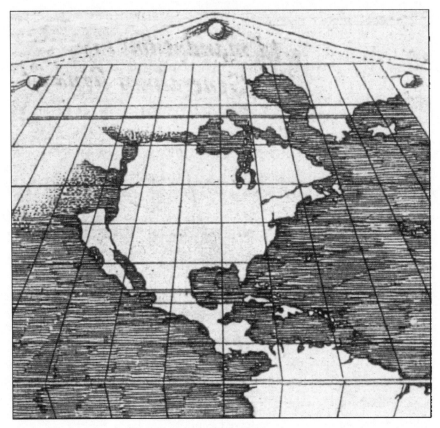

Father Ascension's map (detail)

would be a reward from the English government. Ascension's version probably lost some details in the retelling years later by his colleague, who wrote
that Morera said "a good ships-tender" could get to Spain in forty days;
whereas the veteran pilot de Fuca had carefully noted Morera's details of the
voyage and the information that "one ship of forty tons and a pinnace"
could sail from one end of the passage to the other in thirty days.
Obviously, de Fuca and Ascension could not have formed this concept
unless Morera had been with Drake when he decided to send a quarter of
his company into the northwest passage in his captured Spanish bark and
pinnace.

Moreover, it is hard to credit the idea that Drake would simply have
abandoned a member of his company, or even a captive on the remote
northwest coast of America. Nor, as remarkable as Morera's trek must have

been, is it likely that an experienced navigator, able to obtain his bearings from the stars, would have spent four years wandering about the land if his aim was to trek southward into Mexico. It very much appears, then, that Morera must have been a member of the company that Drake sent home via his supposed strait.

However, the strait came to a dead end 180 miles to the north.* Indeed, its end may not even have been reached. The small vessels with all of the curious objects on them would have made tempting prizes for the *Tlingit* Indians. Morera and his mates may well have been obliged to run for their lives, or they may have found the ice impassable farther up the strait. Whichever the case, they would have had no choice but to return to the careenage and await rescue as instructed by Drake.[12] After waiting for three years, however, the marooned sailors must have begun to despair.

Thus, Morera, who may have been the only one of them who spoke Spanish, had undertaken to try to get through Mexico and back to England with an appeal from his comrades to be rescued. It appears, however, that the Spaniards must have forced him to reveal Drake's discovery of the strait, and once he had divulged this knowledge he would have become an extremely dangerous person to set free. In all probability his life ended as a Spanish prisoner.

As for his stranded shipmates, it appears that Morera had invented the long inland sea passage leading northward from the Gulf of California to distract the Spanish from searching the outer coast for them. It seems safe to assume that despite Drake's best efforts they were never rescued.[13]

That Drake remained convinced he had found the Strait of Anian in spite of his small ships failing to reach England is evident in the enlistment of his relations and other veterans of his voyage both for the follow-up expedition of Fenton and the final attempt, by Richard Hawkins, to complete his discovery. And from Drake's efforts in his maps and leaked information to leave clues to his northern explorations, there can be no doubt that the achievement he most wanted to be remembered for was this voyage to the farthest corner of the globe to discover the Strait.

*Near present-day Skagway, Alaska.

Sir Francis Drake ca. 1594

For Drake to have seen this as the highlight of his life's adventures is completely understandable. Indeed, for those who are familiar with the European voyages to the northwest coast of America in the eighteenth century, it is plain to see that his feat of exploration eclipsed any achieved in that day. Considering the circumstances under which he had to perform his mission, sailing in a small and unimaginably crowded ship with only the crudest of instruments, some 18,000 miles through the uncharted Strait of Magellan and along hostile coasts, even reaching the distant shores of northwest America was by itself an extraordinary accomplishment. And then to have gained, in only a few weeks, a comprehension of this labyrinthine coast that would not be equaled until years after its rediscovery two centuries later was a truly astonishing feat. And finally, to then have sailed another 20,000 miles to bring the *Golden Hinde* home, and yet lose only one man out of sixty to scurvy or any other cause on the final leg of this great odyssey, was yet another remarkable accomplishment.

Altogether, the voyage was a singular display of navigational skill, leadership, improvisation, and sheer tenacity that was unparalleled in that or any subsequent age. Beyond any question, Sir Francis Drake's secret voyage to the northwest coast of America must be regarded as one of the greatest in the history of global exploration.

NOTES

⊰ ABBREVIATIONS ⊱

AGI   Archivo General de Indias, Seville

BL   British Library, London

CDIE Coleccion de documentos inéditos parala historia de España

CSP Spain Calendar of State Papers—Spain (compiled by Martin S. Hume)

PRO   Public Record Office, London

⊰ PROLOGUE ⊱

1. Mendoza to Philip, October 16, 1580, *CSP Spain*, vol. 3, no. 44.
2. Nuttall, *New Light on Drake*, 430.
3. Wagner, *Sir Francis Drake's Voyage Around the World*, 444–45.
4. Hakluyt, *The Principall Navigations, Voyages and Discoveries of the English Nation* (1589), title page.
5. Drake to Elizabeth, January 1, 1593, reprinted in *Sir Francis Drake Revived* (1626).
6. *The World Encompassed by Sir Francis Drake* (1628), title page.
7. This book draws from my academic work *Sir Francis Drake's Secret Voyage to the Northwest Coast of America in A.D. 1579*; hereafter cited as Bawlf, *Secret Voyage* (2001). Since its publication, I have modified my conclusions in some areas. Therefore, unless otherwise noted this book takes precedence over my previous work.

⊰ CHAPTER 1: SAN JUAN DE ULÚA ⊱

1. Hawkins published a narrative of his voyage, *A True Declaration of the Troublesome Voyage of John Hawkins*, in 1569. This and other contemporary accounts of the events are integrated in Williamson, *Sir John Hawkins*.
2. William Camden, *Annales* (1615); excerpt printed in Wagner, *Sir Francis Drake's Voyage Around the World*, 317.
3. Corbett, *Drake and the Tudor Navy*, vol. 1, 97.

4. Hawkins anchored in the darkness just off San Juan de Ulúa while Drake apparently moved farther offshore. Hawkins later complained, "[The *Judith*] forsook us in our great misery," inferring that Drake had abandoned him. Whether true or not, this is all that is recorded of the incident. Some historians argue that Drake must have felt that his first duty was to bring his own crowded ship safely home. During his lifetime, however, Drake's detractors held that this was a case of willful desertion.

5. Quinn and Skelton, eds., *Principall Navigations*, 557–62.

⊰ CHAPTER 2: LETTERS OF MARQUE ⊱

1. There are several excellent modern biographies of Drake, including (in order of publication) those by Mason, Thomson, Sugden, Cummins, and Kelsey noted in the bibliography to this book. For the events of Drake's childhood, I rely primarily on Sugden, *Francis Drake*, 1–9.

2. Sugden, Ibid.

3. Ibid.

4. Ibid.

5. Quoted in Weir, *Elizabeth the Queen*, 221.

6. Quoted in Williamson, *The Age of Drake*, 3–4.

7. Ibid.

8. Parker, *The Grand Strategy of Philip II*, 77–78.

⊰ CHAPTER 3: DRAKE'S PRIVATE WAR ⊱

1. Nearly all that is known about Drake's 1570–71 operations in the Caribbean has been gleaned from Spanish sources assembled in Wright, ed., *Spanish Documents Concerning English Voyages to the Spanish Main, 1569–1580*.

2. Ibid., 32.

3. A narrative of this voyage was published by Drake's nephew under the title *Sir Francis Drake Revived* in 1626, thirty years after Drake's death (ibid., 245–326). Despite the late date of publication, the events it describes are consistent with Spanish reports at the time of Drake's raids. Composed from firsthand accounts by some of the men who accompanied Drake, it was written by Philip Nichols sometime before 1593. Some of the veterans of the voyage sailed on Drake's 1585–86 expedition to the Caribbean, on which Nichols served as chaplain, and most likely he began gathering accounts of their earlier exploits at that time. According to the subtitle of the book, after Nichols completed the draft narrative it was revised by Drake himself "by diverse notes with his own hand here and there inserted" (title page).

4. Sugden, *Sir Francis Drake*, 73.

5. Wright, ed., *Spanish Documents Concerning English Voyages to the Spanish Main, 1569–1580*, 48.

6. Ibid., 326.

7. Corbett, *Drake and the Tudor Navy*, vol. I, 190–91.

8. Ibid., 195–98.
9. Ibid., 191–92.

◄ CHAPTER 4: A PASSAGE TO CATHAY ►

1. Davies, *The Golden Age of Spain*, appendix 2.
2. Lopez de Velasco, *Geographica y Descripcion Universal des Indias* (1576).
3. Taylor, *Tudor Geography*, 111.
4. Williamson, *The Age of Drake*, 12–13.
5. Ibid., 14; Quinn, in Symons, ed., *Meta Incognita, a Discourse of Discovery*, 11–12.
6. Williamson, *The Age of Drake*, 18–27.
7. Sherman, *John Dee*, chap. 1; Starkey, *Elizabeth*, 263–64.
8. Gilbert, *A Discourse of a Discoverie for a New Passage to Cathaia*, circulated in manuscript in 1566, but not published until 1576.

◄ CHAPTER 5: THE SOUTH SEA PROJECT ►

1. Williamson, *The Age of Drake*, 150–53.
2. McDermott, in Symons, ed., *Meta Incognita, a Discourse of Discovery*, 149–50.
3. Corbett, *Drake and the Tudor Navy*, vol. 1, 195.
4. Penzer, ed., *The World Encompassed and Analogous Contemporary Documents*, 166.
5. Ibid.
6. BL Cotton MS Otho E VIII, fols. 8–9; Taylor, "The Missing Draft"; "More Light on Drake."
7. Penzer, ed., *The World Encompassed and Analogous Contemporary Documents*, 166.
8. Ibid.
9. Ibid., 156.
10. Corbett, *Drake and the Tudor Navy*, vol. 1, 205–6.
11. Ibid.
12. Ibid.
13. Quoted in McDermott, *Martin Frobisher, Elizabethan Privateer*, 151–52.
14. The map was printed for inclusion in Best's book, *A True Discourse of the Late Voyages of Discoverie . . . Under the Conduct of Martin Frobisher, General* (London, 1578).
15. van den Broecke et al., eds., *Abraham Ortelius*, 36.
16. McDermott, *Martin Frobisher, Elizabethan Privateer*, 153–56.
17. Ibid., 167–68.
18. Quoted in Savours, in Symons, ed., *Meta Incognita, a Discourse of Discovery*, 27, 34.
19. Rowse, *Sir Richard Grenville of the Revenge*, chap. 5.
20. Ibid.
21. Taylor, *Tudor Geography*, 113.
22. Ibid., 117.
23. Ibid., 114.
24. Ibid., 117; Baldwin, in Symons, ed., *Meta Incognita, a Discourse of Discovery*, 404, 462 n. 12.

25. Taylor, *Tudor Geography*, 116; Wallis, ed., *Sir Francis Drake*, 20.

26. Historians have generally characterized Grenville as Drake's rival for the Queen's consent to a South Sea expedition. However, given William Hawkins's known association with Grenville's first proposal, and the remarkable coincidence of timing and purpose of it and his second proposal to Drake's interest and eventual voyage, there has to be a strong suspicion that Grenville was collaborating with them.

⊰ CHAPTER 6: THE PREPARATIONS ⊱

1. Kelsey, *Sir Francis Drake, the Queen's Pirate*, 83, citing PRO High Court of Admiralty, 25/1, part 2. The bounty was paid by the Crown to private shipowners who constructed armed ships that could be called upon for the defense of the realm.

2. There are no surviving plans of the *Pelican*, later renamed the *Golden Hinde*. However, based on the well-researched replica constructed in 1974, her approximate dimensions probably were:

Length of keel	60 ft.
Rake forward	20 ft.
Rake aft	4 ft.
Length overall (incl. bowsprit)	102 ft.
Draught (laden)	13 ft.
Length at waterline	75 ft.
Breadth (beam)	21 ft.
Depth in hold	12 ft.
Vertical clearances:	
Gun deck	5 ft.
Forecastle and halfdeck	5 ft.
Great cabin	6 ft.
Foremast	46 ft.
Fore topmast	25 ft.
Mainmast	59 ft.
Top mainmast	29 ft.
Mizzenmast	36 ft. 6 in.
Sail area	4,150 sq. ft.

According to a rule attributed to contemporary naval architect Mathew Baker (see Friel, in Symons, ed., *Meta Incognita, a Discourse of Discovery*, 303–6), a vessel's tonnage was calculated as follows:

$$\frac{\text{length of keel} \times \text{beam} \times \text{depth in hold}}{100} = \text{tons burden}$$

Applying this formula to the above dimensions for the *Pelican* yields 151 "tons burden." However, this figure would have represented her carrying capacity only. A reasonable approximation of her gross displacement (incorporating the vessel's structural weight) would be at least 1.5 × tons burden, or 225 tons.

3. Wagner, *Sir Francis Drake's Voyage Around the World*, 503 n. 12.

4. Kelsey, *Sir Francis Drake, the Queen's Pirate*, 81–82.

5. Ibid., 83.

6. Waters, in Thrower, ed., *Sir Francis Drake and the Famous Voyage*, 25–27.

7. Taylor, ed., *A Regiment for the Sea*, 17.

8. Ibid.

9. Unfortunately, there is no surviving record of these discussions. The inference that they must have taken place is derived from subsequent developments, related in chapters 11 and 25 of this book.

10. Quinn and Skelton, eds., *Principall Navigations*, 630. Whether Hall determined their longitude by dead reckoning or by application of the lunar distance method is not clear. Frobisher's men set up some cairns on Christopher Hall Island, at the entrance to the "strait," but these cairns have never been examined in the context of the lunar distance theorem.

11. Nuttall, *New Light on Drake*, xli.

12. Taylor, ed., *The Troublesome Voyage of Captain Edward Fenton*, 49.

13. Sugden, *Sir Francis Drake*, 100.

14. Penzer, ed., *The World Encompassed and Analogous Contemporary Documents*, 2.

15. Kelsey, *Sir Francis Drake, the Queen's Pirate*, 82.

✢ CHAPTER 7: A TROUBLED BEGINNING ✣

1. Corbett, *Drake and the Tudor Navy*, vol. 1, 220.

2. Ibid., 202.

3. Ibid., 210–13, 244.

4. Vaux, ed., *The World Encompassed by Sir Francis Drake*, 171–73.

5. Ibid., 172.

✢ CHAPTER 8: THE COAST OF BARBARY ✣

1. Penzer, ed., *The World Encompassed and Analogous Contemporary Documents*, 3.

2. Ibid., 125.

3. Ibid., 3–4.

4. Ibid.; Wilson, *The World Encompassed*, 53–55.

5. Penzer, ed., *The World Encompassed and Analogous Contemporary Documents*, 91.

6. Ibid., 5.

7. Ibid., 5–6.

8. Ibid., 6–7.

9. Ibid., 95.

10. Ibid., 96.

11. Ibid.

12. Ibid., 97.

13. Ibid., 99–100.

14. Ibid., 98.

15. Ibid., 146–47.
16. Ibid., 168–69.
17. Ibid., 98.

⊰ CHAPTER 9: LAND OF GIANTS ⊱

1. Penzer, ed., *The World Encompassed and Analogous Contemporary Documents*, 103.
2. Ibid., 104.
3. Ibid.
4. Ibid., 103.
5. Ibid., 148.
6. Ibid., 98.
7. Ibid., 108.
8. Ibid., 109.
9. Ibid., 110.
10. Ibid., 110–11.
11. Ibid., 14.
12. Ibid.
13. Ibid., 15.
14. Vaux, ed., *The World Encompassed by Sir Francis Drake*, 166–71.
15. Ibid.; Penzer, ed., *The World Encompassed and Analogous Contemporary Documents*, 150–51.
16. Penzer, ed., *The World Encompassed and Analogous Contemporary Documents*, 120.
17. Ibid., 117.
18. Ibid., 195.
19. Ibid., 153.

⊰ CHAPTER 10: ISLAND OF BLOOD ⊱

1. Penzer, ed., *The World Encompassed and Analogous Contemporary Documents*, 196.
2. Ibid., 20–22, 123–24, 195–96.
3. Ibid.
4. Ibid., 21.
5. Ibid., 22.
6. Ibid., 165, 167.
7. Monson, *Naval Tracts*, 400.
8. There are several indications of Drake's anxiety in the matter, including his subsequent renaming of the *Pelican* and his later remarks to the Spaniard Don Francisco de Zarate. Nuttall, *New Light on Drake*, 208–9.
9. Penzer, ed., *The World Encompassed and Analogous Contemporary Documents*, 155–61.
10. Ibid., 155.
11. Ibid.
12. Ibid.
13. Ibid.
14. Ibid., 156.

15. Ibid.
16. Ibid., 157.
17. Ibid.
18. Ibid.
19. Ibid.
20. Ibid., 25.
21. Ibid., 161.
22. Ibid., 196.
23. Fagan, *The Little Ice Age*, 47–97; Borisenkov, in Bradley and Jones, eds., *Climate Since A.D. 1500*, 171–83.
24. Camuffo and Enzi, in Bradley and Jones, eds., *Climate Since A.D. 1500*, 143–54.
25. Tarusov, in ibid., 505–16.
26. Penzer, ed., *The World Encompassed and Analogous Contemporary Documents*, 163–64.
27. Ibid.
28. Ibid., 166–67.

⊰ CHAPTER 11: INTO THE SOUTH SEA ⊱

1. Penzer, ed., *The World Encompassed and Analogous Contemporary Documents*, 27.
2. More specifically, the number aboard the *Golden Hinde* when Drake exited the strait appears to have been about ninety men and boys. There is no mention of any exchange of manpower between the ships beyond that point, and indeed it is unlikely that there would have been in the circumstances. Then on the coast of Chile and Peru Drake lost two of his crew to scurvy and five more to armed conflict, which would have reduced his company to the low eighties. After these losses one witness, San Juan de Anton, placed the size of Drake's crew at "85, more or less." Nuttall, *New Light on Drake*, 172.
3. The dates of Drake's progress through the strait are taken from Nuño da Silva's log, reprinted in Nuttall, *New Light on Drake*, 282–84; see also Penzer, ed., *The World Encompassed and Analogous Contemporary Documents*, 27.
4. Penzer, ed., *The World Encompassed and Analogous Contemporary Documents*, 28.
5. Ibid.
6. Ibid., 27.
7. Ibid.; Nuttall, *New Light on Drake*, 282.
8. Penzer, ed., *The World Encompassed and Analogous Contemporary Documents*, 129.
9. Ibid., 28.
10. Ibid., 129.
11. Ibid., 130.
12. Ibid.
13. Ibid., 197.
14. Ibid., 133.
15. Ibid., 198.
16. Williamson, ed., *The Observations of Sir Richard Hawkins*, 96.

ᦰ CHAPTER 12: CHILE ᕭ

1. Penzer, ed., *The World Encompassed and Analogous Contemporary Documents*, 139.
2. Ibid., 140.
3. Ibid., 39.
4. Vaux, ed., *The World Encompassed by Sir Francis Drake*, 179.
5. Wagner, *Sir Francis Drake's Voyage Around the World*, 478 n. 14.
6. Penzer, ed., *The World Encompassed and Analogous Contemporary Documents*, 42.
7. Ibid., 43.
8. Ibid.
9. Ibid., 43–44.
10. Nuttall, *New Light on Drake*, 303.

ᦰ CHAPTER 13: PERU ᕭ

1. Williamson, *The Age of Drake*, 140.
2. Nuttall, *New Light on Drake*, 64.
3. Ibid., 10.
4. Ibid.
5. Ibid.
6. Wagner, *Sir Francis Drake's Voyage Around the World*, 356.
7. Nuttall, *New Light on Drake*, 151.
8. Wagner, *Sir Francis Drake's Voyage Around the World*, 361 n. 7.
9. Ibid., 366.
10. Nuttall, *New Light on Drake*, 174.
11. Wallis, ed., *Sir Francis Drake*, 75.

ᦰ CHAPTER 14: NEW SPAIN ᕭ

1. Penzer, ed., *The World Encompassed and Analogous Contemporary Documents*, 47.
2. Nuttall, *New Light on Drake*, 203.
3. Ibid., 204–9.
4. Ibid.
5. Vaux, ed., *The World Encompassed by Sir Francis Drake*, 183.
6. Nuttall, *New Light on Drake*, 213–14.
7. Ibid., 354–57.
8. Ibid., 214.
9. Vaux, ed., *The World Encompassed by Sir Francis Drake*, 176.

ᦰ CHAPTER 15: NEWS FROM THE SOUTH SEA ᕭ

1. Nuttall, *New Light on Drake*, 75.
2. Ibid., 206–9.
3. Ibid., 244.

4. Ibid., 243.

5. Ibid., 303.

6. Wagner, *Sir Francis Drake's Voyage Around the World*, 348.

7. Ibid., 349.

8. Mendoza to Philip, March 31, 1578, *CSP Spain*, vol. 2, no. 486.

9. Allaire and Hogarth, in Symons, ed., *Meta Incognita, a Discourse of Discovery*, 575–88.

10. Best, *A True Discourse of the Late Voyages of Discoverie . . . Under the Conduct of Martin Frobisher,* London, 1578.

11. Ruggles, in Symons, ed., *Meta Incognita, a Discourse of Discovery*, 217.

12. Mendoza to Philip, November 15, 1578; Allaire and Hogarth, in Symons, ed., *Meta Incognita, a Discourse of Discovery*, 577–81.

13. Mendoza to Philip, June 10 and 20, 1579, Kelsey, *Sir Francis Drake, the Queen's Pirate,* 208, citing AGI Patronato 265, ramo 28; and CDIE, 91:262.

14. Nuttall, *New Light on Drake*, 119.

15. Kelsey, *Sir Francis Drake, the Queen's Pirate,* 217–18.

16. Ibid., 401.

17. Sugden, *Sir Francis Drake*, 145.

18. Mendoza to Gabriel de Zayas (Philip's secretary), September 5, 1579, *CSP Spain*, vol. 2, no. 596.

19. Mendoza to Zayas, September 13, 1579, ibid., vol. 2, no. 599.

20. Mendoza to Zayas, September 29, 1579, ibid., vol. 2, no. 604.

21. Mendoza to Philip, December 28, 1579, ibid., vol. 2, no. 611.

22. Mendoza to Philip, February 20, 1580, ibid., vol. 3, no. 5.

◁ CHAPTER 16: THE MOLUCCAS ▷

1. Wagner, *Sir Francis Drake's Voyage Around the World*, 173; Nuttall, *New Light on Drake*, 52.

2. Penzer, ed., *The World Encompassed and Analogous Contemporary Documents*, 64.

3. Lessa, in Thrower, ed., *Sir Francis Drake and the Famous Voyage*, 60–77.

4. Penzer, ed., *The World Encompassed and Analogous Contemporary Documents*, 67.

5. Ibid.

6. Ibid., 70.

7. Ibid., 71.

8. Wagner, *Sir Francis Drake's Voyage Around the World*, 180.

9. Ibid., 181–82.

◁ CHAPTER 17: HOMEWARD ▷

1. Penzer, ed., *The World Encompassed and Analogous Contemporary Documents*, 75.

2. Vaux, ed., *The World Encompassed by Sir Francis Drake*, 183–84. The account, an unsigned manuscript known as the "Anonymous Narrative" [BL Harley MS 280, fols. 81–90] appears to have been adapted from a deposition taken from one of Drake's men soon after their return, and contains a number of details that were

omitted from the later published accounts. Its mention of Maria and her companions being left at this island is corroborated by John Drake's later testimony.

3. Penzer, ed., *The World Encompassed and Analogous Contemporary Documents*, 76.

4. Vaux, ed., *The World Encompassed by Sir Francis Drake*, 176.

5. The "Anonymous Narrative" states that the grounding occurred on January 8, which undoubtedly was the date recorded at the time. When Drake and his crew reached England, however, they discovered that they had lost a day circumnavigating the world from east to west, and the date of the grounding was changed to January 9 in the eventual published accounts. Evidently, it was decided, as with the modern international date line, that the date had skipped forward on the day they crossed the 180th meridian, on the opposite side of the globe from England, in mid-Pacific.

6. The earliest surviving account of Drake's voyage in the Pacific, the "Anonymous Narrative," states that Drake reached Ternate at "ye latter end of November." Allowing for the twenty-eight days he subsequently spent careening his ship at the "island of crabs," it therefore appears that the grounding must have occurred within a few days of his departure from the island. Indeed, this makes perfect sense, because the Bay of Towori is only a short distance from the Banggai Archipelago.

After this manuscript was written, several years passed before an account of Drake's voyage appeared in print. Titled *The famous voyage of Sir Francis Drake*, it was adapted in part from the above-noted anonymous account. For Drake's journey through the East Indies, however, the particulars are taken from a different account, which is now lost. This account evidently stated that Drake reached Ternate on November 14—as much as two weeks earlier than indicated by the anonymous account—and increased the period spent between Ternate and striking the reef on January 9 by an equivalent amount of time. "The famous voyage" states that the time was expended after Drake left the "island of crabs," sailing *northward* in an effort to get around the northern extremity of Celebes.

Another printed account, *The World Encompassed by Sir Francis Drake*, is by far the most detailed and contains many more dates. The original draft of this account, now lost, was adapted from the journal of Francis Fletcher and then served as the principal source for *The famous voyage* from Guatulco onward (see Quinn, "Early Accounts of the Famous Voyage"). The draft was then edited and revised for publication, but it was suppressed and did not finally appear in print until 1628. This version states that Drake arrived at Ternate at an even earlier date: November 4. Thus, the time he spent between there and the mishap on the reef was increased further still, and this was explained very differently than in *The famous voyage*.

According to *The World Encompassed*, when he left the "island of crabs" Drake spent four days sailing westward to Celebes and then became "entangled" in a large bay, undoubtedly the Bay of Towori, for three more days. Then, it says, they turned *southward* and followed the coast for another 22 days before striking the reef somewhere near the southern extremity of Celebes on January 9. After describing their struggle to free themselves, however, the account contradicts itself, stating that the grounding occurred at latitude 2 degrees south, which places the incident back in the Bay of Towori.

These changes to the chronology of the voyage in the published accounts were part of an evolving scheme to displace and conceal up to two months of time that Drake had spent somewhere else prior to arriving in the East Indies, as will be revealed further in the later chapters of this book.

7. Penzer, ed., *The World Encompassed and Analogous Contemporary Documents*, 81–82.

8. *The Oxford Universal Dictionary On Historical Principles*, 3rd ed.: "*Gentile* . . . of a Hindu, as distinct from a Mohammedan."

9. Wallis, ed., *Sir Francis Drake*, 91.

10. Ibid.

11. Drake's "*Portus Java Majoris*," depicted in the upper-right corner of Joducus Hondius's broadside map, has been identified as the port of Cilacap, 400 miles west of Bali near the western end of Java. Departing the Bay of Towori on January 10, Drake had ample time to reach there by February 11. The sailing distance via Lombok Strait, where Bali is located, to Cilacap is approximately 1,300 miles. If one allows for the two days he spent at Bali, this leaves thirty-one days to cover the distance—an average of about 42 miles sailed per day.

12. Wagner, *Sir Francis Drake's Voyage Around the World*, 283–84.

13. Nuttall, *New Light on Drake*, 407–8.

14. Ibid., 409.

❧ CHAPTER 18: "A VERY SHORT WAY" ❧

1. Quinn, *Sir Francis Drake as Seen by His Contempories*, 6.

2. Nuttall, *New Light on Drake*, 54–55.

3. Corbett, *Drake and the Tudor Navy*, vol. I, 307–9.

4. Mendoza to Philip, September 29, 1580; Kelsey, *Sir Francis Drake, the Queen's Pirate*, 211, citing Palencia, *Francisco Draque.*

5. Mendoza to Philip, October 16, 1580, *CSP Spain*, vol. 3, no. 44; Wallis, in Thrower, ed., *Sir Francis Drake and the Famous Voyage*, 121–22, 133.

6. Ibid.

7. Ibid., 122.

8. Nuttall, *New Light on Drake*, 417–18.

9. Ibid., 429.

10. Ibid., n. I.

11. Mendoza to Philip, October 30, 1580; *CSP Spain*, vol. 3, no. 50.

12. Wagner, *Sir Francis Drake's Voyage Around the World*, 306.

13. Mendoza to Philip, January 9, 1581; *CSP Spain*, vol. 3, no. 60.

14. Nuttall, *New Light on Drake*, 55.

15. Wagner, *Sir Francis Drake's Voyage Around the World*, 305.

16. Ibid., 306.

17. Wallis, in Thrower, ed., *Sir Francis Drake and the Famous Voyage*, 137.

18. Ibid., 136.

19. Wallis, ed., *Sir Francis Drake*, 92–93.

20. Nuttall, *New Light on Drake*, 430.

21. Mendoza to Philip, January 9, 1581, *CSP Spain*, vol. 3, no. 61.

22. Mendoza to Philip, January 16, 1581, ibid., vol. 3, no. 65.

23. Mendoza to Philip, April 6, 1581, ibid., vol. 3, no. 77.

⊰ CHAPTER 19: "ISLANDS OF GOOD LAND" ⊱

1. Taylor, ed., *The Troublesome Voyage of Captain Edward Fenton*, 10.

2. Mendoza to Philip, February 9, 1582, *CSP Spain*, vol. 3, no. 211.

3. Wagner, *Sir Francis Drake's Voyage Around the World*, 444–45.

4. Ibid., 218.

5. Taylor, ed., *The Troublesome Voyage of Captain Edward Fenton*, 54.

6. Ibid., 38–40.

7. Manuscript map, "Sʳ Humfray Gylbert knight his charte," drawn by Dr. John Dee, circa 1582. Preserved in the Free Library of Philadelphia.

8. Wallis, ed., *Sir Francis Drake*, 22.

9. Taylor, ed., *The Troublesome Voyage of Captain Edward Fenton*, xxxix.

10. Donno, *An Elizabethan in 1582, the Diary of Richard Madox*, 208.

11. AGI Patronato 266, ramo 49, fol. 49. John Drake's depositions are translated in Eliott-Drake, *The Family and Heirs of Sir Francis Drake*, appendix I, and in Nuttall, *New Light on Drake*, 18–56; see also Kelsey, *Sir Francis Drake, the Queen's Pirate*, 175–76. The translations differ slightly, but the essential details are consistent.

12. Ibid., ramo 54, fol. 8. Translated in Nuttall, *New Light on Drake*, 50–51; see also Wagner, *Sir Francis Drake's Voyage Around the World*, 333 n. 16.

13. Wagner, *Sir Francis Drake's Voyage Around the World*, 333–34.

⊰ CHAPTER 20: "SEEN AND CORRECTED BY SIR DRAKE" ⊱

1. Sugden, *Sir Francis Drake*, 161–62.

2. Ibid., 163–64.

3. Ortelius, *Typus Orbis Terrarum* (1570), printed from the plate as repaired in 1579, with Drake's route added with pen and ink. BL Maps 920.(327). Notably, the inscription concerning Drake's discovery of the islands at the southern extremity of America is in French. Prior to Drake's return, Elizabeth had resurrected a proposal that she marry the Duke of Anjou, brother of the French King. The urgency of an alliance with France was underscored first by King Philip's annexation of Portugal and then was reiterated in December 1580 when the Pope publicly sanctioned the assassination of Elizabeth. Consequently, when a high-level delegation arrived from France at the end of March 1581 to further negotiations for the marriage,

Elizabeth spared no effort to welcome them. Indeed, it was only a short time after the delegation's arrival that she took all of them aboard the *Golden Hinde* for Drake's knighting and enlisted the Seigneur de Marchaumont to assist her in performing the ceremony. It is quite possible then, that Drake had drawn this map, explaining as he did so his abandonment of two ships in Patagonia, for a member of the French delegation at the Queen's behest, as a memento of the occasion.

4. Bawlf, *Secret Voyage* (2001), 35–85. Hondius resided in London from 1583 to 1593, and a contemporary biography states that while there he "drew many fine draughts and master peeces as Sʳ Francis Drakes voyage around the world." Comparison of the scenes in the corners of the Drake Mellon map with those in Hondius's ultimate "master piece" depicting Drake's voyage, *Vera Totius Expeditionis Nautica, 1589* (the Hondius Broadside map), leaves very little doubt that the Drake Mellon map was one of the "many fine draughts" that he drew for Drake over the course of his ten years in London.

5. Ibid., 35–48.

6. Nuttall, *New Light on Drake*, xxvii.

7. Manuscript, circa 1584 (first state), 24 cm × 45 cm, drawn with pen, ink, and watercolor on vellum. Now known as the Drake Mellon map, it is preserved in the Paul Mellon Collection, Yale Center for British Art, New Haven.

8. Wallis, in Thrower, ed., *Sir Francis Drake and the Famous Voyage*, 162 n. 49.

9. Williamson, *Sir John Hawkins*, 411, citing BL Lansdowne MS 49, fols. 9–10.

10. Ibid.

11. Sugden, *Sir Francis Drake*, 173–75.

12. Wallis, in Thrower, ed., *Sir Francis Drake and the Famous Voyage*, 139, quoting from *Calendar of State Papers—Foreign*, compiled by Hume, Elizabeth, vol. 19, 18.

13. Ibid., 123.

14. Ibid., 161 n. 5.

15. BL Harley MS 280, fols. 81–90 and related memoranda. Except for Drake's northern voyage, the account, given in the past tense and containing several accusations against Drake and his sailors, appears to have been copied more or less verbatim from the original deposition. After copying it, the writer crossed out most of the derogatory remarks—apparently to sanitize it for consumption by others—and added several notes concerning matters not covered by the deposition. The handwriting bears a close resemblance to that of Richard Hakluyt, which would make it a very rare example of his work in progress. However, an expert paleographic analysis would be required to confirm this.

16. Ibid. The altered numerals were first discovered by Bob Ward, who drew them to my attention in 1995. I subsequently arranged for them to be examined by the British Library, where the manuscript is preserved, using its Video Spectral Comparator—technology which has proved effective in identifying alterations to handwritten documents. Photos of the numerals under various light conditions created by this device confirmed that the latitude of Drake's northern reach had been altered by the writer. For further details, see Bawlf, *Secret Voyage* (2001), 28–31.

17. Ibid. It appears that the ink may not yet have fully dried when the alterations were made, although this cannot be positively verified.

18. Corbett, *Drake and the Tudor Navy*, vol. I, 40.

19. Sugden, *Sir Francis Drake*, 195–96.

20. Quoted in Sugden, ibid., 197.

21. Quoted in Sugden, ibid., 191.

22. Quinn, *Sir Francis Drake as Seen by His Contemporaries*, 14.

23. Known as the French Drake map because most of the inscriptions are in French, its dimensions and basic scheme are nearly identical to those of the Drake Mellon map, except for the addition of a portrait of Drake with an inscription stating that he was age forty-two at the time. However, it appears to have been drawn by a different artist and has a rather unfinished look. Several of the place-names are incomplete or misspelled, and curiously, the inscription concerning Drake's discovery of Nova Albion is placed adjacent to Greenland. These aspects together with cruder renderings of the corner scenes suggest that it is a rough copy of one of the commemorative maps drawn by Jodocus Hondius for Drake. Nevertheless, it was subsequently engraved in this state by a Nicola van Sype, whose name appears in the lower-right corner. The reason, it appears, is the note along the bottom margin of the map stating that it had been "seen and corrected by the aforesaid Sir Drake." Evidently, the original manuscript map was accompanied by a note, and probably also one or more sketches containing Drake's corrections.

     A family of engravers by the name of van Sype is known to have been active in Germany in the first decades of the seventeenth century, and the surviving copies of the map were all found in either the 1627 or the 1641 French edition of Richard Hakluyt's account of Drake's voyage. Most probably, sometime after the owner's death the manuscript map was found among his papers, and because of the note concerning Drake, van Sype undertook to engrave a faithful copy of it.

24. The addition of a portrait of Drake suggests that the original map from which this one was copied was presented to someone who had never met him. Notably also, the map incorporates two boundaries in North America: One is a line across the continent, expressing a desire to separate North America from New Spain; and the other is a boundary around New France, indicating a wish to acknowledge, but also contain, France's claim to part of the continent. This fits the picture we have of Walsingham in 1585 inviting a dialogue with Henry of Navarre about an alliance, including the sharing of North America. Also, the boundaries leave a space on the Atlantic coast which evidently is reserved for England, but which is not yet named Virginia. Notably, the reconnaissance of that coast to select a site for the colony occurred in the summer of 1584, and then the colony was established in the summer of 1585. It therefore appears that the original from which this map was copied was drawn sometime between those dates. This, coupled with the portrait and the inscriptions in French, leaves little doubt that the map is a copy of the one that was sent to Henry of Navarre in the spring of 1585.

25. The map was bound in Walter Bigges, *Expeditio Francisci Drake*, published in Leyden

in 1588. The only surviving copy is preserved in the Huntington Library, San Marino, California.

26. Bawlf, *Secret Voyage* (2001), 40–48.

27. Ibid., 49–54, 56–61.

28. Ibid.

29. Ibid., 56–61. Titled *Maris Pacifica* (1589). The map on which the place-names were given to Ortelius is lost. However, Hondius engraved a map of his own, titled *Americae* (1589), containing the identical information for northwest America.

30. Ibid.

31. Quoted in Sugden, *Sir Francis Drake*, 208.

32. Quoted in Sugden, ibid., 210.

33. Quoted in Sugden, ibid., 214.

34. Parks, *Richard Hakluyt and the English Voyages*, 248.

35. Titled *Novus Orbis*, [1587].

36. Bawlf, *Secret Voyage* (2001), 54–56.

⊰ CHAPTER 21: "THAT POSTERITY BE NOT DEPRIVED" ⊱

1. Dyke, "The Finance of a Sixteenth-Century Navigator," 111.

2. There is no contemporary documentation that discloses the mission of the *Content*. However, since Cavendish left Peru and New Spain in an uproar, it makes no sense that the crew of the *Content* would attempt to return via Magellan's Strait, and if they were going to cross the Pacific, they would have accompanied Cavendish.

3. Narrative by Francis Pretty. *Principal Navigations* (1600; reprinted Glasgow, 1903–5), vol. 4, 334.

4. Quinn, in Thrower, ed., *Sir Francis Drake and the Famous Voyage*, 33–48.

5. Quinn and Skelton, eds., *Principall Navigations*, xvi–xix.

6. Ibid., xix.

7. Quinn, in Thrower, ed., *Sir Francis Drake and the Famous Voyage*, 40.

8. Ibid., 37.

9. Known as the Drake silver medal, its production was assisted by grants from Parliament funds in the legal years 1588 (which ended March 29, 1589) and 1589. Nine examples survive, one of which is impressed with Mercator's signature as maker and dated 1589. This example is preserved in the Hans P. Kraus Collection at the Library of Congress, Washington. Wallis, in Thrower, ed., *Sir Francis Drake and the Famous Voyage*, 149–51.

10. Quoted in Sugden, *Sir Francis Drake*, 282.

11. Ibid.

12. From Hakluyt's "Note to the Reader," reprinted in Quinn and Skelton, eds., *Principall Navigations*.

13. Ibid.

14. Wallis, in Thrower, ed., *Sir Francis Drake and the Famous Voyage*, 151–55.

15. Ibid.

16. Wallis, ed., *Sir Francis Drake*, 80–81.

17. Petrus Plancio (Peter Plancius), *Orbis Terrarum Typus* (1590).

18. Williamson, *The Age of Drake*, 341.

19. Crino and Wallis, "New Researches on the Molyneux Globes," 14. This first edition of the globe has been lost.

20. Bawlf, *Secret Voyage* (2001), 73–76 and notes thereto.

21. Ibid. The only surviving example of this third edition, once owned by Sir Walter Raleigh, is preserved at Petworth House in Sussex.

22. Wallis, in Thrower, ed., *Sir Francis Drake and the Famous Voyage*, 153.

23. *Blundeville His Exercises* (London, 1594), reprinted in Wagner, *Sir Francis Drake's Voyage Around the World*, 311–13.

24. Sugden, *Sir Francis Drake*, 290.

25. Quinn, in Thrower, ed., *Sir Francis Drake and the Famous Voyage*, 36–38.

26. Drake's letter to Elizabeth is dated January 1, 1592, but—adjusting for the old-style Julian calendar then in use, which extended the year to March 25—was actually written on New Year's Day 1593. Quinn, in Thrower, ed., *Sir Francis Drake and the Famous Voyage*, 16–18.

27. *The World Encompassed by Sir Francis Drake* (1628), reprinted in Penzer, ed., *The World Encompassed and Analogous Contemporary Documents*, 1926, 48–50.

28. "The famous voyage of Sir Francis Drake," inserted in most copies of *The Principall Navigations, Voyages and Discoveries of the English Nation* (1589) sometime after the book's publication.

29. Professor David Quinn, a leading authority on Hakluyt's writings and publications, postulated that the so-called Drake leaves were printed, distributed to the subscribers of *Principall Navigations*, and inserted in the unsold copies of the book in the early months of 1590 (Quinn and Skelton eds., *Principall Navigations*, xxiii–xxv). Wagner (*Sir Francis Drake's Voyage Around the World*, 238–39) and Kelsey (*Sir Francis Drake, the Queen's Pirate*, 85–88) argue that the account could not have been released before 1594 or 1595.

30. Titled *Vera Totius Expeditionis Nautica*, and otherwise known as the Drake Broadside map, it is signed "Jodocus Hondius, Flanders, made in London." Of the six known copies, three were found inserted or bound in English books, and the other three appear to have a Dutch provenance. Wallis, in Thrower, ed., *Sir Francis Drake and the Famous Voyage*, 145–46.

31. The sole example of Hondius's map pasted onto the broadsheet is preserved at the British Library (M.T.6.a.2). The account of Nova Albion on the broadsheet was kindly translated for me by Francis Herbert.

❧ CHAPTER 22: A FORGOTTEN SECRET ❧

1. Williamson, ed., *The Observations of Sir Richard Hawkins*, 8.

2. Ibid., xlix–lii.

3. Ibid., 7.

4. Ibid., xliv–l. Williamson notes that just prior to sending his memoirs to the printer in 1622, Hawkins made a hurried alteration to his opening remarks, which included the purpose of his voyage, and concludes that Hawkins must originally have disclosed something that he subsequently thought it better to suppress. After his capture by the Spanish in 1594, Hawkins told them that once he was clear of Peru his plan had been to repair his ship in the Californias and then cross the Pacific. It hardly seems likely, however, that he would have sailed all that distance north unless his real objective was Drake's Strait of Anian.

5. Sugden, *Sir Francis Drake*, 312.

6. Quoted in Sugden, ibid., 315.

7. Quoted in Sugden, ibid., 316.

8. Quinn, *Sir Francis Drake as Seen by His Contemporaries*, 23.

9. Ibid., 25.

10. Ibid.

11. Ibid., 24.

12. Lope de Vega Carpio, *La Dragontea* (1598).

13. John Davis, *The Worldes Hydrographical Description* (London, 1595).

14. Bawlf, *Secret Voyage* (2001), 73–75.

15. Ibid. The title of Blagrave's book announces that it will contain the map, but none of the surviving copies of the book do. The three surviving copies of the map were all found separately from the book.

16. Titled "The course which Sir Francis Drake held from the haven of Guatulco . . . ," in Hakluyt, *Principal Navigations* (1600), 440–442.

17. Jodocus Hondius, *Globe of the Earth Revised and Corrected in the Year 1600* (Amsterdam).

18. Crino and Wallis, "New Researches on the Molyneux Globes," 15–16.

19. The match between Molyneux's coastline and that behind Vancouver Island was first noticed by Bob Ward, although he thought that Drake's careenage, farther south, was the true site of Nova Albion. Ward's thesis has been that Drake discovered and sailed into the Strait of Juan de Fuca and, concluding that he had found the Strait of Anian, then returned southward, careened the *Golden Hinde* at Whale Cove, and gave the name Nova Albion to the surrounding country.

20. Bawlf, *Secret Voyage* (2001), 119–21, 144 n. 5.

21. Ward, "Churchill Fellowship to examine Drake's maps." The details were incorporated in Dudley's *Carta Particulare, Chart XXXIII* (1647).

22. Bawlf, *Secret Voyage* (2001), 90.

23. Monson, *Naval Tracts*.

24. Ibid., 400.

25. Ibid.

26. Wagner, *Sir Francis Drake's Voyage Around the World*, 477.

27. Monson, *Naval Tracts*, 434.

28. Ibid.

29. Ibid.

30. Wallis, in Thrower, ed., *Sir Francis Drake and the Famous Voyage*, 122–23.
31. Beaglehole, *The Journals of Captain James Cook*, cxxii.

⊰ CHAPTER 23: DRAKE'S STRAIT OF ANIAN ⊱

1. Nuttall, *New Light on Drake*, 302. Nuño da Silva testified that when Drake left Guatulco, he had a crew of "not more than" eighty persons, of whom eight were boys. However, he counted the Negroes—including Drake's manservant Diego, the two Negro men whom they had picked up, and Maria—separately. If one adds the Negroes and Drake, the total company would have been "not more than" eighty-five people.
2. The first mention of Morera's name in the written record comes in the letter that Gaspar de Vargas, the alcade of Guatulco, wrote to Viceroy Enriquez on the evening of Drake's arrival there, in which he states, "All I have been able to find out is that the men on the ship belonging to Juan de Madrid think that the name of the pilot of the ship is Morera." Nuttall, *New Light on Drake*, 214.
3. Bishop, "Drake's Course in the North Pacific," 165.
4. There are no surviving examples of the sixteenth-century charts and sailing directions for the return route from Manila. However, the route remained unchanged for centuries and has been well documented by other means. The earliest surviving chart was seized by British commodore George Anson from the Manila galleon *Nuestra Señora de Covadonga* in 1743, during his voyage around the world.
5. Bishop, "Drake's Course in the North Pacific," 163–65 and map. Drake's course is confirmed by the particulars given in *The World Encompassed by Sir Francis Drake* (Penzer, ed., *The World Encompassed and Analogous Contemporary Documents*, 48) and in John Drake's testimony to the Inquisition at Lima (Nuttall, *New Light on Drake*, 50; see also Wagner, *Sir Francis Drake's Voyage Around the World*, 333, n. 16).
6. Bawlf, *Secret Voyage* (2001), 97–98. Deciphering Drake's cryptographs according to the ten-degree rule—especially the Drake Mellon map, which clearly separates his initial landfall from the location of his future colony—it is clear that he made his landfall at 50 degrees and not 48 degrees as *The World Encompassed* implies. Notably also, 50 degrees was the first latitude written and covered over in the "Anonymous Narrative." Drake later referred to a "Cape of storms" at 50 degrees, which can only be Cape Cook; and Robert Dudley tried to depict a "Cape of storms" at the same latitude, using the drawing he had of Cape Flattery.
7. Penzer, ed., *The World Encompassed and Analogous Contemporary Documents*, 49–50.
8. Oral history related by elders of the *Checleset* Indian band to journalist Arthur Mayse, *Campbell River Gazette*, February 17, 1982.
9. I gratefully acknowledge the assistance of Lt. Comdr. Michael Brooks, former commanding officer of the Royal Canadian Navy sail training vessel *Oriole*, in evaluating the sailing conditions that Drake would have encountered at various stages along the northwest coast of America and subsequently crossing the Pacific, and in reconstructing Drake's probable course at each stage.

10. Penzer, ed., *The World Encompassed and Analogous Contemporary Documents*, 48–49.

11. Bawlf, *Secret Voyage* (2001), 99. Special thanks are due to climate historian Tim Ball for assisting my analysis of the references to freezing weather and snow in the narrative of Drake's voyage.

12. Penzer, ed., *The World Encompassed and Analogous Contemporary Documents*, 49. *The World Encompassed* states that Drake and his men encountered freezing weather at 42 degrees N on June 3, and after sailing two degrees farther north (to 44 degrees), they found the cold and contrary winds so intolerable that they turned eastward, and "the land in that part of America bearing farther out into the West than [we] before had imagined," made their first landfall and anchored in a "bad bay" at 48 degrees on June 5. However, it is inconceivable that they could have encountered, in June, freezing conditions offshore in latitudes 42 degrees to 44 degrees and then found the coast from 48 degrees southward to 38 degrees covered in snow as the narrative states, even during the Little Ice Age. For the latter to have occurred, the coast as far south as San Francisco would have to have been exposed to freezing temperatures for an extended period, not just a freak storm. This would have required average daily temperatures in the latitude of San Francisco at least eight degrees Celsius (fourteen degrees Fahrenheit) colder than the modern norm—an impossibly radical difference. Clearly, the latitude of the freezing weather was altered as part of Drake's effort to tell his story while conforming to the cover up rules.

Evidently, in order to use it as part of the reason for his turning back at 48 degrees, Drake moved the freezing weather ten degrees southward from the true latitudes of 52 degrees and 54 degrees. To complete this alteration, he reversed the order of events. They actually made their first landfall and anchored in the "bad bay" on June 3, and then encountered the cold front further north and made their second landfall on June 5.

Undoubtedly the latitudes that were written over in the "Anonymous Narrative"—50 degrees (Cape Cook) followed by 53 degrees—were the true latitudes of his initial landfalls, with the cold front being met at 52 degrees, prior to the second landfall. Notably, the Queen Charlotte Islands (52 to 54 degrees) lie 150 miles farther west from Cape Cook and this probably accounts for the reference to the land "bearing farther out into the West than [they] before had imagined." Also, on his globe of 1600 Hondius describes the coast at 53 degrees as the "Coast of objections," which accords with the account of Drake's men complaining of the cold weather.

13. Ibid.

14. Boyd, "Demographic History," in Suttles, ed., *Handbook of North American Indians*, vol. 7, *Northwest Coast*, 135–48.

15. Barbeau, *Totem Poles*, vol. 2, 806.

16. Penzer, ed., *The World Encompassed and Analogous Contemporary Documents*, 51.

17. Mann and Streveler, "Final Report on Geological Investigations in Glacier Bay National Park," 20.

18. Swanton, *Tlingit Myths and Texts*, 449.

19. Mann and Streveler, "Final Report on Geological Investigations in Glacier Bay National Park," 8.

20. Penzer, ed., *The World Encompassed and Analogous Contemporary Documents*, 52.

21. MacDonald contacted me and recounted his story in September 2000 after reading about my Drake research (*Vancouver Sun* newspaper, August 6, 2000).

22. Independent sources have corroborated MacDonald's activities in Port Malmesbury in 1954, and that he reported his discovery of the plate to the Juneau Museum and others soon afterward. The diary of anthropologist Henry Bascom Collins confirms that he met with MacDonald at the Smithsonian Institution on April 10, 1956.

23. Unfortunately, no record of the rubbing or of the transcript of the inscription has yet been found at the Smithsonian. Moreover, Collins's diary notes from their initial meeting suggest that MacDonald already knew or believed that the plate bore Drake's name. It therefore appears that there must have been some earlier examination of it that led MacDonald to this belief. He is now in his eighties, and some details of events that occurred half a century ago may understandably have escaped his memory. However, it is not at all unlikely that something left by Drake would have come into the possession of a chief or shaman and been buried with his remains, and it is difficult to believe that a prospector working in a remote area of Alaska at a time when no one was suggesting Drake had been anywhere in the vicinity could have dreamed up this story *and* divined that the plate would have been inscribed in Latin.

24. Penzer, ed., *The World Encompassed and Analogous Contemporary Documents*, 51.

25. Ibid., 52.

26. Ibid., 3. *The World Encompassed* indicates that Drake spent four days at the island of Mogador, during which time the first of his pinnaces was assembled.

27. In June 2001 I visited Port Malmesbury with archaeologists from the U.S. Forest Service and U.S. Parks Service. The *Tlingit* burial caves and several areas along its shores were examined, and soil cores were extracted from two former native habitation sites for dating. No artifacts were found except some strands of *Tlingit* cedar rope in one of the former burial caves. However, the inlet is several miles in length, and only limited areas were examined.

28. The *Tlingit* population residing in Tebenkof Bay prior to European contact likely numbered in the thousands. In the mid–nineteenth century they were all but wiped out by a smallpox epidemic, and the few survivors moved to other areas of the coast. Consequently, there is no oral history specific to the area from the time of Drake.

⊰ CHAPTER 24: NOVA ALBION ⊱

1. Bawlf, *Secret Voyage* (2001), 104–16.

2. Ibid.

3. Ibid.

4. Ibid., 46.

5. Jane, *A Spanish Voyage to Vancouver and the Northwest Coast of America*, 67–68.

6. Wolferstan, *Desolation Sound*, 150, quoting from the diary of Galiano and Valdez.

7. Lamb, ed., *A Voyage of Discovery to the North Pacific Ocean and Round the World, 1791–1795*, vol. 2, 617.

8. Bawlf, *Secret Voyage* (2001), 107–8.

9. Boyd, "Demographic History," in Suttles, ed., *Handbook of North American Indians*, vol. 7, *Northwest Coast*, 135–48. Population estimates for the period prior to eighteenth-century European contact are at best educated guesses. The *Salish* population of the Georgia Basin could well have been as high as 40,000 to 50,000. Just prior to the arrival of the eighteenth-century explorers, a smallpox epidemic spread across the continent and devastated the native population of the basin (Harris, "Voices of Disaster: Smallpox"). By the time Europeans began to record the native population in the nineteenth century, it may already have been reduced by 80 percent or more.

10. Estimate based on discussions with Grant Keddie, curator of archaeology, British Columbia Museum.

11. In the 1790s the *Kwakiutl* Indians of northern Vancouver Island obtained firearms from the maritime fur traders and used them to expand their territory southward. The *Pentlatch* Indians of Comox and Baynes Sound, whose numbers may already have been decimated by disease, were overwhelmed and virtually wiped out. Consequently, there is little surviving oral history for the area prior to that date. The most likely location of Drake's "great post" was either in front of the main village site in Comox Harbor or on nearby Goose Spit. Unfortunately, the former village site has undergone extensive disturbance, becoming part of the modern community of Comox, and Goose Spit has been in use for many years as a military depot. Nevertheless, the silver plate bearing Drake's proclamation of Nova Albion may yet one day be unearthed.

12. The principal alternatives south of Baynes Sound were Northwest Bay, Nanoose Bay, and Nanaimo Harbor. The first two were exposed to strong winds blowing off the mainland, and Nanaimo would have been too difficult to defend.

13. Ortelius, *Maris Pacifici* (1589).

⊰ CHAPTER 25: POINT OF POSITION ⊱

1. Gleeson, *Ozette Woodworking Technology*, 50–52.

2. Ibid., 52–53. Research has shown that the number of Japanese junks that have been wrecked on the northwest coast of America has been exaggerated (Keddie, "The Question of Asiatic Objects on the North Pacific Coast of America"). Surprisingly, the iron tools and blades found at the *Makah* village at Ozette were not subjected to metallurgical tests comparing them to articles of a similar type and date manufactured in Japan and Europe. The British Columbia Museum, the British Museum, and others are now cooperating in the testing of early iron objects found along the coast, and it is hoped that some of the iron found at Ozette will soon be included in these tests.

3. Nuttall, *New Light on Drake*, 160.

4. Ortelius, *Maris Pacifici* (1589); Bawlf, *Secret Voyage* (2001), 58–61, 116. As previously noted, the principal purpose of this map was to provide the highlights of Drake's journey from Nova Albion down the coast to the bay where he careened his ships. More specifically, it is obvious that the map gives particular attention to the defining features of the coast around two of the major rivers that he discovered: the Fraser and the Columbia.

5. Nehalem Valley Historical Society, *Tales of Neahkahnie Treasure*, 1–13.

6. Ibid., 13–18.

7. Costaggini and Schultz, "Survey of Artifacts at Neahkahnie Mountain." Unfortunately, the rock face at the western vertex bearing the Latin words for "heavens" and "predict" has since been removed to enable widening of the Oregon coastal highway. Thanks to Wayne Jensen's foresight, however, the exact position of these inscriptions and the intersecting lines of the triangle was fixed by the above-noted survey. Also, Jensen was able to save the pieces of rock bearing the inscriptions, and they are now preserved in the Tillamook County Museum.

8. BL Sloane MS 3651, fol. 65.

9. The position of the magnetic north pole has shifted over the intervening centuries, so the meridians set up by Bourne and Drake would not align precisely with its present position.

10. Some of the gentlemen in Drake's company—most probably, pilot Thomas Hood, who later became a prominent hydrographer, and Cambridge-educated Francis Fletcher—must have received special instruction from Dr. John Dee or William Bourne in order to set up their observations and make the calculations.

11. To set up the survey, therefore, Drake needed a large site that was cleared of trees. As the entire coast north of the Columbia River was heavily forested, Neahkahnie Mountain, having been regularly burned off by the Indians, was probably the first unforested site found by Drake that had the desired orientation and was large enough for the survey to be laid out.

12. Precisely what the sequence of observations and calculations represented by the layout of the Oregon cairns was, is a question requiring further investigation. Indeed, this is a wonderful puzzle for interested astronomers. The clues include the lunar distance theorem as it was postulated in Bourne's *A Regiment for the Sea*, and the layout of Drake's cairns on Neahkahnie Mountain, which as previously noted has been fixed by modern survey. Therefore, through the medium of computer modeling, the connecting lines can be tested for alignment to the moon and other celestial bodies as of specific dates in the summer of 1579, much as the tides on those dates can be determined (see chapter 26, note 12).

13. Howse, "The Lunar-Distance Method of Measuring Longitude," explains that although the principle was simple, the arithmetic needed to calculate one's longitude was formidable. Allowance had to be made for atmospheric refraction—the bending of light rays as they enter the Earth's atmosphere—and for lunar parallax, be-

cause the observations were made from the Earth's surface rather than its center. Without precise adjustments for these factors the sun and stars would always appear to be higher above the horizon than they truly were, and the moon would appear to be lower than it actually was.

Notably, the entries (Edward Fenton's chaplain) Richard Madox made in his diary in 1582 included a discussion of the problem of light refraction in astronomical observation; and certainly Bourne would have been aware of the need to adjust for lunar parallax, as a similar adjustment was required to observations made to determine one's position in latitude. It is very likely, then, that Bourne's method incorporated formulas to adjust for these factors. As Howse points out, however, the accuracy of Bourne's formulas would have been undermined by the fact that the moon's motion was much more irregular than he could have predicted.

14. Undoubtedly, Drake had charted the northwesterly trend of the coast beyond Cape Flattery, and adjusting for this, he probably reckoned that his Strait of Anian was about 150 degrees west of England. If he believed that Frobisher's entrance to the northwest passage was about 50 degrees west of England, as exemplified by its location on Richard Hakluyt's *Novus Orbis* map of 1587, then he would have reckoned a difference of about 100 degrees in longitude between the two entrances. At latitude 60 degrees, this difference is equivalent to 3,000 miles.

However, the true longitude of Frobisher's "strait" (bay) was actually about 60 degrees west of England, and it seems clear that its placement on a map was subject to rules of secrecy, as admitted by Henry Binnyman in his note to the readers of George Best's account of Frobisher's voyages in 1578 (see chapter 15). Notably, Molyneux's globe also places Frobisher's strait 50 degrees west of England, where it is depicted cutting through the southern tip of Greenland. Ultimately, this effort in disinformation proved so effective that after the principal actors died, the location of Frobisher's strait became a forgotten secret until 1861, when Charles Francis Hall, while searching for the lost Franklin expedition, was led by his Inuit guides to the debris of Frobisher's mine site of Baffin Island.

In all probability, then, Drake knew Frobisher's entrance was nearer to 60 degrees west of England and reckoned the sailing distance between it and his Strait of Anian to be somewhat less than 3,000 miles.

❧ CHAPTER 26: A SORROWFUL FAREWELL ❧

1. Ward, "Lost Harbour Found."
2. Bawlf, *Secret Voyage* (2001), 58–61, 116.
3. Hanna, *Lost Harbour*, 66–82.
4. Ibid., 242–62.
5. Ibid., 214–30.
6. Ibid., 242–62.

7. Ward, correspondence and notes directed to the author. Bob Ward deserves to be congratulated for his twenty-year-long effort to call attention to Whale Cove as the site of Drake's careenage. The story of his investigation, beyond what he has already published, should properly be told by Ward himself.

8. As part of the cover-up of Drake's northern explorations, the dates of his arrival at, and departure from, his careenage were altered or omitted from the published accounts. In *The Famous Voyage* (1589 and 1600), Richard Hakluyt omitted the dates. Then, in the narrative titled *The Course,* which he introduced in his second edition of *Principal Navigations* (1600), he gave the date of arrival as June 17 but omitted the date of Drake's departure. *The World Encompassed,* from which Hakluyt adapted these accounts of the northern voyage, states that Drake arrived on June 17 and departed on July 23, establishing that he spent a little over five weeks at the careenage. However, the "Anonymous Narrative," which gives the true latitude of the careenage and therefore is the most reliable source, states that he departed there at "ye latter end of August."

In all probability, then, the simple expedient of changing the month of Drake's sojourn at the careenage from July–August to June–July (leaving the numerical dates unaltered) was employed in *The World Encompassed* to conceal a month of his secret explorations, and the true dates for Drake's arrival at and departure from the careenage were July 17 and August 23, respectively. This increases the time available to Drake to undertake his northern explorations subsequent to his initial landfall at Cape Cook (50 degrees) from fourteen days to forty-four days.

Is forty-four days a reasonable amount of time for Drake to have completed the reconnaissance described? According to this reconstruction of his route, from Cape Cook to Chatham Strait and back down the coast to Whale Cove, Drake traveled approximately 2,000 nautical miles. Allowing about ten days for intermediate stops means that through the remaining thirty-four days he had to have sailed, on average, about 60 miles per twenty-four-hour day. Considering that Drake, as exemplified by his extraordinarily fast passage through the Strait of Magellan and many other feats of navigation, was among the finest sailors and navigators in his or any era, this does seem reasonable.

9. Penzer, ed., *The World Encompassed and Analogous Contemporary Documents,* 52–53.

10. Ibid., 53.

11. Ibid., 54–55.

12. From his drawing of the spit at high water, it appears that Drake used it as a benchmark to project the optimum tides for moving the *Golden Hinde* on and off the beach. He very likely carried a pocket "compendium" containing a dial which he used for tide projections (photo in Wallis, ed., *Sir Francis Drake,* 47).

In the course of my research, Dr. Tim Ball kindly obtained the use of a computer program that runs the cycles of the moon back in time to reconstruct historical tides, and the times of low and high water in the immediate vicinity of Whale Cove were calculated for each day of July and August 1579. For example, on July 21, 1579 (Julian, or old-style, calendar), high water was reached at seven in the morning and again at a quarter to seven in the evening. The fact that such calculations can now be made with relative ease highlights the potential for further investigation of Drake's survey for longitude (see chapter 25, note 12).

13. Penzer, ed., *The World Encompassed and Analogous Contemporary Documents*, 56.

14. Ibid., 55–58. The "root called *Petah*" would have been the *wapato*, or camas root, a staple of the native diet in Oregon. And "*Tobah*" undoubtedly was tobacco, which was cultivated by tribes on the Oregon coast before European contact (Zenk, in Suttles, ed., *Handbook of North American Indians*, vol. 7, *Northwest Coast*, 573).

15. Penzer, ed., *The World Encompassed and Analogous Contemporary Documents*, 59.

16. Ibid., 61.

17. Ibid., 54.

18. Ibid., 62.

19. Ward, "Lost Harbour Found," 3. The California anchorage sleuths have had some difficulty identifying the "conies" described in the account. They interpret the description as referring to either a gopher or a ground squirrel. However, the California gopher is solitary, never goes abroad for its food, and is seldom seen above ground (Hanna, *Lost Harbour*, 208), and any Englishman would have called a squirrel "a squirrel."

20. Penzer, ed., *The World Encompassed and Analogous Contemporary Documents*, 61–62. Although the match between Whale Cove and Drake's drawing of his careenage is compelling, the identity of the Indians who resided there at the time remains unresolved. The observations of the late-eighteenth-century explorers suggest that by that time the tribes along the Oregon coast had already suffered a wave of smallpox. More epidemics followed, decimating their populations, and then, after unsuccessful efforts to resist the taking of their lands by white settlers, many of the survivors of the various tribes were thrown together on the Siletz Indian Reserve, not far from Whale Cove, where they adopted the trade jargon known as "Chinook" as a common language. Consequently, very little of the individual tribes' oral histories predating that period has survived (Seaburg and Miller, in Suttles, ed., *Handbook of North American Indians*, vol. 7, *Northwest Coast*, 561).

What is of greatest interest is Francis Fletcher's very accurate description of the conical, earth-covered *kekuli* house type, which was widely used in the interior regions of British Columbia, Washington, and Oregon in prehistoric times. By contrast, in 1595, when a returning Manila galleon, the *San Augustine*, stopped in the bay north of San Francisco, that was later named Drake's Bay, her crew found the Indians dwelling in "pits made in the sand and covered with grass, in the manner of the chichimacos Indians [of Mexico]." The details provided in *The World Encompassed* suggest that a tribe that had come from, and retained links to, the interior inhabited the area around Whale Cove in Drake's time. What appear to be several collapsed pit houses have reportedly been found at, and in the vicinity of, Whale Cove, but none has been excavated to ascertain whether they match Fletcher's description. Notably also, Fletcher describes the nearest village as being just three-quarters of a mile from the English camp. Archaeological investigation of these sites would provide an excellent opportunity to learn more about the native culture and perhaps also discover physical evidence of Drake's visit.

21. Ibid., 62. The "Anonymous Narrative," on the other hand, states that Drake "nailed upon this post a plate of lead and scratched thereon the Queen's name" (Vaux, ed., *The World Encompassed by Sir Francis Drake*, 184). In the sixteenth century the term *brass* applied to any metal or alloy that was thought to be imperishable (*The Oxford Universal Dictionary on Historical Principles*, 3rd ed.).

22. Penzer, ed., *The World Encompassed and Analogous Contemporary Documents*, 63. For explanation of the basis of August 23 as the date of Drake's departure, see note 8 above.

23. The copy of this illustration reproduced herewith was found pasted into a volume that belonged to Captain James Cook's one-time covoyager and naturalist Sir Joseph Banks (BL C.115. L.4, additional plate). Although he did not accompany Cook on his voyage to the North Pacific, Banks's interest in the illustration suggests an effort to discover information about Drake's voyage at some point in the planning of Cook's voyages.

24. Penzer, ed., *The World Encompassed and Analogous Contemporary Documents*, 51.

25. Lt. Comdr Michael Brooks (see chapter 23, note 9) plotted Drake's course, taking account of variable wind direction and speed, and reckoned a sailing time of between eleven and fourteen days (averaging between three and four knots) from Whale Cove (latitude 44° 45'N) to the entrance of Chatham Strait (latitude 56° N). Counting August 23 as a sailing day, this would place Drake back in the strait sometime between September 4 and 7. And if he averaged four knots or better over the distance, he may well have made landfall somewhat higher up the outer coast and followed it down to Cape Ommaney, at the southern tip of Baranof Island. If so, this might account for the realistic curvature of the coast depicted beyond latitude 56 degrees on Richard Hakluyt's remarkable *Novus Orbis* map of 1587.

26. Penzer, ed., *The World Encompassed and Analogous Contemporary Documents*, 49. For alternate calculations of the number of men Drake parted company with on the northwest coast, and a review of other theories concerning the reason and their eventual fate, see Hanna, *Lost Harbour*, 54–65.

27. This, it will be recalled, was the inscription that Drake placed on his private commemorative maps at the point where his track reversed southward.

28. Bawlf, *Secret Voyage* (2001), 126–27.

29. The estimate of 9,000 miles breaks down as follows: Guatulco to Cape Cook, 5,000 miles ± (forty-eight days' sailing); Cape Cook to Chatham Strait and then southward to Whale Cove, 2,000 miles ± (thirty-four days' sailing); Whale Cove to Chatham Strait, 1,000 miles (eleven to fourteen days' sailing), and Chatham Strait to Cape Arago, 950 miles (seven to nine days' sailing).

30. No attempt is made in this work to narrate Drake's crossing of the Pacific because there are almost no reliable details in the contemporary sources. *The World Encompassed* states: "Having nothing in our view but air and sea, without sight of any land for the space of full 68 days together, we continued on our course

through the main Ocean, till September 30 following, on which day we fell in ken of certain Islands lying about eight degrees to the Northward of the line [equator]."

Based on the description the narrative gives of the inhabitants, it is likely that Drake made his initial landfall in the western Pacific at the Palau Islands (Lessa, in Thrower, ed., *Sir Francis Drake and the Famous Voyage*). However, it is clear that the date of September 30 is false, and that the time consumed in the crossing was altered as part of the cover-up of Drake's northern explorations.

Notably, from Cape San Lucas at the southern tip of the Baja Peninsula, Cavendish made the 6,600-mile crossing to the Marianas in 42 days (averaging 6.5 knots) and completed his voyage to the Philippines—a total of a little over 8,000 miles—in 56 days. In comparison, starting at Cape Arago, at 43 degrees north, and sailing on an arc south-southwest and then southwest to latitude 14 degrees north, and then due westward to longitude 150 degrees east before veering west-southwest, Drake had to sail about 6,800 miles to reach the Palau Islands, and then another 1,200 miles to reach the Moluccas via the south coast of Mindanao—virtually the identical total distance to that covered by Cavendish in 56 days. Allowing for the seasonal winds and the north equatorial current, Lt. Comdr Brooks (see also chapter 23, n. 9 and chapter 26, n. 25) reckoned that Drake would have made the crossing to the Palau Islands in forty-eight to fifty-seven days, averaging between 5 and 6 knots.

It is much more likely, then, that Drake's whole voyage from Cape Arago to the Mollucas took 68 days, whereas *The World Encompassed* was revised to say that it consumed 104 days. The difference of 36 days therefore would represent part of the time Drake actually spent on his secret explorations on the northwest coast of America. To this may be added the 22 days by which *The World Encompassed* inflates the time spent between Ternate and the grounding of the *Golden Hinde* on the reef off the island of Celebes (see chapter 17, note 6). This yields a total of 58 days, that appear to have been shifted from Drake's exploit on the northwest coast of America to the voyage from there homeward.

Counting July 23—the date on which *The World Encompassed* has him departing the careenage—as a sailing day and adding 57 more days brings one to September 18 as the probable true date of Drake's departure from the coast of America. Then, adding 68 days for his crossing to the Moluccas puts his arrival at Ternate on November 24; or, as the "Anonymous Narrative" states, "at ye latter end of November."

◦ POSTSCRIPT: AN OLD SAILOR'S YARN ◦

1. Lok, "A Note . . . touching the Strait of Sea, commonly called Fretum Anian," in *Purchas, His Pilgrimes* (1905 reprint), 415–21.
2. Ibid., 416–17.
3. Ibid., 418.

4. Ibid., 416–17, with my interjections inserted in brackets.

5. Wagner, *Spanish Voyages to the Northwest Coast of America*, 169.

6. Ibid., 171–76.

7. Ibid.

8. Ascension's story was recounted by Father Jerónimo de Zárate Salmeron in "Relaciones de Nueva Mexico," 1626. A translation of the account is reprinted in Hanna, *Lost Harbour*, 387–88.

9. The background of this pilot Morena or Morera remains something of a mystery. John Drake later testified (1584) that when they departed Guatulco they "set sail with men of their own country only"—meaning, presumably, only persons who had sailed with Drake from England, plus the several Negroes whom they had liberated along the way. There were quite a few renegade Portuguese and Spanish pilots in the service of the English during this period, another being Símon Fernandez, who sailed with Fenton in 1582. Notably, besides Englishmen, Scots, and a few Flemings and Frenchmen, Drake's company when he left England was said to have included a "Biscayan"—possibly meaning a Basque from northern Spain. Perhaps this was Morera. Alternatively, if he was Portuguese, his name would properly be spelled "Moreira."

10. Hanna, *Lost Harbour*, 387–88.

11. The map appeared on the title page of Herrera, *Descriptis Indae Occidentalis* (1622).

12. If, as seems likely, Drake's men did return to Whale Cove to await rescue, one obvious question is: What did they use for dwellings? The descriptions of Drake's camp at the careenage suggest that he set up temporary "huts" or tents, which would not have provided adequate shelter for the winter. And taking up residence at the Indian village three-quarters of a mile inland would have the disadvantage that a passing ship might not be seen.

Unfortunately, the probable site of Drake's fortified camp at Whale Cove was developed as a residential subdivision in the 1960s. However, several acres on the north side of the cove remain undeveloped, and here there appear to be several collapsed pit houses of the *kekuli* type. These may predate Drake's visit; or conceivably they were put up by his stranded mariners with the assistance of the Indians. Whichever the case, they were well located to maintain a continuous watch seaward.

It would be a great shame if these house sites are not, in the interest of possibly retrieving and preserving physical evidence of Drake's expedition, properly and thoroughly investigated by professional archaeologists. For example, if Drake's men eventually departed from the area, they may well have left in one of their dwellings or elsewhere on the site "letters wrapped in a box of lead" as suggested by contemporary William Monson (chapter 22), relating what had happened to them and where they were headed in case a rescue ship did belatedly arrive.

A further problem the stranded mariners would have faced is that Whale Cove is exposed to the southwest gales that regularly collide with the coast in the winter. They would therefore have found it necessary to move their bark and pinnace to a more secure anchorage some distance from the cove, where the vessels would have been vulnerable to looting by the Indians and may eventually have been rendered useless. Conceivably, remnants of these vessels may one day be found.

13. The one expedition that could have reached Drake's men was the company aboard Cavendish's second ship, the *Content*, and the Spanish bark he had captured and renamed the *George*, whose mission undoubtedly was to complete the discovery of the northwest passage via Drake's supposed Strait of Anian, but who were never heard from again. It appears they had planned to have the whole of the summer of 1588 to get through the passage. Departing Cape San Lucas in November, however, they would have known that it was too dangerous to attempt to reach the far northwest coast before the end of winter, and most probably they went looking for a sheltered anchorage on the coast of upper California.

There is compelling evidence that some Englishmen were shipwrecked on Santa Catalina Island, off Santa Barbara, around this time. In 1602 the Vízcaino expedition saw the wreck and reported that many of the Indian youths on the island were "white and blonde." Conceivably the wreck was the captured Spanish bark that Drake sent into his strait in 1579. However, another piece of evidence suggests otherwise: A few years ago four sixteenth-century English cannons—large demiculverin—were unearthed in the mouth of an estuary near Santa Barbara, on the mainland opposite Santa Catalina Island. There can be little doubt they came from the wreck on the island, and it is unlikely that Drake would have depleted his ordnance to such an extent when he faced a long voyage through hostile waters. Moreover, the big guns would have been an unnecessary burden for the voyage through the northern passage. In all probability, then, the wreck was one of Cavendish's missing ships.

It appears the surviving company spent some time on the island salvaging what they could from the wreck, and then ferried the cannons across to the mainland in their remaining ship and left them there, probably because they were heavily laden with men and whatever provisions they had managed to salvage.

Along the mainland coast the Indians made signs to Vízcaino that there were men living in the region who had beards and weapons like the Spaniards'. Precisely where is unclear. If they were Cavendish's men, word of their presence would have spread from tribe to tribe in the intervening fifteen years. Then 170 years later, in 1772, Father Juan Crespi led the first Spanish exploration around the east side of San Francisco Bay and noted on his map: "Around this bay the natives were found to be red-headed, bearded and fair complexioned." Some historians have argued that these people were descendants of Drake's stranded sailors, and indeed they may well have been. After some years waiting at Whale Cove to be rescued, they could have trekked southward in search of a more salubrious climate. However, another intriguing possibility has come to light.

In a recently published book, *1421: The Year China Discovered the World* (London: Bantam Press, 2002), author Gavin Menzies claims that there is the wreck of a "Chinese junk" under a sandbar some distance up the Sacramento River, which drains into the east side of San Francisco Bay. Apparently the existence of the ship has been known for some time, as there have been some investigations. But it has never been fully and systematically excavated, and the evidence in support of Menzies's claim is far from conclusive. Given Father Crespi's report that the Indians in the area were red-headed, bearded, and fair-complexioned, one cannot rule out the possibility that this is Cavendish's other missing ship.

According to Menzies, a magnetometry survey of the site has revealed the presence of an object eighty-five feet long and thirty feet wide, "very similar in size and shape to the trading junks" (ibid., 204). Allowing, however, that the sides of the ship very likely splayed outward under the weight of succeeding aggregations of silt, these dimensions could also represent a European vessel. If so, one might expect her cannons to show up on further investigation, but they may have been removed to a fortification. Menzies also cites the discovery of some pieces of silver gray armor, which, although they have since unfortunately been lost, he speculates were Chinese. Also found were grains of rice, a quantity of seeds, and some pieces of wood, all of which appear to have originated in the Orient (ibid., 203–8). However, all of these items could well have been taken from the returning Manila galleon *Santa Ana*, which Cavendish captured at Cape San Lucas. Indeed, rice undoubtedly was a staple on the return voyages of the galleons.

It is entirely possible, therefore, that careful investigation of this buried vessel and the surrounding area may provide exciting proof that the men aboard either the English-built bark *Content* or the Spanish-built *George* discovered San Francisco Bay in the winter of 1587–88, and subsequently became stuck in the Sacramento River or decided to stay, thereby becoming the first European inhabitants of the modern state of California.

BIBLIOGRAPHY

◄ CONTEMPORARY MANUSCRIPTS ►

Anonymous, *A discourse of Sir Francis Drakes iorney and exploytes after hee had past ye Straytes of Magellan into Mare de Sur, and through the rest of his voyage afterward till hee arrived in England. 1580 Anno* (known as the "Anonymous Narrative") and related memoranda. Harley MS 280, fols. 81–90, British Library, London.

Print of Abraham Ortelius's *Typus Orbis Terrarum* (1570), with manuscript additions depicting and noting Drake's voyage around the world. Maps 920. (327). British Library, London.

◄ CONTEMPORARY PRINTED WORKS ►

Best, George, *A True Discourse of the late Voyages of Discoverie for Finding of a Passage to Cathaya by the North-west Under the Conduct of Martin Frobisher, General.* London, 1578. Reprinted in R. Collinson, *The Three Voyages of Martin Frobisher.* Hakluyt Society, 1867.

Hakluyt, Richard, *Diverse voyages touching the discoverie of America, and the Ilands adiacent.* London, 1582. Reprinted, Hakluyt Society, 1850.

———. *The Principall Navigations, Voyages, and Discoveries of the English Nation.* London 1589. Facsimile edition, 2 vols. eds. D. B. Quinn and R. A. Skelton. Hakluyt Society, 1965.

———. *The Principal Navigations, Voyages, Trafiques, and Discoveries of the English Nation.* London, 1600. Reprinted, 12 Vols., Hakluyt Society, 1903–5.

Monson, Sir William. *Sir William Monson's Naval Tracts.* In Awnsham Churchill, *A Collection of Voyages and Travels.* London, 1704.

Purchas, Samuel. *Purchas, His Pilgrimes.* London, 1625. Reprinted, Glasgow, 1905–7.

Sir Francis Drake Revived. London, 1626. Reprinted in Irene A. Wright, *Documents Concerning English Voyages to the Spanish Main, 1569–1580.* Hakluyt Society, 1932.

The World Encompassed by Sir Francis Drake. London, 1628. Reprinted in N. M. Penzer, *The World Encompassed and Analogous Contemporary Documents.* London, 1926.

⊰ BOOKS, ARTICLES, AND PAPERS ⊱

Allaire, Bernard, and Donald Hogarth. "Martin Frobisher, the Spaniards, and a Sixteenth Century Northern Spy." In Symons, ed., *Meta Incognita, a Discourse of Discovery*, 575–88.

Andrews, Kenneth R. *Drake's Voyages.* London: Weidenfeld & Nicolson, 1967.

Baldwin, Robert. "Speculative Ambitions and the Reputations of Frobisher's Metallurgists." In Symons, ed., *Meta Incognita, a Discourse of Discovery*, 401–76.

Barbeau, Marius. *Totem Poles.* 2 vols. Ottawa: National Museum of Canada, 1950.

Bawlf, R. Samuel. *Sir Francis Drake's Secret Voyage to the Northwest Coast of America, A.D. 1579.* Salt Spring Island, British Columbia: Sir Francis Drake Publications, 2001.

Bishop, R. P. "Drake's Course in the North Pacific." *British Columbia Historical Quarterly* (July 1939): 151–82.

Boyd, Robert T. "Demographic History, 1774–1874." In Suttles, ed., *Handbook of North American Indians*, vol. 7, *Northwest Coast*, 135–48.

Bradley, R. G., and P. D. Jones, eds. *Climate Since A.D. 1500.* London, 1992.

Corbett, Julian S. *Drake and the Tudor Navy.* 2 vols. London, 1898.

Costaggini, P. A., and R. J. Schultz. "Survey of Artifacts at Neahkahnie Mountain." Unpublished paper, Oregon State University, 1980.

Cummins, John. *Francis Drake.* London: Weidenfeld & Nicolson, 1995.

Davies, R. Trevor. *The Golden Age of Spain, 1501–1621.* London, 1964.

Donno, Elizabeth S. *An Elizabethan in 1582, the Diary of Richard Madox, Fellow of All Souls.* Hakluyt Society, 1976.

Dyke, Gwenyth. "The Finance of a Sixteenth-Century Navigator, Thomas Cavendish of Trimley in Sussex." *Mariner's Mirror*, Cambridge, February 1958.

Eliott-Drake, Lady Elizabeth Fuller. *The Family and Heirs of Sir Francis Drake.* 2 vols. London, 1911.

Fagan, Brian. *The Little Ice Age.* New York: Basic Books, 2002.

Friel, Ian. "Frobisher's Ships: The Ships of the North-Western Atlantic Voyages, 1576–1578." In Symons, ed., *Meta Incognita, a Discourse of Discovery*, 299–352.

Gleeson, Paul F. *Ozette Woodworking Technology.* Washington State University, 1980.

Hanna, Warren L. *Lost Harbour: The Controversy Over Drake's California Anchorage.* University of California Press, 1979.

Harris, Cole. "Voices of Disaster: Smallpox Around the Strait of Georgia in 1782." In *Ethnohistory.* American Society for Ethnohistory, 1974.

Howse, Derek. "The Lunar-Distance Method of Measuring Longitude." In William J. H. Andrews, ed. *The Quest for Longitude.* Cambridge, Mass., 1996, 150–62.

Hume, Martin A. S., ed. *Calendar of Letters and State Papers Relating to English Affairs Preserved Principally in the Archives of Simancas.* Vols. 2–4, *Elizabeth, 1568–1603.* London, 1868–99.

Jane, Cecil. *A Spanish Voyage to Vancouver Island and the Northwest Coast of America.* London, 1930.

Jensen, Wayne, et al. *Tales of the Neahkahnie Treasure.* Oregon: Nehalem Valley Historical Society, 1991.

Keddie, Grant. "The Question of Asiatic Objects on the North Pacific Coast of America." In *Contributions to Human History.* Victoria British Columbia Museum, 1990, monograph.

Kelsey, Harry. *Sir Francis Drake, the Queen's Pirate.* New Haven: Yale University Press. 1998.

Kendrick, John. *The Men with Wooden Feet: The Spanish Exploration of the Pacific Northwest.* Toronto: NC Press, 1986.

Krause, Hans P. *Sir Francis Drake, a Pictorial Biography.* Amsterdam: N. Israel, 1970.

Lamb, W. Kaye, ed. *A Voyage of Discovery to the North Pacific Ocean and Round the World 1791–1795.* 2 vols., Hakluyt Society, 1984.

Lessa, William A. "Drake in the South Seas." In Thrower, ed., *Sir Francis Drake and the Famous Voyage, 1577–1580,* 60–77.

McDermott, James. "The Company of Cathay: The Financing and Organization of the Frobisher Voyages." In Symons, ed., *Meta Incognita, a Discourse of Discovery,* 147–78.

———. *Martin Frobisher, Elizabethan Privateer.* New Haven: Yale University Press, 2001.

Mann, Daniel H., and Gregory P. Streveler. "Final Report of Geological Investigations in Glacier Bay National Park." Unpublished paper, 1997.

Markham, Sir Clements Robert. *Early Spanish Voyages to the Strait of Magellan.* Glasgow: Hakluyt Society, 1911.

Mason, A. E. W. *The Life of Francis Drake.* London: Hodder and Stoughton, 1941.

Mathes, W. M. *Vizcaino and Spanish Expansion in the Pacific Ocean.* San Francisco, 1968.

Morison, Samuel Eliot. *The Great Explorers: The European Discovery of America.* New York: Oxford University Press, 1978.

Nuttall, Zelia. *New Light on Drake.* Hakluyt Society, 1914.

Parker, Geoffrey. *The Grand Strategy of Philip II.* New Haven: Yale University Press, 1998.

Parks, George B. *Richard Hakluyt and the English Voyages.* New York: Yale University Press, 1928.

Penzer, N. M., ed. *The World Encompassed and Analogous Contemporary Documents.* London, 1926. Reprint, Amsterdam: N. Israel, 1971.

Quinn, David B. "Early Accounts of the Famous Voyage." In Thrower, ed., *Sir Francis Drake and the Famous Voyage, 1577–1580,* 33–48.

———. "Frobisher in the Context of Early English Northwest Exploration." In Symons, ed., *Meta Incognita, a Discourse of Discovery,* 7–18.

———. *Sir Francis Drake as Seen by His Contemporaries.* Providence: John Carter Brown Library, 1996.

Rowse, A. L. *Sir Richard Grenville of the Revenge*. London, 1937.

Ruggles, Richard I. "The Cartographic Lure of the Northwest Passage: Its Real and Imaginary Geography." In Symons, ed., *Meta Incognita, a Discourse of Discovery*, 179–256.

Savours, Ann. "A Narrative of Frobisher's Arctic Voyages." In Symons, ed., *Meta Incognita, a Discourse of Discovery*, 19–54.

Sherman, William H. *John Dee: The Politics of Reading and Writing in the English Renaissance*. Amherst, 1995.

———. "John Dee's Role in Martin Frobisher's Northwest Enterprise." In Symons, ed., *Meta Incognita, a Discourse in Discovery*.

Starkey, David. *Elizabeth, the Struggle for the Throne*. London: HarperCollins, 2000.

Stewart, Hilary. *Cedar: Tree of Life to the Northwest Coast Indians*. Vancouver: Douglas & McIntyre, 1995.

Sugden, John. *Sir Francis Drake*. New York: Random House, 1990.

Suttles, Wayne, ed. *Handbook of North American Indians*., Vol. 7, Northwest Coast. Smithsonian Institution, 1990.

Swanton, John K. *Tlingt Myths and Texts*. Smithsonian Institution, Bureau of American Ethnology, Bulletin 39. 1908.

Symons, Thomas H. B., ed. *Meta Incognita, a Discourse of Discovery, Martin Frobisher's Arctic Expeditions, 1576–1578*. Canadian Museum of Civilization, 1999.

Taylor, Eva G. R. "Francis Drake and the Pacific: Two Fragments." *Pacific Historical Review* I, no. 2 (1932).

———. "The Missing Draft Project of Drake's Voyage, 1577–1580." *Geographical Journal* 75 (January 1930).

———. "More Light on Drake." *Mariner's Mirror*, (April 16, 1930).

———. *Tudor Geography, 1485–1582*. London: 1930.

———. ed. *The Original Writings and Correspondence of the Two Richard Hakluyts*. Hakluyt Society, 1935.

———. *A Regiment for the Sea and Other Writings on Navigation*. Hakluyt Society, 1963.

———. *The Troublesome Voyage of Captain Edward Fenton, 1582–83*. Hakluyt Society, 1959.

Thomson, George Malcolm. *Sir Francis Drake*. London: 1972.

Thrower, Norman J. W., ed. *Sir Francis Drake and the Famous Voyage, 1577–1580*. University of California Press, 1984.

van den Broecke, Marcel P. R. *Ortelius Atlas Maps*. Netherlands: HES Publishers, 1996.

van den Broecke, Marcel P. R., et al., eds. *Abraham Ortelius and the First Atlas: Essays Commemorating the Quadricentennial of his Death, 1598–1998*. Netherlands: HES Publishers, 1998.

Vaux, W. S. W., ed. *The World Encompassed by Sir Francis Drake, Being His Next Voyage to That to Nombre De Dios*. Hakluyt Society, 1854.

Wagner, Henry R. *Cartography of the Northwest Coast of America to the Year 1800*. 2 vols. San Francisco, 1937.

———. *Sir Francis Drake's Voyage Around the World, Its Aims and Objectives.* San Francisco: John Howell, 1926.

———. *Spanish Voyages to the Northwest Coast of America in the Sixteenth Century.* San Francisco, 1929.

Wallis, Helen. "The Cartography of Drake's Voyage." In Thrower, ed., *Sir Francis Drake and the Famous Voyage, 1577–1580,* 121–63.

———. "The First English Globe: A Recent Discovery." *Geographical Journal* 117 (1951): 275–90.

———. "Further Light on the Molyneux Globes." *Geographical Journal* 121 (1951): 304–311.

———, ed. *Sir Francis Drake: An Exhibition to Commemorate Francis Drake's Voyage Around the World, 1577–1580.* London: British Museum, 1977.

Wallis, Helen, and Anna Maria Crinò. "New Researches on the Molyneux Globes." In *Der Globusfreund* Vienna (1987), 11–18.

Ward, Bob. "Churchill Fellowship to Examine Drake's Maps." *Map Collector* (summer 1992): 14–15.

———. "Drake and the Oregon Coast." *Geographical Magazine* (June 1981): 645–50.

———. "Lost Harbour Found! The Truth About Drake and the Pacific." *Map Collector* (winter 1988): 2–8.

Waters, David W. *The Art of Navigation in England in Elizabethan and Early Stuart Times.* New Haven: Yale University Press, 1958.

———. "Elizabethan Navigation." In Thrower, ed., *Sir Francis Drake and the Famous Voyage, 1577–1580,* 12–32.

Weir, Alison. *Elizabeth the Queen.* London: Random House, 1998.

Williamson, James A. *The Age of Drake.* London: Adam and Charles Black, 1938.

———. *Hawkins of Plymouth.* London, 1949.

———. *Sir John Hawkins, the Time and the Man.* Oxford, 1927.

———, ed., *The Observations of Sir Richard Hawkins.* London, 1933. Reprinted, Amsterdam: N. Israel, 1970.

Wilson, Derrick. *The World Encompassed.* London: Allison & Busby, 1978.

Wolferstan, Bill. *Cruising Guide to British Columbia.* Vol. 2, *Desolation Sound and the Discovery Islands.* Vancouver: Whitecap Books, 1987.

Wright, Irene A., ed. *Spanish Documents Concerning English Voyages to the Spanish Main, 1569–1580.* Hakluyt Society, 1932.

ART CREDITS

Images on the pages noted have been supplied by the following sources.

INDEX

H